THE JOSSEY-BASS READER ON EDUCATIONAL LEADERSHIP

Introduction by
Michael Fullan

JOSSEY-BASS
A Wiley Company
San Francisco

Jossey-Bass books and products are available through
most bookstores. To contact Jossey-Bass directly, call (888)
378-2537, fax to (800) 605-2665, or visit our website at
www.josseybass.com.

Substantial discounts on bulk quantities of Jossey-Bass books
are available to corporations, professional associations, and
other organizations. For details and discount information,
contact the special sales department at Jossey-Bass.

Credits are on pp. 419-421

Library of Congress Cataloging-in-Publication Data
The Jossey-Bass reader on educational leadership.
   p. cm. — (The Jossey-Bass education series)
Includes bibliographical references.
ISBN 0-7879-5281-8
  1. Educational leadership—United States.   2. School management
and organization—United States.   I. Jossey-Bass Inc. II. Series.
LB2806 .J597 2000
371.2'00973—dc21   99-050967

FIRST EDITION

PB Printing 10 9 8 7 6 5 4 3 2 1

The Jossey-Bass
Education Series

CONTENTS

PART ONE
Leadership, Management, and Organizational Behavior

PART TWO
Principals and Superintendents

PART THREE
Diversity and Leadership

PART FOUR
Moral Leadership

PART FIVE
Shared Leadership

SOURCES

CHAPTER ONE
John W. Gardner. *On Leadership*. New York: Free Press, 1990.

CHAPTER TWO
Peter M. Senge. *The Fifth Discipline*. New York: Doubleday, 1990.

CHAPTER THREE
W. Edwards Deming. *Out of the Crisis*. Cambridge, Mass.: MIT Press, 1986.

CHAPTER FOUR
William Glasser. *The Quality School*. New York: HarperCollins, 1990.

CHAPTER FIVE
Educational Administration Quarterly, Vol. 31, No. 2 (May 1995), pp. 224–243.

CHAPTER SIX
Lee G. Bolman and Terrence E. Deal. *Reframing Organizations*. San Francisco: Jossey-Bass, 1991.

CHAPTER SEVEN
Susan Moore Johnson. *Leading to Change*. San Francisco: Jossey-Bass, 1996.

CHAPTER EIGHT
Interstate School Leaders Licensure Consortium, Standards for School Leaders, Adopted by the Full Consortium, November 2, 1996.

CHAPTER NINE
Phi Delta Kappan, May 1968, pp. 654–659.

CHAPTER TEN
Updated version of a paper presented at the annual meeting of the American Educational Research Association in Chicago, March 1997.

CHAPTER ELEVEN
Roland S. Barth. *Improving Schools from Within.* San Francisco: Jossey-Bass, 1990.

CHAPTER TWELVE
Educational Leadership, April 1998, Vol. 55, No. 7, pp. 6–11.

CHAPTER THIRTEEN
Lee G. Bolman and Terrence E. Deal. *Reframing Organizations.* San Francisco: Jossey-Bass, 1991.

CHAPTER FOURTEEN
Phillip C. Schlechty. *Schools for the Twenty-First Century.* San Francisco: Jossey-Bass, 1990.

CHAPTER FIFTEEN
Terrence E. Deal and Kent D. Peterson. *Shaping School Culture.* San Francisco: Jossey-Bass, 1999.

CHAPTER SIXTEEN
James A. Banks and Cherry A. McGee Banks, eds. *Handbook of Research on Multicultural Education.* New York: Simon & Schuster Macmillan, 1995.

CHAPTER SEVENTEEN
Theory Into Practice, Vol. 30, No. 2, 1991, pp. 134–139.

CHAPTER EIGHTEEN
Thomas J. Sergiovanni. *Moral Leadership.* San Francisco: Jossey-Bass, 1992.

CHAPTER NINETEEN
Robert Evans. *The Human Side of School Change.* San Francisco: Jossey-Bass, 1996.

CHAPTER TWENTY
Kevin Ryan and Karen E. Bohlin. *Building Character in Schools*. San Francisco: Jossey-Bass, 1999.

CHAPTER TWENTY-ONE
Frances Hesselbein and Paul M. Cohen, eds. *Leader to Leader*. San Francisco: Jossey-Bass, 1999.

CHAPTER TWENTY-TWO
Ann Lieberman, ed. *Building a Professional Culture in Schools*. New York: Teachers College Press, 1988.

CHAPTER TWENTY-THREE
Educational Evaluation and Policy Analysis, Fall 1994, Vol. 16, No. 3, pp. 287–301.

CHAPTER TWENTY-FOUR
Ann Lieberman, ed. *Building a Professional Culture in Schools*. New York: Teachers College Press, 1988.

ABOUT THE AUTHORS

Cherry A. McGee Banks is an associate professor of education at the University of Washington-Bothell. She also serves as a faculty associate at the Center for Multi-Cultural Education at the University of Washington-Seattle.

Roland S. Barth is a former public school educator and was the founding director of the Principals' Center. He is on the faculty at Harvard University.

Karen E. Bohlin is an assistant professor in the School of Education and director of the Center for the Advancement of Ethics and Character, Boston University.

Lee G. Bolman occupies the Miriom H. Bloch Missouri Chair in Leadership at the Henry W. Bloch School of Business and Public Administration at the University of Missouri, Kansas City.

Steven T. Bossert is dean of the School of Education at Syracuse University in Syracuse, New York.

Joseph Cambone was formerly a professor of education at Wheelock College in Boston.

Terrence E. Deal is the Irving R. Melbo Professor of Education at the Rossier School of Education at the University of Southern California in Los Angeles.

W. Edwards Deming (1900–1993) was a pioneer in the field of quality management and a leader of the rebuilding of Japanese industry after World War II.

Robert Evans is a clinical and organizational psychologist and is director of the Human Relations Service in Wellesley, Massachusetts.

Michael Fullan is dean of the Ontario Institute for Studies in Education at the University of Toronto.

John Gardner, founder of Common Cause and the White House Fellows Program, served as Secretary of Health, Education, and Welfare in the Johnson administration. He now holds the Miriam and Peter Haas Centennial Professorship in Public Service at Stanford University.

William Glasser is a board-certified psychiatrist and founder of the William Glasser Institute in Los Angeles, California.

Susan Moore Johnson is the Carl H. Phorzheimer Jr. Professor of Teaching and Learning at the Harvard Graduate School of Education, where she served as academic dean from 1993 to 1999.

Ann Lieberman is an emeritus professor from Columbia University Teachers College in New York. Currently, she is a senior scholar at the Carnegie Foundation for the Advancement of Teaching and a visiting professor at Stanford University.

Judith Warren Little is professor of education at the University of California, Berkeley, where she serves as chair of the faculty of the Graduate School of Education.

David D. Marsh occupies the Robert A. Naslund Chair in Curriculum and Instruction and is director of the Center for School Leadership at the University of Southern California in Los Angeles.

Matthew B. Miles was a senior research associate at the Center for Policy Research at Columbia University Teachers College before his death in 1996.

Jerome T. Murphy is professor of education and dean of the Faculty of Education at the Harvard Graduate School of Education.

Irene Nowell is superintendent of the Remsenburg-Speonk Union Free School District in Remsenburg, New York, where she has served in that capacity for ten years.

Rodney T. Ogawa is associate dean and professor in the School of Education at the University of California-Riverside. His current research focuses on the intersection of school organization and teacher professionalism.

Andy Perry is principal of the Wilson School in Westfield, New Jersey.

Kent D. Peterson is a professor in the Department of Educational Administration at the University of Wisconsin-Madison and the founding director of the Vanderbilt Principals' Institute at Vanderbilt University.

Kevin Ryan is founder and director emeritus of the Center for the Advancement of Ethics and Character at Boston University.

Ellen R. Saxl is president of Educational Agenda Company, a research and consulting firm.

Phillip C. Schlechty is president and CEO of the Center for Leadership in Education Reform in Louisville, Kentucky.

Thomas J. Sergiovanni is the Lillian Radford Professor of Education and Administration at Trinity University in San Antonio, Texas. He is also a senior fellow at the Center for Educational Leadership and founding director of the Trinity Principals' Center.

Charol Shakeshaft is a professor in foundations, leadership, and policy studies at Hofstra University in Hempstead, New York.

Peter M. Senge is a founding member and is currently the director of the Society for Organizational Learning at the Massachusetts Institute of Technology Sloan School of Management in Cambridge.

Carol H. Weiss is a professor of education at the Harvard Graduate School of Education.

Margaret Wheatley is a partner in the consulting firm of Kellner-Rogers and Wheatley and is a cofounder of the Berkana Institute—a nonprofit research foundation supporting organizational change.

INTRODUCTION

NEVER BEFORE HAS LEADERSHIP in education been more critical for public school systems. Concern about the performance of schools has mounted, while at the same time we are beginning to appreciate the complexities of bringing about school reform. When systems are complex and when the tendencies of such systems are toward overload and fragmentation, the need for leadership to forge synergy and coherence is paramount (Fullan, 1999).

We are beginning to realize that the answer does not lie in locating ad hoc charismatic leaders-as-saviors—they are too few in number and their contributions do not have lasting affects. Compounding this problem is demographics, which until recently have been unfavorable   too little turnover combined with lack of attention to cultivating the next generation of leaders. The result is a shortage of qualified leaders at all levels in the educational system.

The good news, and this Reader is an example of it, is that strong theoretical and practical work has been underway over the past decade which has laid the groundwork for the resurgence of leadership. Thus, as we enter the twenty-first century we recognize the centrality of educational leadership for the success of school systems. We have mapped out much of the territory, including broadening the concept of leadership, and we have put in place higher standards of leadership and have begun to establish programs and leadership academies designed to prepare and sustain leaders.

The burgeoning attention to leadership has produced countless articles over the past decade which are scattered throughout the literature. *The Jossey-Bass Reader on Educational Leadership* provides a much needed anthology that organizes in one place the best of the literature on leadership. Part One contains six groundbreaking articles from leading thinkers in organizational leadership. These are deliberately selected to demonstrate that leadership has a strong conceptual base which is basic in all human situations. John Gardner's classic article on *The Nature of Leadership* introduces the section followed by several featured pieces on theories of quality leadership.

Part Two is no less theoretical but is role specific in looking at the roles of principals and superintendents. These nine articles provide some of the leading research on what leaders in the twenty-first century will face and what they must think about and be able to do to be effective under conditions of uncertainty and complexity. Some of the titles are illustrative of the challenge: "standards for school leaders," "the unheroic side of leadership," "the manager as politician," and "leading a school system through change."

Parts Three and Four delve deeper into issues of equity, values, and moral leadership. In the five articles across these two sections we learn about the difficulties and untapped leadership resources caused by the failure to cultivate women and visible minorities as leaders. Sergiovanni and others talk about the deep moral basis of leadership as stewardships, as authentic role modeling and as builders of "community virtue."

In the final part (Five), we are forcefully reminded that the notion of leadership must not be confined to those holding formal leadership positions. All leadership, if it is to be effective, must have a strong component of *sharedness*. This is a theoretical as well as strategic conclusion. Formal leaders cannot control others in the organization when times are complex, i.e., in times of flux in which innovative, adaptive solutions must be generated and carried out by scores of committed participants. The days of "command and control" says Margaret Wheatley, are over. New forms of shared leadership are emerging with greater roles for principals, teachers, parents, and students.

The phenomenon of leadership has interested humankind for millennia. As we enter the twenty-first century it takes on a renewed interest. The scientific study of leadership has never been greater, nor has the recognition that broad-based leadership is the only way forward. Broad-based leadership will require "leaders of leaders," i.e., those who can help create the conditions for leadership to flourish. *The Jossey-Bass Reader on Educational Leadership* will be of interest to those scores of people who not only want to understand leadership, but also want to participate as part of the shared leadership process itself. This book, in one anthology, marks what we know about educational leadership and where the field is/should be heading. It is a highly significant compendium which will be a widespread interest to all those concerned about the performance of the educational system.

University of Toronto   MICHAEL FULLAN
January 2000

REFERENCES

Fullan, M. (1999) *Change Forces: The Sequel.* London: Falmer Press; Levittown, PA: Falmer Press (Taylor and Francis Inc.).

WELCOME TO the *Jossey-Bass Reader on Educational Leadership*. With the Jossey-Bass education readers we hope to provide a clear, concise overview of important topics in education and to give our audience a useful knowledge of the theory and practice of key educational issues. Each reader in this series is designed to be informative, comprehensive, and portable.

Your feedback is important. If you are familiar with articles, books, or reports that have a national sustained audience and address the topic of this reader, please send us an e-mail at readers@jbp.com.

*In the interest of readability, the editors
have slightly adapted the following selections
for this volume. For the complete text,
please refer to the original source.*

LEADERSHIP, MANAGEMENT, AND ORGANIZATIONAL BEHAVIOR

IN PART ONE, the reader will notice a strong representation of works written by experts in management or business. Why arc these authors, many of whom have never worked in a K–12 environment, included so prominently? They are responsible for theories and practices that were successful in business and were then applied to schools. As many survivors of top-down reform can attest, not all of these movements were embraced or worked the miracles on school systems that their champions touted. However, when talking about leadership in schools, they must be included. Total Quality Management (TQM), which surged from business to the schools in the 1980s, would now be called a fad by many educators. However, the roots and vocabulary of today's pressing reforms—accountability, shared decision making, and the focus on leadership as an invaluable part of school change—can all be traced back to TQM. Therefore, W. Edwards Deming's writing is represented here, as is that of William Glasser. Peter M. Senge's work from *The Fifth*

Discipline is of similar stature. Whether one believes that businesses and schools are similar or that the mantras of the latest management guru can be applied successfully to school-based problems, the legacy of these non-educators in schools cannot be denied. In addition, we have included authors such as John Gardner, who writes eloquently about the principles of leadership. Finally, we take a brief look at organizational behavior and its intersection with leadership, which is discussed by Rodney T. Ogawa and Steven T. Bossert, as well as Lee G. Bolman and Terrence E. Deal.

THE NATURE OF LEADERSHIP

John W. Gardner

LEADERSHIP IS A WORD that has risen above normal workaday usage as a conveyor of meaning. There seems to be a feeling that if we invoke it often enough with sufficient ardor we can ease our sense of having lost our way, our sense of things unaccomplished, of duties unfulfilled.

All of that simply clouds our thinking. The aura with which we tend to surround the words *leader* and *leadership* makes it hard to think clearly. Good sense calls for demystification.

Leadership is the process of persuasion or example by which an individual (or leadership team) induces a group to pursue objectives held by the leader or shared by the leader and his or her followers.

In any established group, individuals fill different roles, and one of the roles is that of leader. Leaders cannot be thought of apart from the historic context in which they arise, the setting in which they function (e.g., elective political office), and the system over which they preside (e.g., a particular city or state). They are integral parts of the system, subject to the forces that affect the system. They perform (or cause to be performed) certain tasks or functions that are essential if the group is to accomplish its purposes.

All that we know about the interaction between leaders and constituents or followers tells us that communication and influence flow in both directions; and in that two-way communication, nonrational, nonverbal, and unconscious elements play their part. In the process leaders shape and are shaped. This is true even in systems that appear to be led in quite autocratic fashion. In a state governed by coercion, followers cannot prevent the leader from violating their customs and beliefs, but they have many ways of making it more costly to violate than to honor their norms, and leaders usually make substantial accommodations. If Julius Caesar had been willing to live more flexibly with the give-and-take he might not have been slain in the Senate House. Machiavelli, the ultimate realist, advised the prince, "You will always need the favor of the inhabitants. . . . It is necessary for a prince to possess the friendship of the people." [1]

The connotations of the word *follower* suggest too much passivity and dependence to make it a fit term for all who are at the other end of the dialogue with leaders. I don't intend to discard it, but I also make frequent use of the word *constituent*. It is awkward in some contexts, but often it does fuller justice to the two-way interchange.

Elements of physical coercion are involved in some kinds of leadership; and of course there is psychological coercion, however mild and subtle, including peer pressure, in all social action. But in our culture, popular understanding of the leadership process distinguishes it from coercion—and places those forms involving the least coercion higher on the scale of leadership.

The focus of this book is leadership in this country today. Examples are drawn from other cultures and many of the generalizations are relevant for all times and places; but the focus is here and now. The points emphasized might be different were I writing fifty years ago or fifty years hence, or writing of Bulgaria or Tibet.

Distinctions

We must not confuse leadership with status. Even in large corporations and government agencies, the top-ranking person may simply be bureaucrat number 1. We have all occasionally encountered top persons who couldn't lead a squad of seven-year-olds to the ice cream counter.

It does not follow that status is irrelevant to leadership. Most positions of high status carry with them symbolic values and traditions that enhance the possibility of leadership. People expect governors and corporation presidents to lead, which heightens the possibility that they will. But the selection process for positions of high status does not make that a sure outcome.

Similarly, we must not confuse leadership with power. Leaders always have some measure of power, rooted in their capacity to persuade, but many people with power are without leadership gifts. Their power derives from money, or from the capacity to inflict harm, or from control of some piece of institutional machinery, or from access to the media. A military dictator has power. The thug who sticks a gun in your ribs has power. Leadership is something else.

Finally, we must not confuse leadership with official authority, which is simply legitimized power. Meter maids have it; the person who audits your tax returns has it.

Leadership requires major expenditures of effort and energy—more than most people care to make. When I outlined to a teenager of my acquaintance the preceding distinctions and then described the hard tasks of leadership, he said, "I'll leave the leadership to you, Mr. Gardner. Give me some of that power and status."

Confusion between leadership and official authority has a deadly effect on large organizations. Corporations and government agencies everywhere have executives who imagine that their place on the organization chart has given them a body of followers. And of course it has not. They have been given subordinates. Whether the subordinates become followers depends on whether the executives act like leaders.

Is it appropriate to apply to leaders the word *elite?* The word was once applied to families of exalted social status. Then sociologists adopted the word to describe any group of high status, whether hereditary or earned; thus, in addition to the elites of old families and old money, there are elites of performance and profession.

Some social critics today use the word with consistent negative overtones. They believe that elite status is incompatible with an equalitarian philosophy. But in any society—no matter how democratic, no matter how equalitarian—there are elites in the sociologist's sense: intellectual, athletic, artistic, political, and so on. The marks of an open society are that elite status is generally earned, and that those who have earned it do not use their status to violate democratic norms. In our society, leaders are among the many "performance elites."

Leaders and Managers

The word *manager* usually indicates that the individual so labeled holds a directive post in an organization, presiding over the processes by which the organization functions, allocating resources prudently, and making the best possible use of people.

Many writers on leadership take considerable pains to distinguish between leaders and managers. In the process leaders generally end up looking like a cross between Napoleon and the Pied Piper, and managers like unimaginative clods. This troubles me. I once heard it said of a man, "He's an utterly first-class manager but there isn't a trace of the leader in him." I am still looking for that man, and I am beginning to believe that he does not exist. Every time I encounter utterly first-class managers they turn out to have quite a lot of the leader in them.

Even the most visionary leader is faced on occasion with decisions that every manager faces: when to take a short-term loss to achieve a long-term gain, how to allocate scarce resources, whom to trust with a delicate assignment. So even though it has become conventional to contrast leaders and managers, I am inclined to use slightly different categories, lumping leaders and leader/managers into one category and placing in the other category those numerous managers whom one would not normally describe as leaders. Leaders and leader/managers distinguish themselves from the general run of managers in at least six respects:

1. They think longer term—beyond the day's crises, beyond the quarterly report, beyond the horizon.

2. In thinking about the unit they are heading, they grasp its relationship to larger realities—the larger organization of which they are a part, conditions external to the organization, global trends.

3. They reach and influence constituents beyond their jurisdictions, beyond boundaries. Thomas Jefferson influenced people all over Europe. Gandhi influenced people all over the world. In an organization, leaders extend their reach across bureaucratic boundaries—often a distinct advantage in a world too complex and tumultuous to be handled "through channels." Leaders' capacity to rise above jurisdictions may enable them to bind together the fragmented constituencies that must work together to solve a problem.

4. They put heavy emphasis on the intangibles of vision, values, and motivation and understand intuitively the nonrational and unconscious elements in leader–constituent interaction.

5. They have the political skill to cope with the conflicting requirements of multiple constituencies.

6. They think in terms of renewal. The routine manager tends to accept organizational structure and process as it exists. The leader or leader/manager seeks the revisions of process and structure required by ever-changing reality.

The manager is more tightly linked to an organization than is the leader. Indeed, the leader may have no organization at all. Florence Nightingale, after leaving the Crimea, exercised extraordinary leadership in health care for decades with no organization under her command. Gandhi was a leader before he had an organization. Some of our most memorable leaders have headed movements so amorphous that management would be an inappropriate word.

The Many Kinds of Leaders

One hears and reads a surprising number of sentences that describe leaders in general as having such and such attributes and behaving in such and such a fashion—as though one could distill out of the spectacular diversity of leaders an idealized picture of The Leader.

Leaders come in many forms, with many styles and diverse qualities. There are quiet leaders and leaders one can hear in the next county. Some find their strength in eloquence, some in judgment, some in courage. I had a friend who was a superior leader in outdoor activities and sports but quite incapable of leading in a bureaucratic setting.

The diversity is almost without limit: Churchill, the splendidly eloquent old warrior; Gandhi, the visionary and the shrewd mobilizer of his people; Lenin, the coldly purposeful revolutionary. Consider just the limited category of military leadership. George Marshall was a self-effacing, low-keyed man with superb judgment and a limitless capacity to inspire trust. MacArthur was a brilliant strategist, a farsighted administrator, and flamboyant to his fingertips. (Eisenhower, who had served under MacArthur, once said, "I studied dramatics under a master.") Eisenhower in his wartime assignment was an outstanding leader/administrator and coalition builder. General Patton was a slashing, intense combat commander. Field Marshal Montgomery was a gifted, temperamental leader of whom Churchill said, "In defeat, indomitable; in victory, insufferable." All were great leaders—but extraordinarily diverse in personal attributes.

The fact that there are many kinds of leaders has implications for leadership education. Most of those seeking to develop young potential leaders have in mind one ideal model that is inevitably constricting. We should give young people a sense of the many kinds of leaders and styles of leadership, and encourage them to move toward those models that are right for them.

Leaders and History

All too often when we think of our historic leaders, we eliminate all the contradictions that make individuals distinctive. And we further violate reality by lifting them out of their historical contexts. No wonder we are left with pasteboard portraits. As first steps toward a mature view of leaders we must accept complexity and context.

Thomas Jefferson was first of all a gifted and many-sided human, an enigmatic man who loved—among other things—abstract ideas, agriculture, architecture and statecraft. He was a man of natural aloofness who lived most of his life in public; a man of action with a gift for words and a bent for research; an idealist who proved himself a shrewd, even wily, operator on the political scene. Different sides of his nature came into play in different situations.

Place him now in the context of the exhilarating events and themes of his time: a new nation coming into being, with a new consciousness; the brilliant rays of the Enlightenment reaching into every phase of life; the inner contradictions of American society (e.g., slavery) already rumbling beneath the surface.

Finally, add the overpowering impulse of succeeding generations to serve their own needs by mythologizing, idolizing or debunking him. It turns out to be an intricately textured story—and not one that diminishes Jefferson.

It was once believed that if leadership traits were truly present in an individual, they would manifest themselves almost without regard to the situation in which the person was functioning. No one believes that any more. Acts of leadership take place in an unimaginable variety of settings, and the setting does much to determine the kinds of leaders that emerge and how they play their roles.

We cannot avoid the bewhiskered question, "Does the leader make history or does the historical moment make the leader?" It sounds like a seminar question but it is of interest to most leaders sooner or later. Corporate chief executive officers fighting a deteriorating trend in an industry feel like people trying to run up the down escalator. Looking across town at less able leaders riding an upward trend in another industry, they are ripe for the theory that history makes the leader.

Thomas Carlyle placed excessive emphasis on the great person, as did Sidney Hook ("all factors in history, save great men, are inconsequential").[2] Karl Marx, Georg Hegel, and Herbert Spencer placed excessive emphasis on historical forces. For Marx, economic forces shaped history; for Spencer, societies had their evolutionary course just as species did, and the leader was a product of the process; for Hegel, leaders were a part of the dialectic of history and could not help what they did.

The balanced view, of course, is that historical forces create the circumstances in which leaders emerge, but the characteristics of the particular leader in turn have their impact on history.

It is not possible to understand Queen Isabella without understanding fifteenth-century Europe (when she was born, Spain as we know it did not exist), or without understanding the impact of the Reformation on the Catholic world and the gnawing fear stirred by the Muslim conquests. But many monarchs flourished on the Iberian Peninsula in that historical context; only Isabella left an indelible mark. Similarly, by the time Martin Luther emerged, the seeds of the Reformation had already sprouted in many places, but no one would argue that the passionate, charismatic priest who nailed his ninety-five theses to the church door was a puppet of history. Historical forces set the stage for him, but once there, he was himself a historical force.

Churchill is an even more interesting case because he tried out for leadership many times before history was ready for him. After Dunkirk, England needed a leader who could rally the British people to heroic exertions in an uncompromising war, and the eloquent, combative Churchill delivered one of the great performances of the century. Subsequently the clock of history ticked on and—with the war over—the voters dropped him unceremoniously. When a friend told him it was a blessing in disguise, he growled "If it is, the disguise is perfect."

Forces of history determined his rise and fall, but in his time on the world stage he left a uniquely Churchillian mark on the course of events.

Settings

The historical moment is the broadest context affecting the emergence and functioning of leaders; but immensely diverse settings of a more modest nature clearly affect leadership.

The makeup of the group to be led is, of course, a crucial feature of the context. According to research findings, the approach to leadership or style of leadership that will be effective depends on, among other things, the age level of the individuals to be led; their educational background and competence; the size, homogeneity and cohesiveness of the group; its motivation and morale; its rate of turnover; and so on.

Other relevant contextual features are too numerous and diverse to list. Leading a corporation is one thing, leading a street gang is something else. Thomas Cronin has pointed out that it may take one kind of leadership to start a new enterprise and quite another kind to keep it going through its various phases.[3] Religious bodies, political parties, government agencies, the academic world—all offer distinctive contexts for leadership.

Judgments of Leaders

In curious ways, people tend to aggrandize the role of leaders. They tend to exaggerate the capacity of leaders to influence events. Jeffrey Pfeffer says that people want to achieve a feeling of control over their environment, and that this inclines them to attribute the outcomes of group performance to leaders rather than to context.[4] If we were to face the fact—so the argument goes—that outcomes are the result of a complex set of interactions among group members plus environmental and historical forces, we would feel helpless. By attributing outcomes to an identifiable leader we feel, rightly or not, more in control. There is at least a chance that one can fire the leader; one cannot "fire" historical forces.

Leaders act in the stream of history. As they labor to bring about a result, multiple forces beyond their control, even beyond their knowledge, are moving to hasten or hinder the result. So there is rarely a demonstrable causal link between a leader's specific decisions and consequent events. Consequences are not a reliable measure of leadership. Franklin Roosevelt's efforts to bolster the economy in the middle-to-late 1930s were powerfully aided by a force that did not originate with his economic brain trust—the winds of war. Leaders of a farm workers' union fighting for better wages may find their efforts set at naught by a crop failure.

Frank Lloyd Wright said, "A doctor can bury his mistakes. An architect can only advise his client to plant vines." Unlike either doctor or architect, leaders suffer from the mistakes of predecessors and leave some of their own misjudgments as time bombs for successors.

Many of the changes sought by leaders take time: lots of years, long public debate, slow shifts in attitude. In their lifetimes, leaders may see little result from heroic efforts yet may be setting the stage for victories that will come after them. Reflect on the long, slow unfolding of the battles for racial equality or for women's rights. Leaders who did vitally important early work died without knowing what they had wrought.

Leaders may appear to have succeeded (or failed) only to have historians a generation later reverse the verdict. The "verdict of history" has a wonderfully magisterial sound, but in reality it is subject to endless appeals to later generations of historians—with no court of last resort to render a final judgment.

In the real world, the judgments one makes of a leader must be multidimensional, taking into consideration great strengths, streaks of mediocrity, and perhaps great flaws. If the great strengths correspond to the needs of a crucial moment in history, the flaws are forgiven and simply provide texture to the biographies. Each leader has his or her own unique pattern of attributes, sometimes conflicting in curious ways. Ronald Reagan was notably passive with respect to many important issues, but vigorously tenacious on other issues.

Leaders change over the course of their active careers as do other human beings. In looking back, it is natural for us to freeze them in that moment when they served history's needs most spectacularly, but leaders evolve. The passionately antislavery Lincoln of the Douglas debates was not the see-both-sides Lincoln of fifteen years earlier. The "national unity" Churchill of 1942 was not the fiercely partisan, adversarial Churchill of the 1930s.

Devolving Initiative and Responsibility

I have already commented on our dispersed leadership and on its importance to the vitality of a large, intricately-organized system. Our most forward-looking business concerns are working in quite imaginative ways to devolve initiative downward and outward through their organizations to develop their lower levels of leadership.

There is no comparable movement in government agencies. But in the nation as a whole, dispersed leadership is a reality. In Santa Barbara County, California, Superintendent of Schools William Cirone is a leader in every sense of the word. A healthy school system requires a vital and involved citizenry. How does one achieve that? Given the aging population, fewer and fewer citizens have children in the schools. How do we keep them interested? Education is a lifelong process. How do we provide for that? These are questions to which Cirone has addressed himself with uncommon energy and imagination.[5]

The leaders of the Soviet Union did not launch the reforms of 1987 because they had developed a sudden taste for grass-roots democracy. They launched them because their system was grinding to a halt. Leader/managers at the lower levels and at the periphery of the system had neither the motivation nor the authority to solve problems that they understood better than the Moscow bureaucrats.

We have only half learned the lesson ourselves. In many of our large corporate, governmental, and nonprofit organizations we still make it all too difficult for potential leaders down the line to exercise initiative. We are still in the process of discovering how much vitality and motivation are buried at those levels awaiting release.

To emphasize the need for dispersed leadership does not deny the need for highly qualified top leadership. But our high-level leaders will be more effective in every way if the systems over which they preside are made vital by dispersed leadership. As I argued in *Excellence,* we must demand high performance at every level of society.[6]

Friends of mine have argued that in view of my convictions concerning the importance of middle- and lower-level leaders, I lean too heavily on examples of high-level leaders. My response is that we know a great deal about the more famous figures, statements about them can be documented, and they are comfortably familiar to readers. No one who reads this book with care could believe that I consider such exalted figures the only ones worth considering.

Institutionaling Leadership

To exercise leadership today, leaders must institutionalize their leadership. The issues are too technical and the pace of change too swift to expect that a leader, no matter how gifted, will be able to solve personally the major problems facing the system over which he or she presides. So we design an institutional system—a government agency, a corporation —to solve the problems, and then we select a leader who has the capacity to preside over and strengthen the system. Some leaders may be quite gifted in solving problems personally, but if they fail to institutionalize the process, their departure leaves the system crippled. They must create or strengthen systems that will survive them.

The institutional arrangements generally include a leadership team. Often throughout this book when I use the word *leader,* I am in fact referring to the leadership team. No individual has all the skills—and certainly not the time—to carry out all the complex tasks of contemporary leadership. And the team must be chosen for excellence in performance. Loyalty and being on the boss's wavelength are necessary but not sufficient qualifications. I emphasize the point because more than one recent president of the United States has had aides who possessed no other qualifications.

NOTES

1. Niccolò Machiavelli, *The Prince* (New York: New American Library, 1952).

2. Sidney Hook, *The Hero in History* (Boston: Beacon Press, 1955).

3. Thomas E. Cronin, *Chronicle of Higher Education* (February 1, 1989), pp. B1–B2.

4. Jeffrey Pfeffer, "The Ambiguity of Leadership" in *Leadership: Where Else Can We Go?* ed. Morgan W. McCall, Jr., and Michael Lombardo (Durham, N.C.: Duke University Press, 1978).

5. William J. Cirone and Barbara Margerum, "Models of Citizen Involvement and Community Education," *National Civic Review* 76, no. 3 (May–June 1987).

6. John W. Gardner, *Excellence,* rev. ed. (New York: W. W. Norton, 1984).

"GIVE ME A LEVER LONG ENOUGH . . . AND SINGLE-HANDED I CAN MOVE THE WORLD"

Peter M. Senge

FROM A VERY EARLY AGE, we are taught to break apart problems, to fragment the world. This apparently makes complex tasks and subjects more manageable, but we pay a hidden, enormous price. We can no longer see the consequences of our actions; we lose our intrinsic sense of connection to a larger whole. When we then try to "see the big picture," we try to reassemble the fragments in our minds, to list and organize all the pieces. But, as physicist David Bohm says, the task is futile—similar to trying to reassemble the fragments of a broken mirror to see a true reflection. Thus, after a while we give up trying to see the whole altogether.

The tools and ideas presented here are for destroying the illusion that the world is created of separate, unrelated forces. When we give up this illusion—we can then build "learning organizations," organizations where people continually expand their capacity to create the results they truly desire, where new and expansive patterns of thinking are nurtured, where collective aspiration is set free, and where people are continually learning how to learn together.

As *Fortune* magazine recently said, "Forget your tired old ideas about leadership. The most successful corporation of the 1990s will be something called a learning organization." "The ability to learn faster than your competitors," said Arie De Geus, head of planning for Royal Dutch/ Shell, "may be the only sustainable competitive advantage." As the world becomes more interconnected and business becomes more complex and dynamic, work must become more "learningful." It is no longer sufficient to have one person learning for the organization, a Ford or a Sloan or a Watson. It's just not possible any longer to "figure it out" from the top, and have everyone else following the orders of the "grand strategist." The organizations that will truly excel in the future will be the organizations that discover how to tap people's commitment and capacity to learn at *all* levels in an organization.

Learning organizations are possible because, deep down, we are all learners. No one has to teach an infant to learn. In fact, no one has to teach infants anything. They are intrinsically inquisitive, masterful learners who learn to walk, speak, and pretty much run their households all on their own. Learning organizations are possible because not only is it our nature to learn but we love to learn. Most of us at one time or another have been part of a great "team," a group of people who functioned together in an extraordinary way—who trusted one another, who complemented each others' strengths and compensated for each others' limitations, who had common goals that were larger than individual goals, and who produced extraordinary results. I have met many people who have experienced this sort of profound teamwork—in sports, or in the performing arts, or in business. Many say that they have spent much of their life looking for that experience again. What they experienced was a learning organization. The team that became great didn't start off great—it *learned* how to produce extraordinary results.

One could argue that the entire global business community is learning to learn together, becoming a learning community. Whereas once many industries were dominated by a single, undisputed leader—one IBM, one Kodak, one Procter & Gamble, one Xerox—today industries, especially in manufacturing, have dozens of excellent companies. American and European corporations are pulled forward by the example of the Japanese; the Japanese, in turn, are pulled by the Koreans and Europeans. Dramatic improvements take place in corporations in Italy, Australia, Singapore— and quickly become influential around the world.

There is also another, in some ways deeper, movement toward learning organizations, part of the evolution of industrial society. Material affluence for the majority has gradually shifted people's orientation toward work—from what Daniel Yankelovich called an "instrumental" view of work, where work was a means to an end, to a more "sacred" view, where people seek the "intrinsic" benefits of work.[1] "Our grandfathers worked six days a week to earn what most of us now earn by Tuesday afternoon," says Bill O'Brien, CEO of Hanover Insurance. "The ferment in management will continue until we build organizations that are more consistent with man's higher aspirations beyond food, shelter and belonging."

Moreover, many who share these values are now in leadership positions. I find a growing number of organizational leaders who, while still a minority, feel they are part of a profound evolution in the nature of work as a social institution. "Why can't we do good works at work?" asked Edward Simon, president of Herman Miller, recently. "Business is the only institution that has a chance, as far as I can see, to fundamentally improve the injustice that exists in the world. But first, we will have to move through the barriers that are keeping us from being truly vision-led and capable of learning."

Perhaps the most salient reason for building learning organizations is that we are only now starting to understand the capabilities such organizations must possess. For a long time, efforts to build learning organizations were like groping in the dark until the skills, areas of knowledge, and paths for development of such organizations became known. What fundamentally will distinguish learning organizations from traditional authoritarian "controlling organizations" will be the mastery of certain basic disciplines. That is why the "disciplines of the learning organization" are vital.

Disciplines of the Learning Organization

On a cold, clear morning in December 1903, at Kitty Hawk, North Carolina, the fragile aircraft of Wilbur and Orville Wright proved that powered flight was possible. Thus was the airplane invented; but it would take more than thirty years before commercial aviation could serve the general public.

Engineers say that a new idea has been "invented" when it is proven to work in the laboratory. The idea becomes an "innovation" only when it can be replicated reliably on a meaningful scale at practical costs. If the idea is sufficiently important, such as the telephone, the digital computer, or commercial aircraft, it is called a "basic innovation," and it creates a new industry or transforms an existing industry. In these terms, learning organizations have been invented, but they have not yet been innovated.

In engineering, when an idea moves from an invention to an innovation, diverse "component technologies" come together. Emerging from isolated developments in separate fields of research, these components gradually form an "ensemble of technologies that are critical to each others' success. Until this ensemble forms, the idea, though possible in the laboratory, does not achieve its potential in practice."[2]

The Wright Brothers proved that powered flight was possible, but the McDonnell Douglas DC-3, introduced in 1935, ushered in the era of commercial air travel. The DC-3 was the first plane that supported itself economically as well as aerodynamically. During those intervening thirty years (a typical time period for incubating basic innovations), myriad experiments with commercial flight had failed. Like early experiments with learning organizations, the early planes were not reliable and cost effective on an appropriate scale.

The DC-3, for the first time, brought together five critical component technologies that formed a successful ensemble. They were: the variable-pitch propeller, retractable landing gear, a type of lightweight molded body construction called "monocque," radial air-cooled engine, and wing flaps. To succeed, the DC-3 needed all five; four were not enough. One year earlier, the Boeing 247 was introduced with all of them except wing flaps. Lacking wing flaps, Boeing's engineers found that the plane was unstable on take-off and landing and had to downsize the engine.

Today, I believe, five new "component technologies" are gradually converging to innovate learning organizations. Though developed separately, each will, I believe, prove critical to the others' success, just as occurs with any ensemble. Each provides a vital dimension in building organizations that can truly "learn," that can continually enhance their capacity to realize their highest aspirations:

Systems Thinking. A cloud masses, the sky darkens, leaves twist upward, and we know that it will rain. We also know that after the storm, the runoff will feed into groundwater miles away, and the sky will grow clear by tomorrow. All these events are distant in time and space, and yet they are all connected within the same pattern. Each has an influence on the rest, an influence that is usually hidden from view. You can only understand the system of a rainstorm by contemplating the whole, not any individual part of the pattern.

Business and other human endeavors are also systems. They, too, are bound by invisible fabrics of interrelated actions, which often take years to fully play out their effects on each other. Since we are part of that lacework ourselves, it's doubly hard to see the whole pattern of change. Instead, we tend to focus on snapshots of isolated parts of the system, and wonder why our deepest problems never seem to get solved. Systems thinking is a conceptual framework, a body of knowledge and tools that has been developed over the past fifty years, to make the full patterns clearer, and to help us see how to change them effectively.

Though the tools are new, the underlying worldview is extremely intuitive; experiments with young children show that they learn systems thinking very quickly.

Personal Mastery. Mastery might suggest gaining dominance over people or things. But mastery can also mean a special level of proficiency. A master craftsman doesn't dominate pottery or weaving. People with a high level of personal mastery are able to consistently realize the results that matter most deeply to them—in effect, they approach their life as an artist would approach a work of art. They do that by becoming committed to their own lifelong learning.

Personal mastery is the discipline of continually clarifying and deepening our personal vision, of focusing our energies, of developing patience, and of seeing reality objectively. As such, it is an essential cornerstone of the learning organization—the learning organization's spiritual foundation. An organization's commitment to and capacity for learning can be no greater than that of its members. The roots of this discipline lie in both Eastern and Western spiritual traditions, and in secular traditions as well.

But surprisingly few organizations encourage the growth of their people in this manner. This results in vast untapped resources: "People enter business as bright, well-educated, high-energy people, full of energy and desire to make a difference," says Hanover's O'Brien. "By the time they are 30, a few are on the 'fast track' and the rest 'put in their time' to do what matters to them on the weekend. They lose the commitment, the sense of mission, and the excitement with which they started their careers. We get damn little of their energy and almost none of their spirit."

And surprisingly few adults work to rigorously develop their own personal mastery. When you ask most adults what they want from their lives, they often talk first about what they'd like to get rid of: "I'd like my mother-in-law to move out," they say, or "I'd like my back problems to clear up." The discipline of personal mastery, by contrast, starts with clarifying the things that really matter to us, of living our lives in the service of our highest aspirations.

Here, I am most interested in the connections between personal learning and organizational learning, in the reciprocal commitments between individual and organization, and in the special spirit of an enterprise made up of learners.

Mental Models. "Mental models" are deeply ingrained assumptions, generalizations, or even pictures or images that influence how we understand the world and how we take action. Very often, we are not consciously aware of our mental models or the effects they have on our behavior. For example, we may notice that a coworker dresses elegantly, and say to ourselves, "She's a country club person." About someone who dresses shabbily, we may feel, "He doesn't care about what others think." Mental models of what can or cannot be done in different management settings are no less deeply entrenched. Many insights into new markets or outmoded organizational practices fail to get put into practice because they conflict with powerful, tacit mental models.

Royal Dutch/Shell, one of the first large organizations to understand the advantages of accelerating organizational learning came to this realization when they discovered how pervasive was the influence of hidden mental models, especially those that become widely shared. Shell's extraordinary success in managing through the dramatic changes and unpredictability of the world oil business in the 1970s and 1980s came in large measure from learning how to surface and challenge managers' mental models. (In the early 1970s Shell was the weakest of the big seven oil companies; by the late 1980s it was the strongest.) Arie de Geus, Shell's recently retired Coordinator of Group Planning, says that continuous adaptation and growth in a changing business environment depends on "institutional learning, which is the process whereby management teams change their shared mental models of the company, their markets, and their competitors. For this reason, we think of planning as learning and of corporate planning as institutional learning." [3]

The discipline of working with mental models starts with turning the mirror inward; learning to unearth our internal pictures of the world, to bring them to the surface and hold them rigorously to scrutiny. It also includes the ability to carry on "learningful" conversations that balance inquiry and advocacy, where people expose their own thinking effectively and make that thinking open to the influence of others.

Building Shared Vision. If any one idea about leadership has inspired organizations for thousands of years, it's the capacity to hold a shared picture of the future we seek to create. One is hard pressed to think of any organization that has sustained some measure of greatness in the absence of goals, values, and missions that become deeply shared throughout the organization. IBM had "service"; Polaroid had instant photography; Ford had public transportation for the masses and Apple had computing power for the masses. Though radically different in content and kind, all these organizations managed to bind people together around a common identity and sense of destiny.

When there is a genuine vision (as opposed to the all-too-familiar "vision statement"), people excel and learn, not because they are told to, but because they want to. But many leaders have personal visions that never get translated into shared visions that galvanize an organization. All too often, a company's shared vision has revolved around the charisma of a leader, or around a crisis that galvanizes everyone temporarily. But, given a choice, most people opt for pursuing a lofty goal, not only in times of crisis but at all times. What has been lacking is a discipline for translating individual vision into shared vision—not a "cookbook" but a set of principles and guiding practices.

The practice of shared vision involves the skills of unearthing shared "pictures of the future" that foster genuine commitment and enrollment rather than compliance. In mastering this discipline, leaders learn the counterproductiveness of trying to dictate a vision, no matter how heartfelt.

Team Learning. How can a team of committed managers with individual IQs above 120 have a collective IQ of 63? The discipline of team learning confronts this paradox. We know that teams can learn; in sports, in the performing arts, in science, and even, occasionally, in business, there are striking examples where the intelligence of the team exceeds the intelligence of the individuals in the team, and where teams develop extraordinary capacities for coordinated action. When teams are truly learning, not only are they producing extraordinary results but the individual members are growing more rapidly than could have occurred otherwise.

The discipline of team learning starts with "dialogue," the capacity of members of a team to suspend assumptions and enter into a genuine "thinking together." To the Greeks *dia-logos* meant a free-flowing of meaning through a group, allowing the group to discover insights not attainable individually. Interestingly, the practice of dialogue has been preserved in many "primitive" cultures, such as that of the American Indian, but it has been almost completely lost to modern society. Today, the principles and practices of dialogue are being rediscovered and put into a contemporary context. (Dialogue differs from the more common "discussion," which has its roots with "percussion" and "concussion," literally a heaving of ideas back and forth in a winner-takes-all competition.)

The discipline of dialogue also involves learning how to recognize the patterns of interaction in teams that undermine learning. The patterns of defensiveness are often deeply engrained in how a team operates. If unrecognized, they undermine learning. If recognized and surfaced creatively, they can actually accelerate learning.

Team learning is vital because teams, not individuals, are the fundamental learning unit in modern organizations. This where "the rubber meets the road"; unless teams can learn, the organization cannot learn.

If a learning organization were an engineering innovation, such as the airplane or the personal computer, the components would be called "technologies." For an innovation in human behavior, the components need to be seen as *disciplines*. By "discipline," I do not mean an "enforced order" or "means of punishment," but a body of theory and technique that must be studied and mastered to be put into practice. A discipline is a developmental path for acquiring certain skills or competencies. As with any discipline, from playing the piano to electrical engineering, some people have an innate "gift," but anyone can develop proficiency through practice.

To practice a discipline is to be a lifelong learner. You "never arrive"; you spend your life mastering disciplines. You can never say, "We are a learning organization," any more than you can say, "I am an enlightened person." The more you learn, the more acutely aware you become of your ignorance. Thus, a corporation cannot be "excellent" in the sense of having arrived at a permanent excellence; it is always in the state of practicing the disciplines of learning, of becoming better or worse.

That organizations can benefit from disciplines is not a totally new idea. After all, management disciplines such as accounting have been around for a long time. But the five learning disciplines differ from more familiar management disciplines in that they are "personal" disciplines. Each has to do with how we think, what we truly want, and how we interact and learn with one another. In this sense, they are more like artistic disciplines than traditional management disciplines. Moreover, while accounting is good for "keeping score," we have never approached the subtler tasks of building organizations, of enhancing their capabilities for innovation and creativity, of crafting strategy and designing policy and structure through assimilating new disciplines. Perhaps this is why, all too often, great organizations are fleeting, enjoying their moment in the sun, then passing quietly back to the ranks of the mediocre.

Practicing a discipline is different from emulating "a model." All too often, new management innovations are described in terms of the "best practices" of so-called leading firms. While interesting, I believe such descriptions can often do more harm than good, leading to piecemeal copying and playing catch-up. I do not believe great organizations have ever been built by trying to emulate another, any more than individual greatness is achieved by trying to copy another "great person."

When the five component technologies converged to create the DC-3 the commercial airline industry began. But the DC-3 was not the end of the process. Rather, it was the precursor of a new industry. Similarly, as the five component learning disciplines converge they will not create *the* learning organization but rather a new wave of experimentation and advancement.

The Fifth Discipline

It is vital that the five disciplines develop as an ensemble. This is challenging because it is much harder to integrate new tools than simply apply them separately. But the payoffs are immense.

This is why systems thinking is the fifth discipline. It is the discipline that integrates the disciplines, fusing them into a coherent body of theory and practice. It keeps them from being separate gimmicks or the latest organization change fads. Without a systemic orientation, there is no motivation to look at how the disciplines interrelate. By enhancing each of the other disciplines, it continually reminds us that the whole can exceed the sum of its parts.

For example, vision without systems thinking ends up painting lovely pictures of the future with no deep understanding of the forces that must be mastered to move from here to there. This is one of the reasons why many firms that have jumped on the "vision bandwagon" in recent years have found that lofty vision alone fails to turn around a firm's fortunes. Without systems thinking, the seed of vision falls on harsh soil. If nonsystemic thinking predominates, the first condition for nurturing vision is not met: a genuine belief that we can make our vision real in the future. We may say "We can achieve our vision" (most American managers are conditioned to this belief), but our tacit view of current reality as a set of conditions created by somebody else betrays us.

But systems thinking also needs the disciplines of building shared vision, mental models, team learning, and personal mastery to realize its potential. Building shared vision fosters a commitment to the long term. Mental models focus on the openness needed to unearth shortcomings in our present ways of seeing the world. Team learning develops the skills of groups of people to look for the larger picture that lies beyond individual perspectives. And personal mastery fosters the personal motivation to continually learn how our actions affect our world. Without personal mastery, people are so steeped in the reactive mindset ("someone/something else is creating my problems") that they are deeply threatened by the systems perspective.

Lastly, systems thinking makes understandable the subtlest aspect of the learning organization—the new way individuals perceive themselves and their world. At the heart of a learning organization is a shift of mind—from seeing ourselves as separate from the world to connected to the world, from seeing problems as caused by someone or something "out there" to seeing how our own actions create the problems we experience. A learning organization is a place where people are continually discovering how they create their reality. And how they can change it. As Archimedes has said, "Give me a lever long enough . . . and single-handed I can move the world."

Metanoia—A Shift of Mind

When you ask people about what it is like being part of a great team, what is most striking is the meaningfulness of the experience. People talk about being part of something larger than themselves, of being connected, of being generative. It becomes quite clear that, for many, their experiences as part of truly great teams stand out as singular periods of life lived to the fullest. Some spend the rest of their lives looking for ways to recapture that spirit.

The most accurate word in Western culture to describe what happens in a learning organization is one that hasn't had much currency for the past several hundred years. It is a word we have used in our work with organizations for some ten years, but we always caution them, and ourselves, to use it sparingly in public. The word is "metanoia" and it means a shift of mind. The word has a rich history. For the Greeks, it meant a fundamental shift or change, or more literally transcendence ("*meta*"— above or beyond, as in "metaphysics") of mind ("noia," from the root "*nous*," of mind). In the early (Gnostic) Christian tradition, it took on a special meaning of awakening shared intuition and direct knowing of the highest, of God. "Metanoia" was probably the key term of such early Christians as John the Baptist. In the Catholic corpus the word metanoia was eventually translated as "repent."

To grasp the meaning of "metanoia" is to grasp the deeper meaning of "learning," for learning also involves a fundamental shift or movement of mind. The problem with talking about "learning organizations" is that the "learning" has lost its central meaning in contemporary usage. Most people's eyes glaze over if you talk to them about "learning" or "learning organizations." Little wonder—for, in everyday use, learning has come to be synonymous with "taking in information." "Yes, I learned all about that at the course yesterday." Yet, taking in information is only distantly related to real learning. It would be nonsensical to say, "I just read a great book about bicycle riding—I've now learned that."

Real learning gets to the heart of what it means to be human. Through learning we re-create ourselves. Through learning we become able to do something we never were able to do. Through learning we reperceive the world and our relationship to it. Through learning we extend our capacity to create, to be part of the generative process of life. There is within each of us a deep hunger for this type of learning. It is, as Bill O'Brien of Hanover Insurance says, "as fundamental to human beings as the sex drive."

This, then, is the basic meaning of a "learning organization"—an organization that is continually expanding its capacity to create its future. For such an organization, it is not enough merely to survive. "Survival learning" or what is more often termed "adaptive learning" is important—indeed it is necessary. But for a learning organization, "adaptive learning" must be joined by "generative learning," learning that enhances our capacity to create.

A few brave organizational pioneers are pointing the way, but the territory of building learning organizations is still largely unexplored. It is my fondest hope that this book can accelerate that exploration.

Putting the Ideas into Practice

I take no credit for inventing the five major disciplines of this book. The five disciplines described below represent the experimentation, research, writing, and invention of hundreds of people. But I have worked with all of the disciplines for years, refining ideas about them, collaborating on research, and introducing them to organizations throughout the world.

When I entered graduate school at the Massachusetts Institute of Technology in 1970, I was already convinced that most of the problems faced by humankind concerned our inability to grasp and manage the increasingly complex systems of our world. Little has happened since to change my view. Today, the arms race, the environmental crisis, the international drug trade, the stagnation in the Third World, and the persisting U.S. budget and trade deficits all attest to a world where problems are becoming increasingly complex and interconnected. From the start at MIT I was drawn to the work of Jay Forrester, a computer pioneer who had shifted fields to develop what he called "system dynamics." Jay maintained that the causes of many pressing public issues, from urban decay to global ecological threat, lay in the very well-intentioned policies designed to alleviate them. These problems were "actually systems" that lured policy-makers into interventions that focused on obvious symptoms not under-lying causes, which produced short-term benefit but long-term malaise, and fostered the need for still more symptomatic interventions.

As I began my doctoral work, I had little interest in business manage-ment. I felt that the solutions to the Big Issues lay in the public sector. But I began to meet business leaders who came to visit our MIT group to learn about systems thinking. These were thoughtful people, deeply aware of the inadequacies of prevailing ways of managing. They were engaged in building new types of organizations—decentralized, nonhierarchical or-ganizations dedicated to the well-being and growth of employees as well as to success. Some had crafted radical corporate philosophies based on core values of freedom and responsibility. Others had developed innova-tive organization designs. All shared a commitment and a capacity to in-novate that was lacking in the public sector. Gradually, I came to realize why business is the locus of innovation in an open society. Despite what-ever hold past thinking may have on the business mind, business has a freedom to experiment missing in the public sector and, often, in non-profit organizations. It also has a clear "bottom line," so that experiments can be evaluated, at least in principle, by objective criteria.

But why were they interested in systems thinking? Too often, the most daring organizational experiments were foundering. Local autonomy produced business decisions that were disastrous for the organization as a whole. "Team building" exercises sent colleagues white-water rafting together, but when they returned home they still disagreed fundamentally about business problems. Companies pulled together during crises, and then lost all their inspiration when business improved. Organizations which started out as booming successes, with the best possible intentions toward customers and employees, found themselves trapped in down-ward spirals that got worse the harder they tried to fix them.

Then, we all believed that the tools of systems thinking could make a difference in these companies. As I worked with different companies, I came to see why systems thinking was not enough by itself. It needed a new type of management practitioner to really make the most of it. At that time, in the mid-1970s, there was a nascent sense of what such a management practitioner could be. But it had not yet crystallized. It is crystallizing now with leaders of our MIT group: William O'Brien of Hanover Insurance; Edward Simon from Herman Miller, and Ray Stata,

CEO of Analog Devices. All three of these men are involved in innovative, influential companies. All three have been involved in our research program for several years, along with leaders from Apple, Ford, Polaroid, Royal Dutch/Shell, and Trammell Crow.

For eleven years I have also been involved in developing and conducting Innovation Associates' Leadership and Mastery workshops, which have introduced people from all walks of life to the fifth discipline ideas that have grown out of our work at MIT, combined with IA's pathbreaking work on building shared vision and personal mastery. Over four thousand managers have attended. We started out with a particular focus on corporate senior executives, but soon found that the basic disciplines such as systems thinking, personal mastery, and shared vision were relevant for teachers, public administrators and elected officials, students, and parents. All were in leadership positions of importance. All were in "organizations" that had still untapped potential for creating their future. All felt that to tap that potential required developing their own capacities, that is, learning. . . .

NOTES

1. Daniel Yankelovich, *New Rules: Searching for Self-fulfillment in a World Turned Upside Down* (New York: Random House), 1981.

2. I am indebted to my MIT colleague Alan Graham for the insight that basic innovation occurs through the integration of diverse technologies into a new ensemble. See A. K. Graham, "Software Design: Breaking the Bottleneck," *IEEE Spectrum* (March 1982): 43–50; A. K. Graham and P. Senge, "A Long-Wave Hypothesis of Innovation," *Technological Forecasting and Social Change* (1980): 283–311.

3. Arie de Geus, "Planning as Learning," *Harvard Business Review* (March/April 1988): 70–74.

CONDENSATION OF THE FOURTEEN POINTS FOR MANAGEMENT

W. Edwards Deming

ORIGIN OF THE 14 POINTS. The 14 points are the basis for transformation of American industry. It will not suffice merely to solve problems, big or little. Adoption and action on the 14 points are a signal that the management intend[s] to stay in business and aim[s] to protect investors and jobs. . . .

The 14 points apply anywhere, to small organizations as well as to large ones, to the service industry as well as to manufacturing. They apply to a division within a company.

1. Create constancy of purpose toward improvement of product and service, with the aim to become competitive and to stay in business, and to provide jobs.

2. Adopt the new philosophy. We are in a new economic age. Western management must awaken to the challenge, must learn their responsibilities, and take on leadership for change.

3. Cease dependence on inspection to achieve quality. Eliminate the need for inspection on a mass basis by building quality into the product in the first place.

4. End the practice of awarding business on the basis of price tag. Instead, minimize total cost. Move toward a single supplier for any one item, on a long-term relationship of loyalty and trust.

5. Improve constantly and forever the system of production and service, to improve quality and productivity, and thus constantly decrease costs.

6. Institute training on the job.

7. Institute leadership. The aim of supervision should be to help people and machines and gadgets to do a better job. Supervision of management is in need of overhaul, as well as supervision of production workers.

8. Drive out fear, so that everyone may work effectively for the company.

9. Break down barriers between departments. People in research, design, sales, and production must work as a team, to foresee problems of production and in use that may be encountered with the product or service.

10. Eliminate slogans, exhortations, and targets for the work force asking for zero defects and new levels of productivity. Such exhortations only create adversarial relationships, as the bulk of the causes of low quality and low productivity belong to the system and thus lie beyond the power of the work force.

11a. Eliminate work standards (quotas) on the factory floor. Substitute leadership.

11b. Eliminate management by objective. Eliminate management by numbers, numerical goals. Substitute leadership.

12a. Remove barriers that rob the hourly worker of his right to pride of workmanship. The responsibility of supervisors must be changed from sheer numbers to quality.

12b. Remove barriers that rob people in management and in engineering of their right to pride of workmanship. This means, *inter alia,* abolishment of the annual or merit rating and of management by objective.

13. Institute a vigorous program of education and self-improvement.

14. Put everybody in the company to work to accomplish the transformation. The transformation is everybody's job.

4

WE NEED NONCOERCIVE LEAD-MANAGEMENT FROM THE STATE SUPERINTENDENT TO THE TEACHER

William Glasser

HAVING SEEN THAT TEACHING is perhaps the most difficult of all management jobs, we are now ready to take a detailed look at the crucial factor in educational reform: replacing boss-management with lead-management so that we can begin the move to quality. Boss-management is wrong because it limits both the quality of the work and the productivity of the worker. And further, as I will explain shortly, its use actually produces most of the discipline problems we are trying to prevent.

In education, where it is used almost exclusively, boss-management has effectively limited the number of students who do acceptable work (many less do quality work) to about 50 percent in the best neighborhoods and up to 90 percent in schools where there is little support for learning in students' homes. Therefore, given the hardest of management jobs, teachers as well as administrators are burdened with a method of management that limits their ability to succeed no matter how competent they are in other respects.

Boss-management is not complicated. Reduced to its essentials, it contains four basic elements:

1. The boss sets the task and the standards for what the workers (students) are to do, usually without consulting the workers. Bosses do

not compromise; the worker has to adjust to the job as the boss defines it.

2. The boss usually tells, rather than shows, the workers how the work is to be done and rarely asks for their input as to how it might possibly be done better.

3. The boss, or someone the boss designates, inspects (or grades) the work. Because the boss does not involve the workers in this evaluation, they tend to settle for just enough quality to get by.

4. When workers resist, the boss uses coercion (usually punishment) almost exclusively to try to make them do as they are told and, in so doing, creates a workplace in which the workers and manager are adversaries.

Viewed as a whole, it is obvious that boss-management is much more concerned with the needs of the boss than of the workers. Because this is so obvious, many bosses have been able to see that boss-management is counterproductive. There is now some softening of this hard line, mostly in high-tech and service industries where the educational and persuasive skills of the worker are paramount to the success of the company. Schools, however, are one of the few "industries" in which boss-management is used pretty much as outlined above.

The most obvious reason for the overwhelming preponderance of boss-managers is tradition. It is "natural" for the strong to try to dominate the weak, and students are always younger and less knowledgeable (therefore weaker) than the teacher. Administrators, especially, tend to see students as subordinates, a situation tailor-made for the boss-management approach. And since schools have always been boss-managed, most teachers and administrators do not question what they do and are not even aware that a better, noncoercive method of management exists.

In industry, we now have extensive research to prove that boss-management is much less effective than lead-management,[1] but this research has had little effect on much of industry and almost no effect on the schools. I believe there are two reasons for this, both of which I address in this book:

1. Managers do not know choice theory and do not know why lead-management works. They therefore tend to distrust it even when they see it working.

2. Managers do not realize that what Deming has taught and demonstrated is that quality is the key to increased productivity.

There is always the fear, especially in education among the measurers and fragmenters who prevail at the top, that if we are too concerned with quality, students will cover less ground. Deming has shown that the opposite occurs: Quality always leads to increased productivity. Many people do not believe this because what Deming has accomplished is so contrary to "common sense."

Boss-management is also difficult to challenge because in most schools there are enough students willing to work that any teacher can say, "Look at all the students who are doing well because they are doing what they are told." But the success of these students is not due to the way they are managed: It is because of the homes they come from. It occurs despite how they are managed: If boss-management were effective, many more students would be successful.

The get-tough, coercive boss approach is the main way in which schools deal with problem students. The persuasive, lead-management approach is not known well enough even to be considered. But even if teachers were aware of this approach, they would be leery of it because they fear it lacks control. Boss-managers are not comfortable with the idea of giving up the control they believe is inherent in their traditional boss approach.

But as much as boss-management promises control, in schools it totally fails to deliver on this promise. There is no shortage of students in most schools who neither work nor follow rules. Teachers who become frustrated by these resistant students tend to request sanctions like detention, suspension, and corporal punishment, but as they use these, they become more boss-like and less effective. They fail to recognize that many students have become hardened to those limited sanctions and have no fear of them. From the students' standpoint, the need-frustrating pain of memorizing low-quality fragments is as great or greater than the pain of whatever sanction they might suffer at the hands of the teacher.

What teachers also fail to see is that these very sanctions stand in the way of achieving the quality that is essential to a highly productive workplace. This is because as soon as a boss uses coercion, especially punishment, the boss and the worker become adversaries. There is no way to keep this from happening. And while people will work for an adversary (huge numbers do and some even work hard), they do so because of their own needs. The boss is ignored, avoided, disliked, or ridiculed and is seen as either unnecessary or as an obstacle to getting the job done.

In such an atmosphere, which prevails in many work situations (schools have no monopoly here), workers will work, but very few will consistently do the high-quality work of which they are capable. Too often, work becomes a wasteful contest. The boss tries to get as much from the workers as possible while giving as little as possible, and the workers give as little as possible and still try to get what they want. This contest uses up a great deal of energy that could be better channeled into productivity and quality.

In school, the adversarial teacher-student relationship that is destructive to quality starts quickly. As early as first grade, any child who does not do as the teacher says is almost always boss-managed, and the coercion starts. It does not make much difference whether it is done subtly or overtly: The child knows when he or she is being coerced. As soon as this occurs, the child's main agenda becomes resistance, the personal power struggle between teacher and pupil begins, and education is left behind. It becomes a vicious cycle: The child learns less and resists more; the teacher coerces more and teaches less. For many children this adversarial relationship is in place by elementary school, and their formal education becomes secondary to a never-ending power struggle in which all involved are losers.

Teachers in elementary schools, however, are much less likely to use boss-management destructively than in the secondary school. The "keep-quiet-and-do-what-you-are-told" boss approach flowers in the higher grades, where teachers are pressured to "produce" and where, with well over a hundred students each day, they have little opportunity to get to know their students personally. By the end of the seventh grade, more than half the students believe that teachers and principals are their adversaries. Quality education thus becomes unavailable except to the dwindling minority who are willing to fit into the boss-defined system. Believing, correctly in most cases, that the system will never adjust to what they want or even try to find out what that is, many students drop out altogether, many more than are reported because our present statistics do not include substantial numbers of middle school dropouts.[2]

Boss-management works better if the boss uses rewards instead of punishment. Even though control remains in the hands of the boss, this tends to reduce the adversarial atmosphere that is the hallmark of boss-management. Schools, however, are largely unable to reward students, so that the best part of boss-management is mostly unavailable to students. There are, for example, no immediate rewards comparable to those in industry, such as pay increases, help from subordinates, promotions, better offices, good parking, and time off.

Even good grades, essentially the only tangible school reward, are far from immediate. Most schools depend on hazy, long-term rewards, such as the promise that students will get into a good college and get a good job if they work hard and get good grades. This is probably true, but these goals are so far in the future that fewer than half of the capable students are willing to work hard now to achieve them. Young people, especially, will not work hard for distant rewards. If they are to put out a lot of effort, they want an immediate payoff.

Therefore, it is almost impossible to coerce students to work hard enough to do quality work when they see school as nonsatisfying. What is needed instead of coercion is a great deal of creativity and patience, both of which tend to be in short supply. This does not mean that all boss-management is ineffective, but it is least effective where workers do not see the job as satisfying. It is most effective where workers and the boss have the same agendas and where the boss uses rewards more than punishment, a situation more prevalent in elementary school than in secondary school.

While boss-management is ineffective at all levels, the higher the level at which it is employed, the more damage it does to the quality of the work and the productivity of the worker. For example, teachers who use boss-management exclusively will limit the learning in their classes. A principal who is a dedicated boss-manager will make it so hard for teachers to use lead-management that the whole school will be negatively affected. A superintendent following this philosophy will cast a shadow on the whole district, and when boss-management is the philosophy in the state office, as it is in the many states that are now demanding that standardized fragments of learning be measured, the whole state will suffer.

As Deming says, "The goal is clear. The productivity of our systems must be increased. The key to change is the understanding of our managers, and the people to whom they report, about what it means to be a good manager."

Lead-Management Is the Basic Reform We Need

In contrast to the coercive core of boss-management, persuasion and problem solving are central to the philosophy of lead-management. The lead-manager spends all his time and energy figuring out how to run the system so that workers will see that it is to their benefit to do quality work. In Deming's words:

1. A manager is responsible for consistency of purpose and continuity to the organization. The manager is solely responsible to see that there is a future for the workers. [It is our responsibility as a society to manage our schools so that almost all students get a high-quality education.]

2. The workers work in a system. The manager should work on the system to see that it produces the highest quality product at the lowest possible cost. The distinction is crucial. They work *in* the system; the manager works *on* the system. No one else is responsible for the system as a whole and improving it.[3] [This means that the administrators, much more than the teachers, are responsible for improving the system.]

Keeping these points in mind, following are the four essential elements of lead-managing:

1. The leader engages the workers in a discussion of the quality of the work to be done and the time needed to do it so that they have a chance to add their input. The leader makes a constant effort to fit the job to the skills and the needs of the workers.

2. The leader (or a worker designated by the leader) shows or models the job so that the worker who is to perform the job can see exactly what the manager expects. At the same time, the workers are continually asked for their input as to what they believe may be a better way.

3. The leader asks the workers to inspect or evaluate their own work for quality, with the understanding that the leader accepts that they know a great deal about how to produce high-quality work and will therefore listen to what they say.

4. The leader is a facilitator in that he shows the workers that he has done everything possible to provide them with the best tools and workplace as well as a noncoercive, nonadversarial atmosphere in which to do the job.

To demonstrate how these elements would work in practice, let me apply them to the teaching of algebra, a subject that many students are having difficulty learning in our predominantly boss-managed math classes. In these classes a boss-teacher sets the agenda, and the students have no say in this process. The students pass the course if the first time they take the test they are able to achieve a minimum score; even low-quality D work is passing. Large numbers of students are failing, however, because they do not do even this much or cannot do it on the only test given.

In contrast, a lead-teacher would start by discussing algebra, defining it, and explaining why it is taught and how the students could use it in their lives. If available, a videotape would be shown in which successful people from various cultural backgrounds explain how they use algebra in their lives and why it was worthwhile for them to learn it. The lead-teacher would tell the class that any student who makes an effort can learn algebra well.

After answering students' immediate questions, the teacher would then explain that much of the work would be done in small cooperative groups (a very need-satisfying way to teach) in which students would help each other. The teacher would try to assign at least one capable student to each cooperative group and would teach these student leaders how to model the problem-solving techniques for the rest of the group. The teacher would emphasize that the purpose of the groups is to help them all to understand algebra, not just to get the problems done. Schools would make an effort to train all the teachers who use cooperative learning to use it well.

The teacher would ask for students' input as to when they are ready to take the tests, based on their results on practice tests that would always precede the real exams. Students who did well on the tests would go on; students who did not do well would then have the chance to continue working on the tested material until they mastered it. Competency and quality would be the rule: Time would never be a factor. The ideal of a quality school would be that no student willing to do the work would need to be concerned about running out of the time needed to learn. This would mean that no one would be asked to go on to new material until he or she had demonstrated a good understanding of what had been covered so far.

In practice, this approach would present difficulties. How would a teacher handle faster and slower students in the same classroom? What we do now is to let the slower students struggle. They either fail or end up doing work of very low quality, hardly a sensible solution to this problem. Or they drop algebra, enroll in general math, and never learn higher mathematics. My solution is to find out early who is not able to keep up in the standard one-year course and offer a two-year course concurrently into which these slower students could transfer. While some of the one-year students might do higher-quality work than the two-year students, quality would also be maintained in the slower course. The difference would be less in the quality of the work than in the time to do it.

In the two-year course, all students who worked would be given sufficient time to complete each unit of the course with competence. As they did, they would gain confidence and begin to work a little faster, and many would go on to higher math. (At present, students who fall behind lose confidence and simply give up.) Students from the one-year course could transfer into the two-year course at specified intervals during the year, knowing that the same quality standards would apply. This might mean that the faster students would have a chance for an additional elective, or they could be enlisted to help tutor the slower students both in and out of class. Given a chance to teach, they would improve their already high-quality skills. . . . In this way, almost all who are willing to try would eventually learn to do quality algebra. And using the approach described here, many more than now would be willing to try.

From the beginning, all students, both as individuals and as a group, would be asked to evaluate the quality of their classwork, homework, and tests and to put this evaluation at the top of all they do. How they would do this would be discussed and agreed on as part of the continual give-and-take that would take place in a lead-managed class. Following Deming, the emphasis would be on involving the students in the evaluation of their own work for quality, and they would be encouraged to keep their own quality record so that they would always know exactly where they were.

The lead-teacher's job would be to facilitate continually, which would mean talking to students and listening to their input on how to keep the classroom a good place to learn and how to make improvements. Once the students discovered that they could actually do quality work in algebra, they would find a satisfaction with math that almost no students get now in their boss-managed classes. It is only the discovery that "I can do quality work" that leads to motivation. . . . There would be no coercion and, therefore, no discipline problems, as they do not occur in a noncoercive atmosphere.

When the above principles are put into practice in school or elsewhere, the worker cannot help but see that the manager is as concerned with the workers' needs as with his or her own. And when the workers are students, they realize that the person they are working for is a teacher, not a boss. This is why lead-managing is so applicable to education: The very definition of good teaching is embodied in the four elements of lead-management.

While in theory the basic tactics of the two types of managers differ markedly, in practice boss-managers are rarely all boss. Few boss-managers approach their job with the coercive zeal of a marine drill sergeant, and even a drill sergeant will at times use some persuasion. On the other hand, lead-managers may be tempted to blend a little coercion into their basic lead approach, but, if they do, they risk losing their effectiveness. For this reason, the best lead-managers make a constant effort never to coerce. Even a little coercion will taint the lead atmosphere and render it adversarial because the manager will be seen as a phony. It takes a long time to persuade workers who have been boss-managed to accept that they can work in a problem-solving, give-and-take atmosphere free of coercion. If there is any coercion at all, this acceptance time is greatly extended.

This does not mean, however, that the lead-manager does nothing if a worker fails to put forth effort or breaks the rules of the workplace. There is much the lead-manager can and should do: His skill is doing it without coercion. How a teacher or administrator can accomplish this [is explained elsewhere], but basically, when there is a dispute between the leader and the worker, the leader makes it clear to the worker that this is a problem they can solve together. The leader emphasizes that problems are never solved by coercion: They are solved by all parties to the problem figuring out a better way that is acceptable to all. If the first solution does not work, the problem is addressed again. Coercion is never an option, so it is almost impossible for the leader and the workers to become adversaries.

While being an effective leader may initially take more time and effort than bossing, in the end it takes much less time and effort because workers find that when they are managed by a leader, quality work is very satisfying. It is certainly possible to learn how to be an effective lead-teacher, but few teachers will make the effort to do so unless they themselves experience the benefit of this approach. This means that lead-management and the concepts of quality will not flourish in our classrooms unless they are implemented at the level of the school principal. He or she is the crucial element in educational reform.

The principal who wants to be a successful lead-manager must learn the social and administrative skills needed to be a buffer between the bosses above and the teachers he or she lead-manages. It would be good if these ideas were accepted at levels above the principal, and I am sure that this will be the case at times. But once we leave the school, the central office power struggles of educational politics almost always intrude. Bossing and kowtowing are so deeply ingrained at the top of the system that my hope for educational reform is to find enough principals willing to give up bossing and start leading. . . .

An Important Word About Style

I have stated that lead-managers are not coercive, but most of us remember great teachers whose style seemed to go against this tenet. Jaime Escalante, the calculus teacher in the movie *Stand and Deliver,* seemed the antithesis of the lead-teacher: he threatened, cajoled, cursed, ridiculed, graded almost capriciously, threw students out of class, put down their interest in other activities such as playing in the band, gave huge amounts of homework, and worked students to the point of exhaustion. A few rebelled, but most revered him and accepted that what he did was for their own good.

What we must realize is that there is a very fine distinction between coercion, which is never caring, and a coercive style of teaching that is, at its core, very caring. If the workers see the manager as caring, then they can accept whatever he does, no matter how coercive it may seem on the surface. To workers, caring means that they believe their welfare is more important to the manager than either his welfare or the welfare of those above him in the organization. Further, they see the manager as desperate, not vindictive. They know that they are not used to doing quality work and that he is only attempting to get them to work harder than most have ever worked before. But they will not see this if they do not also see that the manager himself is working harder than they are used to seeing managers work. The message must come across loud and clear from the manager: No matter how hard I ask you to work, I work as hard or harder.

Therefore, the essence of good managing is caring and hard work. Acting, posturing, dramatizing, shouting, gesturing, and criticizing are styles a manager may choose as he or she attempts to add drama and excitement to what can easily become a boring process. As long as the essence is preserved, any style is within the confines of lead-management. Great leaders all have a style that works for them, and I doubt that it can (or should) be taught or even successfully imitated. It is their unique, creative approach to the difficult problem of persuading people to do what they are reluctant to do.

I believe, however, that the majority of great teachers do not use the coercive style that Escalante used so successfully. When you study great teachers, as I hope you will have a chance to do, you will learn much more from their caring and hard work than from their style. To be a successful lead-manager, you will have to develop your own style; it is the only style that will work for you.

NOTES

1. A good review of the research on what is essentially lead-management (he calls it "system 4") is included in Rensis Likert, *Past and Future Perspectives on System 4,* 1977. This paper can be obtained from Rensis Likert Association Inc., 630 City Center Building, Ann Arbor, MI 48104.

2. Ellen Flax, "New Dropout Data Highlights Problems in the Middle Years," *Education Week,* Vol. VIII, No. 30, April 19, 1989.

3. W. Edwards Deming, *Out of the Crisis* (Cambridge: Massachusetts Institute of Technology, Center for Advanced Engineering Study, 1982).

5

LEADERSHIP AS AN
ORGANIZATIONAL QUALITY

Rodney T. Ogawa
Steven T. Bossert

JOSEPH CAMPBELL (1988) recalled the words of Black Elk, the great shaman of the Sioux: "I saw myself on the central mountain of the world, the highest place, and I had a vision because I was seeing in the sacred manner of the world. But the central mountain is everywhere" (p. 111). Campbell explained, "The center of the world is the *axis mundi,* the central point, the pole around which all revolves" (p. 111).

Background

There are concepts in our society on which much seems to turn. Because they are important, we look for them in special places. Leadership, it seems, is such a concept. It is important, most would agree. We expect it of elected officials, look for it in outstanding students and athletes, and admire those who have it. Moreover, leadership matters. We know that it affects how organizations—from social clubs and athletic teams to corporations and armies—perform.

Following these beliefs, scholars in the field of educational administration have sought to determine how leadership affects school organiza-

Authors' Note: An earlier version of this article was presented at the annual meetings of the American Educational Research Association. We thank the editors and anonymous reviewers for their constructive feedback and helpful suggestions.

tions. They have focused their search for leadership on a particular organizational corner, but they have had little success finding it. In this article we offer a view of leadership that does not treat it as the province of a few people in certain parts of organizations. Rather, we treat leadership as a quality of organizations—a systemic characteristic. To find it, we submit, one must not look in one place or another but must step back and map leadership throughout organizations.

Our central purpose in this article is to argue that leadership is an organizational quality. Our argument extends beyond the obvious point that individuals throughout organizations lead by suggesting the following: Leadership flows through the networks of roles that comprise organizations. The medium of leadership and the currency of leadership lie in the personal resources of people. And, leadership shapes the systems that produce patterns of interaction and the meanings that other participants attach to organizational events.

In making this argument, we build outward from the concept of leadership as an organizational quality. We begin by acknowledging and tracing the roots of this conceptualization. We then briefly review four assumptions that have guided previous theorizing and research on leadership. We discuss how different theoretical perspectives on organizations lead to very different treatments of leadership. We demonstrate this point first by reviewing how the dominant perspective on organizations has contributed to a narrow treatment of the four assumptions on leadership. We then examine the implications of an alternative view of organizations for conceptualizing leadership, noting that it offers an expanded, or organizational, treatment of the four assumptions. Finally, we close by offering some thoughts on the implications of conceptualizing leadership as an organizational quality for future research.

The Conceptual Roots

In this article we offer a conceptualization of organizational leadership that does not treat it as the realm of a few people in certain parts of organizations. Rather, we treat leadership as a quality of organizations—a systemic characteristic.

This perspective on leadership is not new. It simply has been overlooked. The conceptual antecedents can be traced to some of the earliest writings in the modern literature on administration and organization. Barnard (1968) observed that the "authority of leadership" is not confined to those in executive positions, thus acknowledging that leadership may be exerted by anyone in an organization. Similarly, Thompson

(1967), while describing administration rather than leadership, asserted that it is something that flows throughout an organization, spanning levels and flowing both up and down hierarchies.

This perspective was given its fullest expression to date by a group of scholars associated with the Institute for Social Research of the University of Michigan. Viewing leadership as a form of control exerted over organizations' members (Cartwright, 1965), several members of that group treated leadership as a phenomenon that can be found throughout organizations (Cartwright, 1965; Katz & Kahn, 1966; Tannenbaum, 1962). They concluded that leadership is a variable that is measurable at the organizational level. On the basis of Tannenbaum's (1962) empirical work, they established that organizations have different levels of leadership, that leadership varies across organizations and even within organizations over time. Moreover, they claimed that under some conditions a positive relationship exists between the level of organizations' total leadership and their overall performance (Cartwright, 1965; Tannenbaum, 1962).

Thus the notion of leadership as a quality of organizations has been expressed in the past but lost in later discussions. For example, recent reviews of the treatment of leadership in the educational administration literature (Hoy & Miskel, 1991; Immegart, 1988) never mention it. Only very recently has this conceptualization begun to reemerge (Bolman & Deal, 1994).

Four Underlying Assumptions

Arguably, four basic assumptions underlie most treatments of leadership. They attend to four dimensions of leadership: function, role, the individual, and culture. The first assumption is that leadership *functions* to influence organizational performance (Pfeffer, 1978). A second assumption holds that leadership is related to organizational *roles*. A third assumption indicates that leaders are *individuals* who possess certain attributes, act in certain ways, or both. A fourth assumption that has recently found its way into the literature is that leaders operate within organizational *cultures* (Daft & Weick, 1984; Pfeffer, 1981; Schein, 1985; Smircich & Morgan, 1983).

Underlying Conceptions of Organization

Selznick (1957) suggested that how we conceptualize organizational leadership is necessarily rooted in how we conceptualize organizations. Organization theory offers many competing perspectives. Several authors note that these perspectives emphasize different organizational features and thus offer varying explanations of organizational phenomena, including leadership (Burrell & Morgan, 1979; Foster, 1986; Scott, 1992).

Here, we confine our discussion to the implications of two perspectives on organizations for understanding leadership. The first is drawn from a technical-rational theory of organizations; the second is taken from institutional theory. The former rests leadership in certain organizational corners; the latter distributes leadership throughout organizations. We adopt an institutional perspective because we believe that, among emerging conceptualizations, it provides a promising viewpoint for examining the many facets of school organization, including leadership. We encourage others to explicate the views of leadership offered by other emerging theories of organization.

The Dominant View: A Technical-Rational Perspective

Most theories and research on leadership do not explicitly reveal the organizational perspectives from which they are derived. However, an examination of the literature suggests that it has been dominated implicitly by one perspective. That perspective depicts organizations as technically rational systems and thus emphasizes two organizational features: goals and formal structure (Scott, 1992).

From the technical-rational perspective, organizations exist to attain specific, predetermined goals. All else springs from organizations' efforts to reach goals efficiently: They adopt or develop technologies to attain goals; they generate formal structures to enhance the efficient operation of their technologies.

Formal structures are the organizational rules and procedures that govern the behavior of members by precisely and explicitly prescribing roles and role relations (Scott, 1992). Typically, managers located at the top of organizations' hierarchies are authorized to develop formal structures, because they possess the requisite competence and are positioned to comprehend their organizations' overall operations. They develop structures that enhance their organizations' efficiency by rationalizing internal operations and managing relations with external environments.

The Technical-Rational View of Organizational Leadership

The dominance of the technical-rational perspective in the leadership literature is reflected in the treatment of the four assumptions of leadership. Working from this perspective, scholars confine leadership to the narrow corridors of power that exist in the uppermost levels of organizations' hierarchies and emphasize goal attainment as its ultimate product.

THE FUNCTION OF LEADERSHIP

One assumption about leadership is that it functions to influence the performance of organizations by affecting the minds and behaviors of participants. This perhaps is the most fundamental assumption, for it reveals the reason for widespread interest in the phenomenon of leadership. It provides a cause of an important effect: organizational performance (Pfeffer, 1978).

From the technical-rational perspective, performance means goal attainment. Thus successful leaders are those whose organizations reach their goals. This emphasis on goal attainment is evident in mainstream scholarship on leadership. Theories ranging from the work generated by the Ohio State leadership studies and by the University of Michigan Survey Research Center to Fiedler's contingency model and House's path goal theory purport to capture those dimensions of leadership that are linked to organizational performance (Yukl, 1989). In educational administration, research has sought to determine the extent to which leadership affects perceptual and independent measures of school performance, including students' performance on standardized achievement tests (Hoy & Miskel, 1991).

ORGANIZATIONAL ROLES

A second assumption holds that leadership is related to organizational *roles,* or offices. The technical-rational perspective on organizations locates the competence and hence authority for making strategic decisions in managerial positions at the top of organizations' hierarchies. As a consequence, theories and research usually treat leadership as the province of certain roles in organizations. Widespread adherence to this particular expression of this assumption is evident in the designs of leadership studies. Studies of organizational leadership with rare exceptions are studies of top-level managers. For example, studies of leadership in school organizations usually have principals and superintendents as their subjects.

TRAITS AND BEHAVIORS OF INDIVIDUALS

A third assumption is that leaders are *individuals* who possess certain attributes, act in certain ways, or both. Some of the earliest research on leadership attempted to identify the traits that set leaders apart from other group members (Bass, 1981; Hoy & Miskel, 1991; Yukl, 1989). More recent studies sought to chart the behaviors of effective leaders (Bass, 1981; Hoy & Miskel, 1991; Yukl, 1989).

The technical-rational perspective on organizations emphasizes two basic ways in which managers lead: They establish and fix attention on goals, and they develop formal structures to enhance the efficiency with which those goals are attained. These two components are reflected in mainstream theory and research on leadership. For example, House's (1971) path-goal theory emphasizes the role of leaders in affecting subordinates' perceptions of both organizational and personal goals.

The Ohio State leadership studies that produced the Leader Behavior Description Questionnaire, perhaps the most broadly cited conceptualization of leadership in the educational administration literature, highlights two dimensions of leader behavior. One, which is labeled "initiating structure," concerns those behaviors of leaders that define organizations' formal structures (Halpin, 1966). Spurred by the availability of easily administered surveys, numerous studies of the leadership behaviors of educational administrators were conducted (Hoy & Miskel, 1991).

This perspective on leadership is also reflected in the field of educational administration's conceptualization of instructional leadership (Ogawa, 1992). A major component of instructional leadership concerns the development of mission and goals (Murphy, 1989). Scholars also characterize instructional leaders as managing the educational production function by setting schedules and establishing policies and procedures.

THE CULTURAL CONTEXT

A final assumption about leaders is that they operate within organizational *cultures* and affect how other participants interpret organizational events and thus influence how they behave (Daft & Weick, 1984; Pfeffer, 1981; Schein, 1985; Smircich & Morgan, 1983). Resulting from the recent emergence of the cultural metaphor in organization theory, this view of leadership has gained increased attention. This is reflected in the educational administration literature, where scholars have argued that administrators lead by shaping the cultures of their school organizations and thus affect the meanings that other participants fix to organizational events (Bolman & Deal, 1994; Deal & Peterson, 1990; Sergiovanni & Corbally, 1986).

Despite this focus on symbolism and the shaping of meaning, cultural treatments of leadership typically have not escaped the technical-rational emphasis. This is evident in the persistent focus on both high-level managers and goal attainment. For example, the management literature has generally been concerned with how managers frame meaning for subordinates (Pfeffer, 1981; Schein, 1985; Smircich & Morgan, 1983) and how culture is linked to organizations' performance (Deal & Kennedy, 1982). In educational administration, the same tendencies are present. Recent treatments of cultural leadership in schools have continued to focus on principals (Deal & Peterson, 1990; Reitzug, 1994; Reitzug & Reeves, 1992) and have examined the relationships between leadership, school culture, and productivity (Deal & Peterson, 1990).

As Smircich (1983) argued, this reflects but one view of organizational culture. It treats culture as "something an organization has" (p. 347) and thus emphasizes how culture can be manipulated to enhance the efficiency with which goals are attained. Smircich identifies another view, one that treats culture as "something an organization is" (p. 347). It focuses on patterns of symbols and meanings that arise consensually from social interaction and hence focuses on how organization itself is accomplished. This view, then, seems to broaden the scope of inquiry to include the entire organization and escapes the technical-rational emphasis on goal attainment.

INTEGRATED MODELS OF LEADERSHIP

Scholars have made several efforts to link these four assumptions about leadership in comprehensive, integrated models—models intended to exceed the limitations of past treatments of leadership. Yukl (1989) offered an "integrating conceptual framework" that focuses explicitly on managerial leadership and that includes such factors as "leader traits and skills," "leadership behavior," and "criteria of unit effectiveness." Similarly, Immegart's (1988) review of leadership research in the educational administration literature includes culture, activities, and outcomes among other factors in his "model of a broad conceptualization of leadership." Hoy and Miskel (1991) included leadership traits, leader behavior, situational characteristics—including leader role, and effectiveness, organizational and personal—as elements of their schema for the study of leadership.

Clearly, the assumptions regarding function, role, individuals' traits and behavior, and culture are evident in these models. And, although comprehensive, they remain bound to the technical-rational perspective on organizations. That is, they concentrate on the leadership of people in certain roles, namely, those in the highest levels of organizations' hierarchies, and their impact on organizational goal attainment. How might leadership look from a different perspective on organizations?

An Institutional Perspective on Organizations

Institutional theory provides an alternative to technical-rational conceptions of organizations. This perspective on organizations flows from a general institutional theory of social organization, which explains that the behavior of actors, both individual and collective, expresses externally enforced institutions rather than internally derived goals. Institutions are general, societal rules that take the form of cultural theories, ideologies, and prescriptions (Meyer, Boli, & Thomas, 1987). An example of an institution is the belief that human development occurs in a fairly linear, sequential order, which is reflected in the age-graded structure of the vast majority of elementary schools in the United States. From an institutional perspective, then, action is the enactment of broad institutional scripts.

Accordingly, when applied to organizations, institutional theory emphasizes the impact of the institutional environment on the structure of organizations. It explains that in the external environment some structural elements of organizations are institutionalized, or imbued with value (Selznick, 1957). This occurs, in part, because the elements reflect society's cultural theories.

In the absence of clear technologies and competitive markets, some organizations are not well suited to adopting structures to enhance the efficiency of their operations. Instead, they develop structures that reflect institutions to gain social legitimacy (DiMaggio & Powell, 1983; Meyer & Rowan, 1977; Scott, 1987; Zucker, 1987). For example, numerous school districts have adopted school-based management despite the absence of evidence that it affects the academic performance of students, suggesting that school-based management has been adopted in at least some instances to gain legitimacy.

Public schools are clearly marked by the characteristics of highly institutionalized organizations (Meyer & Rowan, 1977): Their technology—teaching and learning—has been characterized as unclear (Cohen, March, & Olsen, 1972). For the most part, they do not compete for clients (Carlson, 1964).

Some institutional theorists argue that legitimacy contributes to organizational effectiveness (DiMaggio & Powell, 1983). They suggest that legitimacy enhances the ability of organizations to attract resources from the environment. Thus it contributes to organizational survival and hence to the attainment of organizations' ultimate, albeit implicit, goal. For example, school districts will cite recently adopted programs, such as the development of site councils, in their campaigns to gain support for bond measures.

The pursuit of legitimacy leads organizations to decouple administrative structures in two ways. First, organizations horizontally decouple structural elements from one another (Meyer & Rowan, 1977). This enables organizations to adopt structures that reflect conflicting or even contradictory values in their environments. For example, school districts may adopt strict discipline policies aimed at moving disruptive students, while also providing alternative programs for students who cannot conform to the norms of conventional educational settings.

Second, organizations vertically decouple administrative structures from activity (Meyer & Rowan, 1977). Because organizations adopt structures to reflect institutionalized rules rather than to enhance internal efficiency, their activities may depart markedly from their adopted structures. Thus they decouple to reduce the likelihood that inconsistencies between structure and activity will be discovered. For example, after a new instructional program is adopted by a school district, it is common for administrators not to monitor its implementation.

Despite the decoupling of structure from activity, institutional theory suggests that the structures may have an indirect impact on the work of organizations in two ways. First, institutions, once adopted by organizations, can serve as the focus of symbolic activity. These symbolic activities can facilitate the development of shared meaning and values among organizations' members (March & Olsen, 1984; Meyer & Rowan, 1977). Shared meaning and values, in turn, can produce commitments to engage in coordinated, or organized, action. Thus individuals at any organizational level can structure work formally or informally. School-based management may provide an example of symbolic action that may have indirect, substantive consequences. There is little empirical evidence that decisions made by school councils affect schools' instructional programs, suggesting that participation on councils is largely symbolic. However, some research suggests that principals, teachers, and parents view opportunities to participate in decision making with enthusiasm, which may carry over to activities that have instructional consequences.

Second, because administrative structure can be decoupled from activity, individuals engaged in the work of highly institutionalized organizations enjoy a great deal of discretion. In fact, Meyer (1983) posited that new structures, or innovations, introduced by individuals at lower, technical levels of organizations are more likely to affect their substantive performance. For example, when school districts adopt reading series that employ particular instructional approaches, teachers have been known to use quite different approaches, while using the materials provided by the adopted series.

We return to the four assumptions about leadership and examine them from the perspective provided by institutional theory. The view, we submit, is quite different.

THE PARAMETERS OF LEADERSHIP

Whereas the function of leadership from the technical-rational perspective is organizational performance and goal attainment, the function of leadership from the institutional perspective is social legitimacy and organizational survival. Rather than the technical-rational focus on affecting the "minds and behaviors of participants," the institutional perspective requires affecting the minds and behaviors of external constituents.

As noted earlier, it is widely assumed that leadership functions to affect the overall performance of organizations. From an institutional perspective, performance involves the survival of the organization. This exceeds the technical-rational emphasis on goal attainment, because survival transcends other, more specific goals. In fact, attaining the wrong, specific goals does not contribute to organizations' survival.

This view of the first assumption, then, clearly fixes the parameters of leadership at the organizational level. If leadership affects the survival of organizations, then it is a phenomenon of nothing less than organizational proportions. This is hardly a startling revelation, but one that is missed by many conceptualizations of leadership—particularly those that treat it as a quality that individuals possess apart from a social context.

Assuming the organizational goal of survival also suggests that leadership is systemically causal. March (1955) and Simon (1957) observed and Cartwright (1965) reminded scholars that social influence, including leadership, is a special instance of causality: "the modification of one person's responses by the actions of another" (p. 3). However, causality, in the case of leadership from the institutional perspective, exceeds the individual level. Survival, after all, depends on both the adoption of institutionalized structures at the administrative level and the development of coordinative mechanisms at the technical level.

Thus leadership must affect more than individuals' actions; it must influence the system in which actions occur. This point has been recognized previously. Early research by Hemphill and Coons (1950) noted that leadership defines patterns of organization. Similarly, Katz and Kahn (1966) observed that leadership changes organizational structure, interpolates structure, and uses structure.

Although the survival of public schools, which have been characterized as domesticated organizations (Carlson, 1964), is largely taken for granted, they face a constant struggle for legitimacy. They rely on state legislatures, federal agencies, and local taxpayers for financial support, but they have difficulty demonstrating their effectiveness and efficiency. Thus public schools are exemplars of highly institutionalized organizations (Meyer & Rowan, 1977). Consequently, their administrators and governing boards embrace new structures, such as school-based management, which have little documented effect on teaching and learning but mark the adopting school systems as progressive and reform minded (Malen, Ogawa, & Kranz, 1990). Meanwhile, teachers establish instructional routines based on the contingencies they face at the technical level of school organizations (Rowan, Raudenbush, & Cheong, 1993).

THE SOCIAL WEB OF LEADERSHIP

A second assumption links leadership to organizational roles. A role is the set of activities expected of the incumbent of a particular social position or office (Gross, Mason, & McEachern, 1958; Katz & Kahn, 1966). This does not seem to square with the institutional perspective, according to which individuals at different levels can exert leadership by affecting how their organizations are structured: individuals working in upper management develop formal structures in response to the institutional environment; individuals working at the technical level develop informal structures to coordinate work activities and adopt new work techniques.

Role theory resolves this potential contradiction and reveals the symmetry of the conceptualization of leadership as an organizational quality. Role theory suggests that role, per se, is not the critical concept in understanding organizations. Rather, the important unit of analysis is the network of relations among roles, because it is the network that comprises the organizational system (Katz & Kahn, 1966; Scott, 1992). Leadership, then, lies in the system of relations among the incumbents of roles and affects organizational legitimacy. Consequently, leadership enhances the likelihood of organizations' survival by affecting their structures, which have been defined as "the regularized aspects of the relationships existing among participants in an organization" (Scott, 1992, p. 16).

Katz and Kahn (1966) suggested that "the essence of organizational leadership [is] the influential increment over and above mechanical compliance with the routine directives of the organization" (Katz & Kahn, 1966, p. 302). Thus it is not leadership when individuals gain the compliance of others simply by virtue of the organizational roles they occupy. Barnard (1968) referred to this as authority of position.

It is leadership, however, when organizational members gain compliance by deploying resources needed by others to enact their roles. Here, again, the system of roles is crucial to organizational leadership because different roles provide access to different resources. For example, information, a staple of modern organizations, is distributed across organizational roles: The incumbents of some roles have greater access to information about external environments (Bass, 1981), whereas the incumbents of other roles have greater access to information regarding internal operations. Organizational members, who possess information needed by others to operationalize their roles effectively, are in a position within the network of roles to exercise influence, or leadership.

In school organizations, district superintendents use their knowledge of state guidelines to influence school boards, principals, and teachers. Principals employ their knowledge of budgets to influence the decisions of both district superintendents and teachers on school councils. Also, teachers use their knowledge of effective instructional techniques to affect principals and district curriculum directors.

From the institutional perspective, the assumption that ties leadership to organizational roles and offices provides conceptual specification concerning leadership as a systemic quality of organizations. It reveals that leadership is embedded not in particular roles but in the relationships that exist among the incumbents of roles. By shifting attention to relationships, this assumption now suggests that organizational members can draw on resources to which their roles provide access to influence others who require those resources to enact their roles successfully. That success, from the institutional perspective, takes the form of social legitimacy and, consequently, organizational survival.

THE CURRENCY AND MEDIUM OF LEADERSHIP

A third assumption about leadership is that it involves individuals' attributes and actions. When viewed from the institutional perspective, both the traits and actions of individuals take on added significance. Traits, rather than simply marking leaders, are resources on which individuals draw in attempting to exert influence. This is consistent with the systemic interpretation of the assumption regarding leadership and organizational roles that leadership is influence that exceeds routine compliance with organizational structures.

Thus leadership requires that organizational actors draw on personal resources. Katz and Kahn (1966), for example, focus on expert and referent power (French & Raven, 1959). Both are based on personal traits of individuals who exert influence. Expertise concerns the possession of task-relevant knowledge. Referent power is based on one's capacity to engender feelings of loyalty. Other traits identified by studies of leadership also provide resources that can be deployed in efforts to exert influence. They include self-confidence, tolerance of stress, creativity, high energy, persistence, willingness to assume responsibility, and cooperation (Yukl, 1989).

Katz and Kahn (1966) claim that, because organizational members possess individual resources regardless of their formal positions and roles, all potentially can lead. In addition, this means that leadership is not a zero-sum game. Depending on the extent to which organizational members use personal resources to exert influence, or leadership, organizations' overall levels of leadership can vary. Tannenbaum (1962) empirically verified this and linked the overall levels of influence in organizations to their performance.

Examples abound in school organizations. People in different roles and at different levels of school organizations' hierarchies employ personal resources to affect others. Specifically, administrators and teachers develop structures and thus affect organizations' outcomes in response to different sets of organizational contingencies (Meyer & Rowan, 1977). Administrators, on the one hand, respond to the institutional environment and establish structures that garner legitimacy (Pitner & Ogawa, 1981) for schools and school districts. Teachers, on the other hand, respond to their immediate environment, including the types of students in their classrooms, and establish instructional routines, or structures (Rowan et al., 1993). Both administrators and teachers exert leadership in their respective domains.

Individuals' behaviors, or actions, also take on new meaning when leadership is seen as an organizational quality. According to the first two assumptions, leadership is systemic and relational. Thus focus shifts from people's isolated actions to their social interactions. The interact, not the act, becomes the basic building block of organizational leadership. Interaction is the medium through which resources are deployed and influence is exerted. And, because leadership affects organizational structure, it affects the interactions of individuals in organizations. In essence, leadership through interactions influences the system of interactions that constitute an organization.

Treating social interaction as the building block of leadership has another implication for examining leadership, one that is consistent with the systemic view of leadership. It underscores what many theorists have observed: Leadership is relational. Consequently, both the leader and followers are important components. As Cartwright (1965) suggested, it is important to consider the parts played by both the agent and subject of influence.

Moreover, because leadership occurs through interaction, influence cannot be assumed to be unidirectional. The agent of influence is, to some degree, also a subject. Coupled with the notion that leadership is not the province of certain roles, the third assumption indicates that leadership can flow, as Thompson (1967) argued, both up and down levels and between organizational components, including roles, regardless of formal prescriptions. In school organizations, teachers can be affected by students, even as they influence their charges. What teacher does not take cues from students as a lesson progresses? Similarly, principals take their lead from teachers on instructional matters, and teachers leave it to their principals to organize work by setting class schedules and introducing instructional initiatives.

Thus the assumption that focuses on the traits and actions of individuals identifies the currency and medium of leadership. Individuals draw on personal qualities as resources to influence organizations. The medium by which leadership is exerted is social interaction. And, ultimately, leadership affects the systems that produce the patterns of interaction that comprise organizations—their structures, which can produce social legitimacy for organizations. Finally, the interactive nature of leadership means that leadership is reciprocal.

THE CONTEXT OF LEADERSHIP

A fourth assumption treats leadership as a cultural phenomenon. Although scholars do not agree on what specifically constitutes organization culture (Smircich, 1983), they acknowledge that organizations have or are cultures and that culture produces patterned behaviors and interactions. Leadership, then, involves shaping organizations' cultures (Deal & Kennedy, 1982; Schein, 1985) and influencing the meanings that people attach to organizational events (Smircich & Morgan, 1983).

This cultural treatment of organizational leadership is congruent with the institutional perspective at two levels. First, institutional theory suggests that organizations erect structures to reflect cultural rules in their external environments. Second, it indicates that organizations conduct activities around those structures to facilitate the development of shared meaning and values among organizations' members, that is, to develop culture.

Sergiovanni (1986), reflecting on the treatment of culture in the educational administration literature, concluded, "Underlying the cultural perspective is the concept of community and the importance of shared meanings and shared values" (p. 8). This interpretation of culture shares much with Durkheim's (1933) concept of mechanical solidarity. Solidarity is the social cohesion and cooperative action directed toward the achievement of collective goals that characterizes groups. Durkheim

(1933) identified two bases of solidarity: organic and mechanical. Organic solidarity is based on the interdependence of highly specialized roles in a complex system of a division of labor. Mechanical solidarity is based on similarity of values and behavior and loyalty to tradition and kinship.

Institutional theory embraces both types of solidarity, suggesting that leaders at different hierarchical levels may effect different forms of solidarity. Top-level administrators are instrumental in adopting structures that reflect the institutional environment and legitimate school organizations among external stakeholders (Pitner & Ogawa, 1981). These administrators and their immediate subordinates, the mid-level managers (e.g., building principals), stage activities around these structures that provide others, including teachers, students, and parents, with shared experiences, which can facilitate the development of shared meanings and values. These meanings and values can serve as the core of shared commitments, or mechanical solidarity.

Meanwhile, at the technical core of school organizations, teachers act on commitments developed during symbolic activities to coordinate, or organize, work-related activity. For example, in districts where administration has adopted school-based management, some teachers involved on site councils eagerly engage, at least initially, in efforts to restructure or reorganize their schools (Malen et al., 1990). In addition, teachers establish instructional routines, or structures, in their classrooms (Rowan et al., 1993). Both efforts to coordinate work and develop routines are forms of organic solidarity because they concern the organization of the substantive work of schools.

AN INSTITUTIONAL PERSPECTIVE
ON ORGANIZATIONAL LEADERSHIP

Much is revealed by institutional theory when it is used to examine the four assumptions on which theories and studies of organizational leadership have been based. It sets leadership's parameters at the level of organization. It reveals the almost contradictory relationship between leadership and organizational roles. It suggests the nature of both the resources on which leadership is based and the social element on which leadership is built. Finally, it embeds leadership in a cultural context. Together, these assumptions reintroduce a perspective on leadership that has been lost by scholars. They reveal that leadership is an organizational quality.

From this perspective, leadership functions to enhance organizations' social legitimacy and their chances of survival. This sets leadership's parameters at the organizational level. Moreover, it treats leadership as causal —a form of social influence. By combining the organizational and causal parameters, we learn that leadership goes beyond influencing individuals; it affects organizations' structures. In a word, leadership is organizing.

The relationship between leadership and organizational roles reveals that leadership is not confined to certain roles in organizations. Rather, it flows through the networks of roles that comprise organizations. Moreover, leadership is based on the deployment of resources that are distributed across the network of roles, with different roles having access to different levels and types of resources.

Thus the currency on which leadership is based lies in the resources possessed by individuals. The medium of leadership is, however, not individual action but social interaction. Leadership affects the systems that produce the patterns of interaction that occur among organizational members; that is, it affects organizations' structures.

The context of leadership from an institutional perspective is largely cultural. Administrators are instrumental in adopting structures to mirror cultural rules in the environment. They then engage other members of their organizations in symbolic activities that focus on these structures. These activities, in turn, shape and reinforce shared values and beliefs, which can produce commitment, or solidarity, leading to coordinated activity.

Implications for Inquiry

The conceptualization of leadership as an organizational quality has implications for how leadership in school organizations is studied. They fall into three rough categories: general research strategies, focus on new dimensions, and promising developments in theory and research.

General Research Strategies

To capture leadership as an organizational quality will require adopting rather paradoxical research strategies that increase the unit of analysis and reduce the focus of inquiry. If leadership is treated as an organizational quality, then studies of leadership must have as their unit of analysis the organization. On the one hand, this will mean taking approaches similar to those employed by researchers at the University of Michigan's Institute for Social Research. Several studies produced by the institute measured the total influence exerted throughout organizations (Tannenbaum, 1962). On the other hand, this will require researchers to trace leadership throughout organizations. They will have to track its flow up and down organizations and within levels. Moreover, institutional theory suggests that leadership may respond to different contingencies and thus produce different outcomes at various levels of organizations' hierarchies. Thus researchers must be sensitive to the variations in leadership's form and substance.

Tracing leadership throughout school organizations will also require researchers to examine micro-organizational events. Data on the network of interactions that occur in organizations must be compiled over time. That will mean recording at least samples of actual interactions that occur between organizational members. The importance of the dimension of time must be emphasized. If leadership involves influencing organizational structures, then time is important. Only time will tell if attempts at leadership affect organizational solidarity. Also, the time that is required for such effects to occur and the duration of the persistence of the effects may be important variables.

Focus on New Dimensions of Leadership

If researchers adopt an institutional perspective for examining leadership, they will necessarily have to focus on organizational dimensions that are underemphasized in existing research. Three come to mind. The first concerns the outcomes of leadership. As we have argued, research conducted from the technical-rational perspective has focused on the impact of leadership on organizational goal attainment. This focus will broaden from an institutional perspective, which depicts organizations as seeking legitimacy, rather than technical efficiency, and ultimately survival. Research might examine how individuals employ social influence to develop structures that do not affect their core technologies but nonetheless enhance external constituents' assessments of their school organizations.

In addition, such research might be forced to address the ethics of this form of leadership. If, as we have suggested, the technical-rational conceptualization of organizations and leadership is itself deeply institutionalized, then what ethical issues may be involved when leaders knowingly direct their organizations to adopt structures that appear substantive but, in fact, are merely symbolic efforts to gain legitimacy?

The symbolic dimension of organizations is a second and related area that should command the attention of researchers seeking to examine leadership from an institutional perspective. Research might explore how organizational actors adopt symbolic structures and use them as the focus of events aimed at building solidarity among participants. In addition, research could closely scrutinize the possible links between the solidarity born of ceremonial activity and efforts by organizational members to coordinate or directly engage in substantive activity, or the work of their organization.

Researchers who attempt to capture leadership as an organizational quality might also examine how varied organizational contingencies evoke leadership from various organizational corners. If leadership does flow throughout organizations, research might begin to tease out the sets of problems, both symbolic and substantive, to which organizations respond and the sets of roles whose incumbents possess the requisite resources to develop routine ways, or structures, for handling these problems.

Promising Developments

Finally, we recognize that the dominant, technical-rational conception of organizational leadership is deeply institutionalized. Following the cultural script, educational researchers focus their studies of leadership on administrators, and practitioners place the responsibility for leadership on the incumbents of administrative offices. Thus efforts to introduce other conceptualizations of leadership will be met with resistance.

However, there are signs of change. Recent research on the leadership of teachers and efforts to implement reforms aimed at empowering teachers and others associated with the educational enterprise mark the change. Similarly, discussions on the development of educational communities and the shared responsibility that characterizes them reflect the change (Sergiovanni, 1994). Perhaps a different conception of leadership is emerging, one that sees it everywhere.

REFERENCES

Barnard, C. I. (1968). *Functions of the executive.* Cambridge, MA: Harvard University Press.

Bass, B. M. (1981). *Stodgill's handbook of leadership: A survey of theory and research.* New York: Free Press.

Bolman, L. G., & Deal, T. E. (1994). Looking for leadership: Another search party's report. *Educational Administration Quarterly, 30,* 77–96.

Burrell, G., & Morgan, G. (1979). *Sociological paradigms and organizational analysis.* Portsmouth, NH: Heinemann.

Campbell, J. (1988). *The power of myth.* New York: Doubleday.

Carlson, R. O. (1964). Environmental constraints and organizational consequences: The public school and its clients. In D. E. Griffiths (Ed.), *Behavioral science and educational administration* (pp. 262–276). Chicago: University of Chicago Press.

Cartwright, D. (1965). Influence, leadership, control. In J. G. March (Ed.), *Handbook of organizations* (pp. 1–47). Chicago: Rand McNally.

Cohen, M. D., March, J. G., & Olsen, J. P. (1972). A garbage can model of organizational choice. *Administrative Science Quarterly, 17,* 1–25.

Daft, R. L., & Weick, K. E. (1984). Toward a model of organizations as interpretation systems. *Academy of Management Review, 9,* 284–295.

Deal, T. E., & Kennedy, A. A. (1982). *Corporate cultures.* Reading, MA: Addison-Wesley.

Deal, T. E., & Peterson, K. (1990). *Symbolic leadership and the school principalship: Shaping school cultures in different contexts.* Washington, DC: U.S. Department of Education.

DiMaggio, P. J., & Powell, W. W. (1983). The iron cage revisited: Institutional isomorphism and collective rationality in organizational fields. *American Sociological Review, 48,* 147–160.

Durkheim, E. (1933). *The division of labor in society.* New York: Free Press.

Foster, W. (1986). *Paradigms and promises: New approaches to educational administration.* Buffalo, NY: Prometheus.

French, J., & Raven, B. H. (1959). The bases of social power. In D. Cartwright (Ed.), *Studies of social power* (pp. 150–167). Ann Arbor, MI: Institute for Social Research.

Gross, N., Mason, W., & McEachern, A. W. (1958). *Explorations in role analysis: Studies of the school superintendency role.* New York: Wiley.

Halpin, A. W. (1966). *Theory and research in administration.* New York: Macmillan.

Hemphill, J. K., & Coons, A. E. (1950). *Leadership behavior description.* Columbus, OH: Ohio State University, Personnel Research Board.

House, R. J. (1971). A path-goal theory of leadership effectiveness. *Administrative Science Quarterly, 16,* 321–338.

Hoy, W. K., & Miskel, C. G. (1991). *Educational administration: Theory, research and practice* (3rd ed.). New York: Random House.

Immegart, G. L. (1988). Leadership and leader behavior. In N. J. Boyan (Ed.), *Handbook of research on educational administration* (pp. 259–278). New York: Longman.

Katz, D., & Kahn, R. L. (1966). *The social psychology of organizations.* New York: Wiley.

Malen, B., Ogawa, R. T., & Kranz, J. (1990). What do we know about school based management? A case study of the literature—A call for research. In W. H. Clune & J. F. Witte (Eds.), *Choice and control in American education* (Vol. 2, pp. 289–342). Bristol, PA: Falmer.

March, J. G. (1955). An introduction to the theory and measurement of influence. *American Political Science Review, 49,* 431–451.

March, J. G., & Olsen, J. P. (1984). The new institutionalism: Organizational factors in political life. *American Political Science Review, 78,* 734–749.

Meyer, J. W. (1983). Innovation and knowledge use in American public education. In W. R. Scott & J. W. Meyer (Eds.), *Organizational environments* (pp. 233–260). Beverly Hills, CA: Sage.

Meyer, J. W., Boli, J., & Thomas, G. M. (1987). Ontology and rationalization in Western cultural account. In G. M. Thomas, J. W. Meyer, F. O. Ramirez, & J. Boli (Eds.), *Institutional structure: Constituting state, society, and the individual* (pp. 12–38). Newbury Park, CA: Sage.

Meyer, J. W., & Rowan, B. (1977). Institutionalized organizations: Formal structure as myth and ceremony. *American Journal of Sociology, 83,* 340–363.

Murphy, J. (1989). Principal instructional leadership. In P. W. Thurston & L. S. Lotto (Eds.), *Advances in educational administration* (pp. 163–200). Greenwich, CT: JAI.

Ogawa, R. T. (1992). Institutional theory and examining leadership in schools. *International Journal of Educational Management, 6,* 14–21.

Pfeffer, J. (1978). The ambiguity of leadership. In M. W. McCall, Jr., & M. M. Lombardo (Eds.), *Leadership? Where else can we go?* Durham, NC: Duke University Press.

Pfeffer, J. (1981). Management as symbolic action: The creation and maintenance of organizational paradigms. In B. Staw (Ed.), *Research in organizational behavior* (pp. 1–52). Greenwich, CT: JAI.

Pitner, N. J., & Ogawa, R. T. (1981). Organizational leadership: The case of the school superintendent. *Educational Administration Quarterly, 17,* 45–66.

Reitzug, U. C. (1994). A case study of empowering principal behavior. *American Educational Research Journal, 31,* 283–310.

Reitzug, U. C., & Reeves, J. E. (1992). "Miss Lincoln doesn't teach here": A descriptive narrative and conceptual analysis of a principal's symbolic leadership behavior. *Educational Administration Quarterly, 28,* 185–219.

Rowan, B., Raudenbush, S. W., & Cheong, Y. K. (1993). Teaching as a nonroutine task: Implications for the management of schools. *Educational Administration Quarterly, 29,* 479–500.

Schein, E. H. (1985). *Organizational culture and leadership.* San Francisco: Jossey-Bass.

Scott, W. R. (1987). The adolescence of institutional theory. *Administrative Science Quarterly, 32,* 493–511.

Scott, W. R. (1992). *Organizations: Rational, natural, and open systems* (3rd ed.). Englewood Cliffs, NJ: Prentice Hall.

Selznick, P. (1957). *Leadership in administration.* New York: Harper & Row.

Sergiovanni, T. J. (1986). Cultural and competing perspectives in administrative theory and practice. In T. J. Sergiovanni & J. E. Corbally (Eds.), *Leadership and organizational culture: New perspectives on administrative theory and practice*. Urbana: University of Illinois Press.

Sergiovanni, T. J. (1994). Organizations or communities: Changing the metaphor changes the theory. *Educational Administration Quarterly, 30,* 214–226.

Sergiovanni, T. J., & Corbally, J. E. (Eds.). (1986). *Leadership and organizational culture: New perspectives on administrative theory and practice.* Urbana, IL: University of Illinois Press.

Simon, H. A. (1957). *Models of man.* New York: Wiley.

Smircich, L. (1983). Concepts of culture and organizational analysis. *Administrative Science Quarterly, 28,* 339–358.

Smircich, L., & Morgan, G. (1983). Leadership: The management of meaning. *Journal of Applied Behavioral Science, 18,* 257–273.

Tannenbaum, A. S. (1962). Control in organizations: Individual adjustment and organizational performance. *Administrative Science Quarterly, 7,* 236–257.

Thompson, J. D. (1967). *Organizations in action.* New York: McGraw-Hill.

Yukl, G. A. (1989). *Leadership in organizations* (2nd ed.). Englewood Cliffs, NJ: Prentice Hall.

Zucker, L. G. (1987). Institutional theories of organization. *Annual Review of Sociology, 13,* 443–464.

6

PEOPLE AND ORGANIZATIONS

Lee G. Bolman
Terrence E. Deal

Vancouver Sun   January 29, 1981

WHISTLE STOPS ANGER OFFICE STAFF

BOISE, Idaho (AP)—Seven times a day, someone blows a whistle at the Idaho health and welfare office. The secretaries have to stop and fill out a form saying what they're doing at the moment.

Administrators in the state department of health and welfare say it's a good way to check office efficiency, part of a drive to eliminate three secretarial positions in an economy move.

Secretaries call it insulting, degrading, and disruptive.

The procedure began on Monday. That was when Theo Murdock, chief of the state's welfare division, instructed aides to blow the whistle—literally—on the secretarial staff. He said the "random moment time study" would enable him to judge how the secretaries spend time on the job.

Complained Angie Stelling: "Yesterday morning, there wasn't a single whistle. They all blew in the afternoon, and everybody was afraid to take a break or go to the bathroom" [Cited in Frost, Mitchell, and Nord, 1986, p. 279].

THE STRUCTURAL PERSPECTIVE focuses on the way that structure develops in response to an organization's tasks and environment. The human resource frame adds an additional dimension—the interplay between organizations and people. It starts from the premise that people's skills, insights, ideas, energy, and commitment are an organization's most critical resource. Organizations, however, can be so alienating, dehumanizing, and frustrating that human talents are wasted and human lives are distorted. Employees may respond by devoting much of their time and effort to beating the system. When a manager starts blowing whistles to find out what the employees are doing, the employees start looking for ways to defend themselves and even to get revenge. But it does not *have* to be that way. At their best, organizations can be energizing, exciting, productive, and rewarding for the individual, as well as for the system.

Literature and film often focus on the alienating and brutalizing aspects of systems. In Franz Kafka's *The Trial,* the protagonist faces a mysterious, impersonal, unpredictable, and hostile organization that destroys individuals at its own time and for its own mysterious reasons. Frederick Wiseman's documentary film *High School* shows a world in which insensitive adults tyrannize students. In such Hollywood films as *Norma Rae, Nine to Five, Silkwood,* and *Wall Street,* organizations are presented, at best, as ineffectual, and, at worst, as oppressive and inhuman, places dominated by insensitive and selfish bosses who care only about accumulating money and power. A similar view is succinctly summarized in the popular song, "Take This Job and Shove It!" How accurate are these popular views of organizations? Is the reality of organizations as bleak as it is often depicted to be? Are human beings inevitably the pawns of organizations, sacrificed to the organization's purposes and thrown out when they are no longer needed? Can individuals only hope to protect themselves or to exploit the system before it exploits them?

These questions are particularly important in light of the enormous size and power of modern institutions. Government spending represents an increasing percentage of the total wealth of virtually every developed nation, and much of that spending goes to support large public bureaucracies. The twentieth century has witnessed an extraordinary growth of large private corporations, including giant multinational companies. General Motors, the world's largest corporation, generates revenues each year that exceed the gross national product of most of the world's nations. In a world whose political and economic decisions are increasingly dominated by such gigantic institutions, how can individuals find freedom and dignity? How can they avoid the fate of Kafka's K, of Wiseman's students?

The answers to such questions are not easy. They require an understanding of people and organizations, as well as of the complex relation between the two. The human resource frame draws on a body of research and theory built around the following assumptions:

1. Organizations exist to serve human needs (rather than the reverse).

2. Organizations and people need each other. (Organizations need ideas, energy, and talent; people need careers, salaries, and work opportunities.)

3. When the fit between the individual and the organization is poor, one or both will suffer: individuals will be exploited, or will seek to exploit the organizations, or both.

4. A good fit between individual and organization benefits both: human beings find meaningful and satisfying work, and organizations get the human talent and energy that they need.

Exploring the fit between people and organizations must, however, begin with a discussion of the concept of *need*—what, in fact, do people need from their experiences with organizations?

Human Needs

The concept of need is controversial. Some scholars reject the whole idea. They argue that the concept of need is too vague, that it refers to something that is difficult to observe, and that human behavior is so heavily influenced by environmental factors that the need concept is really of no help in explaining how people behave (Salancik and Pfeffer, 1977).

From a human resource perspective, the concept of need is important, even though needs are hard to define and difficult to measure. Moreover, the idea that people have needs is a central element in commonsense psychology. Parents talk about the needs of their children, politicians try to respond to the needs of their constituents, and managers try to meet the needs of their workers.

Common sense makes sense in this case, but in everyday language the term *need* is used in a variety of different ways, many of them imprecise and ambiguous. An analogy may help. Gardeners know that every plant has "needs." Certain combinations of temperature, moisture, soil conditions, and sunlight will allow a plant to grow and flourish. Within the limits of its biological capabilities, a plant will do its best to satisfy its basic needs. It will orient its leaves to the sun to get more light. It will sink deeper roots to get more water. A plant's capabilities generally increase as it matures. Highly vulnerable seedlings become more self-sufficient as they reach maturity (for example, they become better able to fend off insect damage and crowding from other plants). Those capabilities decline as the plant nears the end of its life cycle.

Human needs can also be defined as conditions or elements in the environment that allow people to survive and develop. Without oxygen, water, and food, human beings cannot survive. A more complicated question is whether there are also basic psychic needs. There are two sides to this issue. One position is that certain psychological needs are in fact basic to being human. Such needs are presumably present in everyone. The opposing viewpoint is that humans are so molded by environment, socialization, and culture that it is fruitless to talk about generic human needs.

This is one form of the nature-nurture controversy, which has long been a hotly debated issue in the social sciences. The "nature" team argues that human behavior is mostly determined by biological and genetic factors, while the "nurture" team takes the opposite view: human behavior is largely determined by learning and experience.

The debate is often heated because the stakes are high. Is mental illness caused by one's genetic inheritance or by growing up in a disturbed environment? The answer is critical to deciding whether drugs or psychotherapy is a more appropriate form of treatment. Are behavioral differences between men and women determined by biology or culture? (Do women have greater maternal "needs"? Do men have greater needs to engage in combat and competition?) The answers are important in understanding the possibilities for redefining male and female roles.

In their extreme forms, the nature and nurture arguments both mislead. A degree in psychology is not required to know that people are capable of enormous amounts of learning and adaptation or that what people learn is influenced by the situations in which they find themselves. Nor is advanced training in biology needed to recognize that many of the differences among people are present at birth. Since genes determine so many physical characteristics, it is surprising that so many environmentalists are wedded to the argument that differences in behavior are *always* caused by environmental factors.

At present, a consensus is emerging in the social sciences that human behavior results from the interaction between heredity and environment. Genes may determine the initial trajectory, but subsequent learning has a profound effect in modifying or even reversing the original instructions. Nature-nurture interaction suggests another way of thinking about human needs. A need can be defined as a genetic predisposition to prefer some experiences over others. Needs energize and guide behavior, and they vary in strength at different times. We usually prefer temperatures that are neither too hot nor too cold. We do not like being alone all the time, but we are also not happy if we are constantly surrounded by people. Since the genetic instructions cannot anticipate all the specific situations that an individual will encounter, the form and expression of each person's needs will be significantly modified by what happens after birth.

Needs perform other central functions—they influence how we feel and they guide learning. We are likely to have positive emotions—happiness, contentment, joy, and love—in situations that are need fulfilling (Tomkins, 1962). We experience negative emotions—anger, fear, depression, and boredom—in situations where important needs are frustrated. We are also more likely to learn about things that are relevant to our needs. If you are motivated to become a successful manager and believe that organization theory can help you achieve that goal, then you are likely to learn a lot about it. If you have little desire to be a manager, or believe that social science is mostly common sense disguised in polysyllabic words, you are not likely to learn very much.

In sum, people try to satisfy their needs, become unhappy when their needs are frustrated, and are more likely to learn things that are relevant to their needs than things that are irrelevant. Individuals flourish and develop in environments where they can satisfy important needs but become psychologically undernourished in situations where major needs are consistently thwarted.

What Needs Do People Have?

If all human beings have needs, what needs do they have in common? One of the most influential theories about human needs was developed by Abraham Maslow (1954). Maslow started from the notion that human beings have a variety of needs, some more fundamental than others. He noted, for example, that the desire for food dominates the lives of the chronically hungry but that other forms of satisfaction are more significant for those who have enough to eat.

Maslow grouped human needs into five basic categories, arranged in a hierarchy from "lower" to "higher." Lower needs dominate behavior when they are not satisfied. Higher needs become salient only *after* the lower needs have been satisfied. Maslow's categories were:

1. Physiological needs (such as needs for oxygen, water, food, physical health, and comfort)
2. Safety needs (to be safe from danger, attack, threat)

3. Belongingness and love needs (needs for positive and loving relationships with other people)
4. Needs for esteem (needs to feel valued and to value oneself)
5. Needs for self-actualization (needs to develop to one's fullest, to actualize one's potential)

In Maslow's view, lower needs are "prepotent" and have to be satisfied first, although they do not have to be completely satisfied. Once lower needs are satisfied, an individual begins to focus more on higher needs. Maslow acknowledged exceptions. Parents who sacrifice themselves for their children and martyrs who give their lives for a cause are emphasizing higher needs over lower ones. Maslow believed that such exceptions occurred only when lower needs were very well satisfied early in life, so that they fell into the background. Needs for belongingness, esteem, and self-actualization then became dominant.

Maslow's ideas have had an enormous impact on the thinking of both managers and behavioral scientists. While they are intuitively plausible, that does not mean they are right. A number of researchers have tried to assess the validity of Maslow's theory without complete success. The biggest problem is that needs are hard to measure. Testing Maslow's theory requires assessing both the strength and the level of satisfaction of each need. Should you ask people questions such as, "How strong is your need for self-actualization, and to what degree are you are filling that need?" It is not clear how much people know about their own needs. And even if they know what their needs are, will they give truthful answers? What if people think the researcher will have a better opinion of them if they say they are concerned about self-actualization rather than such mundane matters as salary and benefits?

Several systematic attempts to assess the validity of Maslow's theory have failed to show conclusively that Maslow was right *or* wrong (Alderfer, 1972; Schneider and Alderfer, 1973). Still, his is one of the most influential views of motivation in organizations. It has become a widely accepted conception, and its validity is often assumed, despite the lack of convincing empirical evidence.

Theory X and Theory Y

Douglas McGregor (1960) took Maslow's theory of motivation and added another central idea, namely, that the perspective from which a manager views other people determines how they respond. McGregor suggested that most managers subscribed to Theory X. The central proposition of this theory is that managers need to direct and control the work of subordinates. According to Theory X, subordinates are passive and lazy, have little ambition, prefer to be led, and resist change.

McGregor believed that virtually all conventional management practices were built on Theory X assumptions, which limited managers to possibilities ranging from "hard" Theory X to "soft" Theory X. Hard Theory X emphasizes coercion, tight controls, threats, and punishments; in McGregor's view, it results in low productivity, antagonism, militant unions, and subtle sabotage. In contrast, soft Theory X is a permissive style that tries to avoid conflict and satisfy everyone's needs. It may produce superficial harmony but leads to apathy and indifference and causes people to expect more and more while giving less and less. Either way— hard or soft—Theory X creates self-fulfilling prophesies. Both approaches generate signs that the theory is correct and that even more Theory X management is needed to cope with workers who "just don't seem to give a damn any more" and "are never satisfied."

McGregor argued that new knowledge from the behavioral sciences challenged these conventional views. The evidence was inconclusive, he acknowledged, but it suggested a different view, which he called Theory Y. Maslow's need hierarchy was the foundation: "We recognize readily enough that a man suffering from a severe dietary deficiency is sick. The deprivation of physiological needs has behavioral consequences. The same is true—although less well recognized—of deprivation of higher-level needs. The man whose needs for safety, association, independence, or status are thwarted is sick just as surely as the man who has rickets. And his sickness will have behavioral consequences. We will be mistaken if we attribute his resultant passivity, his hostility, his refusal to accept responsibility to his inherent 'human nature.' These forms of behavior are symptoms of illness—of deprivation of his social and egoistic needs" (McGregor, 1960, pp. 35–36).

McGregor argued that managers need a new theory about people. Theory Y, like Theory X, accepted the proposition that "management is responsible for organizing the elements of enterprise . . . in the interest of economic ends" (p. 38). McGregor did not challenge capitalism or the role of private industry; he challenged managers to behave differently. Theory Y argues that people are not passive or indifferent by nature, but that they sometimes become so as a result of their experience in organizations.

The key proposition of Theory Y is that "the essential task of management is to arrange organizational conditions so that people can achieve their own goals best by directing their efforts toward organizational rewards" (p. 61). In other words, the job of management is to arrange things so that the organization's interests and the employee's self-interest coincide as closely as possible. Theory X relies too much on external control of people, while Theory Y relies on self-control and self-direction. Theory X treats people like children, whereas Theory Y treats them like adults.

Personality and Organization

Chris Argyris (1957, 1964) provided another classic statement of the human resource frame. Argyris saw a basic conflict between the human personality and the ways that organizations were structured and managed. Though Argyris did not base his view directly on Maslow, his ideas were similar. He argued that individuals have basic "self-actualization trends" and that they develop in specific directions as they mature from infancy into adulthood. They move from high levels of dependence on others to high levels of independence. They move from a narrow to a much broader range of skills and interests. They move from a short time perspective (in which interests are quickly developed and quickly forgotten, and there is little ability to anticipate the future) to a much longer time perspective. People develop from low levels of self-awareness and self-control to higher levels of both. Argyris proposed that all individuals are predisposed to move from the infant toward the adult ends of all these criteria, "barring unhealthy personality development" (1957, p. 51). That is very much like Maslow's idea that people move up the needs hierarchy unless their lower-level needs are frustrated.

Like McGregor, Argyris saw a conflict between individuals and organizations because organizations often treat people like children. This view was anticipated in Charlie Chaplin's film *Modern Times*. Early in the film, Chaplin's character works furiously in an assembly-line job trying to tighten each bolt on each piece that goes past him. The time perspective of the job can be measured in a few seconds. The range of skills is minimal, and the worker has virtually no control over the pace of his work. A researcher uses Chaplin as the guinea pig for a new machine to increase efficiency. The machine is designed to feed Chaplin his lunch while he continues to tighten bolts, but it goes haywire and begins to assault Chaplin with the food. The message is clear—the logic of industrial organization is to treat adults as much like infants as is technologically possible.

Argyris argued that such problems were built into the traditional principles of organizational design and management. The principle of task specialization carried to its logical extreme leads to defining jobs as narrowly as possible. "You put the right-front tire on the car, Joe will tighten the bolts, and Bill will check to see if it was done right." Task specialization requires a chain of command to coordinate the work of all the people who are doing narrowly specialized jobs. The chain of command requires that people at higher levels be able to direct and control people at lower levels, creating a situation of passivity and dependence. Argyris believed that under such conditions, people experience "psychological failure." They are unable to define their own goals or the way in which they might achieve their goals. Organizations create a situation that is fundamentally in conflict with the needs of healthy human beings. The conflict gets worse as one moves down the hierarchy, as jobs become more mechanized, as leadership becomes more directive, as formal structure becomes tighter, and as people attain increasing maturity.

Argyris added that employees can be expected to find ways to resist or to adapt to the frustration that organizations create. He suggested several options:

1. They might withdraw from the organization—through chronic absenteeism or simply by quitting.

2. They might stay on the job but withdraw psychologically, becoming indifferent, passive, and apathetic.

3. They might resist the organization by restricting output, deception, featherbedding, or sabotage.

4. They might try to climb the hierarchy to better jobs. (But the pyramidal structure of most organizations means that there are far more jobs at the bottom than at the top.)

5. They might create groups and organizations (such as labor unions) that try to redress the power imbalance between person and system. (Argyris cautions, however, that the new organizations are likely to be designed and managed like the old ones. In the long run, the employees may feel equally powerless with company and union.)

6. They may socialize their children to believe that work is unrewarding and that hopes for advancement are slim. (Researchers in the 1960s began to find that the children of farmers were more likely to believe in the merits of hard work than the children of urban, blue-collar workers. One reason that many U.S. companies moved manufacturing facilities south in the 1960s, and off shore in the 1970s, was to find still-uncontaminated rural workers. Argyris's theory predicted, however, that industry would eventually demotivate whatever work force it found unless management practice changed.)

Argyris and McGregor both argued that management practices were inconsistent with employee needs and that this conflict produced resistance and withdrawal. Both believed that managers misinterpreted employee behavior to mean that something was wrong with the employees rather than with the organization. Withdrawal and resistance confirmed Theory X assumptions that employees are lazy, uninterested, incompetent, or greedy. If managers assumed that the problem was "in" the employees, then the solution was to change them.

Argyris described three strategies that managers typically used, all of which made the problem worse instead of better. One approach was "strong, dynamic leadership," an approach based on the assumption that employees are a relatively passive flock of sheep. Argyris saw the strategy as self-defeating—it put more and more responsibility on managers, and less and less on workers. A second solution was to install tighter controls—quality control inspectors, time-and-motion studies, and so forth. But tighter controls deepen and reinforce the conflict between individual and organization and lead to escalating competitive games between managers and employees.

The first two solutions correspond to the tough version of Theory X. The third was softer: human relations programs. These programs often took the form of selling management's philosophy (through company newspapers and films, for example), pseudoparticipation ("make the employees *feel* that their ideas are valued"), and communications programs that rarely communicated what employees really wanted to know. Trying to make employees feel better without solving the underlying problems just made matters worse.

What could be done? Argyris found potential in job enlargement (making jobs more varied and challenging) and participative management, but also saw limits to both. Many employees were already socialized to be passive and dependent at work. They might resent and resist efforts to make their work more challenging and responsible. Ultimately, Argyris said, "reality-centered leadership" was needed—leadership that took account of the actual needs of the employees, as well as the needs of the organization. In addition, Argyris and McGregor both believed that much more needed to be learned about the design and management of organizations in order to reduce the conflict between the system and the individual.

In the three decades since Argyris and McGregor developed their classic statements of the human resource frame, legions of writers, consultants, and managers have pursued the questions that they raised. Their efforts have led in two primary directions, one focuses on individuals and the other on organizations.

Summary

Organizations and people depend on one another. People look to organizations to satisfy a variety of economic, personal, and social needs, and organizations in turn cannot function effectively without the energy and talent of their employees. Human resource theorists argue that the central task of managers is to build organizations and management systems that produce harmony between the needs of the individual and the needs of the organization. When they succeed, both the organization and its employees will benefit. When they fail, one or both sides will suffer. The individuals will feel alienated, apathetic, or exploited. The organization may find that its employees arrive late and leave early, on the days when they even get to work, and put in little effort while they are there.

Human resource theorists argue that managers need to understand and respond to the needs that human beings bring with them to work. Maslow's influential hierarchy of motivation suggests that, as people satisfy lower-level needs for food and physical safety, they move to higher-level needs for self-esteem and self-actualization. Human resource theorists such as Argyris and McGregor note that traditional managers often treat employees like children, satisfying only their lower-level needs. Such techniques as participative management can satisfy higher-level needs and tap higher levels of employee motivation and capacity.

REFERENCES

Alderfer, C. P. *Existence, Relatedness, and Growth.* New York: Free Press, 1972.

Argyris, C. *Personality and Organization.* New York: Harper & Row, 1957.

Argyris, C. *Integrating the Individual and the Organization.* New York: Wiley, 1964.

Frost, P. J., Mitchell, V. F., and Nord, W. R. *Organizational Reality: Reports from the Firing Line.* Glenview, Ill.: Scott, Foresman, 1986.

McGregor, D. *The Human Side of Enterprise.* New York: McGraw-Hill, 1960.

Maslow, A. H. *Motivation and Personality.* New York: Harper & Row, 1954.

Salancik, G. R., and Pfeffer, J. "An Examination of Need-Satisfaction Models of Job Attitudes." *Administrative Science Quarterly,* 1977, *22,* 427–456.

Schneider, B., and Alderfer, C. "Three Studies of Measures of Need Satisfaction in Organizations." *Administrative Science Quarterly,* 1973, *18,* 498–505.

Tomkins, S. S. *Affect, Imagery, Consciousness.* New York: Springer, 1962.

PART TWO

PRINCIPALS AND SUPERINTENDENTS

IF A REPRESENTATIVE of leadership were to be chosen from a school, it would be a principal; from a district, a superintendent. These roles are the most natural places for leadership to reside in a school system. Even though much of the school leadership literature is aimed at or about this population, we were able to include only a small percentage of the seminal works from top authors in this field. In this section we look at Susan Moore Johnson's research on choosing a school leader, the Interstate School Leaders Licensure Consortium's national standards for school leaders, and several pieces by vanguard authors: Jerome T. Murphy, David D. Marsh, Roland S. Barth, Michael Fullan, Lee G. Bolman and Terrence E. Deal, Philip C. Schlechty, and Deal and Peterson. Their subjects range from long-term transformational change to the less glamorous but equally important day-to-day work of an administrator.

7

LOOKING FOR LEADERS

Susan Moore Johnson

WITH A FLOURISH, a January 1989 headline in the Newbridge *Gazette*— "Super Search Begins"—heralded the start of the town's efforts to hire a successor to its superintendent of eighteen years. Intent on acquiring the best, the Newbridge school board asked an educational consultant, Elizabeth James, to run the search. Over the next six weeks James met with twenty-six community groups to learn what kind of person they wanted for the job. She drew up a job description and advertised the position in major newspapers, and she personally pursued prospective applicants. Thirty-seven men and eight women applied. James prepared summaries of the candidates' qualifications and rated each on a three-point scale—very strong, less strong, least strong. With James's assistance, the school board selected and publicly interviewed eight semifinalists.

The *Gazette* quoted James as saying, "In selecting the semi-finalists, the board was looking for individuals with proven leadership ability, with experience working with a diverse population, with budgetary and personnel management skills, and particularly for goodness of fit with the Newbridge schools and the community." The quest, which began by reviewing candidates' skills and experience, soon moved to considering the potential match between individual applicants and the district—its needs, history, locale, and organization. Expectations were high that Newbridge, a small, multiethnic working-class town, would attract and select not only an individual of great talent and experience, but also someone who was particularly drawn to the specific opportunities and challenges of educational leadership the town offered.

In broad outline, the search processes of the twelve districts discussed in this book looked much like that of Newbridge. More than half of them hired consultants to manage the process. Most conducted formal or informal needs assessments to guide their selections. Almost all their search committees included members of interest groups—unions, community agencies, parents of special education students—either as advisors to the consultant or as full-fledged members. All but one district spent over six weeks on the process—advertising widely, attracting an array of candidates, winnowing a large group of applicants down to a small group of finalists, and interviewing them publicly and privately before making a choice. With the exception of Ashmont, a small city district with a history of patronage, where the school board accepted the superintendent's resignation and appointed an insider to succeed him within the first thirty minutes of a regularly scheduled meeting, the processes were as deliberate and measured as one might expect for the important task of selecting a superintendent.

In each case, public deliberation and media coverage highlighted the paper credentials and prior experience of the candidates, but the search committees were actually far more curious about less objective criteria—appearance, sense of humor, ability to listen. Notably, much of this interest was not publicly discussed. Had it been possible to simply determine the exact skills required for the job, assess the candidates according to objective criteria, and then select the individual with the highest cumulative rating, identifying the "best" candidate might have been possible. But in each district the search and selection process proved to be far more intuitive than rational—and far more unpredictable than press accounts revealed. Everyone was looking for leadership, but few could agree on what leadership is or how to appraise a candidate's promise as a leader within their particular setting.

In part the search process is complex because no single candidate can possibly embody all the skills, strengths, and traits sought by school districts. The superintendents' job description reflects the combined wish lists of an array of constituents with varied preferences and priorities. Therefore when school boards consider applicants' qualifications, they must judge how those qualifications will play out in practice and make hard choices about what they value most.

Also, the search and selection process is less than rational because it is embedded within the context of a particular district. Each school district has a unique history of successes and failures that has shaped school officials' beliefs about who can best head their schools. Each community has its own social, economic, and political realities that determine what candidates must know or show in order to get the job, survive, and succeed. And each district has a particular organizational structure, a distinctive culture, and a unique constituency that holds various expectations about what kind of leader the district needs. By saying that those selecting Newbridge's superintendent wanted to achieve a "goodness of fit between the Newbridge schools and the community," James characterized just the sort of match that search and selection committees throughout this study sought to achieve.

Conducting the Search in Context

Three important contexts—a district's history, its community, and the organization of its school system—influence the criteria and process of selection.

The Historical Context

The searches described in this book all occurred during a period of great expectations for superintendents as leaders. During the late 1980s and early 1990s, criticism of public education was intense, sometimes strident. At the same time, education budgets were being cut or imperiled. Citizens often blamed the nation's poor economic performance on the shortcomings of its schools. Many took their cues from vocal critics of schooling who urged the public to recognize its stake in education and become involved in school reform. They hoped that superintendents of heroic stature might rescue the schools from devastation and reverse what appeared to be their precipitous decline. Of course, since diverse groups of citizens held conflicting views about what kind of leader their district needed, broad participation often led to selection processes marked by disputes and prolonged debate.

These features of the period between 1988 and 1992—myriad social and educational needs, great expectations of leaders, and intense involvement by many individuals and interest groups—were fairly consistent across all twelve districts described here. The individual histories of the districts varied in important ways, however, which further influenced their search processes. In particular, a prior superintendent's record had a striking impact on a district's selection process. In determining its priorities, the search committee frequently focused on what had gone wrong or what had been lacking under the previous administration, often to the exclusion of what had gone right. Therefore there was little mention of what should be continued, only talk about what shouldn't happen again.

The influence of prior administrations on the selection of a new superintendent played out in several ways. First, the circumstances of the prior superintendent's departure shaped the immediate context of the search. In some cases, sudden and unexpected events required that a new superintendent be hired quickly; in others, the change was long anticipated. Death and serious illness were the precipitating events in two districts. In four others, the sitting superintendent decided to take a new job, sometimes with the encouragement of the school board. Three superintendents retired after having been in office many years. In the remaining three districts, the superintendent was fired or firmly asked to leave. These districts, in particular, were determined to select someone who would compensate for the predecessor's weaknesses, sometimes at the expense of more objective scrutiny of candidates' knowledge and skills. If the prior superintendent has mismanaged funds, fiscal skills were at the top of that school board's list of priorities; if the prior superintendent had a reputation for being aloof or punitive, interpersonal skills were likely to be one of the board's top concerns; if the former superintendent had suddenly departed, the board sought assurances of a longer tenure.

The retiring superintendent in Newbridge was faulted for being too distant and for, as one administrator said, "exhibiting a lack of communication." A teacher in Millsburg said the retiring superintendent there was a "very outgoing, friendly, charming politician [who] lost sight of the fact that quality education was his primary goal and became satisfied with the status quo." In Oakville, by contrast, the school board judged its schools to be in excellent shape and sought to replace its beloved, retiring superintendent with a "clone." This case, however, was unique. All the other districts were less than satisfied—some were greatly dissatisfied—with the work of their prior superintendent.

Unlike matchmaking for marriage, the search for a new superintendent is rarely expected to lead to a permanent relationship, one that will last until the superintendent retires. Therefore, search committees seek a match not only between a superintendent and a particular place, but also between a superintendent and a particular time. Times change, and communities' needs for school leadership change as well. As one principal observed about Andrew Cronin, the newly hired superintendent in the suburban district of Clayton: "I think for now he's what Clayton really needs. . . . Is he the man of the future for Clayton? I don't know."

The Community and Political Context

Since the superintendent's work is entwined with that of local government officials, hiring the right superintendent also becomes the unofficial business of municipal officials and community leaders. Superintendents must negotiate with mayors, finance committees, and city councils to secure the money they need to run their schools. Contract negotiations with teachers and administrators unions are often linked to prior settlements reached with local fire and police unions. Controversies about sex education, student assignment patterns, or the results of standardized tests spill beyond the boundaries of the schools, affecting civic groups, churches, and real estate offices.

Many mayors will refer to "my superintendent" or "my schools" in interviews, signalling their claim on the public schools. Although some mayors will put their own reputations on the line in supporting particular appointees, others tend to relegate new superintendents to subordinate status in "their" cities and towns. Most municipal officials have lived their lives and built their careers locally; thus they regard most applicants for the superintendency as outsiders. From the start of the search process they assume that it is the new superintendent, rather than they, who must adapt and change. When asked whether he would do anything differently following Louis Antonellis's appointment as superintendent, the mayor of Ashmont said, "No I'm not going to change my approach . . . I say what's on my mind, and I don't get ulcers—I give ulcers. No, I won't change my approach to him. I don't think there's a need to." Territorial boundaries between school departments and local governments are regularly in dispute. While school officials try to secure special status and guarantees of autonomy for their districts, city officials often treat the schools as any other city agency. For new superintendents, this process of jockeying for position and control begins during the search and selection process.

Mayors and other local officials often play key roles in the search process, proposing criteria, personally interviewing candidates, and brokering agreements when a committee reaches an impasse. Even when such officials are not involved directly, their concerns are usually represented by school officials who understand that local support for public education depends on the new superintendent's ability to forcefully and effective advance the schools' interests in the community. The racial and ethnic diversity of urban communities further complicates the community context of the search. Sometimes competition or hostility among groups leads to a racially charged selection process. In the urban district of Millsburg, African-American and Latino groups allied to hire a superintendent from a minority group, contending that white administrators had neglected students of color. In Union, an inner-city district where virtually all the students are African American, there was a decided preference for an African-American superintendent. Reportedly, in some districts candidates are not considered serious contenders if their race or ethnic background does not match that of the local community. Any finalist in a diverse community has to be aware of different groups' concerns and priorities, since success in office often means recognizing schisms and reconciling the differences that inevitably develop between groups of constituents.

Members of the business community also actively participate in the search processes of many districts, reflecting the growing belief that business has a stake in the performance of local schools. The chamber of commerce in Millsburg both financed and greatly influenced the extensive search process. School board members in the other districts kept the priorities of business leaders in mind as they made their decisions. How would this person fare with local Rotarians or leaders of the local business roundtable? Even if board members reject the notion that public schooling should serve the economy, they must realize that business leaders have increasing leverage with the local government officials who control school budgets.

Thus searches often take place within a particular local context in which municipal officials; leaders of racial, ethnic, and religious groups; and influential business people participate directly or indirectly to ensure that their interests are represented. Community members hope that their new superintendent will not only be an effective educator but also an influential and cooperative player in the community.

The Organizational Context: How We Do Things Here

Searches are also influenced by the organizational characteristics of a particular school system. Search committees in highly centralized districts tended to seek superintendents who could exercise hierarchical authority, while more decentralized districts favored candidates who could manage the system effectively while granting considerable autonomy to principals and school staffs. Districts that were more formal and rule-bound expected their superintendents to follow procedures and enforce the chain of command, while more flexible districts showed interest in candidates with records of less formal approaches to administration.

The profile of a district's faculty and administration also influences whom search committees hire. Newbridge, where the faculty were experienced but dispirited, wanted a superintendent with a strong record in staff development. In Union and Millsburg, teachers were said to be retiring on the job, and officials therefore sought candidates with high standards for instructional performance.

School systems' values further shape the selection process. In suburban Highboro, where concerns about African-American students' achievement had intensified during the prior administration, the search committee deliberately sought candidates committed to equity for all students. Officials in Ashmont, who had already reduced the size of the district organization, assumed that anyone holding the superintendency would advocate efficiency.

Finally, districts seek superintendents with the experience and skills to administer current and proposed programs. Fernwood, a small-town district that had begun planning a new high school when their superintendent announced his resignation, looked for a successor who could oversee the process of designing and opening a new building. Summit, a city district involved in a school improvement process, was said to want "someone who was big on organizational development and who knew about organizational change and systemic change over time, someone who could commit to planning." Thus the form, norms, and practices of a school system's organization often influence decisions search committees make as they consider the match between applicants and their district's needs.

Defining a Direction for the Search

With so many individuals and interest groups participating in the process, a search committee is unlikely to settle on a detailed set of criteria. Rather, committee members tend to begin by reaching a broad understanding about the direction they want the superintendent to take—whether they want him or her to introduce change, provide continuity, or stabilize the district.

Looking for Change

Two districts, Millsburg and Newbridge, explicitly sought superintendents who would introduce major change. In each district the incumbent was retiring after many years in office, and respondents in both places characterized their school systems' programs as stagnant and outdated. Members of both districts' search committees intended to hire outside candidates; they thought insiders were too invested in current practices and were unlikely to know about educational reforms taking place elsewhere.

Even a principal whose allegiance to the retiring Millsburg superintendent led him to predict that he would be a "hard act to follow" emphasized the need for change: "I did feel we needed a change. I just felt to continue [by promoting an assistant superintendent from within] would be another continuation of the same old thing."

Although there was consensus on the search committees in Millsburg and Newbridge about the need for change, there was less clarity about what that change should be. "The school board," one Millsburg respondent said, "was looking for a new direction in which to take the whole system." Notably, she did not say that the board was seeking a candidate who would take the district back to basics or toward interdisciplinary learning; no particular direction was specified. But in choosing new leadership, Millsburg would definitely be signing up for a change.

Both Newbridge and Millsburg wanted candidates who were knowledgeable about the latest educational reforms, even when search committee members had little personal knowledge about the reforms. A union leader active in the Millsburg selection process said, "We were looking for someone who could, in fact, move the system forward to face the challenges of the twenty-first century. We all knew that education was in a changing pattern. . . . And all of the research and all of the literature was telling us that the factory model we were using was not the best and obviously was not doing the job it should be doing."

R. O. Carlson (1972) distinguishes between career-bound and place-bound superintendents, portraying the career-bound superintendent as "one who develops an early commitment to the superintendency and engages in deliberate career planning to achieve that goal. Place-bound administrators adopt a more passive orientation toward the superintendency and are less favorably inclined toward mobility" (Miklos, 1988, p. 64). Newbridge and Millsburg were looking for career-bound superintendents.

Both of the successful candidates were conversant with the latest literature on school reform and had experience introducing change. Anna Niles, the new superintendent in Newbridge, had initiated a strategic planning and management process in her former district, and Ben Moreno of Millsburg had introduced participatory decision making in his.

The successful candidates declared that they were, indeed, change agents. Ben Moreno explained that he wanted to head a school system that would not have to be convinced about the need for reform: "I was interested in going to a place that was ready for the bold steps needed to move very, very quickly." He confronted the school board with this expectation and insisted that members not offer him the job unless they were serious about change. That challenge and his confidence were exactly what local Millsburg officials wanted to hear.

Anna Niles also communicated her strong commitment to change. A central office administrator recalled that "they were looking for a change agent, and she presented herself in interviews and the staff visitations that she made as someone who was in the fore in terms of educational practice and theory. She presented certain talents that indicated she would be able to make change."

According to many respondents, each of these districts eventually hired the kind of superintendent it had sought. Looking back, a few respondents described a remarkably precise match between the district's needs and the candidate's qualifications. Most of the time, search committees' expectations were quite broadly framed. They set out looking for change agents, considered what the various candidates proposed to change, and selected finalists who seemed to best fit their district's needs. As emphasized later in this chapter, however, the final selection was driven as much by intuitive judgments about the character and traits of individual candidates as by the particular initiatives those candidates proposed.

Seeking Continuity

While Millsburg and Newbridge looked for change agents, other districts sought candidates who would ensure continuity and steady improvement in their educational programs. Generally those districts were proud of their schools' accomplishments, endorsed prevailing practices, and believed that students could be best served by refining rather than reforming their approach to education.

Three of these districts—Highboro, Clayton, and Oakville—served relatively homogeneous suburban communities that funded public education generously and, over the years, had established national reputations for excellence. They offered extensive and varied academic programs, their students performed well on standardized tests, and they provided considerable support for students with special needs. Respondents in each of these districts suggested ways their schools might be improved, particularly by better meeting the needs of increasingly diverse student populations, but none recommended abandoning or dramatically redirecting their current approach.

Fernwood, which also sought continuity, served a small working-class town that did not fund education generously. Programs and course offerings were limited, and graduates rarely attended prestigious colleges. The most recent superintendent had initiated positive changes in the district, securing funds for a new high school, proposing a grade reorganization, and establishing the district's Reading Recovery program, which was a model for the region. A central office administrator said he had introduced "a comprehensive plan that really amounted to a renaissance for the school system, and we needed someone who would be able to pull that together and build on it and carry us forward aggressively."

In Oakville, where the departing superintendent also enjoyed unusually high approval, a central office administrator said that the board was "interested, number one, in continuing the kind of leadership they had. They were very happy with that. The board certainly wasn't seeking change. If anything, they were seeking evolution or continuation of what they had."

People in Highboro and Clayton, on the other hand, were dissatisfied with the performance of their departing superintendents. The Highboro superintendent, hired during a period of fiscal austerity, had been asked to tighten up the district, which had long granted autonomy to its schools. In response he had assumed an authoritarian and distant approach to management, communicating indirectly with principals through central office administrators and making moves to standardize curriculum and pedagogy throughout the district. He was repeatedly faulted for having poor relationships with staff, exercising weak leadership, and having a meager influence on school practices. When the Highboro search committee first convened, the members did not talk about finding someone who would promote change; rather, they talked about finding someone who would better understand how to lead the district in the direction in which it had long been heading. One school board member stated, "We're not looking to revamp, but to fine-tune." The prior superintendent's appointment was commonly understood to have been a mistake, his tenure an unfortunate detour in an otherwise positive administrative course.

Similarly, in Clayton the prior superintendent was regarded as an aberration. During his administration the district had drifted, making less progress than it might have, but past successes and the strength of the staff carried the schools along respectably. When the search committee considered what their selection would signal about the future, they too decided to hire someone who would provide continuity and progress rather than dramatic change.

Like the successful candidates in the two districts seeking change, the contenders in Highboro, Clayton, Fernwood, and Oakville emphasized how right they were for the position. They praised these systems' prior accomplishments and presented themselves as leaders who could ensure continuous progress.

Searching for Stability

Finally, six districts had experienced disruption of such magnitude that their search committees primarily sought candidates who could stabilize the system. As participants on these search committees saw it, the primary goal of the next superintendent would be to steady the district and get it back on course. Candidates were assessed for their capacity to re-establish order, resolve differences, and return the system to its former state of equilibrium.

Two of these districts, Union and Ashmont, were in the midst of considerable upheaval while searching for a new superintendent. Union was emerging from receivership. A central office administrator explained, "There have been five superintendents within a three-year period, many of them 'interim-acting.' The district has been riddled with indictments of high-level administrative and supervisory staff. A school board had been disbanded." In its search for a new superintendent, Union looked to outsiders who had no political ties and thus could bring order to the feuding factions within the district. A Union teacher reflected on the choice of an outsider: "She brought a bit of stability to the district. As someone from the outside, she did not come clouded with any of the problems the district had."

Ashmont, too, was in a state of tumult. The prior superintendent had resigned in August after a heart attack. The school board, torn with dissension, had no budget. The teachers union began a twelve-day strike, delaying the September opening of school. Everyone expected that the next superintendent would be an insider, since in the past one hundred years only one outsider had been appointed, and that person's tenure was characterized by one principal as "a shock to the system." And everyone knew local politics would be important in determining who that insider would be. Therefore, in seeking stability, Ashmont looked to its own. It appointed Louis Antonellis, who said he was "home bred" and that he had wanted the job "from the day I came in."

Circumstances were less dramatic in Summit and Riverton, two urban districts that had experienced repeated turnover in the superintendency. Just as these districts had become engaged in reform efforts, the superintendents championing the reforms left for more prestigious jobs. A central office administrator in Riverton observed, "Much of the feeling was, people come, get things started, you buy into various programs, and before you have the opportunity to refine what you're doing, you have a new administration with a new philosophy." The effect of such turnover on staff morale was devastating. An administrator in Summit explained, "We had two interim superintendents and a superintendent who didn't do a good job and left. . . . There was just a lot of distrust."

Counting those in acting positions, Summit had had six superintendents in seven years, the most recent having been asked to leave. Riverton had experienced two recent changes in administration, with the most recent superintendent leaving, as one school board member explained, "after barely four years," which seemed far too short a time to many. Notably, this superintendent's tenure actually exceeded the national average for urban districts of this size. But people in Riverton felt he was leaving just as reforms had begun to take hold. Michael Fullan and Suzanne Stiegelbauer (1991), who contend that real reform requires five years' worth of a superintendent's attention, would agree. The most recent superintendent in Riverton emphasized equity and accountability, instituted a strategic management system, and, as one principal observed, "shook up a lot of people who thought mediocrity was okay." Being the first African-American superintendent in the district, his leaving was a particular disappointment to members of minority groups. This principal continued, "People who had supported him felt abandoned and betrayed, almost as if he had jumped ship. . . . Planting seeds for change takes more than a few years to see fruition of one's efforts, and consequently, most of what [he] had initiated never really came to be."

As a result of this turnover, search committees in Summit and Riverton sought candidates who were likely to stay for the long term. Riverton hired insider Maureen Reilly, who had been promoted up through the system and was serving as acting superintendent during the search. Although Reilly did not hold a doctorate (and many people in the district thought the superintendent should), she did have extensive experience in curriculum and instruction. More important, several respondents said, was the certainty that Reilly would not leave before her contract expired. A central office administrator agreed: "The feeling is that now it's time to have someone who will be here, who has knowledge of Riverton at many different levels and has a real commitment to the community, being a resident of the community." Reilly assured them that she was not a "gypsy superintendent."

Respondents understood the hazards of hiring an insider—the inertia resulting from past practices and the possibility that political debts might encumber the new administration—but they also recognized the benefits of their new superintendent's feeling at home in the system and being "a known quantity." A Riverton school board member observed that with an inside candidate, "There was no need to do the transition thing."

Although Summit had also experienced repeated turnover, the board decided to seek an outsider; it seemed more likely that the new expertise the members wanted would be found outside the district. Board members believed that someone without established allegiances within the district could deal more fairly and objectively with competing community groups. The Summit search committee members were no less worried about turnover than their counterparts in Riverton, though, and they considered carefully the commitment each candidate might make. When Wayne

Saunders, their eventual choice, promised to stay for at least five years, committee members were reassured.

Two remaining districts sought candidates who could stabilize their schools after prior superintendents had introduced flurries of programs that seemed to be counterproductive or contradictory. According to a central office administrator in the small, working-class city of Westford, the prior superintendent had "wanted change as his main goal." In promoting change, "he would find pockets where he could institutionalize change or move it and give go-ahead to people, and the system just grew like Topsie. And there was absolutely a loss of central control, lots of duplication of services, but change was what was needed and a lot of change came about."

In Glendale, which one teacher described as "very inbred" ("Everybody in this system went to school in this system; they've known each other since the year one"), people also characterized their former superintendent as a change agent whose reforms had overwhelmed the district. The superintendent was, as one of his many supporters said, "a dynamic, innovative, brilliant, controversial, troublesome, out-of-state superintendent, who was probably the best superintendent we have had in fifty years in this system." Under his direction the district had embarked on school restructuring and districtwide reorganization, but the changes were never fully implemented. One central office administrator in Glendale observed, "We had eighteen trains going on eighteen different tracks, and it was time, I think, to sit back now and say 'Let's get one train going out of the station at a time.'"

Both Westford and Glendale sought superintendents who would steady the schools, as these respondents' comments attest: "They were looking for someone who could bring stability to the educational community." "They were looking for somebody that could bring control to the system, somebody with experience in Glendale, to bring the system back on track. . . . We didn't need a turn-them-upside-down-type superintendent." The newly appointed superintendents promised just what was needed. A central office administrator in Westford said, "Wells came in with a message that 'I can organize things. I can bring focus to it.' And I think that's probably what sold him to the school board." Though not an insider, Wells had been a successful superintendent in a similar community. Glendale sought an insider who, as one principal explained, "hasn't hopped around the nation" and, as another said, would be "a cohesive force within the community, someone well respected."

Thus these communities, too, made what they believed were successful matches between their districts' need for change and the candidates who applied. Of course, search committees' preferences for change, continuity, or stability were not pure and uncomplicated. Districts that sought stability were not giving up on progress; in fact, achieving stability was seen as the first step in preparing for progress. Those embarking on change were not disregarding the importance of order and continuity, but their attention was focused primarily on moving in a new direction.

From this small sample it appears that districts tend to alternate over time between seeking change and preferring stability. The two districts seeking change agents were reacting to long periods of stability, which had in reality become stagnation. The six districts seeking stability sought to establish order after periods of rapid, sometimes chaotic change.

Matching the Person to the Time and Place

The twelve districts' decisions to promote change, maintain continuity, or achieve stability were defined in response to their particular context— their history, local circumstances, and school system organization. But the personal characteristics of the applicants proved to be equally important in determining whom search committees favored. Notably, committees preferred candidates judged to be compatible with the community's self-image. Search committees wanted candidates who were smart and experienced, individuals who could make a good appearance at public meetings and on television. They sought candidates who were likely to work well with people, specifically local people, and who exhibited enough confidence and strength to take on the difficult challenges facing their district. These more personal judgments about the match between candidates and context were largely subjective, only sometimes discussed publicly, and profoundly influential in the selection process.

How Does the Candidate Make Us Feel About Ourselves?

Search committees critically reviewed prospective superintendents as potential emissaries for their communities. Members paid attention to candidates' social class, race, and ethnicity as well as to their values and deportment.

In assessing a candidate on the basis of class, race, or ethnicity, search committee members wondered privately whether a prospective superintendent could become "one of us." For example, Westford, a small, ethnically diverse, working-class city, had three finalists, two men and a woman. One of the men, the favored candidate of four board members, came from a similar working-class community nearby, where local politics were sharply divided along ethnic lines. The woman, who was the choice of four other members, came from an upper-middle-class suburban community. Several who supported the man said they did so because he understood Westford's old-style politics. As one school board member explained, the town the man came from "is comparable to this town, and that's why I was supporting that particular candidate." The woman's supporters liked her because she was more liberal and therefore, they assumed, likely to be responsive to the concerns of new immigrant groups in Westford. She described herself as a "quadrilingual person" with "an appreciation of diversity and multiethnicity." But she was Jewish, and Westford was a town with few Jews. A principal offered these revealing comments about the town's response to her candidacy: "There is some sentiment in the city that we don't have enough affirmative action vis-à-vis women. And I really thought they were going to go with [the woman]. In retrospect, for some reason, she turned an awful lot of people off. It may have been that she was Jewish, and outspokenly so, although with that name she couldn't hide it very well. But she probably spoke about her heritage. It may have been that she was from an elitist community and [people wondered] what in the world would she know about Westford?"

The school board eventually offered the job to a third candidate, Thomas Wells, who had been superintendent in yet another working-class city as well as the headmaster at an international school abroad. Both experiences enabled him to advance as a compromise candidate who appealed to both the conservative ethnic politicians and the liberal champions of new immigrants. Later Wells explained how he had featured both experiences in his interview with the search committee:

> I was able to capitalize on two things: I would gear responses to point out that I was used to dealing with the mayor, that I was used to dealing with city councils, though Westford is more urban than [my former district]. And the second thing was that Westford is now experiencing a significant influx of new immigrants, . . . and so I emphasized the international character of my candidacy. I was coming from a school where we had children from forty-six different nations. I was bilingual and had lived abroad on a number of occasions, and my family was actively involved and familiar with settings where we were minorities and were dealing with minorities.

Wells interpreted the community's interest in him to be about feelings of comfort rather than about particular proposals he might offer: "I think those were more appealing—the city superintendency and the international, multicultural background—than any particular initiative that I espoused."

Class and ethnicity also proved important when Andrew Cronin, a highly qualified candidate from a nearby city, applied to become superintendent in the upper-middle-class suburb of Clayton. Initially many people in Clayton discounted Cronin's candidacy simply because of his urban background. A central office administrator said that many were "predisposed not to like him" when they found out where he came from. Cronin recalled the school board's decision to include him among the ten finalists: "If you asked them at that time why they were including [an administrator from the nearby city] who is Irish, they would say, 'Well, we just thought that was the democratic thing to do, and it looked like he had a good record and good recommendations.'" But Cronin's interview went very well—"I just clicked with them"—and he possessed skills in financial management that people sought. Gradually the search committee's interpretation of his urban experience shifted, and through Cronin's candidacy those hiring Clayton's superintendent began to reconcile the district's past identity with the new reality of its changing demographics. A central office administrator explained that Cronin was "an excellent match—and the reason, for starters, is that Clayton is really moving in a much more urban direction. He is clearly someone with urban school experience and an understanding of urban kids and parents and the issues. We call Clayton an urban-suburban community. We're hanging onto that suburban piece, and certainly, in terms of our values, they're largely suburban. But clearly the reality is we're dealing with a real mix of children in this town, and his coming, to me, signals an acknowledgment of that in a way that Clayton hasn't done before."

Millsburg had diversified significantly over the long tenure of its prior superintendent, a white man. At the start of the search, members of African-American and Latino interest groups allied to press for the appointment of a nonwhite superintendent. The finalists, all outsiders, included one white, one African-American, and one Latino candidate. Confusion arose, however, because many thought the Latino was Italian rather than Puerto Rican, and considerable dissension ensued within the minority coalition when African-American members expected the Latinos to back the African-American candidate. Eventually the Latino candidate, Ben Moreno, won the job, though doubts lingered about whether he truly represented "the community." Given the great diversity of that community, it seemed no candidate's race and ethnic background could satisfy everyone.

Clara Underwood, an African-American woman, was appointed to head the schools in Union, an African-American community. Arthur Holzman, a Jewish man, was hired by Highboro, a community with many

Jewish residents. Insiders, already proven to be compatible with the social and economic character of their communities, were hired in Ashmont, Glendale, and Riverton.

In considering whether prospective superintendents would fit in, committees also paid attention to applicants' values. Often, however, they relied on meager information in deciding what candidates stood for. Typically search committee members were simply seeking reassurance, and candidates' claims—rather than firm evidence about past performance—satisfied them. For example, one member of the search committee in Summit asked the leading candidate, "If you found out you were running a school system that was really two school systems, one for the haves and one for the have-nots, what would you do about it?" The candidate replied that this was the fundamental question in education, and he proceeded to explain how he would address the problem. This, the committee member said, "very much impressed me."

Boards seeking confirmation of their own beliefs generally accepted the word of candidates who espoused the value of diversity or the importance of excellence. Sometimes during board members' visits to candidates' sites, diligent search committee members uncovered evidence contradicting these espoused values and then reported back to the board about the gap between candidates' promises and past actions; but such persistent inquiry was rare, and most boards trusted their intuition in judging the claims of their candidates.

Is This Candidate Smart and Experienced Enough for the Job?

Search committee members tried to judge whether candidates had the intelligence and experience needed for success in a job filled with tremendous demands. They favored candidates who were quick, clever, and experienced in a broad range of administrative responsibilities. Although they valued intelligence, most were wary of pretentiously learned types. According to a principal in Summit, the school board "went with Saunders basically because they felt he was extremely bright. His credentials were very good. He was a graduate of Yale and Harvard." But almost in an effort to disclaim, the principal quickly went on to note that the candidate "also had a tough side to him," having been a hockey player in college and having "done some work in the inner cities." A strong academic record was essential in some communities; it actually became something of a liability in others.

Sometimes districts sought particular strengths, such as administrative experience at both the elementary and secondary levels or a good record working with a teachers union. While evidence of able fiscal management was a common prerequisite during these times of cutbacks, districts often were satisfied with a candidate who could speak confidently about a broad array of experiences. Having seen the finalists in Clayton, a department head was impressed with Cronin's overall intelligence. "He's bright, and Clayton admires brightness. Any system does, but you *really* have to be bright to make it here."

Does This Candidate Look and Sound Good?

The search process is largely a public one. Most of those studied here began in executive session but ended in open session, several under the bright lights of local television. As a result, district officials placed a premium on candidates' ease with the audience and their ability to think quickly and speak fluently. Respondents often commented on how the candidates looked, praising those who were attractive and commanding while criticizing those who seemed uncertain, withdrawn, or rumpled.

Although many search committees gathered extensive information about their candidates through references, phone calls, and site visits, the public interview proved to be the single most important factor in the final selection. Many decisions turned on the candidate's performance in these moments. Successful public interviews clinched the job for particular candidates. Both the candidates and the search committee members acknowledged that these were practiced events in which the questions and answers were rehearsed rather than spontaneous. Nevertheless, public interviews carried great weight. When candidates did not perform well, school board members worried about the effect a weak public speaker might have on the standing of the schools. One principal explained that although the candidate his board eventually hired "didn't get high marks on the interview, everybody liked him because they knew his credentials gave him credibility. They loved the kind of person he was. But it was awkward for him to interview for some reason. And we all accepted that and looked at it accordingly. . . . And the question was, if he's having trouble in the interview process, what kind of image would he project to the public? Would he get their confidence? Would he hold their confidence?"

Similarly, a board member in another district was very disappointed with the leading candidate's interview: "It was the worst interview by an applicant I've seen for a superintendent's job. At that point everyone agreed it was a terrible interview. He made a terrible appearance, and my thought at the time was, 'There's a guy who, if he's ever got to go before the town meeting and present a budget, we're in trouble.'" Search committee members believed that their superintendent's public image would have real consequences for their schools' future. Thus they could not easily ignore a poor performance.

Will This Candidate Work Well with People?

Without exception, the search committees believed their next superintendent should work well with people, since the job demands repeated, often relentless person-to-person encounters. In several districts the prior superintendent was said to have been distant, aloof, and controlling; these individuals had generally been hired to make hard decisions about budgets and jobs, only to be accused of creating poor morale once fiscal cuts were made. As a result, these districts were now determined to find candidates with excellent interpersonal skills.

In several districts respondents said the new superintendent had won the job mainly because he or she was good with people. A respondent in Clayton said, "I think that's why Cronin was hired. His first three concerns are people first, people second, and people always. His emphasis is people, people, people. . . . Is he a great academic thinker? I think not. Is he a great visionary? He's not a visionary person who can look at education in a different way. I think he was hired because he's a people person and he's a very upbeat type of person. Very, very upbeat. [He believes] that people can make a difference."

In Fernwood, where the prior superintendent had the reputation of being authoritarian, Dick Fitzgerald's gentler, more "humanistic" style won him the job. "The town was ripe for it," a principal explained. Similarly, in Glendale, where the prior superintendent's administration was reportedly fraught with "tremendous pressure and tension," a principal said, "Administrators wanted, number one, someone who was pleasant to work with. They wanted someone who had been in the system for many years, someone with wonderful people skills, someone who could bring people together."

Several superintendents were hired explicitly for their skills as peacemakers or mediators. Union, just emerging from receivership, hired Clara Underwood because they thought she could diffuse in-house hostilities and, as one respondent said, bring "quiet to this district in the midst of a storm." In the suburban district of Highboro, which one administrator called "fractured," the school board sought a superintendent who could help them achieve unity. A school board member who praised the prior superintendent nonetheless observed, "One area where there seemed to be a real weakness was in staff relationships. And I said it publicly at the time, and I believe it still to be the case, the most important thing for the new superintendent was to do what he could to sort of beef up staff morale. The previous superintendent, I think, was seen more as a management type. . . . He didn't appear to be a very warm person."

Finally, several districts sought superintendents who would promote greater participation by teachers and administrators in the decisions of the district. As one school board member said, Anna Niles's candidacy offered participation for all parties: "During her interview, she spoke about her prior experience and successes at having done that—including the parents, involving the business community, and her very strong commitment to professional development [for teachers]." A central office administrator believed that Niles's effort to present herself as a leader who could promote participation had worked. "I don't think there's any question that they felt she was a consensus builder. . . . I think at the time that's what this community needed. I think we needed somebody who could make people feel as though they were part of the project." Therefore, search committee members particularly concerned about the limitations of top-down authority considered carefully which of their candidates might engage others most successfully in new initiatives.

Is This Candidate Up To the Job?

There was also considerable recognition that the superintendent's job requires toughness, courage, stamina, and resilience. Here, too, a district's preferences were shaped by current circumstances or by the style of the prior superintendent. Glendale, where labor strife had heightened the board's attention to the need for strong management, hired a candidate whose style, according to one school board member, was "a better match, in the more aggressive style of management, than the other finalist." In Union, which had just emerged from receivership, the newly appointed superintendent, Clara Underwood, said, "They were looking for someone . . . who was not afraid to let people go who weren't pulling their weight, not afraid to speak up to the school board when it's needed, not afraid to involve everybody in the process, not threatened by any faction of the community." Although Underwood seemed confident that she possessed the needed strength, one principal was worried: "I don't know if she has that killer instinct. . . . I mean, you may not have to do it, but the folks have to believe you will. . . . Will she be able to swim in shark-infested waters? Will she be able to survive?"

The search committees recognized that the task of changing schools requires both compassion and tough-mindedness. They conducted their search with the belief that achieving a balance between these two characteristics was both necessary and possible. However, when committee members sensed a weakness in one area, decisions became difficult. For example, in the suburban district of Oakville, a school board member said that the newly appointed superintendent, Mike Ogden, embodied the values of the board—communication and understanding—and that he was the right choice. But the board member asked himself, "'Should I have taken a stronger candidate?' Because there were one or two men in the group who were stronger, but I don't think it would have been the right choice. I think we need a Mr. Ogden here."

Assessing the Candidate as a Person, Not a Professional

In the end, the task of assessing a candidate as an individual was approached intuitively by search committee members. They could compare candidates' paper credentials according to objective criteria, but comparing their strengths and weaknesses as people was a very subjective process. Committee members debated among themselves about the kind of leader their district needed. Most agreed that, ideally, a superintendent should embrace local values; be able to bridge differences within diverse communities; be bright and broadly experienced by local standards; make a persuasive public appearance, by looking good and sounding convincing; work easily with others, engendering optimism among staff and confidence among constituents; and be strong and determined under pressure, doing what must be done for the sake of the district's children.

None of the candidates could offer all this, of course; thus school board members had to carefully weigh their perceptions about the candidates against their priorities for the district. In Newbridge, a school board member recalled, "We got down to two finalists, and it was a difference in style. One of the finalists was more lackadaisical. When you visited his district, you didn't have a sense that there were a lot of systems in there, but you had the sense that he really knew his people. He sort of bumbled around. . . . The system was weak. And at that point in time, given the surrounding circumstances to the hiring process, and the strike and everything, it seemed that we needed someone who was more systems-oriented and would move ahead at a faster clip. . . . Anna Niles was that person."

In Summit, a principal reported that the two finalists had been "neck and neck. The other one [who was not hired] frightened people." He was "too directive, too specific about judgments, possibly too forceful about an opinion, a little too organized." By contrast, Wayne Saunders, who received the appointment, "seemed to be a little more laid back, a little more receptive. There seemed to be a feeling that one could work with him. . . . Truthfully, the school board did not want somebody to tell them what to do. I think they wanted somebody they could talk it over with—a discussion partner, if you will."

Many individuals' final votes turned on these sorts of subjective and undiscussed assessments. A school board member in Westford conceded, somewhat cynically, that in the end "you buy a guy and a style." Another respondent defended these intuitive, subjective judgments, however: "You look for a person who has compassion, understanding, ambition. . . . You cannot hire someone you don't trust and someone you don't respect." If you do, he added, "then you're being very foolish." Although many participated in the search, ultimately it was the school board that made the choice. One board member observed, "Whenever a school board hires a superintendent, it reflects that school board that hired him. I think [our new superintendent] was very much what *we* needed at the time."

Final Days and Decisions

As the searches moved toward completion after two or three months, many of the twelve districts encountered unpredictable events that stalled or sidetracked the process and oddly distorted the outcome. Sometimes the search process unraveled rather than unfolded. Favored candidates dropped out abruptly when job offers materialized from other districts. New, negative information surfaced about some, making once-attractive applicants suddenly unacceptable. Local officials used their political power to augment one individual's chances. Sometimes a hearty list of seemingly strong candidates shrank to a short list of two or three, none of whom seemed right. Reflecting on the selection in one district, a school board member said, "I think that he was hired because the other person was so bad." In another district, the short list of three finalists became a shorter list of one when one candidate withdrew and the board discovered that another had been fired from his previous job.

Such accounts lend support to the view that the search process, as it often transpires in this somewhat haphazard way, is not the best way to select a superintendent; it is clearly not orderly and rational. However, one can also argue that the process, with all its uncertainty, public scrutiny, political influence, and subjective assessment, is not unlike the job of the superintendency itself. And for all the unpredictability and irregularity of the process, the overwhelming majority of respondents thought that their district had made a good match in their choice. They had achieved that "goodness of fit" between the person and the context, which, though not always ideal, was usually perceived to be adequate.

Whether these new superintendents would meet their constituents' expectations over time is another matter. What is clear, however, is that the search and selection process is at once an approach to selecting a new superintendent and an activity of self-definition for the school district; each part affects the other. When it is an open process, it encourages many constituents with varied interests and backgrounds to engage in worthwhile dialogue and to influence the outcome of the search. Commenting on the presidential search process in higher education, Birnbaum (1988) states, "Regardless of the substantive outcome, search and selection is an important and necessary process. It provides people with a sense of participating in important decisions and thereby lessens the power differences in the organization. It stabilizes the organization and leads to satisfaction with the social order by confirming the myth that positions are allocated on meritocratic grounds" (p. 507).

By deciding whether the district is to embark on change, maintain continuity, or introduce stability, a school board assesses its past and charts a general direction for its future. By choosing one individual over others, a school board makes an explicit, illuminating statement about the community and its values. By achieving the best possible match between local needs and candidates' interests, strengths, and weaknesses, a school board can open the way for leadership and change. Jeffrey Pfeffer (1978) speculates that leaders' actual influence on organizations may be less than some expect because the process of search and selection limits the "styles of behavior" that are acceptable within the organization (p. 17). On the other hand, the process of finding a match between the candidate and the district may actually be what makes it possible for a new superintendent to lead. Several of the districts studied could have chosen more venturesome, free-thinking superintendents, but there is no evidence that a new administrator who is seen to be out of sync with his or her constituents can lead effectively.

However it is configured and however successful it turns out to be, the search and selection process creates the conditions for change. It sets the terms for a new administration, identifying both opportunities and constraints and suggesting how a superintendent will be expected to lead in the local context. One of the earliest expectations that many newly appointed superintendents face is to define a vision for change. . . .

REFERENCES

Birnbaum, R. (1988). Presidential searches and the discovery of organizational goals. *Journal of Higher Education, 59*(5), 489–509.

Carlson, R. O. (1972). *School superintendents: Careers and performance.* Columbus, OH: Merrill.

Fullan, M. G., & Stiegelbauer, S. (1991). *The new meaning of educational change.* New York: Teachers College Press.

Miklos, E. (1988). Administrator selection, career patterns, succession and socialization. In N. J. Boyan (Ed.), *Handbook of research on educational administration* (pp. 53–76). New York: Longman.

Pfeffer, J. (1978). The ambiguity of leadership. In M. M. Lombardo & M. W. McCall, Jr. (Eds.), *Leadership: Where can we go from here?* (pp. 3–34). Durham, NC: Duke University Press.

8

STANDARDS FOR
SCHOOL LEADERS

Interstate School Leaders Licensure Consortium
Adopted by Full Consortium
November 2, 1996

Dear Colleague:

For the past two years, the Interstate School Leaders Licensure Consortium (ISLLC), a program of the Council of Chief State School Officers, has been at work crafting model standards for school leaders. Forged from research on productive educational leadership and the wisdom of colleagues, the standards were drafted by personnel from 24 state education agencies and representatives from various professional associations. The standards present a common core of knowledge, dispositions, and performances that will help link leadership more forcefully to productive schools and enhanced educational outcomes. Although developed to serve a different purpose, the standards were designed to be compatible with the new National Council for the Accreditation of Teacher Education (NCATE) Curriculum Guidelines for school administration—as well as with the major national reports on reinventing leadership for tomorrow's schools. As such, they represent another part of a concerted effort to enhance the skills of school leaders and to couple leadership with effective educational processes and valued outcomes.

One intent of the document is to stimulate vigorous thought and dialogue about quality educational leadership among stakeholders in the area of school administration. A second intent is to provide raw material that will help stakeholders across the education landscape (e.g., state agencies, professional associations, institutions of higher education) enhance the quality of educational leadership throughout the nation's schools. Our work is offered, therefore, with these two goals in mind.

It is the desire of the Consortium to raise the bar for the practice of school leadership. Thus the standards and indicators reflect the magnitude of both the importance and the responsibility of effective school leaders.

We encourage you to heavily use this document—circulate it widely to members of the public and the profession as well as to the policy-making community. It is through this shared vision of education that school leaders will be successful and that our children will be assured of the education they will need to carry out the responsibilities of the future.

Sincerely,

Neil Shipman, Director, ISLLC
Joseph Murphy, Chair, ISLLC

PREFACE

OVER THE PAST QUARTER-CENTURY, significant changes have been reshaping our nation. At the same time, new viewpoints have redefined the struggle to restructure education for the 21st century. From these two foundations, educators and policy makers have launched many helpful initiatives to redefine the roles of formal school leaders. In this document, you see the results of one of these efforts—the work of the Interstate School Leaders Licensure Consortium (ISLLC) to establish common standards for school leaders. In this report, we describe the portrait of leadership and the understanding of society and education that guided the work of the ISLLC team. We also provide an overview of ISLLC activity, describing the process we used to develop the standards and discussing central issues embedded in that process. Finally, we present the ISLLC standards and indicators.

Redesigning Leadership

The model of leadership standards one develops depends a good deal on how the design issue is framed. The Consortium tackled the design strategy in two ways. First, we relied heavily on the research on the linkages between educational leadership and productive schools, especially in terms of outcomes for children and youth. Second, we sought out significant trends in society and education that hold implications for emerging views of leadership—and subsequently for the standards that give meaning to those new perspectives on leadership.

An Understanding of Effective Leadership

Formal leadership in schools and school districts is a complex, multifaceted task. The ISLLC standards honor that reality. At the same time, they acknowledge that effective leaders often espouse different patterns of beliefs and act differently from the norm in the profession. Effective school leaders are strong educators, anchoring their work on central issues of learning and teaching and school improvement. They are moral agents and social advocates for the children and the communities they serve. Finally, they make strong connections with other people, valuing and caring for others as individuals and as members of the educational community.

The Changing Nature of Society

Looking to the larger society that envelopes schooling, the Consortium identified a handful of powerful dynamics that will likely shape the future of education and, perforce, the types of leadership required for tomorrow's schools. To begin with, our vision of education is influenced by the knowledge that the social fabric of society is changing, often in dramatic ways. On the one hand, the pattern of the fabric is being rewoven. In particular, we are becoming a more diverse society—racially, linguistically and culturally. On the other hand, the social fabric is unraveling for many children and their families. Poverty is increasing. Indexes of physical, mental, and moral well-being are declining. The stock of social capital is decreasing as well.

The perspective of the Consortium on schooling and leadership is also colored by the knowledge that the economic foundations of society are being recast as well. The shift to a post-industrial society, the advance of the global marketplace, the increasing reliance on technology, and a growing infatuation with market-based solutions to social needs pose significant new challenges for education. We believe that these challenges will require new types of leadership in schools.

An Evolving Model of Schooling

Turning to schooling itself, Consortium members distilled three central changes, all of which augur for a redefined portfolio of leadership skills for school administrators. On one level, we are seeing a renewed struggle to redefine learning and teaching to more successfully challenge and engage all youngsters in the education process. Educators are rethinking long-prevailing views of knowledge, intelligence, assessment and instruction. On a second level, we are hearing strong rumblings that community-focused and caring-centered conceptions of schooling will increasingly compete for legitimacy with more established notions of school organizations as hierarchies and bureaucracies. Finally, stakeholders external to the school building—parents, interested members of the corporate sector and leaders in the community—will increasingly play significantly enhanced roles in education.

ISLLC Initiative

The Consortium's initiative builds on research about skillful stewardship by school administrators and emerging perspectives about society and education. At one level, our work is a continuation of a century's quest to develop a deeper and more productive understanding of school leadership. At the same time, however, primarily because of the fundamental nature of the shift from an industrial to an information society, our work represents one of the two or three major transition points in that voyage.

The Consortium is not alone in its attempt to define the current era of transition in society and schooling and to capture its meaning for educational leadership. Since the 1987 publication of the Leaders for America's Schools by the National Commission on Excellence in Educational Administration, all the major professional associations, both practitioner and university based, have devoted productive energy to this issue. Indeed, the National Policy Board for Educational Administration (NPBEA) was created largely in response to this need and in an effort to generate better and more coordinated purchase on the task. Thus, the work of ISLLC is part of the long tradition of regularly upgrading the profession and, we believe, is a central pillar in the struggle to forge a vision of educational leadership for tomorrow's schools.

The ISLLC initiative began in August 1994. Fueled by the contributions of the 24 member states, a generous foundational grant from The Pew Charitable Trusts, and assistance from the Danforth Foundation and the NPBEA, the program operates under the aegis of the Council of Chief State School Officers. The 24 member states are Arkansas, California, Connecticut, Delaware, Georgia, Illinois, Indiana, Kansas, Kentucky, Maryland, Massachusetts, Michigan, Mississippi, Missouri, New Jersey, North Carolina, Ohio, Pennsylvania, Rhode Island, South Carolina, Texas, Virginia, Washington and Wisconsin. In addition, the following professional associations are affiliated with ISLLC: American Association of Colleges for Teacher Education, American Association of School Administrators, Association for Supervision and Curriculum Development, Association of Teacher Educators, National Association of Elementary School Principals, National Association of Secondary School Principals, National Association of State Boards of Education, National Council of Professors of Educational Administration, National Policy Board of Educational Administration, National School Boards Association, and University Council for Educational Administration.

Representatives of the member states and affiliated organizations have crafted standards and indicators. As noted previously, in the drafting process the Consortium team drew extensively on the research about productive leadership. We also relied heavily on the knowledge of the representatives themselves. Finally, we employed the collective wisdom of colleagues in schools and school districts, institutions of higher education, and various professional associations at both state and national levels to enrich and leaven the work throughout the development process.

Guiding Principles

At the outset of the project, it became clear that our work would be strengthened considerably if we could craft a set of overarching principles to guide our efforts. Over time we saw that these principles actually could serve two functions. First, they have acted as a touchstone to which we regularly returned to test the scope and focus of emerging products. Second, we believe that they help give meaning to the standards and indicators. Here are the seven principles that helped orient all of our work:

Standards should reflect the centrality of student learning.

Standards should acknowledge the changing role of the school leader. Standards should recognize the collaborative nature of school leadership. Standards should be high, upgrading the quality of the profession. Standards should inform performance-based systems of assessment and evaluation school leaders. Standards should be integrated and coherent. Standards should be predicated on the concepts of access, opportunity, and empowerment for all members of the school community.

Comments on the Standards

Many strategies are being used to upgrade the quality of leadership in the educational arena. For example, institutions of higher education have done extensive work on revising preparation programs for prospective school administrators. Many states have also strengthened licensing requirements and revised procedures for approval of university-based preparation programs. The ISLLC team decided at the outset of this project, however, to focus on standards. This strategy made sense for several reasons. First, based on the work on standards in other arenas of educational reform, especially the efforts of the Interstate New Teachers Assessment and Support Consortium (INTASC), we were convinced that standards provided an especially appropriate and particularly powerful leverage point for reform. Second, we found a major void in this area of educational administration—a set of common standards remains conspicuous by its absence. Finally, we believed that the standards approach provided the best avenue to allow diverse stakeholders to drive improvement efforts along a variety of fronts—certification, program approval and candidate assessment.

Within that framework, we began work on a common set of standards that would apply to nearly all formal leadership positions in education, not just principals. We acknowledge full well that there are differences in leadership that correspond to roles, but ISLLC members were unanimous in their belief that the central aspects of the role are the same for all school leadership positions.

While acknowledging the full range of responsibilities of school leaders, we decided to focus on those topics that formed the heart and soul of effective leadership. This decision led us in two directions. First, because we didn't want to lose the key issues in a forest of standards, we deliberately framed a parsimonious model at the standard level. Thus, we produced only six standards. Second, we continually focused on matters of learning and teaching and the creation of powerful learning environments. Not only do several standards directly highlight learning and teaching, but all the standards take on meaning to the extent that they support a learning environment. Throughout, the success of students is paramount. For example, every standard begins with the words "A school administrator is an educational leader who promotes the success of all students by . . ."

Finally, a word about the framework for the indicators is in order. The design we employed (knowledge, dispositions, and performances), is borrowed from the thoughtful work of our INTASC colleagues. While there was little debate about the importance of knowledge and performances in the framework, the inability to "assess" dispositions caused some of us a good deal of consternation at the outset of the project. As we became more enmeshed in the work, however, we discovered that the dispositions often occupied center stage. That is, because "dispositions are the proclivities that lead us in one direction rather than another within the freedom of action that we have" (Perkins, 1995, p. 275),[1] in many fundamental ways they nourish and give meaning to performance. Over time, we have grown to understand that these elements—knowledge, dispositions, and performances—belong together. We also find ourselves agreeing with Perkins (1995) that "dispositions are the soul of intelligence, without which the understanding and know-how do little good" (p. 278).

Standard 1

A school administrator is an educational leader who promotes the success of all students by *facilitating the development, articulation, implementation, and stewardship of a vision of learning that is shared and supported by the school community.*

Knowledge

The administrator has knowledge and understanding of:
- learning goals in a pluralistic society
- the principles of developing and implementing strategic plans
- systems theory
- information sources, data collection, and data analysis strategies
- effective communication
- effective consensus-building and negotiation skills

---

1. David Perkins (1995), *Outsmarting I.Q.: The Emerging Science of Learnable Intelligence.* New York: The Free Press.

Dispositions

The administrator believes in, values, and is committed to:
- the educability of all
- a school vision of high standards of learning
- continuous school improvement
- the inclusion of all members of the school community
- ensuring that students have the knowledge, skills, and values needed to become successful adults
- a willingness to continuously examine one's own assumptions, beliefs, and practices
- doing the work required for high levels of personal and organization performance

Performances

The administrator facilitates processes and engages in activities ensuring that:
- the vision and mission of the school are effectively communicated to staff, parents, students, and community members
- the vision and mission are communicated through the use of symbols, ceremonies, stories, and similar activities
- the core beliefs of the school vision are modeled for all stakeholders
- the vision is developed with and among stakeholders
- the contributions of school community members to the realization of the vision are recognized and celebrated
- progress toward the vision and mission is communicated to all stakeholders
- the school community is involved in school improvement efforts
- the vision shapes the educational programs, plans, and actions
- an implementation plan is developed in which objectives and strategies to achieve the vision and goals are clearly articulated
- assessment data related to student learning are used to develop the school vision and goals
- relevant demographic data pertaining to students and their families are used in developing the school mission and goals

- barriers to achieving the vision are identified, clarified, and addressed
- needed resources are sought and obtained to support the implementation of the school mission goals
- existing resources are used in support of the school vision and goals
- the vision, mission, and implementation plans are regularly monitored, evaluated, and revised

Standard 2

A school administrator is an educational leader who promotes the success of all students by *advocating, nurturing, and sustaining a school culture and instructional program conducive to student learning and staff professional growth.*

Knowledge

The administrator has knowledge and understanding of:
- student growth and development
- applied learning theories
- applied motivational theories
- curriculum design, implementation, evaluation, and refinement
- principles of effective instruction
- measurement, evaluation, and assessment strategies
- diversity and its meaning for educational programs
- adult learning and professional development models
- the change process for systems, organizations, and individuals
- the role of technology in promoting student learning and professional growth
- school cultures

Dispositions

The administrator believes in, values, and is committed to:
- student learning as the fundamental purpose of schooling
- the proposition that all students can learn

- the variety of ways in which students can learn
- life long learning for self and others
- professional development as an integral part of school improvement
- the benefits that diversity brings to the school community
- a safe and supportive learning environment
- preparing students to be contributing members of society

Performances

The administrator facilitates processes and engages in activities ensuring that:

- all individuals are treated with fairness, dignity, and respect
- professional development promotes a focus on student learning consistent with the school vision and goals
- students and staff feel valued and important
- the responsibilities and contributions of each individual are acknowledged
- barriers to student learning are identified, clarified, and addressed
- diversity is considered in developing learning experiences
- life long learning is encouraged and modeled
- there is a culture of high expectations for self, student, and staff performance
- technologies are used in teaching and learning
- student and staff accomplishments are recognized and celebrated
- multiple opportunities to learn are available to all students
- the school is organized and aligned for success
- curricular, co-curricular, and extra-curricular programs are designed, implemented, evaluated, and refined
- curriculum decisions are based on research, expertise of teachers, and the recommendations of learned societies
- the school culture and climate are assessed on a regular basis
- a variety of sources of information is used to make decisions
- student learning is assessed using a variety of techniques

- multiple sources of information regarding performance are used by staff and students
- a variety of supervisory and evaluation models is employed
- pupil personnel programs are developed to meet the needs of students and their families

Standard 3

A school administrator is an educational leader who promotes the success of all students by *ensuring management of the organization, operations, and resources for a safe, efficient, and effective learning environment.*

Knowledge

The administrator has knowledge and understanding of:
- theories and models of organizations and the principles of organizational development
- operational procedures at the school and district level
- principles and issues relating to school safety and security
- human resources management and development
- principles and issues relating to fiscal operations of school management
- principles and issues relating to school facilities and use of space
- legal issues impacting school operations
- current technologies that support management functions

Dispositions

The administrator believes in, values, and is committed to:
- making management decisions to enhance learning and teaching
- taking risks to improve schools
- trusting people and their judgments
- accepting responsibility
- high-quality standards, expectations, and performances
- involving stakeholders in management processes
- a safe environment

Performances

The administrator facilitates processes and engages in activities ensuring that:

- knowledge of learning, teaching, and student development is used to inform management decisions
- operational procedures are designed and managed to maximize opportunities for successful learning
- emerging trends are recognized, studied, and applied as appropriate
- operational plans and procedures to achieve the vision and goals of the school are in place
- collective bargaining and other contractual agreements related to the school are effectively managed
- the school plant, equipment, and support systems operate safely, efficiently, and effectively
- time is managed to maximize attainment of organizational goals
- potential problems and opportunities are identified
- problems are confronted and resolved in a timely manner
- financial, human, and material resources are aligned to the goals of schools
- the school acts entrepreneurially to support continuous improvement
- organizational systems are regularly monitored and modified as needed
- stakeholders are involved in decisions affecting schools
- responsibility is shared to maximize ownership and accountability
- effective problem-framing and problem-solving skills are used
- effective conflict resolution skills are used
- effective group-process and consensus-building skills are used
- effective communication skills are used
- a safe, clean, and aesthetically pleasing school environment is created and maintained
- human resource functions support the attainment of school goals
- confidentiality and privacy of school records are maintained

Standard 4

A school administrator is an educational leader who promotes the success of all students by *collaborating with families and community members, responding to diverse community interests and needs, and mobilizing community resources.*

Knowledge

The administrator has knowledge and understanding of:
- emerging issues and trends that potentially impact the school community
- the conditions and dynamics of the diverse school community
- community resources
- community relations and marketing strategies and processes
- successful models of school, family, business, community, government and higher education partnerships

Dispositions

The administrator believes in, values, and is committed to:
- schools operating as an integral part of the larger community
- collaboration and communication with families
- involvement of families and other stakeholders in school decision-making processes
- the proposition that diversity enriches the school
- families as partners in the education of their children
- the proposition that families have the best interests of their children in mind
- resources of the family and community needing to be brought to bear on the education of students
- an informed public

Performances

The administrator facilitates processes and engages in activities ensuring that:
- high visibility, active involvement, and communication with the larger community is a priority

- relationships with community leaders are identified and nurtured
- information about family and community concerns, expectations, and needs is used regularly
- there is outreach to different business, religious, political, and service agencies and organizations
- credence is given to individuals and groups whose values and opinions may conflict
- the school and community serve one another as resources
- available community resources are secured to help the school solve problems and achieve goals
- partnerships are established with area businesses, institutions of higher education, and community groups to strengthen programs and support school goals
- community youth family services are integrated with school programs
- community stakeholders are treated equitably
- diversity is recognized and valued
- effective media relations are developed and maintained
- a comprehensive program of community relations is established
- public resources and funds are used appropriately and wisely
- community collaboration is modeled for staff
- opportunities for staff to develop collaborative skills are provided

Standard 5

A school administrator is an educational leader who promotes the success of all students by *acting with integrity, fairness, and in an ethical manner.*

Knowledge

The administrator has knowledge and understanding of:
- the purpose of education and the role of leadership in modern society
- various ethical frameworks and perspectives on ethics
- the values of the diverse school community
- professional codes of ethics
- the philosophy and history of education

Dispositions

The administrator believes in, values, and is committed to:
- the ideal of the common good
- the principles in the Bill of Rights
- the right of every student to a free, quality education
- bringing ethical principles to the decision-making process
- subordinating one's own interest to the good of the school community
- accepting the consequences for upholding one's principles and actions
- using the influence of one's office constructively and productively in the service of all students and their families
- development of a caring school community

Performances

The administrator:
- examines personal and professional values
- demonstrates a personal and professional code of ethics
- demonstrates values, beliefs, and attitudes that inspire others to higher levels of performance
- serves as a role model
- accepts responsibility for school operations
- considers the impact of one's administrative practices on others
- uses the influence of the office to enhance the educational program rather than for personal gain
- treats people fairly, equitably, and with dignity and respect
- protects the rights and confidentiality of students and staff
- demonstrates appreciation for and sensitivity to the diversity in the school community
- recognizes and respects the legitimate authority of others
- examines and considers the prevailing values of the diverse school community
- expects that others in the school community will demonstrate integrity and exercise ethical behavior
- opens the school to public scrutiny

- fulfills legal and contractual obligations
- applies laws and procedures fairly, wisely, and considerately

Standard 6

A school administrator is an educational leader who promotes the success of all students by *understanding, responding to, and influencing the larger political, social, economic, legal, and cultural context.*

Knowledge

The administrator has knowledge and understanding of:
- principles of representative governance that undergird the system of American schools
- the role of public education in developing and renewing a democratic society and an economically productive nation
- the law as related to education and schooling
- the political, social, cultural and economic systems and processes that impact schools
- models and strategies of change and conflict resolution as applied to the larger political, social, cultural and economic contexts of schooling
- global issues and forces affecting teaching and learning
- the dynamics of policy development and advocacy under our democratic political system
- the importance of diversity and equity in a democratic society

Dispositions

The administrator believes in, values, and is committed to:
- education as a key to opportunity and social mobility
- recognizing a variety of ideas, values, and cultures
- importance of a continuing dialogue with other decision makers affecting education
- actively participating in the political and policy-making context in the service of education
- using legal systems to protect student rights and improve student opportunities

Performances

The administrator facilitates processes and engages in activities ensuring that:

- the environment in which schools operate is influenced on behalf of students and their families
- communication occurs among the school community concerning trends, issues, and potential changes in the environment in which schools operate
- there is ongoing dialogue with representatives of diverse community groups
- the school community works within the framework of policies, laws, and regulations enacted by local, state, and federal authorities
- public policy is shaped to provide quality education for students
- lines of communication are developed with decision makers outside the school community

9

THE UNHEROIC SIDE
OF LEADERSHIP

NOTES FROM THE SWAMP

Jerome T. Murphy

WHEN I ACCEPTED my current position as associate dean, I had grand ideas about helping to lead the Harvard Graduate School of Education in its dealings with such challenging issues as organizational mission and fiscal stability. Here was a chance to influence the direction of an important institution.

Early on, however, I was abruptly brought down to earth by a fellow faculty member. In the midst of a dinner conversation about world affairs, he suddenly blinked and said, "By the way, what are you going to do about the odor strips?" Sensing my puzzlement, he pressed on, "I am allergic to the new odor strips in the fourth-floor bathroom, and something needs to be done!" I expressed concern and moved off to the bar to ponder the heroic aspects of decanal life at Harvard.

In my ponderings, I recalled a poster I had once seen tacked to the office wall of a seasoned administrator. It read:

NOTICE
The objective of all dedicated department employees should be to thoroughly analyze all situations, anticipate all problems prior to their occurrence, have answers for these problems, and move swiftly to solve these problems when called upon . . .

However . . .

When you are up to your ass in alligators it is difficult to remind yourself that your initial objective was to drain the swamp.

What follows are some observations about educational leadership by a researcher-turned-administrator immersed in the everyday reality of the swamp. I am struck by how the popular view of the leader as hero fails to capture the character of leadership in a world of grand designs and daily problems. Leaders are quiet lambs as much as roaring lions, and leadership is not found only at the top of an organization.[1]

Today's Top Tune

Leadership is back in fashion in education,* and the conventional wisdom suggests a heroic boss who meets at least six expectations. First and most insistently, leaders are supposed to possess a clear personal vision. A sense of purpose is central to success, and center-stage leaders define it for their organizations. Second, leaders are extremely knowledgeable; they have the right answers to the most pressing problems. Third, leaders are expected to be strong: to display initiative, courage, and tenacity. Fourth, leaders communicate forcefully, using their knowledge to convey their vision aggressively and persuasively. Fifth, leaders amass power and use it for organizational improvement. Finally, leaders are take-charge individuals who solve knotty problems along the way as they move toward achieving their personal visions.[2]

In a scathing review of the new literature on leadership, Robert Reich depicts the popular image of corporate heads thus:

> They are crusty, strong-willed characters who have no patience for fools or slackers. They buck the system. They take no crap. They win. . . . [They] are colorful and outspoken. They are the antithesis of the

---

*Within the last year, for example, the National Commission on Excellence in Educational Administration issued its report, *Leaders for America's Schools;* Arkansas Gov. Bill Clinton, as chairman of the Educational Commission of the States, pointed to leadership as the most important, yet least understood aspect of school reform; and the Office of Educational Research and Information announced plans for a $5 million research center to study educational leadership. If belief in leadership as the ticket to organizational success waxes and wanes, it is clearly ascendant at the moment.

gray-flanneled professional of yore. . . . They believe in "hands-on" management. They want to confront people directly, touch them, challenge them, and motivate them through the sheer force of personality. . . . [They] are missionaries. Their stories take on an evangelical tone because these men have been inspired. They have found meaning and value in the services they provide. They manage their enterprises by ensuring that employees share those same meanings and values. . . . The evangelical message is that with enough guts, tenacity, and charisma you too—gentle reader—can be a great manager, a captain of industry.[3]

In a word, the leader is a lion.

Those who lionize leadership miss important behind-the-scenes aspects of day-to-day leadership. They depict the grand designs without the niggling problems. They assume that leadership is the exclusive preserve of the heroic boss.

Those who lionize leadership set unrealistic standards for measuring administrative success. For example, only a relative handful of individuals possess extraordinary vision. Unrealistic standards make it easy to devalue ordinary competence and to view leadership as the only important ingredient in organizational success.

The image of the leader as hero can also undermine conscientious administrators who think that they should live up to these expectations. If leaders are supposed to have all the answers, for example, how do administrators respond when they are totally confused about what to do? If they have learned that leaders are consistently strong, what do administrators think of themselves when they are terrified about handling a difficult situation?

Finally, notions of heroism misconstrue the character of organizational leadership in many situations. Problems are typically so complex and so ambiguous that to define and resolve them requires the knowledge and participation of more than a visionary leader.

At best, the image of the leader as lion depicts only one side of the coin. Moreover, this heroic image ignores the invisible leadership of lower-level staff members throughout effective organizations.

In an attempt to restore balance, allow me to present the *unheroic* side of the six dimensions of leadership that I cited above: developing a shared vision (as well as defining a personal vision), asking questions (as well as having answers), coping with weakness (as well as displaying strength), listening and acknowledging (as well as talking and persuading), depending on others (as well as exercising power), and letting go (as well as taking charge). These unheroic—and seemingly obvious—activities capture the time, the attention, the intellect, and the emotions of administrative leaders who often work off-stage to make educational organizations succeed.

Developing a Shared Vision

As a policy researcher, I am struck by the similarities between the current discussions of vision in organizations and earlier discussions of policy in government. Policy makers made policy, so the theory went, and implementers carried it out. Blueprints for action were carefully laid out by the best and the brightest—and then were installed by presumably less-creative bureaucrats. Similarly today, many observers believe that organizational vision is articulated by the boss and then installed by the staff. Leaders lead; followers follow.

However, the research of the past 20 years on policy implementation demonstrates that this model seldom describes reality. Programs are typically characterized by shifting goals, changing activities, and wide variation across sites. Program priorities and content are determined as staff members learn from experience and as programs adapt to their environments. Purposes and policies are often "discovered" through an evolutionary process. In other words, policies are less often installed than negotiated to maturation over time, and true policy makers can be found both at the top and at the bottom of the system.

Likewise, in educational organizations it is rare to see a clearly defined vision articulated by a leader at the top of the hierarchy and then installed by followers. Top administrators tend to point out a general direction rather than a specific destination; they are more likely to provide a scaffolding for collaboration than a blueprint for action. They take the initiative, set the agenda, establish the pace, and contribute to the conversation—all the while involving other key actors and then clarifying and synthesizing their views. During this process, organizational vision is often discovered, since vision setters, like policy makers, are frequently dispersed throughout an organization.

A close look at the development of organizational vision shows the untidiness, plural parentage, and emergent nature of that process.* Leaders

---

*If this view of organizational vision is accurate, a puzzle still remains: Why do so many accounts of effective schools mention visionary principals? I suspect that three factors are at work. First, in some schools (as in some corporations and government agencies), there are extraordinary visionaries who dominate

act as catalysts. In the words of Ronald Heifitz and Riley Sinder, "A leader becomes a guide, interpreter, and stimulus of engagement." A leader's vision is "the grain of sand in the oyster, not the pearl."[4]

Asking Questions

Striking similarities also exist between the work of researchers, particularly those who do fieldwork, and administrative leaders. Members of both groups spend a great deal of time formulating and asking good questions. Both groups are in the business of seeking knowledge. Both groups establish and nurture intelligence networks.

Gathering intelligence is crucial because administrative life is marked by great uncertainty, confusion, and distortion. Heroes and saints may be in a "state of grace," but administrators are regularly in a "state of ignorance."

Of course, effective administrators bring to their jobs a store of relevant knowledge, such as an understanding of schools and a firm grasp of theories of organizational change. But much of what happens—or *should* happen—in organizations is highly dependent on information that administrators frequently do not possess. This includes "local" knowledge (the histories, key actors, rituals, and contexts of various units within the organization); "situational" knowledge (the who, what, where, when, and how of a given issue); and "people" knowledge (staff members' thoughts and feelings, their perceptions of reality, and the meanings they attach to these perceptions).

These kinds of data are essential. But management information systems typically don't provide such data, because they are confidential, sensitive, verbal, or not generally available. Crucial information is often highly emotional in content, and such information is kept from top administrators. Yet a school administrator would be well-served by knowing such things as the underlying feelings of the parents who oppose a new preschool initiative, the rumors on how an administrator landed his or her job, the level of morale in the English department, what issues cur-

---

their organizations. However, my guess is that such visionaries are in the minority, even among effective principals. Second, the accounts may in part reflect what researchers call "the treachery of recollection" or "the reconstruction of biography." In other words, gaps in stories are filled in with what *might* have happened, and confusing and uncertain plans are recalled as logical, coherent, and rational acts. Finally, respondents often say what the society expects them to say, and our society expects leaders to have a clear sense of purpose, both in their organizational lives and in their personal lives.

rently concern students, the latest word from the grapevine regarding the superintendent's leadership, and the political obstacles to expanding the arts program.

Administrators need to recognize and acknowledge their ignorance and then take action. They need to develop an informal "system" of constantly gathering information—from meetings, chance encounters, and casual conversations (by phone or in person) with candid and knowledgeable colleagues. Administrators need to recognize that the ability and willingness to ask good questions is central; administrators, like researchers, should be judged by the quality of their questions.[5]

There are limits, of course. Administrators need to ask questions freely, but they also need to know when to stop. Too much knowledge, or the endless pursuit of knowledge, stalls action. Not knowing all the complexities is sometimes a good thing. As Albert Hirschman has noted:

> The only way we can bring our creative resources fully into play is by misjudging the nature of the task, by presenting it to ourselves as more routine, simple, undemanding of genuine creativity than it will turn out to be. Or, put differently: since we necessarily underestimate our creativity, it is desirable that we underestimate to a roughly similar extent the difficulties of the tasks we face.[6]

Too much information, as well as too little, can be a problem.

Coping with Weakness

"Great man" theories of leadership—the leader as lion—are making a comeback. Deep in the swamp, however, exceptional leaders not only draw on their strengths, but also accept their weaknesses and develop a capacity to cope.

To deal with personal deficiencies in skills, knowledge, attributes, or disposition, four coping strategies seem particularly useful. Those strategies are matching, compensation, candor, and acceptance.

Matching. Wise administrators recognize that administrative positions differ significantly in their requirements. Some positions require rhetorical artistry, for example, while others call for political skill, creative genius, or a flair for coordination. Administrators who succeed hold positions that match their talents and their personalities. As a corporate head once put it, "You can't grow lemons in Antarctica."

Compensation. Successful leaders have the capacity to recognize their own shortcomings, and they take steps to compensate for them. They surround themselves with staff members who have complementary skills and inclinations, and they rely on these individuals. They often hire staff members whose knowledge of particular areas exceeds their own—people who are able and willing to criticize the boss's pet ideas.

Candor. Administrators need to acknowledge to close associates their weaknesses and the feelings that those weaknesses engender. I am not advocating detailed confessions, but forthright and critical self-disclosure on significant job-related issues. A leader who is unwilling to treat subordinates as colleagues and to share self-assessments and feelings with them cannot expect shared confidences in return. Without candid exchanges, crucial intelligence will be withheld, jeopardizing decision making and implementation efforts.

Acceptance. Psychologists say that one must recognize, acknowledge, and accept one's weaknesses and the feelings associated with them before one can move beyond them. If an administrator is fearful of giving negative feedback to a subordinate, for example, the administrator is wiser to accept those feelings and act within that framework than to try to banish the feelings as signs of weakness. Though it is counterintuitive, "giving in seems to allow one to move forward and act successfully."[7]

These coping strategies are far easier to advocate than to implement. Individuals who function superbly in one administrative position may be tempted to think that they can handle any administrative position, ample evidence to the contrary notwithstanding.[8] It can be threatening to be surrounded by smarter people. Because leaders tend to be lionized, they often find it difficult to acknowledge a need for help. Moreover, because they have learned that leaders are consistently strong, administrators often have trouble accepting the emotional upheavals of administrative life. Paradoxically, the more a leader acknowledges and accepts personal weaknesses and feelings, the more effective he or she becomes.

At the heart of all these coping strategies, of course, are self-knowledge and the capacity to act on it. These traits are rare, I suspect, among those who aspire to positions of leadership. John Gardner is on target when he says:

> It is a curious fact that from infancy on we accumulate an extensive knowledge of the effect others have on us, but we are far into adulthood before we begin to comprehend the impact we have on others. It is a lesson young leaders must learn.[9]

Young leaders must also learn the impact they have on themselves.

Listening and Acknowledging

That leaders should be good listeners seems obvious. Yet very little high-quality listening goes on in the swamp. Why is listening such a problem for leaders?

The heroic image of leadership is one source of the problem. When leaders believe that they possess—or should possess—all the important information and knowledge, they do not see listening to others as essential. Can-do administrators persuade others to adopt their visions, and they give short shrift to alternative perspectives. To such administrators, listening is passive, reactive, and thus unappealing. To listen is to appear uninformed, weak, and inactive. To be a lion, one cannot act like a lamb.

In addition, good listening fails to occur because administrators often make faulty assumptions about others. They assume, for example, that their colleagues share—or *should* share—their own worldview. They assume that confrontations signify ill will, rather than a misunderstanding or a differing perspective. Recognizing that people are different and giving others the benefit of the doubt are behaviors that facilitate listening.

Administrators also underestimate the skill and effort that are required to listen well.[10] Good listening involves an active effort to understand the world from another's perspective. It requires both an instant analysis of what has been said (and of the accompanying tone and body posture) and a sense of what has been left unsaid. Good listening involves testing aloud what one has heard, to make certain that the speaker's meaning has been captured. Good listening requires the ability to act as if the speaker's topic is central—even when the listener is preoccupied with other matters. To listen well takes practice, patience, energy, and hard work.

Clearly, good listening is essential for gathering information about organizational activities. In my experience, however, listening is crucial for other reasons as well.

First, when an administrator fails to understand the varying perspectives of others, organizational problems do not get solved—and new ones are likely to be created. It is not enough to know just the facts; a leader also needs to understand the feelings, the meanings, and the perceptions that are tied to those facts. Such understanding requires careful listening to what is said and careful reading between the lines.

At a more emotional level (and administrative work is highly emotional), listening is frequently the *best* thing that an administrator can do. Colleagues often want only an opportunity to express their concerns. Many professionals are passionate about their work; not surprisingly, they get upset when things go wrong. Sometimes they get upset when nothing is wrong, simply because no one is listening to them. The very process of verbalizing frustrations and having them acknowledged often enables these individuals to move forward. Asked about his job change, a former therapist who is now a dean smiled and replied, "Now my patients have tenure."

Moreover, since demands on organizational resources typically outstrip the supply and even reasonable demands cannot be met, listening is often the *only* thing an administrator can do. Under these circumstances, there is a big difference between a disappointed employee (who can deal with the limited resources) and an employee who feels unheard (and therefore angry).

Finally, one rule of thumb in administrative life invariably turns out to be correct: if you don't listen to others, they won't listen to you. A key to effective persuasion, then, is the capacity to listen to the perspectives of others. To be a lion, one must first be a lamb.

Depending on Others

The study of policy implementation has demonstrated that different levels of government are highly dependent on one another and on competing interests. In our federal system of shared power, hierarchical strategies based on assumptions of centralized authority are simply inadequate in promoting change. Softer strategies are required—strategies that mix authority, persuasion, and incentives; strategies that take other interests into account. Even for Presidents, orders don't work, as Richard Neustadt documented more than 25 years ago.[11]

Likewise, top administrators in educational organizations are surprisingly dependent on others to bring about change.[12] In part, this is a matter of shared power and the current shift toward empowering teachers. But it is also a matter of skill: teachers and other staff members possess expertise and information that are crucial for defining problems and making progress. And it is a matter of will: if those at the bottom don't accept responsibility for resolving problems, change efforts will come unglued.

Thus educational organizations are increasingly marked by a high level of mutual dependence. The superintendent's success depends on the actions of the principals within the school system; the dean's success, on the actions of the tenured faculty; the principal's success, on the teachers— and vice versa.

While hierarchical strategies for promoting change are becoming outmoded, new strategies that are based on an assumption of mutual dependence need further development. Administrators need to find better ways to involve teachers and other staff members and to help them adjust to conflicting interests. Even when they are not required to do so, administrators need to depend on others for active leadership because, by sharing power and asking for help, they can tap latent resources in an organization. By relying on staff members, administrators give them a greater sense of efficacy, responsibility, and control. That leads, in turn, to organizational progress.

The capacity for dependency is rare among top administrators, however. Having been taught that top administrators exercise power, they don't want to appear weak. Paradoxically, when power within an organization is shared and leadership is shifted among various staff members, the administrator's position is often strengthened, reflecting what sociologists call the norm of reciprocity: if you share your power, I'll share my power in return. In other words, leaders can often achieve results by acting like followers and depending on followers to act like leaders

Letting Go

An important dimension of organizational leadership is dealing with what John Dewey called problem situations. Such situations come in various forms: student test scores continue to decline; the boiler has broken down; a teacher is livid about his treatment by a parent; the history department is ignoring the new curriculum; faculty members are complaining about inadequate resources. Such situations are the everyday stuff of ordinary leadership—punctuated occasionally by loftier issues. How does an administrator respond, as he or she skips, in the words of Henry Rosovsky, "from the sublime to the ridiculous five times a day"?[13]

One crucial step is deciding who should address a problem situation. Many times, of course, an issue is important enough to demand the intense involvement of a take-charge leader. Often, however, the lion needs to let go. The administrator's "problem" is not usually solving problems per se, but helping others define and resolve problems—doing what Russell Ackoff calls "managing messes."[14]

Insuring that messes end up on the right desks is surprisingly complicated, however. Employees typically view the top administrator as the chief problem solver. I have dubbed the outcome the "goose theory of leadership." Honking and hissing like geese, faculty and staff members will cruise into the boss's office, ruffle their feathers, poop on the rug, and leave. It then becomes the boss's job to clean up the mess.

This happened to me one summer day when a program director phoned me at home at 7:30 A.M. to announce: "We've got some big dormitory problems. A student says his room is filthy, with ashes on the floor and two used condoms under his bed!" Indeed, this matter deserved prompt attention. But sensing that the problem was headed my way and believing that the program director should take responsibility instead, I raised some questions and then closed with the words, "I know you can handle it."

Some administrators unwittingly adopt the goose theory of leadership because they like to solve problems and therefore take them on. (Administrators often reach the top because of their problem-solving skills, and it is always rewarding to do what one knows how to do.) Many administrators also believe that their job is to be responsive to demands; therefore, they automatically assume responsibility for any problem dumped on their rug.

The challenge is to be responsive while simultaneously developing a sense of responsibility in others. This involves encouraging subordinates to take risks—and back them up when they fail. It means working hard to make other people successful—and giving them the credit.[15] In short, taking charge involves letting go.

In letting go, administrators must decide to ignore issues that they believe ought not to be ignored and to do some things superficially that ought to be done with careful attention. A conscientious leader always has more high priorities to address than time and organizational resources allow. In the face of competing demands, deciding to do some things badly, letting go before the time seems right, and coping with the consequences are all ingredients of leadership behavior.

Administrative leadership involves both grand designs and careful attention to the mundane. High-minded intentions are inextricably intertwined with such everyday problems as allergies to odor strips.

Perhaps it feels less than heroic to help develop a shared vision, to ask questions, to acknowledge weakness, to listen carefully, to depend on others, and to let go. Yet, where heroism is concerned, less can be more. To be a lamb is really to be a lion.

NOTES

1. Many of the ideas herein grew out of conversations with and out of the writings of Louis B. Barnes and Barry C. Jentz. See, for example, Louis B. Barnes and Mark P. Kriger, "The Hidden Side of Organizational Leadership," *Sloan Management Review*, Fall 1986, pp. 15–25; and Barry C. Jentz and Joan W. Wofford, *Leadership and Learning: Personal Change in a Professional Setting* (New York: McGraw-Hill, 1979).

2. For a similar portrayal of the conventional wisdom on leadership, see Ronald A. Heifetz and Riley M. Sinder, "Political Leadership: Managing the Public's Problem Solving," in Robert B. Reich, ed., *The Power of Public Ideas* (Cambridge, Mass.: Ballinger, 1987).

3. Robert B. Reich, "The Executive's New Clothes," *New Republic*, 13 May 1985, p. 26.

4. Heifetz and Sinder, pp. 194, 197.

5. For ideas that can be adapted to fit the information-gathering needs of administrators, see Jerome T. Murphy, *Getting the Facts: A Fieldwork Guide for Evaluators and Policy Analysts* (Santa Monica, Calif.: Goodyear, 1980).

6. Quoted in Robert T. Nakamura and Frank Smallwood, *The Politics of Policy Implementation* (New York: St. Martin's Press, 1980), p. 175.

7. Jentz and Wofford, *Leadership and Learning.* . . .

8. See, for example, Jameson W. Doig and Erwin C. Hargrove, eds., *Leadership and Innovation: A Biographical Perspective on Entrepreneurs in Government* (Baltimore: Johns Hopkins University Press, 1987).

9. John W. Gardner, *Leadership Development* (Washington, D.C.: Independent Sector, Leadership Papers, No. 7, June 1987), p. 20.

10. Jentz sand Wofford, *Leadership and Learning.* . . .

11. Richard E. Neustadt, *Presidential Power: The Politics of Leadership* (New York: John Wiley and Sons, 1960). .

12. This dependence on others seems typical of even the most hierarchical organizations. In the army, for example, generals depend on the leadership of lower-ranking soldiers to carry out objectives. See Louis B. Barnes, "Leadership from Strange Places," paper presented at the Wingspread Invitational Seminar on Leadership Research, Racine, Wis., 23–26 April 1987.

13. Henry Rosovsky, "Deaning," *Harvard Magazine*, January/February 1987, p. 37.

14. Quoted in Donald A. Schön, *The Reflective Practitioner: How Professionals Think in Action* (New York: Basic Books, 1983), p. 16.

15. I am particularly indebted to Harold Howe II for this thought.

10

EDUCATIONAL LEADERSHIP FOR THE TWENTY-FIRST CENTURY

INTEGRATING THREE ESSENTIAL PERSPECTIVES

David D. Marsh

THE ROLE OF the school principal has evolved dramatically over the last decade (Caldwell and Spinks, 1992; Odden, 1995; Murphy and Louis, 1994). The ideal principal in the 1980s was an instructional leader who focused on four key elements of reform. First, principals, as instructional leaders, were supposed to be responsible for defining the mission of the school and setting school goals (Murphy, 1990). The goals emphasized traditional student achievement which effective principals communicated to audiences both within and outside the school and allocated time at the school so that the vision could be attained.

Second, instructional leaders were to manage what Murphy (1990) called the education production function: coordinating the curriculum, promoting quality instruction, conducting clinical supervision and teacher evaluation/appraisal, aligning instructional materials with curriculum goals, allocating and protecting instructional time, and monitoring student progress. Third, principals were to promote an academic

Updated from a paper presented at the annual meeting of the American Educational Research Association in Chicago in March, 1997.

learning climate by establishing positive high expectations and standards for student behavior and for traditionally-defined academic achievement, maintaining high visibility, and providing incentives for teachers and students. They were also supposed to promote and manage professional development efforts that often were isolated from instructional practice.

Finally, principals were to develop a strong culture at the school that included a safe and orderly work environment, opportunities for meaningful student involvement, strong staff collaboration and cohesion, additional outside resources in support of the school goals, and stronger links between the home and the school. As it often turned out, the focus on culture was quite disconnected from the instructional process at the school. In short, the tendency during this era was to place the burden for improvement upon the principal as the individual "strong instructional leader" in the organization.

Recent studies from many countries, however, report that school principals did not actually carry out this role, and conclude that the role may no longer be appropriate for contemporary schools. In synthesizing this research, Murphy (1994) points to dramatic changes in the work environment including a turbulent policy environment, an overwhelming scale and pace of change, and a new view of teacher involvement and expertise. The result has been role ambiguity of massive proportions for the school principal. The same summary of research on the school principal also captured the role overload for school principals. They report that the job is much more difficult than expected, that a new repertoire of skills is needed to function effectively, and that they have significantly changed their patterns of behavior. Murphy reports that this rampant, "role overload and role ambiguity often led to increased stress for school administrators involved in fundamental change efforts" and "led to a personal sense of loss for principals, a loss of control and a loss of professional identity" (pp. 24–25).

This chapter is designed to explore the role of the school principal, especially as the role relates to educational leadership in highly effective schools over the next decade. The chapter is organized into several sections. First, it explores several themes in educational reforms that are likely to emerge and grow across national settings over the next ten years. Then, it presents three interconnected perspectives on educational leadership and how these must be fit together if leadership is to survive the decade. Finally, it presents practical applications and principal competencies that follow from this integrated view of the new educational leadership at the school level. This last part of the paper is a view to the future: the competencies presented are my hunch as to what will have been important educational leadership strategies as viewed 10 years from now. The hunch is not a direct extension of patterns seen in schools today. In fact, my hunch conflicts in some respects with reports of current practice as summarized by Murphy and Louis (1999), Murphy (1994), and Gurr (1995) about educational leadership in transforming schools.

Directions in Educational Reform Over the Next Decade

In the next decade, educational reform as seen across national boundaries is likely to have several common themes relevant to the role of the principal as an educational leader. First, standards for student results are increasingly going to be defined and assessed at the system level, with dramatically improved technology for assessing important student performance (Tucker and Codding, 1998; Caldwell and Spinks, 1992; Odden, 1995). At the same time, customer satisfaction will matter more as competition for students increases and choice becomes more prevalent. Customer satisfaction and school performance will become more synergistic because of societal trends common across countries, because customers care about student performance, and because the value a school adds to student performance will matter more than it has before to customers. Of course, customers will continue to care about other dimensions of school quality: parents care about a safe and supportive environment for their student, and universities and employers care what students know and are able to do after leaving the school.

Second, the shift from a rule-driven to a results-driven system will intensify—local schools have much greater authority and control of resources, within a framework worked out at the system level (Marsh and Codding, 1998). This shift will continue the expansion of leadership roles and organizational support needed within the school, create a very different culture, and value much different views of expertise and collaboration. Third, after years of inertia, teaching and learning will change in truly revolutionary ways. The push for "value-added" schooling and much higher student performance for all students will force schools to dramatically change the way teaching and learning take place. The enhanced clarity about student performance standards and the improved assessment technology will act both to prod schools and to finally provide the assessment support needed to clarify how students are doing. At the same time, new approaches to curriculum design linked to the standards, stronger efforts at finding "best" instructional practices by using benchmarking in an international context, and powerful uses of technology that enhances school learning and links it to the resources of the learning society will become dominant. Yet, these new approaches to assessment, curriculum and instruction/technology will only be successful if the school restructuring and reculturing happens as implied above.

The next decade will also be characterized by political, economic, and social issues of stunning complexity and tenacity. These issues will evolve with rapid speed, but are likely to accelerate the reshaping of schools themselves as well as the world "beyond" the school. Schools are likely to have new strategic partnerships with families and community agencies characterized by new approaches to incentives and accountability, and shared but limited resources (see Tucker and Codding, 1998; Carnegie Council on Adolescent Development, 1995). All these trends have strong implications for the nature of educational leadership needed by school principals.

Rethinking the Role of the School Principal as an Educational Leader

It is clear that the old role of the principal as the solitary instructional leader is inadequate for the new directions in educational reform over the last decade. That view—which emphasizes the directive and clinical view of instructional leadership—no longer fits the realities of time and work load for principals. That view also blocks the development of the collective leadership, culture, and expertise needed for success in the reforms, and assumes that reforms can be aligned and packaged in outdated and rigid ways.

Several premises underlie this new view of the educational role for school principals. Before the end of the next decade, the educational role of school principals will be critically important to the success of their schools. While the role ambiguity and overload described by principals in schools embarking on massive change are currently dominant, successful principals will evolve the role to include setting the strategic direction for the school—a direction that requires considerable insight about education and the new interface between management support and educational reform. Pressures for accountability and "value-added" will also push schools to improve in ways that require fundamental paradigm shifts in the nature of schooling. The paradigm shifts will involve major change and new patterns of leadership, but also the significant educational leadership of the school principal—the reforms won't be successful without this educational leadership from the principal.

Also, the new educational role for school principals will need to be reinvented—mere extensions of previous views of the role will inform but not suffice as the basis for the new role. Instead, the educational leadership role of the school principal will be reinvented within three perspectives of emerging thought and practice. But, what will it take for the school principal to be successful in the next decade?

The Cultural/School Transformation Perspective

An important view of the educational role of the school principal is that of a transformational leader (Murphy and Louis, 1994; Fullan, 1993). Sergiovanni (1991) identifies transformational leadership in terms of three leadership components: building, bonding, and banking. Building entails empowerment, symbolic leadership, and charisma that leads to raised expectations of leaders and followers so that they are motivated to higher levels of commitment and performance. For Sergiovanni, bonding elevates organizational goals and purposes through a covenant that binds together leader and followers in a moral commitment. This type of leadership involves cultural leadership, moral leadership, covenant building and followership. Finally, Sergiovanni thinks of transformation as banking where improvements are turned into the routine so that they become second nature in the school. This leadership is carried out through institutional leadership, servant leadership, and leadership by outrage.

This new view of culture and learning organization draws heavily on the notion of a complex dynamic world involving both continuous change and continuous conservation (Senge, 1990). Schools as organizations are viewed as organic where values (Sergiovanni, 1991) and moral passion (Fullan, 1993) rather than objectives are the basis for the school's orientation. Relationships in this learning organization are a community of inter-connected web of relationships in which all processes are reciprocal (Lambert, et al., 1995; Caldwell and Spinks, 1992; Odden, 1995).

In these organizations/communities, leaders work from the middle rather than the top of the organization (Kouzes and Posner, 1995; Murphy, 1994; O'Toole, 1995). They work to facilitate ongoing change through problem solving (Leithwood and Steinbach, 1995), conceptual thinking (Hallinger, Leithwood, and Murphy, 1993), reflection (Sergiovanni, 1991), and creating a learning community (Fullan, 1993; Senge, 1990). Leaders are effective when they create a culture where practitioners can be successful. The image is one of empowering and building capacity.

Moreover, a new form of expertise is needed for all participants. All members of the organization need skills in working together as well as expertise in inventing new arrangements for teaching and learning. Acquiring this expertise is more a matter of culture and reflection rather than of technical skills (Fullan, 1993) and includes norms of experimentation, risk taking, common technical language, and collaboration (Little, 1993).

It is in this view of transformational leadership that Murphy noted the emerging role ambiguity and work overload of principals in transforming schools (Murphy, 1994). Murphy (1994) and Gurr (1995) report that principals in these schools have diminished their former role in instructional leadership.

The Strategic/Results-Driven Perspective

Leaders in restructured schools typically work in educational systems which increasingly are tightly coupled around results and loosely coupled around means for attaining these results (Caldwell and Spinks, 1992; Marsh, 1995; Odden, 1995). These desired results are typically a combination of system-defined student performance standards and locally-defined views of market niche and customer satisfaction. Successful schools are finding that the two views of results are mutually enhancing rather than contradictory, as first imagined. Arriving at this understanding is a hallmark of successful educational leadership.

In some national settings, the system is already targeted toward high student performance, even as it continues to evolve in dynamic ways. In the somewhat unique case of the United States, however, the system focus on high student performance standards and high stakes assessment that matters both to the school and the student is still being developed. Many issues still abound: should the standards be defined at the local school or system level, should they be the same for all students, and should they have high stakes consequences for the school and/or the student? Many states are moving toward a view of statewide standards common for all students in at least some academic subjects, and with some pressure/accountability for the school, and perhaps the student.

Conversely, Marsh (1996) reports that individual schools working in isolation are having more difficulty in consolidating a clear view of desired results. Tucker (1994a, 1994b, 1994c) has proposed, and many states are considering adopting, a new high school diploma which is based on performance not course completion, engages students to work hard to meet the standards, and has strong incentives for high performance both for the school and the student. This new diploma is similar to that found in most other western countries.

Assuming that this result orientation is established—the combination of system-defined student performance indicators/accountability and local customer satisfaction/niche—schools will need two types of strategic leadership that are not found in the transformational leadership: a) leadership focused on results-indicators/accountability within the tightly-coupled educational and social system, and b) substantive leadership for reshaping the school as an organization to help all students meet the high performance standards while also achieving quality/market goals.

The reshaping of the school will involve planning backward from intended results in a dynamic and powerful way that builds on the strengths of the school as a learning organization rather than on the installation of proven new programs (Odden, 1995). Drawing on the work of Mohrman, Wohlstetter, and Associates (1994), Odden (1995) portrays this reshaping as including four interrelated segments:

- Recognizing the need for fundamental change
- Forming an organizational strategy to respond
- Redesigning the work and structure of the organization—the vision of teaching and learning, and
- Implementing the design, assessing impacts, and refining and changing over time

These strategies for fundamental redesign of the organization have special importance for leadership in restructured schools.

For restructured schools, mobilizing understanding of the need for change and developing the commitment to engage in fundamental reform will have a special quality. Odden (1995) reports that in the private sector, "pressures to engage in fundamental change derive from the environment and international competition. Corporations and work teams work within them either understanding that in order to stay in business, they must deliver services or make products that are better or lower priced, or they quickly lose market share and are forced out of business" (p. 293). In contrast, pressure in education for reform is likely to be a combination of system-defined results indicators coupled with a local commitment and understanding supported by moral passion to change the schools to high performing organizations (Odden, 1995). Forming an organizational strategy to respond will require new approaches to the change process and reform. Odden summarizes numerous authors in reporting that fast-paced large scale change will require a more decentralized, team-driven organizational response.

It is the redesigning of work and structure of the organization that requires the new educational leadership paradigm. This task involves building a fundamentally fresh understanding of the student learning and performance problems, and developing powerful new ways of seeing how schools might be organized and conducted to resolve those problems. Mohrman (1994) suggests this means "a willingness to challenge professional practices and create new ones with confusion and stress." Odden (1995) reports that after developing a shared understanding of the problem, school-based teams then need to construct a common vision of teaching and learning and school organization. This vision needs to focus on results and on linking dramatically improved teaching and learning to those results. Redesigning the work and structure of the organization will include a delicate balancing of examining effective programs while recognizing how those programs must be dramatically reworked to meet the needs of the local setting. In Odden's terms, "The vision created should be viewed as tentative, as something with high potential that will be tried, but more likely will need to be redesigned and modified more than once over time" (p. 297).

Finally, Mohrman proposes the need for implementing the design, assessing impact, refining and redesigning over time. Characteristics of this new change process include: a) a learning organization focused on resolving problems and on needed high performance results, and b) substantial ongoing training and professional development. These characteristics are discussed in more detail later in this paper.

Linking Management Support to Educational Improvement Perspective

The third perspective required in the new approach to educational leadership is the linkage of management support to the new educational improvement. Traditional management functions such as personnel and budgeting will have to be redesigned in dramatic new ways if these functions meaningfully support the new educational reform effort. Characteristics of the new support system include:

1. Definition and design of the purposes of management function in terms of the strategic direction adopted. For example, the problem with information systems is not simply to decentralize information to the local school but also to rethink what information is needed— an educational leadership issue. For example, assessments of student work are important new types of information that are not easily quantified and stored on a computer.

2. The system has to be usable by support staff and high performance work teams. The system must be user-friendly in terms of inputing, storing, retrieving, and utilizing information. This includes:

- *Access*—Redesign how the management functions are carried out so that large numbers of staff have appropriate access to designing and operating the management function and the function itself is user-friendly. For example, the budgeting system of the management information system at the school level is easily used for a variety of purposes that support high performance work teams.

- *Educational program focused*—Redesign all management functions so that they better serve the high performance work teams and the dynamic ongoing change processes in the organization in order to achieve high student results. Management functions must be much more tightly aligned with student results if they are to adequately serve the leadership in highly effective schools.

- *Synergism of support services*—Reconnect various management functions so that, for example, management information, budgeting, and personnel work synergistically both to increase their impact and to increase their operational efficiency.

3. The system must be highly efficient, use technology in powerful ways, [and] provide fast response and flexibility in displaying information. It must also provide strong assistance to users, including:

- Changing the culture and technical support provided by the system so that schools can be effective in carrying these management functions.

- Changing the culture and technical support at the school to enhance the efficiency of the system and allow multiple participants in the system as opposed to having only the principal be involved at the school level.

4. Information must be accessible by external audiences ranging from community members to policy makers and monitors, in appropriate fashions.

Overall, the management functions have to support the central mission of the educational program in a much more direct fashion. The critical educational issue will be the interface of the support services with educational improvement efforts—the strategic issue is understanding this interface and helping collective leaders at the schools use the system effectively.

Marsh (1992) studied the connection of management support to educational leadership, and found that school principals progressed through three stages in their ability to make these connections. The 3 stages in the development of strong educational leaders able to link management support services with educational improvement are portrayed in Figure 10.1.

Educational leaders at Stage 1 focus primarily on the "nuts and bolts" of school management. They learn to operate these management functions at the school level as discreet pieces—the master schedule is not linked to the personnel and teacher evaluation system, for example. In addition, Stage 1 educational leaders have no focus on educational leadership.

Stage 2 leaders are typical of school principals across many national settings. Here, they have greater capacity for carrying out management functions. They are also good at carrying out the pieces of educational leadership and reflecting about management functions or these educational leadership pieces. They have a fragmented view of educational

---

**Figure 10.1. School Principals as Educational Leaders:
Developmental Stages.**

STAGE 1: GETTING STARTED

    Initial socialization into the role of site administrator

    Development of routine management skills

    No real focus on educational leadership

    Reflection about the nuts and bolts of school management and own role in the school

STAGE 2: DOING THE PIECES OF EDUCATIONAL LEADERSHIP

    Enhancement of management capability

    Mastery of pieces of educational responsibilities

    Fragmented views of educational leadership

    Reflection about management and educational leadership pieces

    School change is incremental and fragmented

STAGE 3: UNDERSTANDING THE WHOLE OF EDUCATIONAL
LEADERSHIP

    Integration of management and educational leadership

    Integration of educational leadership pieces (activities and functions)

    Deepening and integration of views of educational leadership

    Reflection about integrated educational leadership and school life

    Transformation of the school in relation to the vision; the school is substantially changed

leadership, but they are quite good at carrying out pieces of work in the education setting.

Stage 3 leaders are different from Stage 2 not so much by their overt actions, but rather by their understanding of the whole. This whole includes the integration of management functions and educational leadership, that is, they see how functions such as budgeting and personnel can be linked to the teaching and learning and high performance work teams, for example. Moreover, they are quite insightful about the integration of various educational leadership pieces and are reflective about the integration of educational leadership and school life, especially towards student results. It is only Stage 3 leaders who are able to manage the interface between management functions and the educational program both in terms of designing these support services for high performing work teams and operating these management functions, even if the operational details are ultimately delegated to other participants at the school.

Practical Applications and Competencies: A View from the Future

The view of educational leadership described above has a number of implications for the practical application and the knowledge and skills that principals will need over the next decade. This last part of the chapter is a view to the future: the competencies presented are my hunch as to what will have been important educational leadership strategies as viewed 10 years from now, and so I have written them in the past tense as viewed from that future point. These hunches are not a direct extension of patterns seen in schools today. In fact, my hunch conflicts in some respects with reports of current practice as summarized by Murphy and Louis (1999), Murphy (1994), and Gurr (1995) about educational leadership in highly effective schools, as discussed above. These hunches, however, do fit very well with Caldwell's (1996) evolving stages of leadership needed for schools of the future. The competencies and strategies for principals that follow are written as lessons learned as viewed a decade from now: lessons from the 21st century for leadership in schools.

Leading from the Middle Still Required a Substantive Leader

Principals in successful schools combined both personal and positional educational leadership in their schools. At a personal level, they developed over time a very deep understanding of teaching and learning and the way that relates to the new student outcomes. This learning was credible to teachers and parents and built on a moral base linked to student results. Successful principals were able to persuade others through mentoring, coaching, and planning, but in the end, their influence was both substantive educationally as well as collaborative and transforming.

At the same time, successful principals used their positional power to structure the school so that deep problems, important results and school restructuring hinged on a powerful view of student results. In their positional role, these leaders sorted out governance structures from management and implementation structures, even as these evolved continuously. They helped governance groups focus on student results and monitor these results, while the groups stayed out of micromanaging the school (see Marsh, 1995; Tucker and Codding, 1995). Conversely, the principals established a set of cross-role groups that provided a variety of implementation and management structures, as will be discussed below. Finally, these successful principals created structures where many leaders emerged at the school—all with an important educational focus which successful principals built into the structure, culture, and results focus.

Reframe the Right Problems

Fullan (1993) finds that successful and fundamental change efforts entail a love of problems. Other researchers have found that schools that avoided or denied problems were typically schools with poor student performance relative to the capacity of that school. In turn, successful schools embraced problems and believed it took a long time and hard work to create meaningful resolution of those problems. Successful leaders in highly effective schools had more guidance from the system about critical student outcomes, which would account for success at the school. Successful principals helped the school internalize the importance of those system results and understand them in educational as well as political terms. At the same time, these principals were excellent at reframing problems within the school to identify the most powerful means to help students reach those systemically-defined student results. Successful principals also married the concept of market niche, customer satisfaction and student results through reframing problems so that all three became interrelated and mutually supporting priorities.

One way successful principals reframed the problems is through the use of the four lenses proposed by Deal and Kennedy (1982). In reframing the problems, the lenses helped illuminate different dimensions of the problem itself as well as the desired resolution. Successful principals had a "nose" for the right problems. Schools faced many problems and often were almost paralyzed by the overwhelming number and interconnected-ness of the problems. Unsuccessful school leaders attempted to solve these problems one at a time. Successful school principals reframed patterns of problems into fewer large problems focused directly on student results and the means to help students achieve them.

Focus on the Best Results and Sustain the Focus

Successful principals thought about results and quality of the school in several ways (Schmoker, 1996). They were able to combine system de-fined student performance results with local indicators of student growth and customer satisfaction. This connection was both political and educa-tionally powerful, grew out of the collective view of important education at the school as stimulated by the principal, and served to focus strategic and operational efforts at the school. Successful principals were able to understand and articulate the deep meaning of these results while ex-plaining them in concrete terms to various audiences.

Successful principals also thought in terms of "value added" and im-provement targets for their student results and quality indicators. Conse-quently, the school was frequently focused on performance for all students, in the context of students at other schools as well as the relative improve-ment these students had made, and the role the school had played in ac-complishing that. Successful principals helped the school use these indicators of success as anchors for decisions, program priorities and sup-port services. Since the world was increasingly dynamic and fast-changing, successful principals were able to anticipate changes in societal directions and anticipate the consequences for the indicators.

At the same time, the school had a vision of teaching and learning that mattered—the vision represented the "best bets" as to what schooling conditions would help students achieve the desired student results. Stated differently, the key indicators at the school operated at two levels—the learning environment indicators as part of the vision, and the result in-dicators which this vision was designed to achieve. On the one hand, the vision was robust in incorporating many dimensions of teaching and learning while on the other hand remained flexible and continually rethought in relation to the results. Moreover, the vision itself had indi-cators of success and became more than a vague picture of the desired school. Faculty, staff, community, and others could map the relative suc-cess of the school in accomplishing its vision both in terms of the vision being implemented and the vision being powerfully related to student re-sults. In short, the school had clear results indicators with improvement targets and a view of value added for all students. Linked to this was a powerful and integrated school vision which had indicators of implementation and ongoing flexible mechanisms for connecting vision to results. The connections represent the best of reflection, of learning community and cultural and transformation view of leadership.

Developed Strategic Thinking/Planning That Mattered

Successful principals developed strategic and system thinking in a way that was infectious across the organization. They engaged cross-role work teams in creating strategic plans for their own team as well as school-wide plans, all driven by result indicators. The plans linked the organizational and governance changes in the school to the instructional improvement and ultimately student results, customer satisfaction and quality indicators, and represented a compact between various constituencies responsible for the school. The plans embodied long-term strategic planning linked to action planning on a yearly basis as proposed by Caldwell and Spinks (1992) and Holmes and Davies (1994). The planning/thinking also linked management resources to the substance of the schools, and had revision cycles that mattered in terms of resource allocation, program assessment, and accountability. Finally, the plans were short, results-focused, easily understood by all the groups, and publicly acknowledged and displayed.

Successful principals needed many skills and competencies to make the strategic thinking/planning effective. They needed a deep understanding of the results of the school and the possible effects of various alternative strategic directions. They needed process skills in engaging others in this thinking and ways to portray and reframe problems within the strategic thinking/planning period. They needed to engage others in taking seriously the planning/thinking process as the basis for access to resources and accomplishments of their workgroups. Finally, principals needed to help identify results while clearly staying out of micromanaging the process to achieve those results.

Restructured and Recultured in a Powerful Synergy

Successful principals worked in ways similar to Mohrman's (1994) view that schools must be restructured and recultured into high performance work teams before the actual changes in teaching and learning are carried out. Establishing these meaningful work structures distinguished successful principals over the decade—other principals tried to reculture without restructuring at the same time, and achieved little in the end. Aside from the personal dimensions of establishing work groups, principals needed to align responsibility, authority and accountability so that individuals are designated groups who are responsible for efforts and also have the authority and accountability for their accomplishment. Successful principals helped establish these workgroups not by management functions, but rather by integrating the various dimensions of an effective learning environment so that a group of students could be successful. Principals need to help define the appropriate size of workgroups, including establishing small school units where personal connection and communication could be maximized. Successful principals also helped realign incentives and support structures for these workgroups.

Linked Management Support to Work Structures and Organizational Redesign

As described above, Marsh (1992) found that Stage 3 educational leaders had a holistic understanding of the interface of management supports to the educational efforts of the school as linked to strong student results and institutional success. These leaders were distinguished by their ability to understand the connections—an understanding composed of educational connections, political savvy, and organizational dynamics. What made these principals strong educational leaders was their ability to structure support services connected to important work structures that helped students learn. These connections entailed, in part, redirecting traditional functions such as fiscal and personnel so that work teams had greater control of the decisions in these support areas. Moreover, successful principals helped design and transform the way these support services are carried out through greatly enhanced technology and efficiency, a wider set of meaningful users of the support services, and easier access to the support services in user-friendly modalities. For example, successful schools were able to establish new and dramatically better information support services that decentralized information from the district office and made it much more accessible and useful within the school. These new management information systems also included new kinds of information found in student learning portfolios that greatly enhanced instruction that helped students learn effectively.

Additionally, successful principals were able to increase the management support services and fiscal resources available in service of the critically important educational program. They carefully distinguished cash cows from vitally important educational services (see Davies and Ellison, 1994). They also developed strong management support staff closely integrated with the high performance work teams so that the principal as an individual was not operating the management support services. The principal did, however, manage the linkage of the management support services to the high performance work teams in ways that greatly enhanced and empowered team performance.

Powerfully Expanded Teaching and Learning Linked to the New Results

Successful principals knew the attributes of good teaching/learning and the pragmatics of what teaching and learning ought look like in various subjects and for various grade levels. The value of this understanding was not to have the principal serve as expert who demanded or monitored improvement for individual teachers. Instead, this understanding led to collaboration with team leaders of high performance work teams able to carry out powerful instruction and instructional improvement efforts — the principal's role was more strategic than clinical and very different from the previous instructional leadership paradigm. Successful principals also focused teaching and learning on the success for all students through moral persuasion, use of data, structuring work teams to accommodate varieties of students and a culture that promoted student success, whatever it took.

Successful principals also had networks and a strong understanding of emerging but promising learning approaches that would greatly enhance the power of teaching and learning at the school. They helped the school benchmark its most successful practices across the whole world. For example, many schools recently have benefited extensively from the thinking about teaching and learning found in China and Japan (see Stevenson and Stigler, 1992; Stigler and Hiebert, 1999). This provocative and helpful view of curriculum design, teacher collaboration, and careful instructional practice has deeply influenced teachers in many other countries. As Odden (1995) reports, principals are going to need to view "effective programs" in several ways: as the best available insight about powerful teaching and learning while also as only an approximation of what might ultimately be the most effective learning environments linked to the school's own particular students and results. Moreover, successful principals worked to plan backwards from desired student learning and therefore, provide tools for targeting and teaching learning on these results.

Principals helped work teams establish and carry out improvement strategies such as evaluation, aligning instructional materials with curriculum, and managing information about student and program performance.

Successful principals also created new partnerships for teaching and learning—a strategic approach to engaging students and the community more powerfully as direct support for strong student performance. At best, the student and the school's learning environment are in a delicate "dance of learning" where both partners must work together in a complex and unique way. Schools that intended to improve teaching and learning only through the improvement of high performance work teams and instructional strategies missed the opportunity to get the equal participation from students. Successful principals understood the need for student motivation and hard work and the community organization and family supports that helped students be engaged in this way. Consequently, successful principals transformed partnerships with community agencies from bureaucratic connections to support services for powerful student learning. At the same time, they widened the available school resources to beyond the school setting and the school day. These new partnerships require more than communication; they required focus on student learning and the interrelated set of strategies and supports that helped students do well.

Created Professional Capacity and Learning Communities Driven by Results

Successful principals worked hard to help colleagues build professional capacity and effective learning communities at the school. The stronger capacity was needed by the high performance work teams in the form of expertise and inventiveness that helped them do their work. Principals helped with building networks and multiple collaboration arrangements that supported teacher connection outside and within the school. Capacity building of several forms was promoted: training that included modeling, practice, and feedback; collaboration and planning; inquiry and problem-solving. The capacity building also used the criteria proposed by Little (1993) for good professional development: a) meaningful intellectual, social, and emotional development with ideas and materials, b) explicit accounting of the context of teaching and the experience of teachers, c) support for informed dissent, d) classroom practice in the larger contexts of school practice and purposes, e) supported techniques and perspectives of inquiry, and f) governance that featured bureaucratic constraint and balanced individual and institutional interests.

What will make this leadership distinctive for leaders in self-managed schools are several features. First, these leaders will have linked the professional development and learning community work to the student performance and other results in a powerful and accountable way. Second, these schools will have created high performance work teams so that the organizational/change process context will be especially rich for the capacity and learning communities. Finally, these principals will have redesigned the management support functions to support professional development and learning, and will have redirected resources controlled by the high performance work teams to invest heavily in professional development, and incentives for high performance (Odden, 1995). Bold redirection of resources and very strong learning communities driven by results were among the most distinctive strategies of successful school principals.

Conclusion: A New View of Educational Leadership

In conclusion, my hunch is that from the perspective of hindsight as viewed from a decade in the future, successful principals will have invented a new form of educational leadership. These leaders will have joined the transformational power of collaboration and leading from the middle to the high performance work teams where a new form of expertise and learning community driven by results are dominant. With the new interface of management support for the educational efforts at these schools, these principals will have had a strategic influence on internalizing the results, and planning backwards to redesign the school to help all students meet high performance expectations. These schools will be able to dramatically improve teaching and learning, not because the principal set others to do the work; but instead, because the principal had a new form of educational leadership that provided substantive and cultural leadership to the transformation of the school linked to the high performance organizational arrangements that support the results-driven collective focus.

REFERENCES

Caldwell, B. J. (1996, September). *Beyond the self-managing school.* A paper presented as the Keynote Address at the Annual Conference of the British Educational Management and Administration Society in Coventry, England.
Caldwell, B. J., and Spinks, J. (1992). *Leading the self-managing school.* London: Falmer.

Carnegie Council on Adolescent Development (1995). *Great transitions: Preparing adolescents for a new century.*

Davies, B., and Ellison, L. (Eds.) (1994). *Managing the effective primary school.* London: Longman.

Deal, T., and Kennedy, A. A. (1982). *Corporate cultures: The rites and rituals of corporate life.* Reading, MA: Addison-Wesley.

Fullan, M. (1993). *Change forces: Probing the depths of educational reform.* London: Falmer.

Gurr, D. (1995). *The leadership role of principals in selected "Secondary Schools of the Future": Principal and teacher perspectives.* Unpublished Ed.D. thesis, University of Melbourne, Melbourne, Australia.

Hallinger, P., Leithwood, K., and Murphy, J. (Eds.) (1993). *Cognitive perspectives on educational leadership.* New York: Teachers College Press.

Holmes, G., and Davies, B. (1994). Strategic management in primary schools. In B. Davies and L. Ellison (Eds.) (1994). *Managing the effective primary school.* London: Longman.

Kouzes, J., and Posner, B. (1995). *The leadership challenge: How to keep getting extraordinary things done in organizations.* San Francisco: Jossey-Bass.

Lambert, L., Walker, D., Zimmerman, D., Cooper, J., Lambert, M. D., Gardner, M., and Slack, P. J. (1995). *The constructivist leader.* New York: Teachers College Press.

Leithwood, K., and Steinbach, R. (1995). *Expert problem solving: Evidence from school and district leaders.* Albany, NY: State University of New York Press.

Little, J. W. (1993). Teachers' professional development in a climate of educational reform. *Educational Evaluation and Policy Analysis, 5* (2), 129–151.

Marsh, D. D. (1992). Enhancing instructional leadership: Lessons from the California school leadership academy. *Education and Urban Society, 24* (3), 386–409.

Marsh, D. D. (1995). *Restructuring for results: High performance management in the Edmonton public schools.* Washington, D.C.: The National Center on Education and the Economy.

Marsh, D. D. (1996). Making school reform work: Lessons from successful schools. *Thrust for educational leadership.*

Marsh, D. D., and Codding, J. B. (1998). *The new American high school.* Thousand Oaks, CA: Corwin Press.

Mohrman, S. (1994). Making the transition to high-performance management. In S. Mohrman, P. Wohlstetter, and Associates (1994). *School-based management: Organizing for high performance.* San Francisco: Jossey-Bass.

Mohrman, S., Wohlstetter, P., and Associates (1994). *School-based management: Organizing for high performance.* San Francisco: Jossey-Bass.

Murphy, J. (1990). Principal instructional leadership. *Advances in Educational Administration: Changing Perspectives on the School, 1,* 163–200.

Murphy, J. (1994). Transformational change and the evolving role of the principal: Early empirical evidence. In J. Murphy and K. S. Louis (Eds.), *Reshaping the principalship: Insights from transformational reform efforts.* Thousand Oaks, CA: Corwin Press.

Murphy, J., and Louis, K. S. (Eds.) (1994). *Reshaping the principalship: Insights from transformational reform efforts.* Thousand Oaks, CA: Corwin Press.

Murphy, J., and Louis, K. S. (Eds.) (1999). *Handbook of research on educational administration* (second edition). San Francisco: Jossey-Bass.

Odden, A. R. (1995). *Educational leadership for America's schools.* New York: McGraw-Hill.

O'Toole, J. (1995). *Leading change: Overcoming the ideology of comfort and the tyranny of custom.* San Francisco: Jossey-Bass.

Schmoker, M. (1996). *Results: The key to continuous school improvement.* Alexandria, VA: ASCD.

Senge, P. (1990). *The fifth discipline: The art and practice of the learning organization.* London: Doubleday.

Sergiovanni, T. J. (1991). *The principalship: A reflective practice perspective, second edition.* Boston: Allyn and Bacon.

Stevenson, H., and Stigler, J. (1992). *The learning gap: Why our schools are failing and what we can learn from Japanese and Chinese education.* New York: Touchstone.

Stigler, J. W., and Hiebert, J. (1999). *The teaching gap: Best ideas from the world's teachers for improving education in the classroom.* New York: Free Press.

Tucker, M. (1994a). *States begin developing the Certificate of Initial Mastery.* Washington, D.C.: The National Center on Education and the Economy.

Tucker, M. (1994b). *The Certificate of Initial Mastery: A primer.* Washington, D.C.: The National Center on Education and the Economy.

Tucker, M. (1994c). *The international experience with school leaving examinations.* Washington, D.C.: The National Center on Education and the Economy.

Tucker, M. and Codding, J. (1995). *Organizing alliance schools for results.* Washington, D.C.: The National Center on Education and the Economy.

Tucker, M. and Codding, J. (1998). *Standards for our schools.* San Francisco: Jossey-Bass.

LEARNING TO LEAD

Roland S. Barth

IN ORDER NOT ONLY to survive but to flourish, principals need to be able to discuss promising school practices without fear of violating a taboo; they need to learn to share problems without worrying about appearing inadequate. They need to recognize that adult learning is not only legitimate but essential. They need help clarifying and becoming confident about their goals, ideas, and practices so they can act thoughtfully.

This constellation of crucial and largely unmet needs led in 1981 to the creation of the Principals' Center at Harvard. Over 100 other centers have been established in the United States and abroad. A National Network of Principals' Centers—with its headquarters at the Harvard Graduate School of Education—now supports emerging and existing centers through newsletters, conferences, an annual journal, and year-long informal interactions.

What Is a Principals' Center?

While there is no orthodox model of a "principals' center," while diversity among centers is part of the energy that propels the Network, the Principals' Center at Harvard shares with others many common purposes:

- To provide helpful assistance to principals and other school leaders that will enable them to become more successful in fulfilling their goals and providing leadership to their school

- To help principals cope with the changing realities of school administration, including increased time demands, collective bargaining, declining resources, and new state and federal guidelines

- To bring together principals from across districts to share experiences, ideas, concerns, and successes

- To identify promising school practices and arrange for principals who wish to engage in similar practices to visit one another's schools

- To encourage the formation of networks among principals, school districts, state departments, private foundations, professional associations, and universities

- To provide a mechanism for practitioners to take responsibility for promoting their own professional growth

- To provide assistance to principals in sharing leadership with teachers, parents, and students within their schools

- To provide a national forum for discussion of school leadership and professional training

- To bring attention to the relationship of principals' professional development to good schools

- To explore new conceptions of school leadership

Teacher centers in the 1960s and 1970s demonstrated that practitioners can take an active role in determining their professional training needs and provide a significant portion of that training. Although principals' centers frequently draw on the resources of universities, central offices, and state departments of education, they too are places where school practitioners play the major role in their own professional development. In short, a principals' center is *principal-centered*. Its activities emanate from the concerns and aspirations of the principals themselves, and its vitality relies heavily on the resources principals have to offer one another.

Like teachers, principals have a great capacity to stimulate professional growth and improved practice in their colleagues because they occupy the same rung on the bureaucratic ladder. They neither evaluate nor are evaluated by one another. In short, principals constitute a potential cohort— a potential "group 3." However, because the culture of schools neither rewards nor encourages the sharing of ideas and resources among principals any more than among teachers, there is a pronounced need for a mediator leading toward their professional interdependence.

Principals are capable of interdependence and learning if the conditions are right. Considering the importance of the principalship, of the professional development of principals, the lack of success with principals' staff development, and the host of impediments that prevent leaders from becoming learners, what have we learned at the Principals' Center at Harvard during the past decade about the conditions necessary for principals' learning? A major proposition underlies our efforts: *Principals will be seriously involved in designing and conducting their professional development.* It is our belief that the critical element in principals' learning—indeed in anyone's learning—is ownership. Learning must be something principals do, not something others do to or for them. The questions asked at the Principals' Center at Harvard, then, are the following: Under what conditions will principals become committed, lifelong learners in their important work? Under what conditions will principals assume major responsibility for their learning? And, What conditions can principals devise to encourage and support their own learning?

As I have mentioned, our conviction that a principals' center must be principal-centered led to enlisting twenty-eight Boston-area principals as designers of the Center. After six months of deliberations, this group came up with several building blocks for the Center, each of which, ten years later, surprisingly is still in place, attached to the cornerstone of principals' involvement and ownership. Let me share what these principals put in place.

There are no more important decisions affecting principals' staff development than those determining the content and format of activities. An advisory board, chaired by a principal and joined by eighteen other Boston-area principals and four Harvard faculty members, was established to ensure that the major voice about the program was the principals'. Discussions at board meetings follow a common pattern: brainstorming about issues about which principals want to learn more (for example, new technologies, dealing with diversity); sharpening questions related to each theme (for instance, How can a new Apple II be used both as a management tool and an instructional tool?, or How can the principal come to use differences of age, gender, race, and ability within a school as opportunities for school improvement?). The board then identifies consultants, university professors, and principals as possible resources. Then members develop an idea, select resource persons, and devise formats. Finally, a staff member of the center, often a doctoral student interested in the principalship, takes the plan and invites speakers, secures a room, advertises the seminar, and evaluates the session.

Many observers initially questioned the wisdom of turning responsibility for programs over to principals, fearing that their decisions, like those made by some high schoolers in an "open campus," might be frivolous. Many feared that the Principals' Center would offer what principals "want" rather than what they "need." Conversely, principals were suspicious that the Center would be a disguised attempt by Harvard to "inservice" them. Over time, suspicions abated as principals demonstrated enthusiasm and inventiveness in planning programs for their colleagues. A list of some of the themes addressed at the Center would probably pass muster in most quarters:

Curriculum improvement

Shared leadership

Using and not being used by the national reports

New conceptions of school leadership

Adult development

Staff development within the school

Special needs students and mainstreaming

Gifted and talented students

Dealing with minimum competency requirements

The impact of standardized testing

Issues facing a woman principal

Instructional skills

Proposal writing for grants

Pupil and teacher evaluation

Supervision of teachers

Involving parents productively in a school

Constructing a budget

Decision making

Priority setting

Time management

Dealing with stress

Assertiveness training

Self-understanding

Racial and cultural awareness

Vision

We are finding that principals, like teachers, carry with them extraordinary insights about their work that are seldom explicit for them, let alone accessible to others. The work of the Center is to reveal this abundance of thinking and practice so it may be more widely available to improve schools. We have engaged in a long and difficult struggle against the belief held by many practitioners that one's success in schools is a private matter, best kept from potential competitors or critics. Equally difficult to overcome is the belief harbored by some principals that the knowledge base for improving schools lies more in universities than within themselves. Many worried, for instance, that when principals talked they would reveal, not craft knowledge, but war stories. But more and more principals are acknowledging the importance of what they know and finding ways of making it available and valuable to others.

In our attempts to involve principals as givers as well as receivers, we are finding that the process of being helpful to others is one of the most powerful ways of generating respect and recognition for oneself as well as for those one helps. We find too that often the most sophisticated form of staff development comes not from listening to the good words of others but from principals sharing with others what they know. Every principal I know is good at *something*. By reflecting on what the principal does, by organizing it, by sharing and articulating that knowledge, principals learn.

Principals choose to participate in the Center's activities as members. Each principal decides to spend $120 to become a member for a year and selects events to attend from a list of forty or fifty presented annually. For their membership fee they receive a catalogue and access to activities, several editions of a newsletter edited and contributed to by member principals, a parking permit in a nearby garage, a library card at the Harvard School of Education, and preference for attending limited-enrollment events such as the National Summer Institute for Principals.

Initially, some superintendents offered to subsidize principals' participation if they could decide which principals to send and for what sort of "remedy." Even a PTA offered to send its principal if we would promise to "fix" him! The board has resisted these offers. By placing the decision for participation squarely on each principal's shoulders, we find that those who participate want to participate. Activities are refreshingly free of back-row cynics because with the choice to attend comes an openness to learn. The board remains adamant in believing that if the activities of the Center are worthwhile, people will come.

By the end of the first year, the Center had nearly 100 members, but there was concern that it was becoming an elitist organization for only "the top ability group" of principals. As had been the case with many teacher centers, it appeared that "those who need it the most would not come; those who came did not need to." We have watched and waited. Today the Center has over 600 members, perhaps 10 percent of whom attend each session. Membership has become generally representative of men, women, novice, veteran, elementary, middle, high school, urban, suburban, with a cross section of interests and abilities.

Principals continue to prefer the neutral territory of the university for their activities, finding that a university-based Center provides a protected setting where a secretary is unlikely to intrude with a worried look and a phone message to "call your building immediately." The atmosphere of an emergency room is not conducive to learning. A contemplative place in the ivory tower is as welcome and valuable for schoolpeople as for academics.

The education business seems to thrive as a sorting enterprise, attempting to narrow the range of human characteristics that appear within any group. The board has firmly tilted in the other direction, toward heterogeneity and diversity. Few activities are grouped. Indeed, when more than 200 principals from across the nation applied for the 100 seats at our first Summer Institute, we were faced with the problem of selection. The usual Harvard criteria such as recommendations, transcripts, and test scores were considered—and abandoned. We decided to make these selection decisions each year with the goal of *maximizing* diversity within the group. Sitting in small groups, talking at lunch, and sharing a dorm with other principals who differ markedly in their geographical region, size of school, length of service, gender, race, income, and ability contributes to a powerful and unique learning experience. During the school-year activities, about one-third of the participants in discussions are not principals at all. Superintendents, teachers, board members, university faculty, and graduate students further extend the boundaries of diversity.

For principals there appear to be few alternative solutions to the same gnawing problems. What do I do with a "marginal teacher"? How do I respond to the parent who wants to remove a child from one classroom and place the child in another? We find that the wider the range of participants and the greater the diversity, the wider the universe of new ideas and possible solutions. We ask of differences not how we can "group them out" but rather how we can generate them and make deliberate use of them to promote learning for principals, teachers, parents, and students. A community of learners is, above all, a heterogeneous community.

Too often, attempts at professional development for principals are group activities. The assumption is that all principals need the same skills before Thursday and all will have them after Thursday. However, principals, like other learners, have "preferred" learning styles and different attention spans, interests, and needs. Consequently, the board attempts to vary activities along several important dimensions—for example, those led by principals, Harvard faculty, graduate students, and outside consultants; long-term, one-shot, small-group, large-group, and individual participation; low-risk (large-group addresses), modest-risk (small-group discussions), and high-risk (writing groups, pairing to exchange school visits) activities. Principals match their styles as practitioners and as learners to these different formats. In the process, many learn something about themselves as learners—the conditions under which they learn best—as well as new content and skills.

Principals' centers then attempt to improve the quality of life and learning in schools by encouraging different ways of thinking about common problems; by transforming school problems into opportunities for school improvement; by encouraging clarification of assumptions guiding practice by offering opportunities for shared problem solving and reflection; and by providing a context of mutual support and trust in which personal and professional relationships may be developed. Many centers rest on similar assumptions:

- The principal is a central figure in determining the quality of a school.
- It is possible and desirable for school heads to be effective educational leaders, as well as building managers.
- The role of the principal and the nature of schools are becoming more complex and problematical.
- Every principal is very good at something.
- Principals have the capacity and need for personal and professional growth—as much after they have assumed their position as before.
- The principal who is a committed learner is likely to have a school full of students and adults who are committed learners.

The Impact of Principals' Centers

We often ask ourselves in what ways the Center may be contributing to school improvement and having a demonstrable influence on pupils. Put another way, what difference does it make to a fourth-grade youngster in Watertown, Massachusetts, that the child's principal visits the Principals' Center at Harvard once or twice a month? We suspect it does make a difference. For instance, we see the crucial influence of principals modeling learning. I visited one principal, a member of the Center, and as I entered her office was overwhelmed to see her name on the door followed in large bold letters by her title, "Head Learner." What a message that must convey each day to parents, students, teachers, and central office officials! Another principal observed: "My staff this year is enrolling in record numbers in the local staff development program. Whether this is a reflection of my participation in the Center and my own new commitment to learning, I'm not sure. I think it is."

"Do as I do" is a powerful formula in transforming schools from places with older, learned people and younger, learning people into a community of learners where everyone is both a teacher and a learner. One principal put it this way: "At the beginning of the school year, I put together a portfolio of relevant readings for myself and for each teacher. I have been adding to that portfolio regularly. I've encouraged staff members to share anything they read that would be of interest."

Principals are voluntarily joining the Center and attending in large numbers. They report enthusiasm for what they experience and learn, carry these conversations back to their schools and systems, and establish their own professional networks. Many transport Center activities back to their own faculty meetings. In short, most appear to be experiencing professional growth that releases and generates energy as well as consumes it.

The concept of a principals' center seems capable of providing recognition and a sense of professionalism for principals. Recognition comes from inviting principals to share their craft knowledge with colleagues, from empowering principals with major decisions affecting the Center, from helping them write about their important work, and from offering affiliation with a major university that enlists them as speakers in classes and as members of committees and that recently has offered faculty appointments to several principals.

Recognition comes to a number of principals from around the country who teach at the Summer Institute. Others serve for a half or full year as visiting practitioners at the Center, contributing their skills to the staff and providing resources to members while they reflect and write about their professional experience. Many of these school leaders return home to establish centers of their own.

Although not part of the original plan, the Center is contributing to the evolution of a community of school leaders in the Boston area. Principals, like teachers, need and treasure collegiality and peer support. Yet, perhaps even more than teachers, principals live in a world of isolation—and sandboxes. There is often a huge distance between adjoining classrooms; the distance across town to the next school is even greater. When principals associate with peers, it is often at an administrators' meeting. But just as it is forbidden for principals to "not know" within their individual school, principals often have trouble "not knowing" with peers. Seldom is time or setting conducive to collegial support or the exchange of ideas and concerns.

As the bridges provided by generic issues begin to transcend professional chasms, members of this community of school leaders are recognizing a shared sense of purpose. Recently, a Boston high school principal was featured in an hour-long television documentary. The next day I happened to be at the Principals' Center and found this program the focus of discussion. Two things were clear: Almost every principal had watched and almost every principal had cheered for one of their own—both unthinkable a few years ago.

Strengthening of collegial relationships, then, appears to be among the major outcomes for principals at principals' centers. A decade ago, few suburban principals talked with urban principals; elementary administration did not talk with those at high schools, even within the same district; men administrators did not talk with women administrators; public school personnel did not talk with their private school counterparts; and no one talked with those in parochial schools. Now, conversations among these groups in the Boston area are common and infused with fresh vigor, expanding the repertoire of different responses to similar school problems. And that is the essence of what principals seek as they strive to improve their leadership. When principals learn and share their learning with other principals, they not only feel professional, they become more professional.

We see more and more indication that fostering a culture of reflection, learning, cooperation, and professionalism among educators outside their schools contributes to a similar culture among adults and students within schools. Principals who once experience these qualities do not want to relinquish them when they enter the schoolhouse door.

School principals have an extraordinary opportunity to improve public schools. A precondition for realizing this potential, I believe, is for
principals to put on the oxygen mask—to become head learners. The
Center is beginning to demonstrate that there are conditions under which
school practitioners are not only educable but will take responsibility for
and voluntarily engage in activities that promote their learning and the
learning of others. In so doing, they telegraph a vital message: Principals
can become learners and *thereby* leaders in their schools.

An outline of a conceptual model for the professional development of
principals is beginning to emerge that is quite different from the venerable
training models of list logic:

engage in practice

reflect on practice

articulate practice

better understand practice

improve practice

If ways can be devised to help principals reflect thoughtfully about the
work they do, analyze that work, clarify and reveal their thinking through
spoken and written articulation, and engage in conversations with others
about that work, both they and their colleagues will better understand
their complex schools, the tasks confronting them, and their own styles
as leaders. And understanding schools is the single most important precondition for improving them.

12

LEADERSHIP FOR THE TWENTY-FIRST CENTURY

BREAKING THE BONDS OF DEPENDENCY

Michael Fullan

Wanted: A miracle worker who can do more with less, pacify rival groups, endure chronic second-guessing, tolerate low levels of support, process large volumes of paper and work double shifts (75 nights a year out). He or she will have carte blanche to innovate, but cannot spend much money, replace any personnel, or upset any constituency.[1]

○

THE JOB OF THE PRINCIPAL or any educational leader has become increasingly complex and constrained. Principals find themselves locked in with less and less room to maneuver. They have become more and more dependent on context. At the very time that proactive leadership is essential, principals are in the least favorable position to provide it. They need a new mindset and guidelines for action to break through the bonds of dependency that have entrapped those who want to make a difference in their schools.

The Context for Dependency

Dependency is created by two interrelated conditions: overload and corresponding vulnerability to packaged solutions. First, the system fosters dependency on the part of principals. The role of principals in implementing innovations more often than not consists of being on the receiving end of externally initiated changes. The constant bombardment of new tasks and the continual interruptions keep principals off balance. Not only are the demands fragmented and incoherent, but even good ideas have a short shelf life as initiatives are dropped in favor of the latest new policy. Overload in the form of a barrage of disjointed demands fosters dependency.

These demands have recently taken on an even more intrusive quality as school boundaries become more permeable and transparent. In the third book in our trilogy, *What's Worth Fighting For Out There,* Andy Hargreaves and I document how very different the school environment is today compared to even five years ago (1998; see also Fullan 1997 and Fullan and Hargreaves 1996). The walls of the school have come tumbling down, metaphorically speaking. "Out there" is now "in here" as government policy, parent and community demands, corporate interests, and ubiquitous technology have all stormed the walls of the school. The relentless pressures of today's complex environments have intensified overload.

The situation just described makes principals and other leaders especially vulnerable to the latest recipe for success—the second aspect of dependency. Providers of management theories and strategies are only too happy to oblige the demand for instant solutions. Management techniques, like so many fads, have a terrible track record. Part of the problem lies in the nature of the advice. As Micklethwait and Wooldridge (1996) say about the "guru business": "it is constitutionally incapable of self-criticism; its terminology usually confuses rather than educates; it rarely rises above basic common sense; and it is faddish and bedeviled by contradictions" (p. 12).

Where does that leave the modern boss? ask Micklethwait and Wooldridge:

> The simple answer is, overworked. He [or she] faces a far more complex challenge than his [or her] predecessors: today's boss is expected to give power away while keeping some form of control, and to tap the creative talents of . . . employees while creating a common culture within the company (p. 172).

The most serious problem, however, is not that the advice is wrong, but that there is no answer out there. Mintzberg (1994), who wrote the definitive critique, *The Rise and Fall of Strategic Planning,* observes only half-facetiously, "Never adopt a [management] technique by its usual name" (p. 27). Farson (1997), the author of *Management of the Absurd,* advises, "Once you find a management technique that works, give it up" (p. 35). These authors drew these odd conclusions because they wanted to stress that there is no external answer that will substitute for the complex work of changing one's own situation.

Contrary to what management books would have us believe, organizations did not become effective by directly following their advice. Evans (1996) notes:

> It is one thing to say in most successful organizations members share a clear, common vision, which is true, but quite another to suggest that this stems primarily from direct vision-building, which is not. Vision-building is the result of a whole range of activities (pp. 208–209).

Educators and business leaders have wasted precious time and resources looking for external solutions. Times of uncertainty and relentless pressure prompt an understandable tendency to want to know what to do. The first insight is that there is no definitive answer to the "how" question. Take, for example, the very clear research finding that student achievement increases substantially in schools with collaborative work cultures that foster a professional learning community among teachers and others, focus continuously on improving instructional practices in light of student performance data, and link to external standards and staff development support (Newmann and Wehlage 1995). To know and believe this does not tell educators *how* to change their own situation to produce greater collaboration. They can get ideas, directions, insights, but they can never know exactly how to go about it because such a path is exceedingly complex, and it changes as they work with their organization's unique personalities and cultural conditions.

Realizing that there is no answer, that we will never arrive in any formal sense, can be quite liberating. Instead of hoping that the latest technique will at last provide the answer, we approach the situation differently. Leaders for change get involved as learners in real reform situations. They craft their own theories of change, consistently testing them against new situations. They become critical consumers of management theories, able to sort out promising ideas from empty ones. They become less vulnerable to and less dependent on external answers. They stop looking for solutions to the wrong places.

Giving up the futile search for the silver bullet is the basic precondition for overcoming dependency and for beginning to take actions that do matter. It frees educational leaders to gain truly new insights that can inform and guide their actions toward greater success, mobilizing resources for teaching and learning with children as the beneficiaries. We formulated four such novel guidelines in *What's Worth Fighting For Out There* (1998):

1. Respect those you want to silence.
2. Move toward the danger in forming new alliances.
3. Manage emotionally as well as rationally.
4. Fight for lost causes.

Respect Those You Want to Silence

Reform often misfires because we fail to learn from those who disagree with us. "Resistance" to a new initiative can actually be highly instructive. Conflict and differences can make a constructive contribution in dealing with complex problems. As Maurer (1996) observes:

> Often those who resist have something important to tell us. People resist for what they view as good reasons. They may see alternatives we never dreamed of. They may understand problems about the minutiae of implementation that we never see from our lofty perch atop Mount Olympus (p. 49).

Thus, for example, it is a mistake for principals to go only with like-minded innovators. Elmore (1995) puts it this way: "Small groups of self-selected reformers apparently seldom influence their peers" (p. 20). They just create an even greater gap between themselves and others that eventually becomes impossible to bridge. In turbulent times the key task of leadership is not to arrive at early consensus, but to create opportunities for learning from dissonance. Mobilizing people to tackle tough problems is the key skill needed these days: "Instead of looking for saviors we should be calling for leadership that will challenge us to face problems for which there are no simple painless solutions—problems that require us to learn in new ways" (Heifitz 1994, p. 2).

Move Toward the Danger in Forming New Alliances

I have said that the boundaries of the school have been permanently penetrated. I also conclude that this is a good and necessary development because school reform cannot succeed without community reform. Healthy neighborhoods and healthy schools go hand in hand (Schorr 1997), and school-community relationships are key. The problem is, What do you do if you do not have a strong relationship with the community? Here leaders have to do the opposite of what they feel like doing. Instead of withdrawing and putting up barricades, they must "move toward the danger." Today's environment is dangerous, but it is also laced with opportunities:

> In a school, where mistrust between the community and the administration is the major issue, you must begin to deal with it by making sure that parents are present at every major event, every meeting, every challenge. *Within the discomfort of that presence* the learning and healing could begin (Dolan 1994, p. 6, emphasis added).

The same is true with other dimensions of the new environment. For example, educational leaders must directly address state policy that results in student performance data being generated and published. The way to deal with potential misuses of student performance data is to become assessment-literate. Schools put themselves in the driver's seat when they invest in professional development and collaborative cultures that focus on student learning and associated improvements in instructional practices.

In all cases, the new leadership requires principals to take their school's accountability to the public. Successful schools are not only collaborative internally, but they also have the confidence, capacity, and political wisdom to reach out, constantly forming new alliances.

Manage Emotionally as Well as Rationally

Leaders moving their staff toward external dangers in a world of diversity cannot invite disagreement without attending to their own emotional health.

As Maurer (1996) says, "Dealing with resistance can be very stressful. People attack you and your precious ideas. Sometimes they seem to show no respect for you" (p. 59). Someone will always be dissatisfied with the leader's performance. Relaxation exercises, physical fitness, recalling a higher purpose, teaming up with a supportive peer, separating self from role, and ignoring the temptation to get even are some of the remedies Maurer suggests.

The emotionally intelligent leader also helps teachers, students, parents, and others create an environment of support, one in which people see problems not as weaknesses but as issues to be solved. Managing emotionally means putting a high priority on *reculturing,* not merely *restructuring.* Restructuring refers to changes in the formal structure of schooling in terms of organization, timetables, roles, and the like. Restructuring bears no direct relationship to improvements in teaching and learning. Reculturing, by contrast, involves changing the norms, values, incentives, skills, and relationships in the organization to foster a different way of working together. Reculturing makes a difference in teaching and learning.

Reculturing, because it is based on relationships, requires strong emotional involvement from principals and others. It also pays emotional dividends. It contributes to personal and collective resilience in the face of change. It helps people persist as they encounter the implementation dip when things go wrong. Principals who manage emotionally as well as rationally have a strong task focus, expect anxiety to be endemic in school reform, but invest in structures and norms that help contain anxiety. Collaborative cultures promote support, but they also elevate expectations.

Fight for Lost Causes (Be Hopeful When It Counts)

In *What's Worth Fighting For Out There* Andy Hargreaves and I carefully examine the fascinating concept of "hope." It turns out that the best definition of *hope* is "unwarranted optimism." Vaclav Havel, president of the Czech Republic, captures this best:

> Hope is definitely not the same as optimism. It is not the conviction that something will turn out well, but the certainty that something makes sense, regardless of how it turns out. It is hope, above all, that gives us strength to live and to continually try new things, even in conditions that seem hopeless (1993, p. 68).

Principals with hope are much less likely to succumb to the daily stresses of the job. They place their problems in a loftier perspective that enables them to rebound from bad days. Once leaders realize that having hope is not a prediction, that it is independent of knowing how things might turn out, it becomes a deeper resource. Leaders with hope are less likely to panic when faced with immediate and pressing problems.

It is especially important that leaders have and display hope, that they show they are prepared to fight for lost causes, because they set the tone for so many others. Teachers are desperate for lifelines of hope. They understand that hope is not a promise, but they need to be reminded that they are connected to a larger purpose and to others who are struggling to make progress. Articulating and discussing hope when the going gets rough re-energizes teachers, reduces stress, and can point to new directions. Principals will be much more effective (and healthier) if they develop and pursue high hopes as they reculture their schools and their relationships to the outside.

Scale Up

As we approach the next century, the big question preoccupying policymakers and others is how to scale up. We have witnessed pockets of innovation, but little that could be characterized as large-scale patterns of success. The main problem, I would say, is not the spread of good ideas. Making reform widespread is related to replicating the *conditions* of successful change, not to transferring products (Healey and DeStefano 1997). These conditions involve scores of principals and other educational leaders breaking the bonds of dependency that the current system fosters. The societal context for educational reform has radically changed. To be successful, future leaders of the school, district, or other levels will require very different characteristics than those expected of leaders in the last decade.

Dependency is a function of insecurity, which can never be resolved under conditions of uncertainty. The education leader of the 21st century, paradoxically, will find greater peace of mind by looking for answers close at hand and reaching out, knowing that there is no clear solution.

"Life is a path you beat while you walk it," wrote the poet Antonio Machado, and DeGues (1997) calls this line of poetry "the most profound lesson in planning and strategy that I have ever learned." Breaking the bonds of dependency involves grasping this basic truth: "It is the walking that beats the path. It is not the path that makes the walk" (p. 155).

NOTES

1. Evans, R. (April 12, 1995). "Getting Real About Leadership." *Education Week* 14, 29: 36.

REFERENCES

DeGues, A. (1997). *The Living Company*. Boston: Harvard School Business Program.

Dolan, P. (1994). *Restructuring Our Schools*. Kansas City, Mo.: Systems and Organizations.

Elmore, R. (1995). "Getting to Scale with Good Educational Practice." *Harvard Education Review 66,* 1: 1–26.

Evans, R. (1996). *The Human Side of School Change.* San Francisco: Jossey-Bass.

Farson, R. (1997). *Management of the Absurd.* New York: Simon and Schuster.

Fullan, M. (1997). *What's Worth Fighting For in the Principalship?* 2nd ed. New York: Teachers College Press.

Fullan, M., and A. Hargreaves. (1996). *What's Worth Fighting For In Your School.* New York: Teachers College Press.

Hargreaves, A., and M. Fullan (1998). *What's Worth Fighting For Out There.* New York: Teachers College Press.

Havel, V. (October 1993). "Never Against Hope." *Esquire,* 65–69.

Healey, H., and J. DeStefano. (1997). *Education Reform Support: A Framework for Scaling up School Reform.* Washington, D.C.: Abel 2 Clearinghouse for Basic Education.

Heifitz, R. (1994). *Leadership Without Easy Answers.* Cambridge, Mass.: Harvard University Press.

Maurer, R. (1996). *Beyond the Wall of Resistance.* Austin: Bard Books.

Micklethwait, J., and A. Wooldridge. (1996). *The Witch Doctors: Making Sense of Management Gurus.* New York: Time Books, Random House.

Mintzberg, H. (1994). *The Rise and Fall of Strategic Planning.* New York: Free Press.

Newmann, F., and G. Wehlage. (1995). *Successful School Restructuring.* Madison, Wisc.: Center on Organization and Restructuring of Schools.

Schorr, L. (1997). *Common Purpose: Strengthening Families and Neighborhoods to Rebuild America.* New York: Doubleday.

13

THE MANAGER AS POLITICIAN

Lee G. Bolman
Terrence E. Deal

THE MANAGERS WHO decided to launch the space shuttle *Challenger* did not believe they were making a decision that would destroy the shuttle and kill seven astronauts. Everyone knew that there were risks, but there are *always* risks and judgments *always* have to be made about which risks are acceptable. Even in areas that are highly technical, momentous judgments can be distorted by political pressures. How can we try to prevent such catastrophes?

Many believe that the answer is simply to get politics out of management. Consider Benno Schmidt, whose leadership style as president of Yale University was described as "hard-nosed practicality doled out with a notable lack of levity" (Radin, 1989, p. 20). Criticized for being uncompromising and for not understanding the political dimension of his job, Schmidt's response was crisp: "I am not a politician. And I resist political measures of this job or this institution. In this job, the test of success is substance, not form, not posturing. I want to represent a different point of view: objectivity, principle as distinct from politics. I am resistant to a lot of the style and trappings people have come to associate with leadership of any sort in this society" (p. 20).

Though we wish Schmidt well (one of us is a Yale alumnus), we are skeptical about his philosophy of university leadership. Politics will not go away whenever the basic conditions of the political frame are present: enduring differences, scarce resources, and interdependence. Enduring differences mean that people will interpret events and situations differently and will often have difficulty agreeing on what is important or even what is true. Scarce resources mean that no one can have everything that he or she wants and that decisions about who gets what must constantly be made. Interdependence means that people cannot simply ignore one another: they need each other's assistance, support, and resources. Under these conditions, attempts to eliminate politics drives them under the rug and into the closet, where they become even more counterproductive and unmanageable. We need instead to develop an image of positive politics and of the manager as constructive politician.

Two Faces of Politics

McClelland (1975) describes two faces of power. The negative face is power as exploitation and personal dominance. The positive face is power as a means of creating visions and collective goals. Might there be two faces of politics as well? Everyone knows the negative face. The positive one is more elusive. Politicians and politics are widely scorned. What good can be said about a perspective that emphasizes power, conflict, bargaining, and self-interest? Consider the following case: "'Doris Randall' was the new head of backwater purchasing department that she feared would join personnel and public relations as the 'three Ps' of women's ghettoized job assignments in the electronics industry. But she eventually parlayed technical information from users of the department's services into an agreement from her boss to allow her to make the first wave of changes. No one in her position had ever had such close contacts with users before, and Randall found this a potent basis for reorganizing her unit into a set of user-oriented specialties" (Kanter, 1983, p. 219).

Doris Randall is a constructive politician. Starting from a weak position, she built a support base by establishing relationships with the people whose assistance she needed. She understood the essentials of effective leadership and management. Leaders and managers can never fully escape a fundamental dilemma: how to confront the realities of diversity, scarcity, and self-interest, and still channel human action in cooperative and socially valuable directions.

Kotter (1985) contends that too many managers are either naive or cynical. The naive see the world through rose-colored glasses; they never want to believe that people are selfish, dishonest, or exploitative. The cynical believe the opposite: everyone is selfish, everything is political, and "get them before they get you" is the best guide to conduct. Kotter believes that, in America, the naive outnumber the cynical but that neither stance is effective: "Organizational excellence . . . demands a sophisticated type of social skill: a leadership skill that can mobilize people and accomplish important objectives despite dozens of obstacles; a skill that can pull people together for meaningful purposes despite the thousands of forces that push us apart; a skill that can keep our corporations and public institutions from descending into a mediocrity characterized by bureaucratic infighting, parochial politics, and vicious power struggles" (p. 11).

Kotter's view suggests that it is in the best interests of both individual and organization for managers to be "benevolent politicians." For Kotter, this requires steering a course between naiveté and cynicism: "Beyond the yellow brick road of naiveté and the mugger's land of cynicism, there is a narrow path, poorly lighted, hard to find, and even harder to stay on once found. People who have the skill and the perseverance to take that path serve us in countless ways. We need more of these people. Many more" (Kotter, 1985, p. xi).

What does that path look like? Why would anyone choose to follow it? Kotter's answer is primarily pragmatic. The reason to follow the path is that it works, both for the individual and for the larger society. But staying on the path requires the ability both to understand and diagnose diversity and complexity and to accumulate and use power effectively. Kotter believes that following such a path is a moral undertaking, but his distinction between leadership and cynicism emphasizes results rather than ethics: leadership produces collective action in the service of organizational goals, while cynicism leads to parochial politics.

Skills of the Manager as Politician

What political skills does a manager need? In a world of scarcity, diversity, and conflict, the politically astute manager needs to develop an agenda, build a base of support for that agenda, and learn how to manage relations with those who might support or resist the agenda. This requires understanding and skill in three major areas: (1) agenda setting (Kanter, 1983; Kotter, 1988; Smith, 1988); (2) networking and forming coalitions (Kanter, 1983; Kotter, 1982, 1985, 1988; Smith, 1988); and (3) bargaining and negotiating (Bellow and Moulton, 1978; Fisher and Ury, 1981; Lax and Sebenius, 1986).

Agenda Setting

Kanter (1983), in her study of internal entrepreneurs in American corporations, Kotter (1988), writing about effective corporate leaders, and Smith (1988), writing about effective U.S. presidents, all concluded that the first step in effective leadership is setting an agenda. In Kotter's view, effective leaders create an "agenda for change" that has two major elements: a *vision* of what can and should be, which considers the legitimate long-term interests of the parties involved, and a *strategy for achieving that vision,* which considers the relevant organizational and environmental forces. The agenda must provide a sense of direction while addressing the concerns of both the leader and other major stakeholders. The manager as politician needs to be familiar with the major stakeholders and understand their values, goals, and local agendas.

Kanter (1983) argues that "active learning to the information circulating in the neighborhood is really the first step in the generation of an innovative accomplishment" (p. 218). Only by knowing what others care about can you fashion your agenda in a way that will respond to their concerns: "While gathering information, entrepreneurs can also be 'planting seeds'—leaving the kernel of an idea behind and letting it germinate and blossom so that it begins to float around the system from many sources other than the innovator. Problem identification often precedes project definition, for there may be many conflicting views in the organization about the best method of reaching the goals. Discovering the basis for these conflicting perspectives while gathering hard technical data is critical at this stage" (p. 218).

A vision is inert without a strategy to make it happen. The strategy has to reflect a sound understanding of the major forces that work for and against the agenda. Smith (1988) makes this point about the American presidency: "In the grand scheme of American government, the paramount task and power of the president is to articulate the national purpose: to fix the nation's agenda. Of all the big games at the summit of American politics, the agenda game must be won first. The effectiveness of the presidency and the capacity of any president to lead depends on focusing the nation's political attention and its energies on two or three top priorities. From the standpoint of history, the flow of events seems to have immutable logic, but political reality is inherently chaotic: it contains no automatic agenda. Order must be imposed" (p. 333).

Almost no job has an automatic agenda. The bigger the job, the more difficult it is to wade through all the issues clamoring for attention and to bring order out of chaos. Contrary to Woody Allen's dictum, success in management requires a good deal more than just showing up. High office, even if the incumbent has great personal popularity, is no guarantee of success. Smith (1988) asserts that President Ronald Reagan was remarkably successful in his first year as president because he followed a classic strategy for winning the agenda game: "First impressions are critical. In the agenda game, a swift beginning is crucial for a new president to establish himself as leader—to show the nation that he will make a difference in people's lives. The first one hundred days are the vital test; in those weeks, the political community and the public measure a new president— to see whether he is active, dominant, sure, purposeful" (p. 334).

Reagan began with a vision but not a strategy. He was not gifted as a manager or strategist, though he had extraordinary ability to simplify complex issues and paint a picture in broad, symbolic brush strokes. Reagan's staff had painstakingly studied the first 100 days of his four predecessors. The staff concluded that it was essential in the early days to move with speed and focus. Pushing other agenda items to one side, they focused on two things: cutting taxes and cutting the federal budget. They also discovered a secret weapon in David Stockman, the only person in the Reagan White House who really understood the federal budget process. Stockman himself later admitted that he was astounded by the "low level of fiscal literacy" of Reagan and his key advisers (Smith, 1988, p. 354). According to Smith, "Stockman got a jump on everyone else for two reasons: he had an agenda and a legislative blueprint already prepared, and he understood the real levers of power. Two terms as a Michigan congressman plus a network of key Republican and Democratic connections had taught Stockman how to play the power game" (pp. 351–352). Reagan and his advisers had the vision. Stockman gave them the strategy.

Networking and Coalition Building

The *Challenger* disaster occurred even though engineers at both Morton Thiokol and NASA had been aware of the O-ring problem for a long time. They had tried to call it to their superiors' attention, mostly by writing memos. Six months before the *Challenger* accident, Roger Boisjoly, an engineer at Morton Thiokol, wrote a memo saying, "The result [of an O-ring failure] would be a catastrophe of the highest order—loss of human life" (Bell and Esch, 1987, p. 45). Two months later, another engineer at Thiokol wrote a memo that opened, "HELP! The seal task force is constantly being delayed by every possible means" (Bell and Esch, 1987, p. 45). That memo went on to detail the resistance that the task force was getting from other departments in the company.

A memo to your boss is sometimes an effective political strategy, but it more often is a sign of powerlessness and lack of political skill and sophistication. Kotter (1985) suggests four basic steps for dealing with the political dimensions in managerial work:

1. Identify the relevant relationships (figure out who needs to be led).

2. Assess who might resist cooperation, why, and how strongly (figuring out where the leadership challenges will be).

3. Develop, wherever possible, relationships with those people to facilitate the communication, education, or negotiation processes needed to deal with resistance.

4. When step three fails, carefully select and implement more subtle or more forceful methods.

The political frame emphasizes that no strategy will work without a power base. Managers always face a "power gap": managerial jobs never come with enough power to get the work done (Kotter, 1985). Managerial work can only be done with the cooperation of other people, often large numbers of people. Moving up the ladder brings more authority, but it also brings more dependence because the manager's success depends on the effort of large and diverse groups of people, sometimes numbering in the hundreds or thousands (Kotter, 1985, 1988). Rarely will those people provide their best efforts and fullest cooperation merely because they have been told to. If you want their assistance, it helps a great deal if they know you, like you, and see you as credible and competent.

The first task in building networks and coalitions is to figure out whose help you need. The second is to develop relationships with those people. You want them to be there when you need them. Kanter (1983) found that middle managers seeking to promote change or innovation in a corporation typically began by getting preliminary agreement for an initiative from their boss. They then moved into a phase of "preselling" or "making cheerleaders": "Peers, managers of related functions, stakeholders in the issue, potential collaborators, and sometimes even customers would be approached individually, in one-on-one meetings that gave people a chance to influence the project and the innovator the maximum opportunity to sell it. Seeing them alone and on their territory was important: the rule was to act as if each person were *the* most important one for the project's success" (p. 223).

Once you have cheerleaders, you can move on to "horse trading," that is, promising rewards in exchange for resources and support. This builds the resource base that lets you go to the next step of "securing blessings"—getting the necessary approvals and mandates from higher management (Kanter, 1983). Kanter found that the usual route to success at that stage was to identify the senior managers who had the most to say about the issue at hand, and develop a polished, formal presentation to get their support. The best presentations responded to both substantive and technical concerns, because senior managers typically cared about two questions: (1) Is it a good idea? (2) How will my constituents react to it? Once innovators got the blessing of higher management, they could go back to their boss to formalize the coalition and make specific plans for pursuing the project (Kanter, 1983).

The basic point is simple: as a manager, you need friends and allies to get things done. If you are trying to build relationships and get support from those friends and allies, you need to cultivate them. Hard-core rationalists and incurable romantics sometimes react with horror to such a picture. If what they want is right, why should they have to play political games to get it accepted? Like it or not, however, political dynamics are inevitable under conditions of ambiguity, diversity, and scarcity. Those are conditions that most managers, including the president of Yale, face every day.

Mistakes can be very costly. Smith (1988) reports a case in point. Thomas Wyman, the board chairman of the CBS television network, went to Washington in 1983 to lobby the U.S. attorney-general, Edwin Meese. An emergency at the White House forced Meese to miss the meeting, and Wyman was sent instead to the office of Craig Fuller, one of Meese's top advisers:

> "I know something about this issue," Fuller suggested, "Perhaps you'd like to discuss it with me."
>
> But Wyman waved him off, unaware of Fuller's actual role, and evidently regarding him a mere staff man.
>
> "No, I'd rather wait and talk to Meese," Wyman said.
>
> For nearly an hour, Wyman sat leafing through magazines in Fuller's office, making no effort to talk to Fuller, who kept working at his desk just a few feet away.
>
> Finally, Meese burst into Fuller's office, full of apologies that he simply wouldn't have time for a substantive talk. "Did you talk to Fuller?" he asked.
>
> Wyman shook his head.
>
> "You should have talked to Fuller," Meese said. "He's very important on this issue. He knows it better than any of the rest of us. He's writing a memo for the president on the pros and cons. You could have given him your side of the argument" [Smith, 1988, pp. xviii–xix].

Wyman missed an important opportunity because he failed to test his assumptions about who had power, who could help, and who could not.

Bargaining and Negotiation

Bargaining is often thought to apply primarily to commercial, legal, and labor relations settings. From a political perspective, though, bargaining is central to decision making in organizations. The horse trading that Kanter describes as part of the coalition-building process is just one of many examples. Negotiation is called for whenever two or more parties have some interests in common and other interests in conflict. Labor and management both want an organization to do well enough to provide jobs for its employees but they often strongly disagree on how resources should be divided between management and workers. Engineers and top managers at Morton Thiokol had a common interest in the success of the shuttle program. They differed sharply on how to balance technical and political considerations in making hard decisions.

The fundamental dilemma in negotiations is the choice between "creating value and claiming value" (Lax and Sebenius, 1986):

> Value creators tend to believe that, above all, successful negotiators must be inventive and cooperative enough to devise an agreement that yields considerable gain to each party, relative to no-agreement possibilities. Some speak about the need for replacing the win-lose image of negotiation with win-win negotiation. In addition to information sharing and honest communication, the drive to create value can require ingenuity and may benefit from a variety of techniques and attitudes. The parties can treat the negotiation as solving a joint problem; they can organize brainstorming sessions to invent creative solutions to their problems [Lax and Sebenius, 1986, pp. 30–31].
>
> Value claimers, on the other hand, tend to see this drive for joint gain as naive and weak-minded. For them, negotiation is hard, tough bargaining. The object of negotiation is to convince the other guy that he wants what you have to offer much more than you want what he has; moreover, you have all the time in the world, while he is up against pressing deadlines. To "win" at negotiation—and thus make the other fellow "lose"—one must start high, concede slowly, exaggerate the value of concessions, minimize the benefits of the other's concessions, conceal information, argue forcibly on behalf of principles that imply favorable settlements, make commitments to

accept only highly favorable agreements, and be willing to outwait the other fellow [Lax and Sebenius, 1986, p. 32].

One of the best-known "win-win" approaches to negotiation was developed by Fisher and Ury (1981) in their book, *Getting to Yes*. They argue that the basic problem in negotiations is that most people routinely engage in "positional bargaining": they take positions and then make concessions to reach agreement. Fisher and Ury give the example below of a conversation between a customer and the proprietor of a secondhand store (pp. 3–4):

Customer: How much do you want for this brass dish?
Shopkeeper: That is a beautiful antique, isn't it? I guess I could let it
                go for $75.
Customer: Oh, come on, it's dented. I'll give you $15.
Shopkeeper: Really! I might consider a serious offer, but $15
                certainly isn't serious.
Customer: Well, I could go to $20, but I would never pay anything
                like $75. Quote me a realistic price.
Shopkeeper: You drive a hard bargain, young lady. $60 cash,
                right now.
Customer: $25.
Shopkeeper: It cost me a great deal more than that. Make me a *serious* offer.
Customer: $37.50. That's the highest I'll go.
Shopkeeper: Have you noticed the engraving on that dish? Next year
                pieces like that will be worth twice what you pay today.

Fisher and Ury argue that positional bargaining is inefficient and often produces poor outcomes: the parties, for example, may miss the opportunity to create an agreement that would benefit both of them. Fisher and Ury propose an approach to "principled bargaining" that is built around four strategies. The first is to "separate the people from the problem" (1981, pp. 3–4). The stress and tension of negotiations easily escalate into anger and personal attacks. The result is that negotiators sometimes want to defeat or hurt the other person at almost any cost. Since every negotiation involves both substance and relationships, the wise negotiator will "deal with the people as human beings and with the problem on its merits" (p. 40).

Fisher and Ury's second recommendation is to "focus on interests, not positions" (p. 11). If you get locked into a position, you might overlook other ways to achieve what you want. An example was the Camp David treaty between Israel and Egypt in 1978. The two sides were at an impasse for a long time over where to draw the boundary line between the two countries. Israel wanted to keep part of the Sinai, while Egypt wanted all of it back. Resolution became possible only when they looked at each other's underlying interests. Israel was concerned about security: no Egyptian tanks on their border. Egypt was concerned about sovereignty: the Sinai had been part of Egypt from the time of the Pharaohs. The parties agreed on a plan that gave all of the Sinai back to Egypt, while demilitarizing large parts of it (Fisher and Ury, 1981).

Fisher and Ury's third recommendation is to invent options for mutual gain, that is, to look continually for new possibilities that might bring advantages to both sides. Parties often consider only the first few alternatives that come to mind. But if they make the effort to generate more options, the chances of a better decision increase. The final recommendation is to "insist on objective criteria"—standards of fairness for both substance and procedures. When a school board and a teachers' union are at loggerheads over the size of the teachers' pay increase, the two sides can try to find objective criteria for a fair settlement, such as the rate of inflation or settlements in other districts. The classic example of looking for a fair procedure is two brothers deadlocked over how to divide a pie between them. They finally agreed that one would cut the pie into two pieces, and the other could choose the piece he wanted.

Fisher and Ury devote most of their attention to strategies for creating value, that is, how to find solutions that are better for both parties. They downplay the equally important question of claiming value—how negotiators can maximize their individual gains. In many ways, "win-win" bargaining is more consistent with a human resource than a political view of the world. By contrast, a bargaining tactics stance may better represent the political frame. A classic example is Schelling's (1960) essay on bargaining, which focuses particularly on the problem of how to make credible threats.

Suppose, for example, that I want to buy a house from you, and I am willing to pay $150,000 for it, although you do not necessarily know what my highest offer is. If I want to convince you that I am willing to pay only $125,000, how could I make my offer credible? Schelling notes that, contrary to a common assumption, I am not always better off in such a situation if I am stronger and have more resources. If you know that I am very wealthy, you might take my threats less seriously than if you know (or I can get you to believe) that it is barely possible for me to scrape up $125,000. Common sense also suggests that I should be better off if I have considerable freedom of action. Yet I may get a better price if I can convince you that my hands are tied—for example, that I am negotiating for a very stubborn buyer who will not go above $125,000, even if the house is worth more. Such examples suggest that the ideal situation for the bargainer is to have considerable resources and freedom to act but to be able to convince the other side that just the opposite is true. This gives us the following picture of the bargaining process:

1. Bargaining is a mixed-motive game. Although both parties want an agreement, they have very different preferences about which agreement.

2. Bargaining is a process of interdependent decisions, and what each party does affects the other. Each player wants, as much as possible, to be able to predict what the other will do while limiting the other's ability to do the same.

3. The more player A can control player B's level of uncertainty, the more powerful A is.

4. Bargaining primarily involves the judicious use of *threats* rather than sanctions. Players may threaten to use force, to go on strike, to break off negotiations, and so forth. In most cases, however, they much prefer not to have to carry out the threats.

5. A critical bargaining skill is the ability to make threats credible. A threat will only work if your opponent believes you, and noncredible threats may even weaken your bargaining position.

6. Calculation of the appropriate threat level is also critical. If I "underthreaten," I may weaken my own position. If I "overthreaten," you may not believe me, may break off the negotiations, or may escalate your own threats.

Bellow and Moulton (1978) present a fascinating account of negotiations between lawyers for the U.S. Department of Justice and lawyers for then Vice-President Spiro Agnew. A legal case against Agnew developed by accident. A group of federal attorneys investigating local corruption in Baltimore County, Maryland, initially had no idea that the trail would lead them to the vice-president.

But Agnew himself made an early tactical error. Only a few weeks after the prosecutors began to subpoena witnesses, Agnew expressed concern about the investigation to the attorney general. Although the prosecutors had no reason to suspect Agnew at that point, they immediately became interested. If the vice-president was nervous, they wanted to know why.

The federal investigators then got a break. An attorney for William Fornoff, a potential defendant, came to the prosecutors and said, "I know you have A, B, and C, but what else do you have?" The prosecutors had nothing else but chose not to say so. They played a hunch—that an unknown case would be more threatening than a known one. They tried to control Fornoff's uncertainty and it worked. They insisted that they would make a deal only after Fornoff told them what he knew. He did, providing information that led the investigators to several of Agnew's political associates in Baltimore. They, in turn, provided evidence against Agnew.

When Agnew realized that some of his old friends were cooperating with the prosecutors, he sent his attorneys to negotiate. Both sides preferred to make a deal. The attorney general, Eliot Richardson, and Agnew both owed their jobs to the same man, President Richard Nixon. Richardson wanted Agnew out of office before something occurred that might permit him to become president. (Richardson's fear was justified; Nixon's resignation in the Watergate scandal would have made Agnew president.) Agnew wanted to avoid a trial and possible conviction. Both sides thus had reasons to avoid a trial, which would create uncertainties that neither side could control. The bargaining came down to three issues: whether Agnew would resign as vice-president, how much Agnew would admit in court, and whether Agnew would go to jail. Initially, the prosecutors and Agnew's lawyers could not agree on any of the three questions.

During these negotiations, a newspaper broke the story that plea bargaining was under way. Someone in the prosecutor's office apparently leaked the information, perhaps to increase the pressure on Agnew. Agnew responded by promising that he would not resign, even if indicted. He was using a common tactic in adversarial bargaining: trying to convince the opponent that you have adopted an unchangeable position. He knew Richardson dreaded the possibility of a convicted felon in the office of the vice-president. The prosecution, meanwhile, kept much of its evidence secret—continuing to use the so-called black box technique to pressure Agnew.

In public, Agnew complained that he was being harassed and tried in the press. In private, he sent his attorneys to try again for a plea bargain. Most members of the prosecution wanted to hold out for a full public confession, if not a jail term. They reasoned that Agnew had to make a deal, but Agnew's attorneys refused to budge. Richardson finally agreed to settle for a resignation and minimal admissions in court. Richardson's decision was softer than his subordinates wanted, but he had little desire to bring an incumbent vice-president to trial. The deal was struck. Agnew resigned, appeared briefly in court, and made a nationwide television appearance in which he minimized any wrongdoing on his part.

We have now seen two dramatically different approaches to the question of bargaining—what Lax and Sebenius (1986) call "creating value" and "claiming value." But how does a manager choose between them? One approach is to ask how much opportunity is there for achieving a win-win solution, and if one will have to work with these people again. If everyone will be much better off with an agreement than without one, it makes sense to emphasize creating value. If the manager will have to work with the same people again in the future, it would be very dangerous to use value-claiming tactics that leave anger and mistrust in their wake. Managers who have a reputation for being manipulative and self-interested will have a hard time building the networks and coalitions that they need to be successful in the future.

Axelrod's (1980) research suggests that, when negotiators must work together over time, a strategy of "conditional openness" is most effective. This strategy tells the negotiator to start with open and collaborative behavior and to maintain this approach if the other party does too. If the other party becomes adversarial, however, the negotiator should respond in kind and remain adversarial until the opponent makes a collaborative move. It is, in effect, a friendly and forgiving version of tit for tat—do unto others exactly as they do unto you. In Axelrod's experimental research, this conditional openness strategy worked better than even the most fiendishly diabolical adversarial strategies (Axelrod, 1980).

One other criterion can be applied to the question of choosing collaborative or adversarial tactics, namely, what is the *ethical* thing to do? Bargainers often deliberately misrepresent their positions, even though few actions are more universally condemned than lying (Bok, 1978). This leads to a profoundly difficult question for the manager as politician: What actions are ethical and just?

Morality and Politics

Block (1987), Burns (1978), and Lax and Sebenius (1986) all explore ethical issues in bargaining and organizational politics. Block's view rests on the assumption that individuals can empower themselves through an understanding of politics: "The cornerstone of this book is the idea that the process of organizational politics as we know it works against people taking responsibility. We empower ourselves by discovering a positive way of being political. The line between positive and negative politics is a tight-rope we have to walk" (p. xiii).

Block argues that there is a bureaucratic cycle in organizations that often leaves individuals feeling vulnerable, powerless, and helpless. If we give too much power to the organization and to people around us, he says, we fear that power will be used against us, and we begin to develop indirect and manipulative strategies to protect ourselves. To escape the dilemma, managers need to support organizational structures, policies, and procedures that promote empowerment, and they must also make personal choices to empower themselves.

Block urges managers to build an "image of greatness" for their department or unit—an image of what the unit can contribute that is meaningful and worthwhile. "A vision is an expression of hope and idealism. The anxiety we feel means we are moving against the culture or working to recreate the culture, and that is what makes our vision a positive political act" (1987, p. 115).

Having created a vision, the manager needs to focus on building support for that vision. Block views this as a matter of negotiating agreement and trust. He suggests that managers need to differentiate between those with whom agreement and trust are initially high (allies and bedfellows) and those with whom they are low (adversaries and opponents). Adversaries, he says, are both the most difficult and the most interesting people to deal with. He argues that it is usually ineffective to pressure them and that the effective strategy is to "let go of them." He offers four steps for letting go: (1) tell them your vision of the organization, (2) state in a neutral way your best understanding of their position, (3) identify your own contribution to the problem, and (4) end the meeting by telling them what you plan to do but without making any demands on them.

To empower ourselves, Block argues, we have to believe that our well-being and survival are in our own hands, that we have an underlying purpose, and that we are committed to achieving that purpose *now*. Then, says Block, managers can choose between maintenance and greatness, caution and courage, and dependency and autonomy. Bureaucracy, in his view, nudges us in the direction of maintenance (holding on to what we already have), caution, and dependence.

Block recognizes that such a strategy might seem naively suicidal but argues that "war games in organizations lose their power when they are brought into the light of day" (p. 148). The political frame, however, questions that assumption. Block may be right in the case of political games that result merely from a misunderstanding or an unduly narrow understanding of one's self-interest. But in situations where resources really are scarce, and where there are real and durable differences in values and beliefs among different groups, bringing politics into the open may simply make everyone more tense and uncomfortable. Conflict may become more obvious and overt, but no more resolvable. Block's message about the importance of personal commitment to a vision for oneself and one's organization is important. Nevertheless, his view of politics disregards basic propositions of the political frame.

Burns's (1978) effort to develop a conception of positive politics is more complex. He considers examples as diverse and complex as Franklin Roosevelt and Adolph Hitler, Gandhi and Mao, Woodrow Wilson and Joan of Arc. He recognizes the reality of differences and conflict and argues that both conflict and power are central to the concept of leadership and management. Searching for firm moral footing in a world of cultural and ethical diversity, Burns turned to social science and specifically to the motivation theory of Maslow (1954) and the ethical theory of Kohlberg (1973). From Maslow he borrowed the idea of the hierarchy of motives. Moral leaders, he argued, appeal to higher levels on the need hierarchy.

From Kohlberg he adopted the idea of stages of moral reasoning. At the lowest stage, the "preconventional" level, moral judgments are based primarily on perceived consequences: an action is right if you are rewarded and wrong if you are punished. Kohlberg found preconventional reasoning primarily in children. In the next two stages—the "conventional" level—the emphasis is on conforming to authority and established rules. At the two highest stages—the "postconventional" level—ethical judgments rest on more general principles. At the fifth stage, ethical reasoning emphasizes the social contract and the greatest good for the greatest number. At the sixth and last stage, individuals base ethical judgments on universal and comprehensive moral principles.

Maslow and Kohlberg thus provided an ethical foundation on which Burns (1978) constructed a positive view of politics:

> Leaders are taskmasters and goal setters, but they and their followers share a particular space and time, a particular set of motivations and values. If they are to be effective in helping to mobilize and elevate their constituencies, leaders must be whole persons, persons with fully functioning capacities for thinking and feeling. The problem for them as educators, as leaders, is not to promote narrow, egocentric self-

actualization, but to extend awareness of human needs and the means of gratifying them to improve the larger social situation for which educators or leaders have responsibility and over which they have power.

What does all this mean for the teaching of leadership as opposed to manipulation? "Teachers"—in whatever guise—treat students neither coercively nor instrumentally but as joint seekers of truth and of mutual actualization. They help students define moral values not by imposing their own moralities on them but by positing situations that pose moral choices and then encouraging conflict and debate. They seek to help students rise to higher stages of moral reasoning and hence to higher levels of principled judgment [pp. 448–449].

In other words, Burns argues that positive politics evolve when individuals choose actions that appeal to higher motives and higher stages of moral judgment.

For Lax and Sebenius (1986), ethical issues are inescapable for the manager as negotiator, and they provide a set of questions to help managers decide whether an action is ethical:

1. Are you following rules that are understood and accepted? (In poker, for example, everyone understands that bluffing is part of the game.)

2. Are you comfortable discussing and defending your action? Would you want your colleagues and friends to be aware of it? Your spouse, children, or parents? Would you be comfortable if it were on the front page of a major newspaper?

3. Would you want someone to do it to you? To a member of your family?

4. What if everyone acted that way? Would the resulting society be desirable? If you were designing an organization, would you want people to act that way? Would you teach your children to do it?

5. Are there alternatives that rest on firmer ethical ground?

While these questions do not provide an ethical framework, they do embody several important principles of moral judgment:

1. Mutuality—are all parties to a relationship operating under the same understanding about the rules of the game?

2. Generality—does a specific action follow a principle of moral conduct that is applicable to all comparable situations?

3. Caring—does this action show care for the legitimate interests of others?

These questions attempt to illuminate and clarify ethical and moral judgments. They raise issues that managers need to consider and that should be part of an ongoing conversation both in schools and at work about the moral dimension of management and leadership. Porter (1989) notes, however, that such a conversation is often absent or impoverished: "In a seminar with seventeen executives from nine corporations, we learned how the privatization of moral discourse in our society has created a deep sense of moral loneliness and moral illiteracy; how the absence of a common language prevents people from talking about and 'reading' the moral issues they face. We learned how the isolation of individuals—the taboo against talking about spiritual matters in the public sphere—robs people of courage, of the strength of heart to do what deep down they believe to be right. They think they are alone in facing these issues" (p. 2).

Organizations and societies may choose to banish moral discourse and to leave managers to face ethical issues alone, but they invite dreary and brutish political dynamics when they do so. In an increasingly pluralistic and secular world, the solution is not for organizations to impose a narrow ethical framework on their employees. Such an approach would not work and would not be desirable if it did. But organizations can take a moral stance. They can make it clear that they expect ethical behavior, and they can validate the importance of dialogue about the moral issues facing managers. Positive politics absent moral dialogue and a moral framework is as likely as successful farming without sunlight or water.

Summary

The question is not whether organizations will have politics, but what kind of politics they will have. Politics can be and often is sordid and destructive. But politics can also be the vehicle for achieving noble purposes, and managers can be benevolent politicians. Organizational change and effectiveness depend on such managers. The constructive politician recognizes political realities in organizations and knows how to fashion an agenda, build a network of support, and negotiate effectively both with those who might advance and with those who might oppose the agenda.

In the process, managers inevitably encounter a dilemma that is both practical and ethical—when to adopt strategies that are open and collaborative and when to choose tougher, more adversarial approaches. They will need to consider the potential for collaboration, the importance of long-term relationships, and most importantly, the values and ethical principles that they endorse.

REFERENCES

Axelrod, R. "More Effective Choice in the Prisoner's Dilemma." *Journal of Conflict Resolution*, 1980, 24, 379–403.

Bell, T. E., and Esch, K. "The Fatal Flaw in Flight 51-L." *IEEE Spectrum*, Feb. 1987, pp. 36–51.

Bellow, G., and Moulton, B. *The Lawyering Process: Cases and Materials*. Mineola, N.Y.: Foundation Press, 1978.

Block, P. *The Empowered Manager: Positive Political Skills at Work*. San Francisco: Jossey-Bass, 1987.

Bok, S. *Lying: Moral Choice in Public and Private Life*. New York: Vintage Books, 1978.

Burns, J. M. *Leadership*. New York: Harper & Row, 1978.

Fisher, R., and Ury, W. *Getting to Yes*. Boston: Houghton Mifflin, 1981.

Kanter, R. *The Change Masters: Innovations for Productivity in the American Corporation*. New York: Simon & Schuster, 1983.

Kohlberg, L. "The Claim to Moral Adequacy of a Highest Stage of Moral Judgment." *Journal of Philosophy*, 1973, 70, 630–646.

Kotter, J. P. *The General Managers*. New York: Free Press, 1982.

Kotter, J. P. *Power and Influence: Beyond Formal Authority*. New York: Free Press, 1985.

Kotter, J. P. *The Leadership Factor*. New York: Free Press, 1988.

Lax, D. A., and Sebenius, J. K. *The Manager as Negotiator*. New York: Free Press, 1986.

McClelland, D. C. *Power: The Inner Experience*. New York: Irvington, 1975.

Maslow, A. H. *Motivation and Personality*. New York: Harper & Row, 1954.

Porter, E. "Notes for Looking for Leadership Conference." Paper presented at Looking for Leadership Conference, Graduate School of Education, Harvard University, Dec. 1989.

Radin, C. A. "New Haven Blues: Yale President's Colors Not True to Tradition." *Boston Globe*, Apr. 23, 1989.

Schelling, T. *The Strategy of Conflict*. Cambridge, Mass.: Harvard University Press, 1960.

Smith, H. *The Power Game*. New York: Random House, 1988.

14

LEADING A SCHOOL SYSTEM THROUGH CHANGE

KEY STEPS FOR MOVING REFORM FORWARD

Phillip C. Schlechty

IN ONE OF HIS many books, C. Wright Mills tried to convey what he would do if he were to assume a variety of positions in the national life and his goal were to avert a nuclear holocaust. (See Mills, 1985.) In one chapter, Mills indicated the kind of sermon he would preach if he were a member of the clergy, which he certainly was not, and which he never, to my knowledge, promised or threatened to be.

In writing the present chapter I feel something like Mills might have felt in composing his sermon. I am going to write as if I were a superintendent of schools, which I am not, and which I never threaten to be. I have, however, worked with many superintendents; some have been exemplary. From working with, and for, a number of very good superintendents I have learned quite a bit about the strengths and weaknesses of the office as well as something of the qualities of the men and women I have observed in this office.

In this chapter I am more interested in considering the qualities of the office than I am in discussing the qualities of any particular occupant. I know, as does anyone who thinks about the matter, that strong superintendents will take advantage of the positions they occupy; weak superintendents will be overwhelmed by the responsibilities imposed by the office. Similarly, even the strongest superintendents are constrained by the limitations of the office (and some school boards, state agencies, and legislatures constrain superintendents more than others). And even weak superintendents will have a considerable impact (for good or ill) on the lives of teachers and children.

Where I Would Begin

There are two things I know about the office of superintendent. First, whatever moral authority resides in, or is bestowed upon, the school system, that authority resides in the office of the superintendent. Second, the superintendent can delegate to others nearly anything he or she wants to delegate (so long as the board consents) except the moral authority that resides in the office of superintendent. In the long run, therefore, who the superintendent is, what the superintendent values, and the style of operation supported by the superintendent will be manifest throughout the school system.

Superintendents who do not use their office to lead will create a school system incapable of leadership in the community. So long as the community does not look to the schools for leadership and so long as the school board does not want, or will not tolerate, leadership from the schools, such superintendents survive and do quite well. Superintendents who use their office as a forum from which to lead will create an organization capable of leadership.

There are two caveats. First, if the board and the community prefer a passive, perhaps even submissive, role for schools and school personnel, strong leaders will not last long—or if they do survive, they will cease to be strong leaders. Second, if the prior superintendent was strong and developed a commitment to a shared vision, the new superintendent had better take the predecessor's vision into account or his or her tenure is likely to be short. Strong leaders build cultures that outlive them; they lead even when they are gone.

Given these beliefs about the office of superintendent, I would want to be sure that the board of education and the union leadership of the district are willing to support strong leadership from the superintendent. The problem I would anticipate—especially in a system where the history of leadership has been less than outstanding—is that many in the audience I would want to address (board members and union leaders) would take *strong* leader to mean *authoritarian* leader.

I would first make it clear that authoritarian leaders are, as leaders, weak. That is why they are authoritarian. Weak leaders must use the power of their office (that is, they must use authority) because they do not have the capacity to get action from others by any other means. An authoritarian is nothing less than a person who resorts to his or her authority to compel others to act. Moreover, authoritarians seem to enjoy compelling others to obey.

Given the tendency to confuse strong leaders with authoritarian leaders, I would need to be careful in explaining what I mean by strong leader. And from the outset I would need to be educating all who would listen that while I am committed to participatory leadership, I do not view a participatory leader as a laissez faire leader. Nor is a participatory leader a democratic leader. A participatory leader is a leader who invites others to share the authority of the office and expects those who accept the invitation to share the responsibility as well. A participatory leader is a leader who is strong enough to trust others with his or her fate, just as he or she expects their trust in return.

Unfreezing the System

Having established the desire for leadership, I would begin to assess the system's belief structure. At the same time, I would begin to express my views of the world of education. I would talk with many people regarding their beliefs. I would review old statements of mission and philosophy to see if there had, in the past, been an effort at developing a shared expression of authentic beliefs. I would not, however, be overly impressed with the typical school philosophy that expresses the desire to educate each child to the maximum of the child's potential and to prepare each for a productive life in a democracy. I am in favor of such goals, of course, but they do not drive an organization toward excellence.

I would seize every opportunity to express my beliefs about school and the purposes of schooling. These statements would be sensitive to local language and local custom, but they would also be jarring sometimes and initially a bit off-putting. I would choose this course because I believe that one of the superintendent's roles is to serve as chief educator in the community. If the education the superintendent is to provide includes a fresh or more powerful vision, then it is important to use language that is educative.

Familiar language is not a good instrument for setting forth a new vision. A new vision requires a new language, at least until the old language can be unloaded of its prior meanings and recharged with new meaning. The word *teacher,* for example, is strongly associated with the idea of giving instruction, imparting knowledge, providing information. The word *student* often connotes a passive role and subservience to traditional authority. Such meanings need not attach to these words, but, at present, terms like *teacher, student,* and *school* connote images that should not be implied if a new vision is to be set forth. Therefore, I would insist on linking the word *student* to active terms like *worker, knowledge worker,* and *customer.*

The purpose of the school system I envision is to get students actively engaged in working on and with knowledge. I would link *teacher* to words like *executive* and *leader* because such terms convey the leadership posture I believe teachers must assume in the schools of the future. Furthermore, such terms place teachers in that category of professionals with whom they have the most in common (professional executives) and dissociate them from the service-delivery professions like law and medicine which I believe are inappropriate models for teachers in coming years. I would insist on describing schools as knowledge-work organizations if for no other reason than that such language links schools to the future of American society and conveys the notion that schools are about something purposeful—doing schoolwork.

This I Believe: What About You?

Shortly after deciding to set on a restructuring course, I would begin to compose my version of a belief statement for the district. Since I do not have a particular school district in mind, I am not certain exactly how this statement would come to be framed. But I do know that it should contain at least the following principles:

WE BELIEVE

1. Every student can learn, and every student will learn, if presented with the right opportunity to do so. It is the purpose of school to invent learning opportunities for each student each day.

2. Learning opportunities are determined by the nature of the schoolwork (knowledge work) students are assigned or encouraged to undertake. It is the responsibility of teachers and administrators to ensure that students are provided with those forms of schoolwork at which they experience success and from which they learn those things of most value to them, to the community, and to the society at large.

3. All school activity should be focused on the creation and delivery of schoolwork at which students are successful and from which they gain skills and develop understanding that will equip them to participate fully in an information-based, knowledge-work society.

4. Properly conceived, schools are knowledge-work organizations. Students are central to the operation of schools for they are the primary recipients of what the school has to offer—the opportunity to work on and with knowledge and knowledge-related products.

5. Teachers are leaders just as executives are leaders; principals are leaders of instructors or leaders of leaders. The curriculum is the raw material upon which students work, and all parts of the school system are to be organized in whatever fashion produces the greatest likelihood that students will be successfully engaged in working on and with knowledge.

6. The primary role of the superintendent is to educate the community about education, to promote the articulation and persistent pursuit of a compelling vision, and to ensure that results, rather than programs, dominate the attention of all.

7. Teachers and principals are accountable for results, and the results expected are that all students will be provided schoolwork at which they experience success and from which the students gain knowledge and skills that are socially and culturally valued.

8. It is the obligation of the superintendent, the board of education, and all members of the community to provide teachers, principals, and students with those conditions and forms of support that ensure optimal conditions for performance, continuing growth, and development.

9. As a responsible and ethical employer, the school system has an obligation to ensure working conditions that confirm the professional status of all educators and the importance of the tasks assigned to all who work in and around schools.

10. Continuous improvement, persistent innovation, and a commitment to continuing growth should be expected of all people and all programs supported by school district resources, and school district resources should be committed to ensure that these expectations can be met.

Next Steps

Immediately after I had composed a belief statement with which I was satisfied and others might endorse (I would be doing a great deal of management by roaming and talking while I was drafting the statement), I would approach the board of education with four proposals. First, I would ask the board to commit to the development of a system-wide mission statement based on the beliefs I had outlined. The time frame for the completion of such a draft would be nine months (a school year).

Second, I would propose that the board develop a policy statement assuring that, within a reasonable time period, at least 2 percent of the school system's operating budget would be committed to human resource development. (At present, the human resource budget for most school systems is substantially less than 1 percent.) If the district is a collective bargaining district, I would also work with the union leadership to negotiate a supporting provision in the union contract, thereby symbolizing even more clearly my intent to institutionalize a commitment to human resource development. And, depending on the maturity of the union/management relationships in the district, I would be persuaded to advocate some sort of governance arrangement that guaranteed the union a say in the way these funds are expended. My goal would be to signify that human resource development is a high-priority, permanent commitment of the district.

Third, I would ask the board to create a new position in the school district that I will here call an enrichment/demonstration teacher. During the first year, the number of these positions should represent 1 percent of the regular teaching force, but within three years the number should be at least 2 percent of the teacher work force. These special teachers would be employed on a twelve-month contract. They would be specially trained and supported. Their job would be to develop and implement in any classroom in the district a self-contained lesson or series of lessons (perhaps organized like a workshop) that would constitute an enrichment activity for the students and a demonstration lesson for other teachers. More specifically, the lesson should be so fine-tuned that no student would get this material unless a demonstration teacher were available to provide it. Moreover, it should be designed to show other techniques and materials they can incorporate into their regular work should they choose to do so.

The demonstration teachers would also serve as substitute teachers to support the training and development functions that would be going forward in the district. When teachers are taken from their classrooms for developmental work, their students would get an enrichment lesson rather than an ill-prepared substitute teacher. In addition to making it possible for regular classroom teachers to participate in developmental activities without compromising their own success in the classroom, the role of demonstration teacher would be inherently developmental throughout the system. Apart from the obvious training opportunities provided by having demonstration teachers present in the schools on a regular basis, these teachers would themselves be undergoing continuous development and training. Indeed, if the role were constructed so that esteem attached to being appointed a demonstration teacher, and if such appointments were temporary (two to three years), such roles could do much to enrich the school system's reward structure and provide for the continuing growth and development of outstanding teachers in the district.

Fourth, the board would be informed that, in the long run, I would want to establish a high-level office in the district responsible for coordinating all human resource development and school improvement activity, as well as supporting local school initiatives to improve their capacity to produce results and to seek other sources of support and cooperation for the district's efforts to invent schools for the twenty-first century. Though I would not expect action immediately, I would request that the board approve, in concept, the direction proposed.

Finally, I would present the board with my action plan for the following nine months. This plan is described below.

The First Year

We have been assuming that I would be functioning as a newly hired superintendent. Actually, such an assumption is not necessary. If I were an established superintendent who had come to the conclusion that I needed to move the system in a different direction—and many superintendents are coming to such a conclusion—I would do pretty much the same things.

What is important, I think, is that during the initial period of a change effort everything must be done with sufficient drama and flair that people *believe* things are going to change. The system must be unfrozen before it can be put together in new ways. This process of unfreezing creates uncertainty, fear, and anxiety and can threaten the tenure of the superintendent, board members, and others. But without such activity things will surely not change much.

As part of the unfreezing process, I would indicate to the board that I did not intend to spend as much time, during the first year, on the matters that often occupy superintendents. Insofar as possible I would delegate responsibility for the day-to-day routine of running the school district to others and would provide only general supervision. If the school district already had a tradition of participatory leadership and true team management, this would not be a new departure. If, however, the system had previously operated as a top-down bureaucracy, such a move would be sufficiently alarming to require discussion. If the prior situation was top-down bureaucracy, I would probably be accused by some of "not doing my job"—until it was learned that I was in the process of redefining my job.

During the first year of implementing a plan to reinvent schools, I see the superintendent's role as primarily concerned with teaching, listening, reacting, developing, and learning. Indeed, during this first year the superintendent must not only be head of the school district but also the head of human resource development, marketing, and product (vision) development. Obviously I need help. How do I get it?

The first step would be to take the board and top union officials (if a collective bargaining unit) or other elected teacher leaders away on a retreat. Its focus would be on my statement of beliefs. (I might hire an outside consultant to facilitate this meeting if I were not confident that someone inside could do the job.) My goal would be to ensure that those in attendance fully understood what I meant by these statements and why I made them. Moreover, I would want to see how this audience reacted to my proposal and I would want to hear how these beliefs could be modified to gain the strongest possible support.

Following the retreat with the board and union leaders, I would rewrite the belief statement in light of the comments I had received. Copies of the revision highlighting these changes, along with copies of the initial statement, would be sent to all who had participated in the retreat. (It is not enough to hear people; they must see and hear themselves being heard.) If a particularly strong piece of advice were not taken—there is no obligation to take all advice—I would make sure that the person understood why the advice was rejected. He or she might not like my reasoning, but would know I took his or her views seriously. Watching strong superintendents at work, I have observed that people are more concerned that their advice be heard and taken seriously than that it be acted on. Most people—except the unreasonable and those who fasten on single issues at the expense of all other considerations—understand that the complexity of school life makes it difficult to do everything everybody wants all the time.

Simultaneously I would call a meeting, again probably in a retreat setting, with all central office department heads and all those who have, or think they have, authority at the district level. With these people I would repeat the process I initiated with the board and the union. And I would again revise the statement based on their comments and again inform everyone who attended about my revisions. Next, in cooperation with the union president, I would hold meetings with principals and building representatives. The purpose of these meetings would be to repeat the process yet another time. At this point, though, I would begin to shift tactics. Once I had been through a round with the principals and building representatives, I would work with the president of the board, the union president, key leaders among the principals, and key influentials from the central office hierarchy and the union hierarchy to enlist members for a steering committee. This committee would take the revised revision (or the revised revised revision) of the belief statement and rewrite it, taking into account the views of building-level faculties. Principals would be instructed to work with key teachers to lead their faculties through an exercise similar to the process the principals themselves had been through. Faculties would then be asked to rewrite the belief statement in a way that would satisfy local concerns.

Here my goal is to get ideas from each building. It is also to help principals develop skills as developmental leaders. (Depending on the circumstances, I or someone I had confidence in would probably conduct workshops to prepare principals for this task.) Another goal would be to encourage collaboration between teacher leaders and principals. Through such a process, one could develop a belief statement that is officially endorsed by the board and the union—a statement in which most teachers and administrators believe and in which they are involved. It is upon such a foundation that schools of the future might be built.

Translating Beliefs into Action

Humankind aspired to go to the moon for many generations. It was not until the 1960s, however, that such a goal became attainable. And at the time this goal was set, it was not in fact attainable—the technology was not in place, and there were many things scientists had yet to learn if moon travel was to be possible. Tang, the orange-flavored fruit drink, had not been thought of, for example, and some of the problems of reentry were beyond imagining. Yet a president pointed to the moon and said, "We'll be there within this decade." And we made it.

Of course, many factors contributed to the success of the United States' moon program. But one should never underestimate the significance of the fact that scientists and laymen had a relatively clear notion of where the moon was and what the moon was. And through the exercise of strong leadership, John F. Kennedy and Lyndon B. Johnson were able to develop and sustain a commitment doing whatever was necessary, including inventing yet to be imagined technologies, to achieve the vision they had set.

One of the greatest barriers to school reform is the lack of a clear and compelling vision. One cannot get to the moon if one does not know what the moon looks like or where it is. A belief statement like the one set forth above provides a moral equivalent to the moon. Such a belief statement indicates a world that one wants to invent, to create, to make real. Surely we know that under present circumstances every child cannot learn. The belief statement asserts that it is possible to invent a world in which every child will learn. And I could go on.

Unlike Presidents Kennedy and Johnson, school superintendents must first invent the moon before they can turn their attention to devising the means of getting there. It is for this reason that superintendents must exercise strong leadership in developing and articulating throughout the school system a shared vision that is at once compelling and inspiring. Teachers will not be inspired by goals like reducing dropout rates or improving test scores. They will, however, respond to the challenge to invent schools in which both teachers and students have increased opportunities for success—schools in which every teacher is a leader, every leader is a teacher, and every student is a success. At least I have found that teachers and principals and custodians and board members will respond to such visions. But such visions are only compelling when they have the moral authority of the superintendent's office behind them.

Beliefs and visions alone are not enough, however. Beliefs must be supported by actions that translate a vision into concrete reality. What then does one do once the vision has been inculcated to the point that, in Peters and Waterman's (1982) terms, it is held bone deep by most of those who work in and around the school district? First of all, such a dramatic event does not occur overnight or even in a year. Action to translate beliefs into reality must begin even before the vision is widely shared. Indeed, it is in the act of translating the vision that it comes to be shaped and embraced. It is in the act of translating the vision that it takes on meaning for all who participate in the organization.

Second, and probably more important, the specific actions that are needed will depend on the dynamics that surround the creation of the vision. One must learn to think in the long term (strategic thinking) and plan in the short term (tactical planning). Engaging in strategic planning and developing detailed action agendas to achieve a long-term goal may be fine in theory and textbooks, but as the creators of strategic planning models (General Electric Corporation) have discovered, strategic planning is not all it is cracked up to be. Selecting a future and pursuing it with all the energy, wisdom, and resources at one's command require strategic thinking in the long run and purposeful action in the short run.

If a plan is effective, its implementation will change the environment in ways that cannot be anticipated in the short term. Since long-term plans must be made in the short term and are based on assessments of present reality, rather than on the reality that is being invented, long-term plans are necessarily based on faulty assumptions. This is why strong leaders understand that planning is an act of implementation and that one cannot separate planning from doing. Planning *is* doing—and what one does affects future plans.

There are, however, two observations that would guide my short-term actions toward the long-term agenda. First, if schools are to become the dynamic organizations they must be to satisfy the conditions of the twenty-first century, then the school's management and leadership style must shift from management-by-programs (making sure people do things right) to leadership-by-results (insisting that people do the right things and giving them latitude to judge what those things are). Second, productivity in knowledge-work organizations is productivity through people. To improve the productivity of knowledge-work enterprises, one must invest in people, support people, and develop people. Indeed, human resource development becomes the linchpin upon which all improvement efforts are based. The strategy of the knowledge-work enterprise begins and ends with people—the support of people, the development of people, and the creation of an environment in which people feel free to express themselves as creative individuals and feel supported when they try and fail.

Given these observations, my early efforts to restructure the school district would focus on two priorities (in addition to creating a compelling vision statement). First, I would want to improve the school district's capacity to lead by results. Second, I would want to ensure that the district had a human resource development capacity that was adequate to the tasks set by a results-oriented leadership system committed to continuous improvement and perpetual change.

Creating a Results-Oriented System

Most discussions of results-oriented management in education proceed from the tacit assumption that students are products of the school—in other words, the factory model of schooling. David Kearns, the CEO of Xerox Corporation and a thoughtful advocate of restructuring in schools, makes this assumption clear when he asserts that the reason for restructuring schools is that they are producing too many defective products, by which he means students. A results-oriented management system will have little chance of success so long as students are viewed as products. Such a view allows for too much scapegoating, and it is based on assumptions that are not believable to teachers and administrators.

In an effective results-oriented management system, those who are held accountable for results believe that these results are important and that they themselves can do something about them. The results most commonly advocated by those who would make school systems and teachers "more accountable" are results such as test scores and dropouts—results over which teachers and administrators feel they have little direct control and in which they have little confidence as useful measures of quality. In the short term at least, it is probably preferable to avoid such measures if one's intention is to develop the confidence of teachers and administrators in the concept of leading by results.

To many teachers and to many administrators, the reason for low test scores is that the "raw material" they start with is not very good. As I indicated earlier, this means that the children were born to poverty, their parents are less supportive of the schools than they should be, television is distracting them, and on it goes. There is, furthermore, considerable evidence to support the educator's view on these matters, which makes it even more tempting to blame the victim. (In a recent national survey conducted by the Carnegie Foundation for the Advancement of Teaching, nearly 80 percent of the teachers interviewed believe that most of the causes for school failure have to do with things over which teachers have little control—parental support, nutrition, child abuse, and so on.)

The advocates for accountability and results regard the educator's reluctance to use these "obvious" results to assess school performance as irresponsible. Many, in fact, think such reluctance is evidence that teachers and administrators are trying to escape accountability. To these critics, especially members of the business community and the press, schools are not producing the results that are needed and these results are best indicated by test scores, dropout rates, and the like. These critics, therefore, push schools to produce better test scores and lower dropout rates.

Some go so far as to suggest that merit pay will help since the real problem is that teachers are not working as hard as they could. Just put a little money on the line and test scores will improve. Nonsense! Schools will never improve if educators allow others to put them into the test-score, keeping-children-in-school, reducing-vandalism-rates, and reducing-suspensions business. And educators who put themselves in this business are playing a dangerous game. In the short term, certain things can in fact be done to improve test scores marginally. By articulating the curriculum with the test, for example, a euphemism that means teaching to the test, one can improve scores. And as some districts and teachers have shown, there are even more direct means of improving test scores, not the least appealing of which is to cheat.

Test scores, dropout rates, vandalism rates, and suspension rates are results toward which school systems need to be managed. Such measures indicate whether the school is doing its business as it should. If students do not come to school or if they do come to school and tear the school apart or tear each other apart, there is something wrong with the way the school is doing its business. Test scores and dropout rates can be used to indicate that something is wrong—just as profit margins and market share can be used to indicate that something is wrong at Ford or General Motors—but such scores cannot be used to indicate *what* is wrong. Furthermore, there is little that teachers and building-level administrators can do in a direct sense to affect these scores, any more than a first-line manager at Ford can directly affect profit or market share.

What teachers and administrators can do is ensure that the school does its business right. And what is the business of the school? To produce schoolwork that will engage the young to the point that they try it, stick with it, and succeed at it. If students do this work but test scores do not improve, dropout rates do not decrease, and vandalism rates do not diminish, it may be that students are being given the wrong work. The fact remains that the students most likely to fail are those the schools are not getting engaged in doing schoolwork—the dropouts, the truants, those who are euphemistically termed "at risk." Furthermore, even those who are doing well on tests are sometimes not challenged to excel at the schoolwork they are assigned, for the schoolwork assigned is work they can do without succeeding. (Recall that I defined success as an achievement in an area where the outcome is problematic—that is, where there is some risk of failure.) Many of the most talented children in school will resist restructuring, too, because restructuring will place them "at risk" in that they will have to learn to do forms of schoolwork that will stretch their talents and cause them to learn things they would not have learned outside of school.

The results by which school systems must be led are the results that are consistent with the purpose of school, as that purpose is articulated in the school's vision statement and belief structure. In schools as knowledge-work enterprises, the school's business is to ensure that each child, each day, is successfully engaged in working on and with knowledge and knowledge-related products. The results by which schools should be led, therefore, are results that are clear indicators of student success.

Those who would manage by results in school must understand that student learning is a result of student success in doing schoolwork; evidence of learning is not a short-term indicator of student success any more than a quarterly profit statement is an indicator of the quality of an automobile. Quality indicators have to do with the nature of the product itself—and in schools as knowledge-work organizations that product, simply stated, is schoolwork.

What is needed is a results-oriented management system that focuses internal attention on producing quality schoolwork for children. If this can be accomplished, test scores, dropout rates, and so on will improve, just as Ford Motor Company and Xerox have found that as they began to emphasize customer needs and product quality, rather than engineering and accounting, profits began to increase.

Clearly one of the new technologies that must be put in place is a means of measuring the qualitative aspects of schoolwork, for it is by such qual itative results that schools of the future must be led. This problem is too important to turn over to the measurement specialist. The inventors of these measures must be the people who will use them and be directed by them—that is, teachers, principals, and superintendents. It is hard work and it is heady work. Such work takes time, and it is never completed, for measures wear out just as slogans wear out and just as today's innovations become stale and routine next year.

Measures must focus attention on elements of systems that people believe can make a difference in the results toward which the system is managed. If teachers believe that doing homework increases learning, for example, then homework results need to be measured. Do students do the homework? Are there certain kinds of homework students are more likely to do than others? At what rate and frequency are various kinds of homework assignments turned in? These are results teachers can believe in— and teachers can invent measures of such results in which they can have confidence.

What is needed is a style of leadership that insists on the creation of such measures and provides the training and support necessary to ensure that the measures are constantly being invented. Thus if I were a superintendent, one of the first things I would do is to educate myself and others about the problems and prospects of quality measures. If I went outside the school district for help, I would be very cautious about turning to conventional education measurement specialists, for most of these experts are by training and inclination psychometricians. Psychometric procedures have their place in the education enterprise, just as accounting procedures have their place in business. But businesses that are run by the accounting department usually fail, and I suspect that one of the reasons for our present distress in education is that we have too long allowed the psychometric interests to determine how our schools are led and evaluated.

Human Resource Development

If teachers and school administrators are to behave as leaders rather than as managers and technicians, then school systems must invent leadership development systems that are at least as sophisticated as those in the business sector. Teachers are not independent professionals as are physicians and attorneys. Teachers are, of necessity, part of a "corporate" structure, and their effectiveness is at least partly determined by the way the "corporations" in which they work are organized and managed. Teachers have effects, but schools have effects as well.

The continuing education of teachers and administrators is, or should be, the responsibility of the employer, just as is the case with other corporate employers (including hospitals and law firms). Teachers and administrators should be expected to participate in continuing education because it is part of their job, not because it is a requirement to keep their certificates or licenses current. If it is part of the job, it must be viewed that way, not as a nonessential requirement to be satisfied in some ritual fashion. The quality of work in continuing education, for example, should be as much a part of an employee appraisal system as is the quality of work in any other part of the work of the teacher or administrator. Participation in continuing education is not enough; quality participation is expected—or so it should be. Work days and work years should be adjusted to accommodate this expectation.

In large systems, this probably means creating a facility to support human resource development, school improvement, and leadership development activity, perhaps something like the Jefferson County Public Schools/Gheens Professional Development Academy in Louisville, Kentucky. This organization, which I helped to create, is designed to function much like a leadership development center for a large corporation combined with certain characteristics that have come to be associated with teacher centers. Besides carrying out a variety of training and development programs, the academy is officially charged with encouraging local school faculties in the effort to restructure their schools. At the same time, the academy works with district personnel to create a supportive environment at the top as well. (See Kyle, 1988.) In smaller school districts, providing appropriate support may mean creating a consortium arrangement with other school districts to invent a human resource development system that can meet the needs of a variety of school districts and maintain quality at a level that might be impossible in a single small district. Alternatively, state education agencies might create organizations that could respond to the human resource development needs of smaller school districts. Illustrations of such systems abound in the United States. In any case, school districts must have a clear vision of where they are going so that existing organizations might better serve them. And where these organizations do not exist, new organizations can be invented. Moreover, it is critical that the organizations designed to serve teachers and administrators in local schools be responsive to these schools as opposed to some externally imposed mandates.

Another possible source of support for human resource development is local institutions of higher education. Assuming that these institutions are oriented toward schools as customers for their services, and assuming that their reward structure is such that qualified faculty are encouraged to provide responsive support to schools, universities and colleges can be valuable allies in the quest for superior human resource development programs. Unfortunately, it often turns out that these institutions are structured in ways that discourage professors from responding to the human resource development needs of school districts. Furthermore, these structures often discourage faculty from linking their private agendas to the larger cause of school reform. Unless such links exist or can be created, efforts to use higher education's resources to support human resource development in schools can be more bother than benefit—at least I have found it so.

As a superintendent, I would approach the university as if I were a customer for services. I would try to negotiate with leaders in the various departments to provide the training and support my school district's programs seemed to need. I would listen to their advice. I would however, be prepared to commit the school district to producing what was needed if a preferred-customer arrangement could not be worked out. Moreover, I would ensure that the products and materials the university delivered to the school district were tailored to meet the system's needs. I would not take any old course, workshop, or seminar that was sitting on the shelf waiting for someone to buy it.

If schools of education and universities are going to contribute to reinventing our schools, they too must become inventive. There is much that colleges and universities can do, and should do, to help restructure schools, but in many instances such help will not be available until higher education, especially that part of higher education which has to do with the education of teachers and administrators, has undergone its own form of restructuring. School leaders must do all they can to support reform in higher education, but school leaders must also be prepared to move on their own if higher education cannot be restructured to provide the support that is needed. (See Schlechty, 1989, for a detailed discussion of the restructuring of teacher education.)

Above all, I would keep in mind that local teachers and local administrators are the greatest resources available for increasing the human resource development capacity of the school district. What we need are structures and commitments that liberate the potential that is already there.

The Restructuring Agenda

Creating the capacity to assess results by which one can lead and by which decisions can be disciplined is an essential prerequisite to the systematic restructuring of schools. Without such a capacity, one has no basis for determining how well restructuring decisions are working in practice and no basis for analyzing what parts of the system need to be further restructured. Creating a human resource development capacity is essential to assuring that the needed training and support system will be available when restructuring efforts place strains on individuals and systems. But neither measuring results more effectively nor creating an improved human resource development system constitutes school restructuring. School restructuring begins with a vision that is compelling and satisfies values held by those who live and work in schools. Restructuring occurs when rules, roles, and relationships are altered in whatever way seems appropriate to assuring that the vision can be pursued in progressively more effective ways.

What, then, must be restructured? As a beginning I would nominate the following elements as likely candidates. First, the pattern of decision making that typifies schools probably needs to change. Participatory leadership will be the mode of operation in healthy school districts committed to student success. I would, therefore, be likely to assess all schools and departments in terms of their capacity for and commitment to shared decision making. I would encourage results-oriented, shared decision making in every area of school life and would orient the human resource development unit in a way that would provide whatever training and support would be required to ensure that this operating style could be implemented.

Second, I would explore ways of reorienting the school district departments that are not located in school buildings but are staffed with people whose skills would be useful to building-level principals and teachers in their efforts to invent schoolwork for students. The role of the central office supervisor or curriculum coordinator, for example, might be restructured so that these positions were locked into building-level work teams which principals and teachers might establish for the purpose of creating new curriculum materials or for studying alternative uses of technology to support local instructional activity. The critical point is that I would want to structure the central office so that its personnel were responsive to building-level initiatives rather than being in a position to control or direct (except through expert advice) these initiatives. This would mean, I suspect, that few central office personnel would have independent budgets beyond what they need to support their personal activities (such as access to a pool secretary). I would, of course, want to have central coordination of effort. In a small school district, the superintendent alone could probably provide the coordination. In a larger district some assistance would be needed, but my goal as superintendent would be to have a lean and responsive central staff. The focus of this group would be to support building-level initiatives, to provide a collection and monitoring point for the assessment of results, to serve as a catalyst for innovation, and to facilitate the exchange of information about improvements and advances.

Third, eventually I would want a thorough review of policies, procedures, rules, and regulations. My goal would be to identify pointless constraints on building-level decisions. Subsequently, a strategy for changing these constraints would be developed. Special attention would be given to providing training and support where changes in policy called upon teachers and building-level administrators to assume responsibilities that had heretofore resided in the central office. A strategy for creating political coalitions with the teachers' union and superintendents from other school districts, as well as with local legislators, would also be developed, since many of the more constraining elements in school district life have their origin in state law and state regulations. It would be my intent to assert the legitimacy of the superintendent in the political arena as well as in the educational arena, since in a democracy politics and education are necessarily interwoven.

Fourth, public education dealing with education issues and the building of alliances with local groups and agencies concerned with the quality of education would be a high priority. If a local education foundation did not exist, I would work to have one established. This foundation would serve as the conduit and coordinating point for school/business partnerships and would energetically seek developmental funding from nongovernment sources (such as local foundations). I would also work closely with the media. I might try, for example, to write a regular super-intendent's column in the local newspaper, based more on the style of Albert Shanker's column in the *New York Times* than on the style of a local education "puff piece." The column's purpose would be to educate the community about education. Similarly, I might try to have a local education issues program on radio or television. I would certainly take advantage of opportunities to speak to local groups regarding my assessment of the local situation within the national context and with regard to prospects and problems as I see them. In my view, superintendents who tell the community what the problems are and invite community help in solving them do better, in the long run, than those who try to conceal the problems until they can deal with them. Sometimes a strategy of candor will backfire, but in over twenty years of superintendent watching I have seen fewer superintendents get in trouble for their candor than for their efforts to conceal.

Finally, I would try to see that each employee, department, administrative unit, and school faculty would be required to submit a growth and improvement plan. The plan would clearly focus on one interrelated set of questions: What can I do differently next year to increase the rate and frequency of student success in my area of responsibility? If I do these things, what will I need to know that I do not know now and what support will I need in order to learn it? If I do these things, how will I know that what I thought would work did in fact work, and will others be convinced? The same plan would contain a deletion clause that called upon every person and unit to indicate one thing they were prepared to quit doing because they had found better ways to spend their time, energy, and resources.

Such a procedure could not be, and should not be, installed without a great deal of support and training. It needs to be modeled from the top. Therefore, the superintendent should expect to file a similar plan. (It would not be a bad idea for board members as well.) And the goals of the exercise should be kept clearly in mind: to maintain a focus on results; to encourage innovation and continuous improvement; and to promote growth and development in all parts of the system.

Concluding Remarks

Obviously, if I were superintendent there would be many things I could not do. There would also be many things I would need to do that I would prefer not to do. And time would often preclude my being as thorough as I would like. But of the actions I have listed above, there is not one that

.I have not seen some superintendent do in some form and with considerable effect. There are men and women in superintendents' offices who are as deserving of recognition as any of the CEOs who appear in the popular books on leadership. The school reform movement depends, in large measure, on the ability of these strong leaders to find their voice in the national debate on education reform. In my opinion, this voice is now muted. Most of what is heard from superintendents in the national debate comes from the reactionary, rather than the progressive, members of the superintendents' ranks.

REFERENCES

Kyle, R. M. *Innovation in Education: A Progress Report on the JCPS/Gheens Professional Development Academy.* Louisville: Gheens Foundation, 1988.

Mills, C. W. *The Causes of World War Three.* (2nd ed.) Armonk, N.Y.: M. E. Sharpe, 1985.

Peters, T. J., and Waterman, R. H. *In Search of Excellence: Lessons from America's Best Run Companies.* New York: Harper & Row, 1982.

Schlechty, P. C. *Reform in Teacher Education: A Sociological View.* Washington, D.C.: American Association of Colleges for Teacher Education, 1989.

15

EIGHT ROLES OF SYMBOLIC LEADERS

Terrence E. Deal
Kent D. Peterson

CULTURE ARISES IN response to persisting conditions, novel changes, challenging losses, and enduring ambiguous or paradoxical puzzles. People create culture; thereafter it shapes them. However, school leaders can nudge the process along through their actions, conversations, decisions, and public pronouncements.

Effective school leaders are always alert to the deeper issues agitating beneath a seemingly rational veneer of activity. They read between the lines to decipher complex cultural codes and struggle to figure out what's really going on. Once they get a bead on a situation, they ponder over whether and how to try to shape or reshape existing realities. In effect, they are asking three basic questions: (1) What is the culture of the school now—its history, values, traditions, assumptions, and ways? (2) What can I do to strengthen aspects of the culture that already fit my idea of an ideal school? and (3) What can be done to change or reshape the culture, when I see a need for a new direction?

As they labor to meld past, present, and future into a coherent cultural tapestry, school leaders assume several symbolic roles in their work to shape features of the culture.

Reading the Current School Culture

How do school leaders read and shape the cultures of their respective schools? To find that out, we borrow from anthropology and coin our own metaphors for school leaders' roles: historian, anthropological sleuth, visionary, symbol, potter, poet, actor, and healer.

It is important to remember the formidable nature of school leaders' unofficial power to reshape school culture toward an "ethos of excellence" and make quality an authentic part of the daily routine of school life. School leaders must understand their school—its patterns, the purposes they serve, and how they came to be. Changing something that is not well understood is a surefire recipe for stress and ultimate failure. A leader must inquire below the surface of what is happening to formulate a deeper explanation of what is really going on. To be effective, school leaders must read and understand their school and community culture.

Reading culture takes several forms: watching, sensing, listening, interpreting, using all of one's senses, and even employing intuition when necessary.

First, the leader must listen to the echoes of school history. The past exists in the cultural present.

Second, the leader should look at the present. More important, the leader must listen for the deeper dreams and hopes the school community holds for the future. Every school is a repository of unconscious sentiments and expectations that carry the code of the collective dream—the high ground to which they aspire. This represents emerging energy that leaders can tap and a deep belief system to which he or she can appeal when articulating what the school might become.

A school leader can get an initial reading of the current culture by posing several key questions about the current realities and future dreams of the school (Deal and Peterson, 1990):

What does the school's architecture convey? How is space arranged and used? What subcultures exist inside and outside the school? Who are the recognized (and unrecognized) heroes and villains of the school? What do people say (and think) when asked what the school stands for? What events are assigned special importance? How is conflict typically defined? How is it handled? What are the key ceremonies and stories of the school? What do people wish for? Are there patterns to their individual dreams?

Shaping a School Culture: The Roles of School Leaders

When school leaders have reflected and feel they understand a school's culture, they can evaluate the need to shape or reinforce it. Valuable aspects of the school's existing culture can be reinforced, problematic ones revitalized, and toxic ones given strong antidotes.

Everyone should be a leader. The eight major leadership roles to be listed next can be taken on by principals, teachers, staff members, parents, and community leaders. Cultural leaders reinforce the underlying norms, values, and beliefs. They support the central mission and purpose of the school. They create and sustain motivation and commitment through rites and rituals. It is not only the formal leadership of the principal that sustains and continuously reshapes culture but the leadership of everyone. Deep, shared leadership builds strong and cohesive cultures.

School leaders take on eight major symbolic roles:

> *Historian:* seeks to understand the social and normative past of the school
>
> *Anthropological sleuth:* analyzes and probes for the current set of norms, values, and beliefs that define the current culture
>
> *Visionary:* works with other leaders and the community to define a deeply value-focused picture of the future for the school; has a constantly evolving vision
>
> *Symbol:* affirms values through dress, behavior, attention, routines
>
> *Potter:* shapes and is shaped by the school's heroes, rituals, traditions, ceremonies, symbols; brings in staff who share core values
>
> *Poet:* uses language to reinforce values and sustains the school's best image of itself
>
> *Actor:* improvises in the school's inevitable dramas, comedies, and tragedies
>
> *Healer:* oversees transitions and change in the life of the school; heals the wounds of conflict and loss

School Leaders as Historians

Effective school leaders probe deeply into time, work, social, and normative events that have given texture to the culture of a school. They realize that echoes of past crises, challenges, and successes reverberate in the present. Leaders perpetuate an understanding of where the school has been as a key factor in interpreting present practices and ways. Staff and parents take on this role whenever new people arrive or new parents join the community.

One of the best ways of tracking the past is to construct an "organizational timeline" that depicts the flow of events, ideas, and key personages over several decades. This provides a chronological portrait of the events, circumstances, and key leaders who shaped the personality of the school.

School Leaders as Anthropological Sleuths

Anthropological sleuths are just what the name depicts—a cross between Margaret Mead and Columbo—serious students of the culture as well as dogged detectives. Both roles are important, as school leaders listen and look for clues and signs to the school's present rituals and values.

School leaders must unearth the pottery shards and secret ceremonies of daily activity in teachers' lounges, workrooms, and hallway greetings that reflect deeper features of the culture. Nothing is ever as it seems, and one must look for unexpected interpretations of common human activity.

For example, in one innovative school teachers started wearing the drug program badge that states, "Just Say No." They did it, not to reinforce drug awareness week but to uphold their desire to slow the pace of curricular change for a little while. Knowing the meaning of the badge was important to understanding the culture.

School Leaders as Visionaries

In addition to their role as historian or anthropologist, school leaders must also be visionaries. Through a careful probe of past and present, they need to identify a clear sense of what the school can become, a picture of a positive future. Visionary leaders continually identify and communicate the hopes and dreams of the school, thus refocusing and refining the school's purpose and mission. To arrive at a shared vision, they listen closely for the cherished dreams that staff and community hold. They probe for the latent sentiments, values, and expectations for the future and bring these to the front for public discussion, consideration, and enactment.

Developing a shared vision for the school can motivate students, staff, and community alike. It is not simply for the leader; it is for the common good. By seeking the more profound hopes of all stakeholders, school leaders can weave independent ideas into a collective vision (Deal and Peterson, 1994).

Visionaries can be found anywhere in a school. For example, in Chicago's Piccolo Elementary School the president of the local school council, who was a parent and community leader, joined with the principal to identify and communicate the hopes and dreams for the school. Together they worked to focus on developing a caring, safe, and academically focused learning environment. Another example: At Hollibrook Elementary, the principal and the teachers jointly shared and protected the vision for the school, even as staff and administration changed. When Suzanne Still, the principal, and some teachers left for other positions, remaining staff leaders helped preserve the dream by pulling the new principal into the collective vision.

School Leaders as Symbols

Everyone watches leaders in a school. Everything they do gets people's attention. Educational philosophy, teaching reputation, demeanor, communication style, and other characteristics are important signals that will be read by members of the culture in a variety of ways. Who school leaders are—what they do, attend to, or seem to appreciate—is constantly watched by students, teachers, parents, and members of the community. Their interests and actions send powerful messages. They signal the values they hold. Above all else, leaders are cultural "teachers" in the best sense of the word.

Actions of leaders communicate meaning, value, and focus. We rarely "see" an action's symbolic value at the time it occurs. More often we realize it later, as it soaks in. For example, the principal's morning "building tour" may be a functional walk to investigate potential trouble spots or building maintenance problems. In some schools, teachers and students see the same walk as a symbolic event, a ritual demonstrating that the principal cares about the learning environment. Similarly, the visit of a teacher-leader to another's class to observe a unique and successful lesson can send the message that instruction is valued.

Schools are filled with many routine tasks that often take on added significance. Routine tasks take on symbolic meaning when leaders show sincere personal concern for core values and purposes while carrying them out. A classroom visit, building tour, or staff meeting may be nothing more than routine activity—or it can become a symbolic expression of the deeper values the leader holds for the school.

Almost all actions of school leaders can have symbolic content when a school community understands the actions' relevance to shared values. Seemingly innocuous actions send signals as to what leaders value. This is done in many ways, but five possibilities are as follows:

Symbolize core values in the way offices and classrooms are arranged. A principal's office, for example, sends strong messages. Its location, accessibility, decoration, and arrangement reflect the principal's values. One principal works from her couch in an office in the school's entryway; another is hidden in a corner suite behind a watchful and protective secretary. One principal decorates her office walls with students' work; another displays athletic trophies, public service awards, posters of favorite works of art, and photographs of his family. These social artifacts signal to others what the principal sees as important.

The arrangement of classrooms also sends a powerful message. Is student work displayed? Is it current? Is there a wide variety of learning activities, materials, and books readily available? Do teachers have a professional library, awards, or certificates for professional institutes nearby? Physical arrangements reverberate with values.

Model values through the leader's demeanor and actions. What car a leader drives, his or her clothes, posture, gestures, facial expression, sense of humor, and personal idiosyncrasies send signals of formality or informality, approachability or distance, concern or lack of concern. A wink following a reprimand can have as much effect on a child as the verbal reprimand itself. A frown, a smile, a grimace, or a blank stare—each may send a potent message. Do staff interact with students and parents when they cross into school territory? Are energy and joy apparent in the faces of teachers?

Use time, a key scarce resource, to communicate what is important, what should be attended to. How leaders spend their time and where they focus attention sends strong signals about what they value. A community quickly discerns discrepancies between espoused values and true values by what issues receive time and attention. The appointment book and daily routines signal what a principal values. And whether staff attend and engage in discussions with parents during Parent Association Meetings or site-based council gatherings shows what the culture holds most dear.

Realize that what is appreciated, recognized, and honored signals the key values of what is admirable and achievable. School leaders signal appreciation formally through official celebrations and public recognition and rewards. Informally, their daily behavior and demeanor communicate their preference about quality teaching, correct behavior, and desired cultural traditions. Staff and students are particularly attentive to the values displayed and rewarded by various school leaders in moments of social or organizational crisis.

Recognize that official correspondence is a visible measure of values and reinforces the importance of what is being disseminated. The form, emphasis, and volume of memos and newsletters communicate as strongly as what is written. Memos may be a source of inspiration, a celebration of success, or a collection of bureaucratic jargon, rules, and regulations. Class or departmental newsletters can send a message to parents that communication and connection are important. Even the appearance of written material will be noticed, from the informality of the penciled note to the care evidenced by the new color inkjet printer. Pride, humor, affection, and even fatigue displayed in writing send signals as to what a school's leaders value.

Taken together, all these aspects of a leader's behavior form a public persona that carries symbolic meaning. They come with the territory of being a school leader and play a powerful role in shaping the culture of a school.

School Leaders as Potters

School leaders shape the elements of school culture (its values, ceremonies, and symbols), much the way a potter shapes clay—patiently, with skill, and with an emerging idea of what the pot will eventually look like. As potters, school leaders shape the culture in a variety of ways. Four illustrations of how leaders shape school culture follow:

They infuse shared values and beliefs into every aspect of the culture. It often falls to the principal, formally and informally, to articulate the philosophical principles that embody what the school stands for. A valuable service is rendered if the principal and other leaders can express those values in a form that makes them memorable, easily grasped, and engaging. But teachers are also powerful communicators of values whenever they meet parents in the hallway, run into a school board member in the grocery store, or jog with a local businesswoman. What they say and do sends messages about the school and its values as compellingly as if they were giving a speech.

Values are often condensed into slogans or mottos that help communicate the character of a school. Of course, to ring true they must reflect the school's practices and beliefs. Examples are (1) "Every child a promise" (2) "A commitment to People. We care. A commitment to Excellence. We dare. A commitment to Partnership. We share" and (3) "A Community of Learners" (Deal and Peterson, 1990). In some schools, symbols take the place of slogans but play a similarly expressive role. One middle school's values are embodied in the symbol of a frog. The frog reflects the school's commitment to caring and affection that eventually can turn all children into "princes and princesses."

They celebrate heroes and heroines, anointing and recognizing the best role models in the school. There are important individuals in most schools, past and present, who exemplify shared virtue. Heroes and heroines, living and dead, personify values and serve as role models for others. Students, teachers, parents, and custodians may qualify for special status and recognition through words or deeds that reflect what a school holds most dear. Like stories about Amelia Earhart or Charles Lindbergh, the stories of these local heroes help motivate people and teach cultural ways. When heroes exemplify qualities a school wants to reinforce, leaders can recognize these individuals publicly. Schools can commemorate teachers or administrators in pictures, plaques, or special ceremonies just as businesses, hospitals, or military units do.

They observe rituals as a means of building and maintaining esprit de corps. School leaders shape culture by encouraging rituals that celebrate important values. As noted earlier, everyday tasks take on added significance when they symbolize something special. School activities may become rituals when they express values and bind people in a common experience.

These rituals are stylized, communal behavior that reinforces collective values and beliefs. Here is an example:

> A new superintendent of schools opened his first districtwide convocation by lighting a small lamp, which he labeled the "lamp of learning." After the event, no one mentioned the lamp. The next year, prior to the convocation, several people inquired: "You are going to light the lamp of learning again, aren't you?" The lighting of the lamp had been accepted as a symbolically meaningful ritual.

Rituals take various forms (Deal and Peterson, 1990). Some rituals are social and others center around work. Americans shake hands, Italians hug, and French people kiss both cheeks when greeting or parting. Surgical teams scrub for seven minutes, although germs are destroyed by modern germicides in thirty seconds. Members of the British artillery, when firing a cannon, still feature an individual who holds his hand in a position that once kept the horse from bolting because "that's the way it has always been done."

Meetings, parties, informal lunches, and school openings or closings provide opportunity for rituals. As we saw earlier, Herring closed meetings by offering an opportunity for anyone to share stories of positive events. In this setting, issues can be aired, accomplishments recognized, disagreements expressed, or exploits retold. These rituals bond people to each other—and connect them with deeper values that are otherwise difficult to express.

They perpetuate meaningful, value-laden traditions and ceremonies. Schoolwide ceremonies allow us to put cultural values on display, to retell important stories, and to recognize the exploits and accomplishments of important individuals. These special events tie past, present, and future together. They intensify everyone's commitment to the organization and revitalize them for challenges that lie ahead.

When an authentic ceremony is convened in a hallowed place, given a special touch, and accorded a special rhythm and flow, it builds momentum and expresses sincere emotions. Planning and staging these events is often done with extreme care. Encouraging and orchestrating such special ceremonies provide still another opportunity for leaders to shape—and to be shaped by—the culture of the school. Here is an example:

> One group of parents—with input from the high school leadership—planned a joyous celebration for the school's teachers. They decorated the cafeteria using white tablecloths and silver candle holders. They went to the superintendent and asked permission to serve wine and cheese and arranged for a piano bar where teachers and parents could sing together. Each teacher was given a corsage or a ribbon. The supper was potluck, supplied by the parents. After dinner the school choir sang. Several speakers called attention to the significance of the event. The finale came as the principal recognized the parents and asked everyone to join her in a standing ovation for the teachers. The event was moving for both the teachers and the parents and has become a part of the school's tradition.

School Leaders as Poets

We should not forget the straightforward and subtle ways that leaders communicate with language—from memos to mottoes to sagas and stories, as well as in informal conversation. Words and images invoked from the heart convey powerful sentiments. "The achievement scores of my school are above the norm" conveys a very different image from "Our school is a special temple of learning."

Acronyms can separate insiders from outsiders to the school community and tighten camaraderie. (They can also exclude people.) PSAT, CTBS, or NAEP may carry different meanings to educators than to their public. Idioms and slogans ("Every child a promise" or "We Care; We Dare; We Share") may condense shared understandings of a school's values. However, hypocrisy in such slogans can alienate those who hear them. Consider the principal in the satirical book *Up the Down Staircase* (Kaufman, 1966) who would say, "Let it be a challenge to you" in the face of problems that were obviously impossible to solve.

Metaphors may provide "picture words" that consolidate complex ideas into a single, understandable whole. Whether students and teachers think of a school as a factory or a family will have powerful implications for day-to-day behavior.

One of the highest forms of culture-shaping communication is the story. A well-chosen story provides a powerful image that addresses a question without compromising its complexity. Stories ground compli-cated ideas in concrete terms, personifying them in flesh and blood. Sto-ries carry values and connect abstract ideas with sentiment, emotions, and events.

Stories told by or about leaders help followers know what is expected of them. They emphasize what is valued, watched, and rewarded for old-timers and greenhorns alike. For example, the parents of a third-grade student informed the principal that they were planning to move into a new house at Christmas and would therefore be changing schools. He suggested they tell the teacher themselves, since she took a strong per-sonal interest in each of her students. They returned later with the sur-prising announcement that they were postponing their move. The principal asked why. The mother replied, "When we told Mrs. Onfrey about our decision she told us we couldn't transfer our child from her class. She told us that she wasn't finished with him yet."

By repeating such stories, leaders reinforce values and beliefs and so shape the culture of the school. Sagas—stories of unique accomplish-ment, rooted in history and held in sentiment—can convey core values to all of a school's constituents. They can define for the outside world an "in-tense sense of the unique" that captures imagination, engenders loyalty, and secures resources and support from outsiders.

School Leaders as Actors

Cultures are often characterized as theater, that is, the stage on which im-portant events are acted out. If "all the world's a stage," then aspects of the life of a school are fascinating whether they are comedy, tragedy, drama, or action. Technically, they have been called "social dramas"; the various stages of activity in the school cross all forms of theater.

Much of this drama occurs during routine activities of the school. Pe-riodic ceremonies, staged and carefully orchestrated, provide intensified yet predictable drama in any organization. In crises or in critical incidents (like the murder of students in a school yard or the explosion of the space shuttle Challenger) are moments of unforeseen school drama.

A critical incident like a school closing gives leaders a significant opportunity to act in a social drama that can reaffirm or redirect cultural values and beliefs. An example: A principal was concerned about the effect of a school merger on the students and the community. He convened a transition committee made up of teachers and community members to plan, among other things, a ceremony for the last day of school. On that day, the closing school was wrapped in a large red ribbon and filmed from a helicopter. When wreckers had demolished the building, each student, teacher, parent, and observer was given one of the bricks tied with a red ribbon and an aerial photograph of the school tied with a red bow (Deal and Peterson, 1990).

Such drama provides a heightened opportunity to make a historical transition and reaffirm cultural ties within the school community. Rather than inhibiting or stifling such dramas, school leaders may seize them as an opportunity to resolve differences and redirect the school.

Social dramas can be improvisational theater with powerful possibilities to reaffirm or alter values. In a political sense, such events as faculty or student conflicts are arenas—with referees, rounds, rules, spectators, fighters, and seconds. In the arena, conflicts are surfaced and decided rather than left lingering and seething because they have been avoided or ignored. Such avoidance often leads to the development of toxic cultures or subcultures. Critical incidents from this perspective provide school leaders with a significant opportunity to participate in a social drama that can reaffirm or redirect the values and beliefs of the school.

School Leaders as Healers

Most school cultures are stable but not static, and changes do occur. School leaders can play key roles in acknowledging these transitions—healing whatever wounds they create and helping the school adapt to change in terms of its traditions and culture. Leaders serve as healers when

They mark beginnings and endings. Schools celebrate the natural transitions of the year. Every school year has a beginning and an end. Beginnings are marked by convocations to end the summer and outline the vision and hopes for the coming year. Endings are marked by graduations, which usually unite members in a common celebration of the school culture.

They commemorate events and holidays of cultural importance. The observation of national and seasonal holidays, from Cinco de Mayo to Presidents Day, may make the school an important cultural center for events in the local community and reaffirm the school's ties to the wider culture. One school convenes a schoolwide festival each fall, winter, and spring, at which they demonstrate the way the students' religions honor a particular holiday. Because of the diversity among students, such festivals provide an opportunity for students to learn different customs and foods. Such observances create a schoolwide unity around differences that would otherwise become divisive.

They remember and recognize key transitional events in the occupational lives of staff. The beginning and end of employment are episodic transitions that a principal may use to reaffirm the school's culture and its values. What newcomers must learn about the school is a good definition of what is important in its culture. Even transfers, reductions in force, terminations, and firings for cause are transitions that can be marked by cultural events. In one Massachusetts elementary school, primary students named hallways after teachers who had been let go in the wake of a taxpayer rebellion that required tremendous cost reductions in nearly every school in the state (Deal and Peterson, 1990).

They deal directly and openly with critical, difficult, challenging events in the lives of staff and students, always aware of the message they are sending. Unpredictable, calamitous events in the life of the school, like a death or a school closing, will be upsetting to all members of the school community. These transitions require recognition of pain, emotional comfort, and hope. Unless transitions are acknowledged in cultural events, loss and grief will accumulate. For example, at one school following the death of several classmates by two snipers, the school and its community came together at funerals, services, and informal gatherings to remember and eulogize the students. They came together to grieve over the loss of friends, the loss of classmates, the loss of innocence. These events helped the culture cope with their pain and sadness.

School leaders as healers recognize the pain of transitions and arrange events that make the transition a collective experience. Drawing people together to mourn loss and to renew hope is a significant part of a leader's culture-shaping role. Too often, the technical side of leadership eclipses available time and willingness for its much-needed cultural aspects. As a result schools become sterile, incapable of touching the hearts of students and teachers, or securing the trust and confidence of parents and local residents. By expanding their repertoire of symbolic roles, school leaders can make a real difference. Their artistry can help galvanize a diverse group of people into a cohesive community whose members are committed to a beloved institution.

Symbolic leadership is especially needed when schools are new or when they require considerable transformation to serve their students.

REFERENCES

Deal, T. E., and Peterson, K. D. *The Principal's Role in Shaping School Culture.* Washington, D.C.: Office of Educational Research and Improvement, U.S. Department of Education, 1990.

Deal, T. E., and Peterson, K. D. *The Leadership Paradox: Balancing Logic and Artistry in Schools.* San Francisco: Jossey-Bass, 1994.

Kaufman, B. *Up the Down Staircase.* New York: Avon, 1966.

PART THREE

DIVERSITY AND LEADERSHIP

WOMEN MAKE UP a large percentage of the teaching staff and a much smaller percentage of the administrative staff. Our nation, and especially our schools, become increasingly diverse. In Part Three we take a brief look at these trends and their impact on school administration and leadership. Charol Shakeshaft, Irene Nowell, and Andy Perry look at the reasons for the gap in percentages between women teachers and women administrators. Cherry A. McGee Banks examines the effect of gender and race on leadership roles.

16

GENDER AND RACE AS FACTORS IN EDUCATIONAL LEADERSHIP AND ADMINISTRATION

Cherry A. McGee Banks

THIS CHAPTER IS A REVIEW of the status and characteristics of women and people of color in educational leadership and administration. The author's primary intention is to acquaint readers with significant studies and provide a broad overview of the characteristics and experiences of women and people of color who are superintendents and principals. The chapter reflects a dual concern for research and expert opinion. Theories and research are discussed, but the chapter also includes personal insights, interpretations, and recommendations for improving opportunities for women and people of color in educational leadership.

Available research on women and people of color in educational leadership does not support equal coverage of both groups on all of the topics covered in the chapter. Some sections of the chapter are primarily concerned with women; others focus on people of color. A major aim of the chapter is to identify gaps in the research, compare and contrast the experiences of women and people of color, and explore possible linkages between their experiences.

A major theme running throughout the chapter is the relationship of social context to the underrepresentation of women and people of color in educational leadership positions. A primary objective of this chapter is to review what we have learned and are learning about women and people of color in educational leadership and to identify ways in which a multicultural approach can help extend our knowledge by providing new insights and perspectives on leadership.

The Nature of Leadership

Leadership is a relatively new field of study (Yukl, 1981). Scientific research on leadership did not begin until the late 20th century. Several of the major theories in leadership, such as social exchange theory and situational theories, were not conceptualized until the 1950s and 1960s.

Women and people of color were almost completely absent from the study of leadership until the late 1970s (Bass, 1981). The lack of research on women and people of color was not viewed as problematic because race and gender were not considered differences of consequence (Bass, 1981). Researchers seemed to assume that their findings could be applied without regard for race and gender. Theories used to frame research, such as McGregor's Theory X and Theory Y and Argyris's Model I and II, were silent on issues of race and gender (McGregor, 1960; Argyris & Schön, 1974).

Leadership theory and practice are evolving and the traditional leadership paradigm is being challenged. Scholars are working to broaden the study of leadership to include women and people of color. They are also developing preservice and continuing education programs to prepare leaders to address the changing context of educational leadership and administration (Cunningham, 1990).

Definitions

Leadership is a broad concept with many different meanings (Burns, 1979; Hemphill & Coons, 1957; Stogdill, 1974; Rost, 1991). While there is no universally accepted definition of leadership, most definitions share two assumptions. They assume that leadership is a group phenomenon and that leaders exercise intentional influence over followers (Yukl, 1981; Janda, 1960). Definitions of leadership differ in terms of who exercises influence, the reasons why influence is attempted, and the ways in which influence is exercised (Yukl, 1981; Immegart, 1988).

One widely used definition of leadership states that leadership is "the initiation and maintenance of structure in expectation and interaction" (Stogdill, 1974, p. 411). This definition incorporates two key categories of leadership behavior: *consideration* and *initiating structure* (Fleishman,

1957; Halpin & Winer, 1957; Hemphill & Coons, 1957). Consideration and initiating structure include a number of specific behaviors. Three questionnaires, the 40-item Leader Behavior Description Questionnaire (LBDQ), the Supervisory Behavior Description Questionnaire (SBDQ), and the Leader Behavior Description Questionnaire XII (LBDQ XII), were constructed by Ohio State University researchers to measure leadership behavior (Fleishman, 1953; Stogdill, 1963; Hemphill & Coons, 1957).

The LBDQ, which was normed on male samples, is still used as a research protocol. In a meta-analysis of studies that examined differences in male and female responses to the LBDQ, Shakeshaft (1979, 1985) found that there were no differences between the two sexes. Shakeshaft (1987) notes that perceptual studies using instruments like the LBDQ, as opposed to behavioral studies, may not pick up real differences in the behavior of male and female leaders. Other researchers have criticized the LBDQ for having a halo effect, reporting implicit theories and stereotypes instead of actual leader behavior, and not relating to leaders' self-descriptions of their behavior (Bass, 1981).

Current State of Leadership

There are radically different views on the status of leadership as a discipline. In a comprehensive review of research and theory on managerial leadership, Yukl (1981) concluded that the field is in a state of ferment and confusion. Yukl's concerns center on three issues: (a) the lack of agreement in the field about leadership as a concept; (b) the lack of agreement in the field as to the ability of a leader to exercise substantial influence on performance in an organization; and (c) the conceptual weaknesses of current theories of leadership and their lack of clear empirical support. Immegart (1988, p. 266), however, argues that leadership is not the "barren ground nor the frustrating arena" portrayed by critics like Yukl. In a review of research on leadership and leader behavior, Immegart notes that the knowledge base in leadership is growing, scholars are building on previous research, and the field's understanding of leadership is increasing.

Research on and conducted by women and people of color in educational leadership is growing. Women and people of color are adding an exciting element to the study of leadership. Their work raises new questions (Scott, 1983; Lomotey, 1989), challenges traditional leadership theory (Evers & Lokomski, 1991), redefines old concepts and presents new language to describe leadership (Ortiz & Marshall, 1988; Shakeshaft, 1987), and is helping to create a new vision of leadership (Astin & Leland,

1991). However, there continues to be a dearth of research on both groups. Of the research that is available, there is considerably more on women than on people of color.

Major Research Approaches

Research on leadership can generally be classified into four approaches: the power-influence approach, trait approach, behavioral approach, and situational approach (Yukl, 1981). The power-influence approach regards power as a relationship that involves persuasion, coercion, indoctrination, and other forms of reciprocal influence (Bell, 1975). Leader effectiveness is measured in terms of the amount and source of power available to leaders and the ways in which power is used (French & Raven, 1960).

At the turn of the century and in the early 1900s, and then again in the 1960s and 1970s, trait theories were a topic of considerable interest in leadership. Trait theories assume that leaders can be differentiated from followers by their personality, character, and other qualities. Personal qualities such as intelligence, self-confidence, high energy, and persuasive skill are commonly identified as traits of leaders (House & Baetz, 1979; Jago, 1982; Stogdill, 1974). Trait theories are no longer in vogue. However, the idea that effective leaders have characteristics traditionally associated with men still has currency and continues to influence contemporary views of women leaders.

Behavioral approaches and situational approaches are somewhat related. Researchers use behavioral approaches to examine what leaders do (Pelz, 1952; Bales, 1950). They are particularly concerned with identifying and understanding effective behaviors and activities of leaders. Situational approaches, which are also known as contingency theories, highlight the importance of context in determining effective leadership (Fiedler, 1967; Vroom, 1976; Vroom & Yetton, 1973). For example, a specific behavior, such as praising a subordinate, is not always effective. In some cases praise may result in the desired outcome, while in other cases it may not. Situational theorists argue that effective leaders must be able to contextualize their behavior (Hersey, 1984).

It is interesting that even though situational theories were created in a society in which racism and sexism are salient, they are silent on issues of race and gender. This is especially perplexing since community factors, cultural values, and other commonly studied situational variables frequently involve issues of race and gender. Situational analysis can help increase our understanding of the behaviors of people of color and women in leadership positions as well as the behaviors of others toward them. It can also enhance our understanding of the ways in which race and gender serve as moderator variables in situations that require personal commitment, risk taking, and a quest for justice and equality.

Barbara A. Sizemore, a former superintendent of schools in Washington, D.C., argues that scholarly work on Black superintendents must be interpreted in the larger social reality of Black life and the historical context of the struggle of Blacks for education. The history of African Americans and their struggle to attend public school and gain access to jobs and positions in public schools is necessary for an informed analysis of Black educational leaders (Sizemore, 1986). Sizemore uses Black schools in Pittsburgh to illustrate her point. She states that after the Black segregated school in Pittsburgh was closed in 1867 no Black teachers were hired until 1933. The first Black principal since 1867 was hired in 1962.

Social and Role Theory

Social and role theory can help explain the status of women and people of color in leadership theory and their underrepresentation in educational leadership positions. Role theory provides a basis for examining role socialization and for explaining the behaviors of people in occupational roles such as principals and superintendents. Role theory is based on the idea that a role defines how individuals are expected to behave, how individuals occupying roles perceive what they are supposed to do, and the actual behavior of individuals (Toren, 1973; N. Gross, Mason, & McEachern, 1958).

Scholars, practitioners, and gatekeepers (those who control entry into educational leadership) are socialized and participate in a society that makes cultural assumptions about women and people of color. Those cultural assumptions grow out of societal norms and values that marginalize these two groups. Norms and values are products of socialization, and part of the process of role socialization that begins in infancy and continues through adulthood. Decisions about who is the focus of research, who is recruited and hired, and who does or does not get promoted are made within a social context in which women and people of color experience an inferior social status and are often objects of negative stereotypes.

Role socialization is commonly viewed as a two-way process in which both the socializer and the person being socialized may be changed in significant ways (Goslin, 1969). This characteristic of role socialization is particularly important when race and gender are incorporated into the study of educational leaders. On one hand, leaders learn to accept and adopt appropriate values, rules, and policies through their socialization into the profession and participation in professional organizations (E. Gross & Etzioni, 1985). Weber (1968) refers to this process as legitimation. On the other hand, women and people of color also have the potential to change the institutions in which they work and their colleagues. More research is needed to increase understanding of this dynamic interchange.

Racism and Sexism as Factors in Socialization

Women and people of color both experience prejudice and discrimination. Racism and sexism are unconscious ideologies and integral parts of the American identity (Franklin, 1993; West, 1993; Freeman, 1984). The values and norms that legitimate prejudice and discrimination are internalized and transmitted to new members of U.S. society through socialization. However, while racism and sexism are both forms of discrimination, they are not necessarily evidenced in the same way. From a sociological perspective, the prejudice and discrimination that women and people of color experience have different origins and different consequences. Developing and implementing effective strategies to reduce prejudice and discrimination require that we acknowledge and work to understand the similarities and differences in the social genesis and maintenance of gender and racial prejudice and discrimination.

Unlike people of color, women are not a numerical minority. Women are a majority in the U.S. population. They are considered a minority group because, like people of color, they lack access to power. However, even though White women lack social, political, and economic power, they enjoy a privileged status in U.S. society based on their race (McIntosh, 1988; hooks, 1990). Women of color experience discrimination based on two factors: race and sex (Butler & Walter, 1991; DuBois & Ruiz, 1990).

Women have more social contact with men and boys who are members of their ethnic or racial group than minorities have with Whites. Men and women interact with each other from birth, whereas most minorities and Whites have little voluntary social contact with each other. Children learn about sex roles directly from parents, friends, and other close associates, but most acquire information about different racial and ethnic groups from secondary sources such as books, television, and individuals who are not members of their primary groups.

Race socialization frequently privileges White characteristics and marginalizes characteristics associated with people of color (Sleeter, 1993). It is particularly pernicious because it frequently occurs in an environment where racism is a powerful though often unidentified variable in the socialization process. Racism affects individual as well as institutional responses to people of color (West, 1993; Franklin, 1993; C. McCarthy & Crichlow, 1993). Selective perception and reinforcement and other such processes are used to deny variability among people of color in areas such as intellect and accomplishment (H. J. Scott, personal communication, 1993). As a result, it is not uncommon for all members of a group to be reduced to one-dimensional representatives of their phenotype. These representations are codified in images that are presented in media, texts, and other communicative elements in society that forefront racism as an important element in race socialization.

On an institutional level, racism results in barriers that restrict people of color from access to power and privilege within the institution. Racism and its impact on race socialization make it impossible for people of color to dream their dreams free from the dire reality that color is the key that opens the door to the full range of opportunities and benefits of American citizenship (II. J. Scott, personal communication, 1993).

For the most part, race and sex socialization have been explored as independent processes. Researchers who are interested in race have basically disregarded gender and researchers who have examined issues of gender have tended to overlook race (C. McCarthy & Crichlow, 1993). This tendency ignores women of color as an integrated whole and presents them in fragments (Pinar, 1993; Dugger, 1991). Exploring race and sex as a collectivity offers exciting possibilities for future research.

Persistence of Prejudice and Discrimination

Schools reflect the race and gender stratification that exists in the wider society (Gaertner, 1980). Both women and people of color are underrepresented in educational leadership positions in schools. In 1992, 97.1 percent of superintendents were White and 89.5 percent were male (Saks, 1992). Female administrative aspirants interviewed by Edson (1987) stated that "they had to be far superior to male candidates just to be considered for an administrative position and, even then, school boards still showed a preference for hiring men" (p. 265).

Efforts to combat prejudice and discrimination, such as affirmative action, have been disappointingly ineffective for people of color and only marginally effective for women (M. McCarthy & Zent, 1981). In 1992 women held 10.5 percent of superintendencies while people of color held only 2.9 percent. African Americans constituted 1.9 percent of those superintendencies and Hispanics constituted .5 percent (Saks, 1992). Whites also held most school principalships.

Sex Roles

Over the years, researchers have used the concept of sex roles to explain why women are underrepresented in educational leadership (Schmuck, 1980). The concept of sex roles grew out of social theory and Blau's (1976) research on social exchange. Holter (1970) defines sex roles as the roles that are assigned to men because they are men and women because they are women. Sex roles are acquired through socialization in environments where there are different expectations for men and women. Each sex is socialized in ways that are consistent with specific gender expectations (Holter, 1970). Early investigations of sex roles focused on sex-role identity in terms of attitudes, values, beliefs, and behaviors (Millett, 1969/1980). These investigations were followed by studies that explored the relationship between sex and the experiences of women and men in organizations (Biklen & Brannigan, 1980).

Schmuck (1980) organized research on sex roles into three broad categories, each representing a specific perspective: the individual perspective, the social perspective, and the organizational perspective. Schmuck notes that individual perspectives on sex roles draw heavily on psychological research and focus on individual attitudes and aspirations. According to Schmuck, the individual perspective is limited by its lack of attention to societal norms, folkways, and traditions. The social perspective focuses on men's and women's work. Schmuck argues that our society maximizes the differences between men's and women's work and gives women's work less status, value, and pay. Even though most institutions in the United States have both male and female workers, Schmuck states that men generally hold the more influential positions. From an organizational perspective, competent women are often discriminated against because they are viewed as threatening and are marginalized with terms such as "girls" and "honey" (Hagen & Kahn, 1975).

The women's movement in the 1960s and 1970s increased awareness of and sensitivity to sex roles and the expectations and norms related to them (Friedan, 1963). An increased awareness of sex roles led to questions about the validity of men's investigating and interpreting research on sex roles (Schmuck, 1980). Researchers such as Huber (1973) and Rossi (1970) argue that much of the research on sex-role characteristics reflects male perspectives and is stereotyped. They question research that creates a dichotomy between males and females by suggesting, for example, that males are frank and straightforward in social relations, intellectually rational, and competent, and that females are interested in social amenities, emotional warmth, and affective matters (Huber, 1973; Rossi, 1970). Feminists have also criticized research that uses male models of organizational behavior to evaluate females. They note that even though most women are clerical or service workers, most of the research on women in organizations focuses on the roles and behavior of women in male-dominated professions (Astin, 1969; Bernard, 1964; J. White, 1967). Research on sex roles in organizations has become more diverse within the last decade. It includes studies that explore gender differences in graffiti styles, portrait posing, and assertive acts of toddlers (Loewenstine, Ponticos, & Pauldi, 1982; Mills, 1984).

Sex-Role Stereotypes

The presence of sex-role stereotypes in our society has been extensively researched and is well documented (Fernberger, 1948; Komarovsky, 1973). Sex-role stereotypes, however, may be changing. Research on sex-role stereotypes conducted in the 1980s suggests that while sex-role stereotypes seem to remain strong, sex-biased attitudes appear to be less polarized (Ruble, 1983). Nevertheless, sex-role stereotypes continue to be pervasive.

The relationship between sex-role stereotypes and leadership is complex and has not been fully defined. However, we know that sex-role stereotypes are integrated into the self-concepts of men and women (Broverman, Vogel, Broverman, Clarkson, & Rosenkrantz, 1972). O'Leary (1974) reported that the career aspirations of women are influenced by societal sex-role stereotypes and attitudes about their competency. As late as the mid-1970s, Bem and Bem (1975) found that one third of all working women were concentrated in seven jobs: secretary, retail sales clerk, household worker, elementary school teacher, waitress, and nurse.

Many women internalize societal sex-role stereotypes and attitudes. They express these attitudes and stereotypes in role conflict, as fear of failure, and in low self-esteem (Horner, 1987; O'Leary, 1974). In investigating the relationship between sex-role stereotypes and leadership, Petty and Miles (1976) found that both males and females subscribe to sex-role stereotypes for leadership roles. Research on sex-role stereotypes suggests that there is a tendency to attribute a higher social value to behaviors that are considered masculine than to those that are considered feminine (L. T. White, 1950). Women as well as men attribute higher social value to male behaviors even when they work in female-dominated cultures, such as elementary schools. Broverman et al. (1972) found that, compared with men, women are perceived as less competent, independent, objective, and logical. Men are perceived as lacking interpersonal sensitivity, warmth, and expressiveness (Broverman et al., 1972; Williams, 1982).

Interestingly, sex-role stereotypes cause the same traits to be perceived differently in men and women (Bayes & Newton, 1978). Consequently, sex-role stereotypes can result in a no-win situation for women. Women are expected to exhibit behaviors associated with sex-role stereotypes in order to be viewed as women, and yet those very behaviors are often seen as being antithetical to effective leadership. Women who behave in ways traditionally associated with males may be passed over for promotions. L. K. Brown and Klein (1982) found that women were only allowed to advance into administrative positions when they were able to play the roles of peacemaker and nurturer as well as supervisor. Sex-role stereotypes can limit women's access to and effectiveness in leadership positions.

Since the late 1960s much of the research on sex-role stereotypes has been conducted using the Stereotype Questionnaire (Broverman, Broverman, Clarkson, Rosenkrantz, & Vogel, 1970). Researchers using the Stereotype Questionnaire have found that sex-role stereotypes are commonly found in a variety of groups throughout the nation and are deeply ingrained in U.S. society. Research by Millham and Smith (1981), however, indicates that sex-role stereotypes may be different for African Americans than they are for Whites. In their study comparing sex-role differentiation among Black and White Americans, Millham and Smith concluded that "Blacks are generally less concerned with traditional sex-role differentiation as defined by the White majority" (p. 89).

Role Stress and Conflict

Role stress is a construct that describes a feeling of conflict that results from the inconsistent demands of a role (Goode, 1960; Merton, 1957; Parsons, 1951; Popenoe, 1971). Gross et al. (1958) found that superintendents experience conflict when they try to satisfy the conflicting desires of teachers, parents, and school board members. Conflict also results from the multiple roles minorities and women in educational administration are expected to assume. Role conflict among White males entering their first administrative positions tends to be lower than that of women and minorities entering their first administrative positions (Ortiz, 1982).

Ortiz (1982) examined the socialization processes of 350 school administrators in California. Her work is particularly important in understanding the relationship between career patterns and role conflict of women and minorities in school districts. Ortiz investigated some of the intervening processes between status and role conflict and found that organizational position can increase as well as decrease role conflict. Women and minority administrators may experience role conflict as a result of the "organization's expectations regarding their ascribed roles such as being feminine or ethnic" (p. 138). This form of role conflict is reduced when "minorities and women accentuate the positions' characteristics and when they refuse to be shattered in the face of conflicting expectations" (p. 138). Ortiz also found that role conflict is dependent on the way minorities participate in their organizations. The potential for role conflict is reduced when minorities are highly competent, limit their area of expertise to issues involving ethnicity and social bias, and do not compete with White males.

The reform role that many Black superintendents are expected to fill can also result in role stress and conflict (Sizemore, 1986) Minority administrators are challenged to maintain loyalty simultaneously to bureaucratic, personal, and community ideologies that often involve incompatible expectations, attitudes, and beliefs. Peterson (1985) makes the following comment on the role of superintendents in school reform in his book on the politics of school reform:

> Reform superintendents were neither heroes nor devils, but they had an agenda that placed them at odds with a diversity of opponents that changed according to the issue at stake and the political context in which it was raised. (p. 155)

Educational administrators are frequently expected to take on the roles of educational superperson, technical manager, and democratic leader (Cunningham & Nystrand, 1969). In his book on Black superintendents, Scott (1980) states that "the relationship Black superintendents have with other Blacks and many Whites is a manifestation of contemporary racial attitudes in America" (p. 57). Scott concludes that African American superintendents are charged with tempering Black hostility and distrust while simultaneously providing the leadership necessary to reform urban school districts.

The small number of women and people of color in educational leadership is another potential source of role stress and conflict. Kanter (1977) argues that three dynamics may result when there are small numbers of women in leadership positions: (a) women in those positions may receive more attention; (b) the additional attention may lead to more pressure to perform; and (c) the organization's cultural boundaries may be heightened due to polarization and the exaggeration of differences between males and females. Women may be channeled, through affirmative action, into special roles set aside for them. The smaller the number of individuals from other groups, the more they are seen as representatives of their group rather than as individuals. That perspective, along with the assumption that minority persons are only interested in appointments in areas such as human rights, immigration, and social assistance, limits them from being considered seriously for advancement.

Gender and Race Stratification in Educational Leadership

Even though both women and people of color have experienced long tenure in the field of education, there are important differences in the social contexts and experiences of the two groups. Programs designed to increase the number of people of color and women in educational leadership positions will continue to be ineffective until a better understanding is gained of the ways in which history and social context influence their underrepresentation (Ortiz & Marshall, 1988; Sizemore, 1986). This section identifies some of the key factors in the backgrounds of the two groups and provides some statistics on their past and current representation in educational leadership positions.

Effect of Gender and Race on Opportunities for Leadership

Leadership opportunities for women in school administration began to increase in the 1980s. However, women continue to be underrepresented in higher-level positions in school administration (Saks, 1992). During the 1981–1982 school year, 25 percent of the school administrators in the United States were women. From 1981 to 1984, the percentage of female elementary and high school principals increased from 12 percent to 17 percent (Marshall, 1984). During that same period, the percentage of female assistant superintendents increased from 9 percent to 15 percent. By 1986, 27 percent of principals and assistant principals were women (U.S. Bureau of the Census, 1992). In 1992 women held 12.1 percent of high school principalships, compared to 7.6 percent in 1991 (Saks, 1992). The percentage of female superintendents increased from less than 1 percent in 1971 to 1.8 percent in 1981–1982, 2.7 percent in 1984–1985, 7.5 percent in 1991, and eventually to 10.5 percent in 1992 (Saks, 1992).

The number of minorities in school administration did not change substantially from 1975–1976 to 1984–1985 (Snyder, 1989). During that period, the number of African American male principals declined .12 percent and the number of Black female principals increased 1.85 percent. By 1986 only 8 percent of all school administrators and 13 percent of elementary and secondary principals and assistant principals were Blacks (U.S. Bureau of the Census, 1992). A national survey of school administrators, conducted in 1985 by the American Association of School Administrators (AASA), found that African Americans held 1 percent of the superintendencies and 6.5 percent of the assistant superintendencies; Hispanics held 1.4 percent of the superintendencies and 1.8 percent of the assistant superintendencies; American Indians held .5 percent of the superintendencies; and Asian Pacific Islanders held .1 percent of the superintendencies (AASA, 1985). By 1991 the number of African American superintendents had increased only to 2.5 percent. The percentage of African American superintendents dropped to 1.9 percent in 1992 (Saks, 1992).

Historical Context of Underrepresentation

Historically, women and people of color have had limited career options. For many years education was one of the few careers open to them. Education offered an aura of respectability and professionalism, a realistic career goal, financial independence, and an opportunity to serve the community. Women constituted almost 98 percent of all elementary school teachers and 61.7 percent of elementary school principals in 1905 (Shakeshaft, 1987). By 1920 education was the seventh-ranked field of work for African American women (Shakeshaft, 1987).

Virtually all school administrators are initially recruited from the ranks of teachers (Clement, 1975). Several states require teacher certification as a prerequisite for administrative certification. For many years minorities were not hired as teachers in public schools. Even in the rural South, teaching and administrative positions in segregated schools did not open for Blacks until the first half of the 20th century (Perkins, 1989; Clifford, 1982). In a study of the early history of Black superintendents, Jones (1983) found that the first Black superintendents served in all-Black school districts between 1930 and 1958. Most of those districts were in the South. Sizemore (1986) notes that the Black superintendency did not become a reality in mixed school districts until 1954.

Teaching opportunities for African Americans began to decline during the 1960s and 1970s. Schools were integrated during those years and Black students were transferred from Black schools to White schools. African American teachers and administrators who worked in Black schools were not generally transferred to White schools. Consequently, many lost their jobs.

During the 1980s scholarships and other forms of financial aid for students entering higher education began to decrease. As a result, the number of students of color entering college and available to select education as a major decreased as well. As opportunities opened up for employment in other fields, such as business, students of color began to choose majors outside education (Perkins, 1989). In 1977, African Americans were more likely than Whites to major in education; by 1989 Whites were more likely than Blacks to select education as their major (National Center for Educational Statistics, 1991). Between 1985 and 1990, less than 1 percent of American Indians, 1 percent of Asian Americans, 2 percent of Latinos, and 5 percent of African Americans were hired in teaching positions (Feistritzer, 1990).

The underrepresentation of women in educational leadership, like that of minorities, is embedded in a compelling historical context. After World War II the number of women administrators decreased as more men went into education. During that period, school boards tended to limit new hires to heads of households. School boards also frequently replaced retiring female principals with males (Neely & Wilson, 1978). Decision makers tended to view men as having characteristics that were more favorable in educational administration. The percentage of male elementary teachers increased from 12.8 percent in 1957–1958 to 14.6 percent during the 1967–1968 school year. During that period there was an increase of male teachers at the secondary level from 50.5 percent to 52.9 percent. In 1990 males represented approximately 15 percent of elementary school teachers and almost 46 percent of secondary teachers (U.S. Bureau of the Census, 1992).

Determining Underrepresentation

While both women and people of color are underrepresented in educational leadership positions, the determination of their underrepresentation is derived in different ways. Justification for increasing the number of women in educational administration is frequently based on the disproportionate number of women who hold administrative positions. Jones and Montenegro (1990) found that even though most teachers are women, men hold 96 percent of superintendencies, 77 percent of assistant superintendencies, 88 percent of high school principalships, and 71 percent of elementary principalships.

Increasing the number of minorities in educational administration is frequently justified on the basis of the growing number of students of color in the public schools. The majority of students enrolled in public schools in California are students of color. By 2020 almost half of the students attending public school in the United States will be students of color (Spencer, 1986).

Placement of Minorities in Educational Administration

Many minorities enter administration through special projects and work on minority issues. They frequently work in schools with high minority enrollment and occupy the least powerful positions in the administrative hierarchy. In a national study of high school principals, Byrne, Hines, and McCleary (1978) found that most minority principals served in school districts with more than 20 percent minority enrollment. In a national survey of 210 Black school administrators, Holden (1977) found that 58 percent of the Black administrators worked in predominantly Black school districts with fewer than 10,000 students.

Most minority superintendents are hired in school districts that have a high proportion of students of color. The probability of African Americans being hired as superintendents increases as the number of minority students in school districts increases (Moody, 1971; Jones, 1983; Scott, 1983). By the late 1980s most Black superintendents were located in cities (Sizemore, 1986). Scott (1983) predicts that those school districts with high minority populations, critical financial conditions, and educational problems will have unwanted superintendencies, and those superintendencies will be available to Blacks.

In one of the first national studies of Black superintendents, Moody (1971) found that 72.2 percent of the school districts with Black superintendents were predominantly Black. Many of those districts were large urban school districts. Black superintendents have served in Chicago, Detroit, Minneapolis, Rochester, Washington, DC, Atlanta, Baltimore, Newark, and New Orleans (Scott, 1983). However, it is important to note that most school districts that have a majority of African American students do not have Black superintendents. In 1982, 66 percent of predominantly Black districts in the United States had White superintendents (Scott, 1983).

Role of School Boards in Underrepresentation of Women

School boards reflect the values of their communities and play an important role in the selection of administrators (Peshkin, 1978). In a 1986 survey of superintendents, personnel directors, and school board presidents, Phillips and Voorhees found that attitudes of school board presidents differed from those of superintendents and personnel directors on the ability of women to advance in educational administration. The superintendents and personnel directors believed women had the ability to advance in educational administration. The board presidents, however, believed that women could be placed in elementary administration, but should not be placed in positions such as assistant superintendent or superintendent.

In a survey of Connecticut school board members, Taylor (1971) found that board members were more likely to appoint women to positions in central office administration and as elementary principals than to positions as superintendents or secondary principals. Taylor found that female school board members, like male board members, favored males for administrative positions. However, those attitudes may be changing. In a 1978 study of California school board members, Beck found that the attitudes of male board members toward women administrators were significantly more traditional than the attitudes of female board members.

Working with women administrators seems to moderate negative attitudes toward them. Male board members who have worked with a female administrator had more favorable attitudes toward women administrators than male board members who have not worked with women administrators. Beck (1978) found that there was a positive correlation between the percentage of women hired in administrative positions and more liberal attitudes toward women.

The number of female school board members remains relatively low. In 1987, 39 percent of school board members were women. By 1992 that percentage had increased only to 39.9 percent. Minority representation on school boards is much lower than female representation. In 1987, 3.6 percent of school board members were Black, 1.5 percent were Hispanic, .1 percent were American Indian, and .2 percent were Asian American. By 1992 the percentage of African American school board members had fallen to 3.1 percent. It increased to .8 percent for American Indians. The percentage of Hispanic and Asian American board members remained the same in 1992 as it was in 1987 (Saks, 1992).

Characteristics of Women and Minorities in Educational Leadership

The assumption that leadership requires male characteristics has led to a body of research in which women and people of color are compared to White men. This research results in men being held up as the ideal to which women and people of color are compared. Conceptualizing research on leadership as a mirror in which women and people of color are expected to be a reflection of White men ultimately marginalizes these two groups because they are viewed as having fewer skills and less power. In a review of empirical studies on male and female leaders, S. M. Brown (1979) concludes that "one of the popular reasons given for the differential treatment of women in management stems from stereotyping females as ineffective leaders . . . trait studies consistently supported the traditional attitude that women lack adequate leadership characteristics" (p. 595). In addition to marginalizing women and people of color, research comparing male and female leaders diverts attention away from issues like discrimination in the workplace (Fierman, 1990).

Male and Female Leaders Compared

Researchers frequently use survey instruments to gather data on the personal characteristics of male and female educational leaders. The availability of such data enables researchers to create a profile of women and men who reach high levels in school administration. In general, studies that compare male and female leaders do not demonstrate a clear pattern of difference in leadership style between the sexes (Bass, 1981; C.A.M. Banks, 1991). On occasion, however, individual studies have identified differences in leadership style. In a meta-analysis of 50 studies that compared the leadership styles of male and female principals, Eagly, Karau, and Johnson (1992) found that there is some evidence that men and women have different styles. Women tended to display a democratic and participatory style and to be more task oriented than men. However, Eagly et al. state that there are men who practice democratic leadership and women who exercise autocratic leadership. Male and female leadership styles overlap and there are considerable intragroup differences in leadership style.

Studies comparing personal characteristics and experiences of male and female leaders have had mixed results. Some studies suggest that there are differences between male and female leaders, while others suggest that there are no significant differences (Adkinson, 1981; Frasher & Frasher, 1979; Shakeshaft, 1987). Age is one variable on which differences have been consistently noted. Researchers have found that women entering school administration are older and have more school experience than men (Johnson, Yeakey, & Moore, 1980; N. Gross & Trask, 1976). Males generally have taught 5 to 7 years and females have generally taught 15 years before they enter educational administration (N. Gross & Trask, 1976).

Studies have also shown that women leaders share many commonalities. Stevens (1988) interviewed 10 women who held superintendencies in Washington State school districts. Most of the women came from homes where they were expected to achieve. Nine of the 10 female superintendents were the oldest child in their families, and 5 began their educational careers as teachers in junior high schools. All of the superintendents saw themselves as collaborative leaders.

The following studies illustrate some of the key factors found in research comparing the personal characteristics of male and female educational leaders. N. Gross and Trask (1976) conducted a major study of men and women elementary school principals. The study was part of the National Principalship Study that was carried out at Harvard University and supported by the U.S. Office of Education. Gross and Trask used a cluster sampling procedure that gave them a representative sample of 189 elementary principals in cities with a population of 50,000 or more. Secondary principals were not included in the study because the number of female junior and senior high school principals was too small. Data were gathered using a personal and school background questionnaire, a role questionnaire, and a three- to five-hour personal interview.

The average age of the women in the study was 54.3 years, with 59 percent of them between 50 and 59 years old. The average age of the men was 49.2 years. The largest group of men (4 percent) was between the ages of 40 and 49. Ninety-six percent of the women and 92 percent of the men were White. With one exception, the remaining individuals in the study were African American.

The N. Gross and Trask (1976) study revealed a number of important characteristics of school administrators. Over 95 percent of the men in the study were married, but only about one third of the women were married. Kanter (1977) notes that some high-level positions, such as superintendent of schools, seem to require two individuals: the individual hired for the position and a spouse to handle its social aspects. Traditionally, women have provided an extra hand in support of their husbands' careers. Women who are married as well as women who are not married generally have to handle both the social and professional components of their positions.

Women in the N. Gross and Trask (1976) study reported higher academic performance than the men. Twenty-three percent of women and 12 percent of the men indicated that their academic work was far above average; 1 percent of the men and none of the women reported that their academic work was below average. The women also stated that they went into teaching because they were influenced or persuaded by someone else. Men indicated that they went into teaching for financial reasons and for upward mobility. The women in the study reportedly had lower aspirations for career advancement than did the men.

Douglas and Simonson (1982) studied the life experiences and leader behaviors of 25 male and 25 female superintendents. They found that male and female superintendents did not exhibit different leader behaviors; however, they did find other differences. Four times as many male superintendents as female superintendents earned $50,000 or more. Female superintendents were less likely to be married than were male superintendents—92 percent of the men were married, compared to 72 percent of the women. All of the married male superintendents had children, but 28 percent of the married female superintendents had no children. The female superintendents had an average of 11.7 years of teaching experience, compared to 3.2 years for men. Fifty-four percent of the men in the study moved into superintendencies within 10 years after they started teaching. None of the women moved into superintendencies within 10 years after they started teaching. At the other extreme, 36 percent of the women and 4 percent of the men in the study became superintendents 26 or more years after their first teaching experience. Men served an average of 13.2 years in a superintendency, compared to 4.5 years for women.

In a nationwide study of 791 male and 191 female superintendents, Schuster (1987) found that males and females differ on personal and career variables, politics, and job-related costs and satisfactions. Women superintendents were more often firstborn than were male superintendents. They were more likely to be politically liberal and single, and had on average fewer children than did male superintendents. Females also read more professional books and held more doctoral degrees than did male superintendents. Increasingly, a significantly larger number of women than men sat on school boards that hired female superintendents.

In 1990 C.A.M. Banks surveyed 31 superintendents of the largest public school districts in the United States to gather data on their career patterns, personal and educational characteristics, and perceptions of managerial and leadership styles and skills (C.A.M. Banks, 1991). The respondents included 2 female superintendents and 29 male superintendents—15 European Americans, 13 African Americans, and 3 Hispanic Americans. She found that there was no significant relationship between the gender or race of the superintendents and their perceptions of their leadership styles and skills.

Hollander and Yoder (1978) reviewed research on gender and leadership and concluded that there were general areas where men and women differ in their leadership. They found that men focus more on achieving success in tasks while women seek interpersonal successes; women put more energy into creating a positive group effort; men focus on displaying recognizable leader behavior. They concluded that the differences that they noted in male and female leader behavior are related to role expectations, style, and situational characteristics.

Chapman (1975) compared the leadership styles of males and females. He concluded that differences in male and female leader behavior may result from pressures to display behaviors that are consistent with societal and cultural expectations. In a study of supervisor ratings, female supervisors received higher scores than men in the areas of being friendly, expressing appreciation for good work, and agreeing on values. In addition, female supervisors were less likely to be avoided by subordinates than were male supervisors (Munson, 1979). The Chapman and Munson studies suggest that societal expectations of appropriate female and male behavior are implicated in the ways in which leaders are evaluated. Women are expected to be warm, sympathetic, aware of others' feelings, and helpful. Men are viewed as self-assertive and dominant (Ashmore, Del Boca, & Wohlers, 1986; Williams, 1982).

Morsink (1970) measured 12 dimensions of leader behavior. There were no significant differences between male and female secondary principals on 2 of the dimensions: tolerance of uncertainty and consideration. Male principals in the study were perceived as having a greater tolerance of freedom than did women principals. While the difference was not significant, female principals were viewed as demonstrating a higher level of consideration than male principals. They generally spoke and acted as a representative of their group, maintained cordial relations with their superiors, and tried to influence them. The idea that females focus on consideration is supported by Josefowitz's (1980) finding that female managers were twice as accessible as male managers. Josefowitz noted that female managers, unlike male managers, tended to maintain an open-door rather than a closed-door policy, did not use their secretaries to screen their calls, and encouraged telephone calls to their homes in the evenings and on weekends.

Pitner (1981) observed three women superintendents for one week to determine whether male and female superintendents focus on different work activities. She found that the nature of the work that men and women superintendents performed was essentially the same. There were, however, some differences in the ways that they handled routine paper work and the ways in which they observed in schools. The female superintendents in the study interacted more frequently with their peers and female counterparts and used a more informal communication style and language than did males. They also spent more of their unscheduled time working on curriculum and instruction and tended to eat lunch alone at their desks instead of in restaurants.

Pratt (1980) used case studies of critical incidents in leaderless task-oriented small groups to examine seven leadership factors, including the leadership style of males and females. She found that there were no differences between males and females on any of the seven factors, including leadership style. Pratt concluded that, in general, there are more similarities than there are differences between male and female leaders.

In the 1980s women began to challenge openly the idea that masculine characteristics are associated with effective leadership. They argued that intuitiveness, caring, and other characteristics that are typically associated with women make for better managers and leaders (Helgesen, 1990; Loden, 1985; Rosener, 1990). While this line of research presents female characteristics in a more positive light, it maintains the dichotomy between males and females and reinforces a monolithic view of women. That limited view of women is related to their underrepresentation in educational leadership positions (Nichols, 1993). If a decision maker accepts the idea that men are self-assertive and women are caring, it is understandable why a man would be selected over a woman for a job that requires an assertive leader.

Studies of the kind reported here have several limitations. They tend not to focus on the variations within groups of males and females even though there is tremendous intragroup variation (Epstein, 1988, 1991; Fierman, 1990). Some males are more similar to females than to males and some females are more similar to males than to other females. Intragroup differences as well as similarities need further exploration. By focusing on differences between males and females we essentially deny the variation that exists within each group.

The lack of attention to variation within groups is further complicated by the methodology employed in many studies. Most use a form of survey research. Surveys rely on self-report data and are limited to the respondents' frame of reference. Research on the actual behavior of male and female managers does not always support the self-report perceptions through which male and female leaders describe themselves (Epstein, 1988, 1991).

Minorities and Educational Leadership

Research on minorities in school administration is almost exclusively on African Americans. The author was able to locate only two dissertations completed between 1964 and 1989 that were on Latino school administrators. None were located that focused primarily on Native Americans or Asians. Data on Asian Americans, Native Americans, and Latinos are limited to a small number of broad-based surveys of school administrators. In general, those studies simply indicate the number of minorities that serve in specified job categories. They do not provide information on the characteristics of Latino, Asian, or Native American administrators (Lovelady-Dawson, 1980).

Compared to women and White males, there are relatively few studies on minorities in educational leadership. Available research, however, suggests that there are significant differences in the experiences of minority, women, and White male leaders. One of the primary differences involves community relations. African American school administrators tend to be very closely tied to the minority community. Johnson, Yeakey, and Holden (1979) found that African American superintendents often reflect the needs and priorities of their client communities, and that those communities are largely Black. African American principals, to a greater extent than their White colleagues, involve parents and members of the community in school activities (Monteiro, 1977). In a study of African American principals, Lomotey (1989) found that one of the characteristics of African American principals in more successful elementary schools was "a deep compassion for, and understanding of, their students and of the communities in which they work" (p. 150).

Characteristics of Minority Female School Administrators

Edson (1987) has conducted several studies that included minority women in school administration. She argues that there may be a connection between the small number of studies on minority women in school administration and the low number of minority women actually in school administration. This intriguing hypothesis ties together two important realities: Minority females are underrepresented in leadership research and in educational administration. The lack of research on minority female school administrators makes identifying their characteristics much more problematic than identifying the characteristics of White administrators. In a national survey of school superintendents, Schuster (1987) found that no single category of minority women held more than 2 percent of any school administrative position. Revere (1985) found that out of 16,000 public school superintendents, only 29 were African American women. Research that highlights the nature of minority female underrepresentation in educational leadership will not only publicize this problem; it can also serve as a departure point for action to rectify it.

Research on minority women is often incorporated into larger studies of women. Edson's (1987) comprehensive study of female administrative aspirants included 36 minority females; 27 of the women were Black,

7 were Hispanic, 1 was Asian, and 1 was American Indian. Both the minority and White women in Edson's study agreed that race and gender significantly affected their career aspirations. They also acknowledged that competition exists between minority and White females. This finding raises an important question about the extent to which White women and women of color will support and cooperate with each other in what could be called a zero sum game. The reality of competition in the workplace may result in the perception that the advancement of one group of females may hinder the advancement of other groups. Edson (1988) concludes her discussion of minority female administrative aspirants by stating, "Until the field of administration welcomes all female candidates, no matter what their color, minority issues will continue to complicate the lives of minority and nonminority women alike" (p. 193).

Minority females embody two status roles—one related to gender and one related to ethnicity. Doughty (1980) argues that those status roles have negative consequences for Black women who want to enter educational administration. She states that African American female administrators have to cope with the popular myth that Black women are superhuman, capable of solving any problem and dealing with any crisis, and stronger than other women and African American men.

In 1980 Doughty surveyed Black administrators in school districts with populations of 100,000 or more. Data were collected from 1,004 Black administrators. Of those administrators, 250 were Black females. Doughty found that Black females tended to be at the bottom of the administrative hierarchy. White men held top positions such as superintendent and Black males were next, followed by White females. Black females were last. Black females in the study held positions such as supervisor, administrative assistant, and elementary principal.

Doughty (1980) also found that Black and White females who enter educational administration share a number of characteristics. Like White women, Black female administrators tend to be older than male administrators. Most of the women in the study were in their middle 40s to middle 50s before they became administrators. Also like White females, Black female administrators, as compared to males, have more education and have spent more time teaching before moving into administration. Doughty also found that the Black females she studied had positive perceptions of themselves and their ability to do their jobs. They tended to reject descriptions of themselves as tokens and felt that they were hired and promoted because of their credentials and past performance.

In an article on Black professional women, Epstein (1972) argued that Black women were in great demand in the labor market because they satisfy two affirmative action criteria, sex and race. Doughty (1980) responded to Epstein in an article on Black female administrators. She argued that Department of Labor statistics clearly indicate that the dual status of minority and female results in lower earning power for Black women than for Black men, White women, and White men. Doughty concludes that the perception that Black women get top jobs because they are minority women is a myth. She challenges her readers to carefully look at the positions Black women hold in educational administration. She notes that they are usually assistants to superintendents, supervisors, vice principals, or elementary principals. Doughty's position that African American women may be doubly challenged by the dual barriers of gender and race is supported by Ortiz (1982) and Korah (1990). They also conclude that while women and minorities encounter barriers to leadership positions, minority women confront both gender and racial barriers.

The Effect of Race and Gender on Career Patterns

Data developed by AASA (1960, 1985) suggest that access to high-level administrative positions is limited to individuals who have followed specific career patterns (1960). While career patterns leading to superintendencies vary over time, two patterns are commonly followed. In school districts with 100,000 or more students, the typical career pattern of superintendents is teacher/principal/central office administrator/superintendent. In smaller school districts, the most common career pattern leading to a superintendency is teacher/principal/superintendent.

In a survey of 78 Black superintendents and on-site interviews with 6 of the superintendents, C. M. Banks (1988) found that Black superintendents progressed through a career path that included teacher, principal, assistant superintendent, and superintendent. Most of the Blacks in the survey were in their first superintendency and had served in that position for an average of 6.6 years. The superintendents indicated that their career development had been aided by mentors who took a personal interest in their careers.

Keim (1978) compared the career paths and expectations of 470 male and female superintendents in Pennsylvania. She found that there were significant differences between male and female career paths leading to superintendents. Women tended to teach longer before entering administration and had more certificates and doctorates than did the men in the study.

Revere (1985) conducted one of the few studies investigating the career patterns of minority women. Based on data from her interviews, she concluded that there was no single career pattern that described the accession of minority women to the superintendency. The factors that led to their rise to the superintendency were their self-confidence, industriousness, productivity, and ability to work well with people. Most of the women in the study were married and felt that their husbands were an important source of support.

In another study on the career paths of minority women, Bulls (1986) used ethnographic case studies to investigate the behavioral strategies used by nine Black female leaders to attain superintendencies. Attaining access to high-level administrative positions requires that African American females engage in highly purposeful behavior. For example, Bulls concluded that a doctorate was essential for African American females to become superintendents. Securing mentors, balancing feminine and masculine qualities, networking with other Black female superintendents, and obtaining a visible position in the central office were also identified as critical steps for career advancement.

Ortiz (1982) found that White males, unlike women and minorities, were socialized as teachers to enter administration. When they were assigned to vice-principalships, they were able to move away gradually from work with children and instruction and to assume more administrative responsibilities. As work demands increased, men generally had a supportive and compassionate environment in which to assimilate a new understanding of themselves and their work.

Women were more likely to move into positions where they would continue to see children as central to their work (Ortiz, 1982). Role conflict can occur when women are placed in administrative positions if they believe their children and instruction are supposed to be their primary concern. Ortiz concludes that this role conflict is often viewed as incompetency. She states that one serious consequence of this role conflict is that women may try to resolve it by accentuating male behaviors, an adaptive behavior that is often viewed as unfeminine and may result in increased role conflict.

Minorities frequently enter educational administration through special project positions (Ortiz, 1982). In general, their prior administrative work has focused on working with minorities or on minority issues. These kinds of administrative positions do not prepare them to move away from children and instruction as a primary concern and to administer and manage other adults from a wide range of ethnic groups. In similar fashion, most Whites are not given an opportunity to develop the skills and knowledge necessary to work effectively with traditional minorities and to address minority issues.

Key Factors in the Underrepresentation of Minorities and Women Educational Leaders

Educational administration is highly stratified by race and gender (Ortiz, 1982; Ortiz & Marshall, 1988). The high number of female teachers and the low number of female administrators is an example of stratification by gender (Ortiz & Marshall, 1988). A number of explanations have been offered to account for the low numbers of women and minorities in educational administration. One commonly accepted explanation is that women and minorities are not motivated to enter administration. The research, however, does not support that claim. Diaz (1976) studied male and female teachers and found that women are more highly motivated than males to become administrators. Ortiz and Covel (1978) found that women have high career aspirations. After an extensive case study of a female principal, they concluded that "women have the same career ambitions as men, but they do not have the same opportunities" (p. 214). This conclusion is supported by Valverde (1974), who found that women and minorities held high career aspirations.

In a review of research on women in educational administration, Ortiz and Marshall (1988) concluded that women are underrepresented in educational leadership because of the way in which school administration has developed. They state that over the years school administration developed into a field that favors men over women. They identify four themes that dominated the development of educational administration: (a) teaching and administration were increasingly seen as separate but mutually dependent professions, with women in classroom teaching positions and men in administrative positions; (b) the structure of schools changed, making them more hierarchical and professional; (c) open competition decreased as sponsorship became viewed as the way to build a career in educational administration; and (d) the discussion of gender and power issues was discouraged (Ortiz & Marshall, 1988).

Research conducted by Pavan (1982) suggests that the low number of female administrators is not due to women's lack of qualifications. She found that a number of qualified females in the administrative job pool in Pennsylvania did not hold administrative positions. The women were not selected for administrative positions for several reasons, including sex-role stereotyping. Sex-role stereotyping can exist in employee selection, placement, disciplinary decisions, and preferences for supervisory behaviors (Rosen & Jerdee, 1974a, 1974b, 1974c, 1975). The extent of sex-role stereotyping is related to variables such as the percentage of women on the school board (Forlines, 1984) and the extent to which the individuals involved in the selection process have worked with a female administrator (Mack, 1981).

Woo (1985) surveyed 450 top women educational leaders. He found that many of the factors that were identified in earlier research as important variables in increasing or negating success for women were not identified as such by the women he surveyed. For example, the women in Woo's sample did not believe that affirmative action, flexible working hours, fear of success, mentors, and the "Cinderella syndrome" had any effect on their careers. They did, however, believe that factors such as assertiveness training and career guidance had a small effect on their careers. They believed the greatest obstacle to their career advancement was the lack of job opportunities.

In a 1979 nationwide survey of men and women superintendents, Richardson found that both males and females believed gender was a factor in their career development. Males believed their gender helped them attain administrative positions. Females believed their gender was of no help or was a hindrance. Even though both males and females believed that gender was a factor in access to administrative positions, affirmative action programs were not viewed positively by White males. Nasstrom and Butler (1975) found that male educators have a negative attitude toward affirmative action programs for female educators. Their attitudes were based on: (a) their belief that women were not prepared to hold a wider role, (b) perceived differences in leadership behavior between males and females, and (c) concern for their job security.

In 1979 Edson (1988) began a longitudinal study of 142 women who were seeking their first principalship. The initial data collection occurred in 1979–1980. A career update was conducted in 1984–1985. Edson's study of these 142 women provides some important information about the goals, attitudes, career progress, and concerns of women pursuing administrative careers. The subjects varied in age, race, and marital status. They lived all over the United States in cities, suburbs, and rural communities located in the South, West, Northwest, Midwest, Southeast, and Northeast. The women gave three reasons for seeking administrative careers: personal growth and challenge, concern about what was happening to children in schools, and their belief that they could do a better job than current administrators.

Edson's (1988) findings contradict earlier studies that concluded that (a) women were not interested in administration; (b) they would not move to further their careers; (c) family responsibilities were a burden and made career advancement difficult for women; and (d) female educators were uncomfortable with decision and policy making and therefore preferred support, not line, positions (Lesser, 1978; Paddock, 1981). The women Edson studied wanted careers in educational administration and the power and authority to change schools. Twenty-seven percent of the women in the study wanted to become superintendents, 13 percent hoped to become assistant superintendents, 14 percent identified secondary principalships as a career goal, and 26 percent named elementary school principalships as their highest career goal.

Unlike women in earlier studies, the women in the Edson (1988) study were not place-bound. Seventy-five percent of the women in the Edson study indicated that they would move out of their districts and 40 percent indicated that they would move out of their state for improved career opportunities. Only 26 percent of the 42 subjects indicated that their family responsibilities were a problem. Edson's findings on family responsibility are supported by McCamey (1976) who, in a study of African American and White female administrators, found that the women administrators did not believe that they had trouble combining family life and marriage with a career.

Epstein (1970) identified several processes by which male-dominated professions limit the participation of women. Those processes include institutionalized channels of recruitment and protégé systems that are not easily available to women. One of the pressures that women confront when they enter a male-dominated occupation is the inability to obtain information through the "good old boy" network (Harragon, 1977). Surveys of female educators often, although not always, identify the lack of mentors as an important reason why more women are not school administrators (Diaz, 1976; Jones & Montenegro, 1982; Schmuck, Charters, & Carlson, 1981). Pavan's (1987) survey of women administrators in Pennsylvania suggested that men and women have about the same number of mentoring experiences. More women than men, however, reported that mentoring functions were helpful.

The importance of sponsorship and mentoring has been documented in several studies (Collins, 1983; Misserian, 1982; Valverde, 1980; Villani, 1983). While the two concepts are frequently used interchangeably, there are subtle differences between them (Villani, 1983). Sponsors help locate their protégés in positions where they receive informal career socialization experiences. These informal experiences include meeting and interacting with members of the administrator group (Valverde, 1980; Villani, 1983). Valverde (1980) interviewed six mentors to gather information on the sponsor-protégé process. He found that mentors provide 4 basic functions: exposure, advice, protection, and sanction. Misserian's (1982) survey of women managers resulted in a list of 14 mentoring behaviors. Collins (1983) surveyed 400 women and identified a similar list of 15 mentoring behaviors. Mentoring can thus be viewed as a more personal, complex process than sponsorship.

The Future Study of Educational Leadership

A review of dissertations completed between 1964 and 1989, conducted by the author, indicates that studies of educational leaders were very limited in their scope. They tend to focus on educational leaders in a region or state. They also tend to focus on one key variable such as gender, ethnicity, leadership style, or career patterns. They do not usually examine several variables or attempt to identify intersections among them. Future research needs to have a broader scope and to reflect the dynamics of race and gender within the changing nature of our society. As a socially constructed phenomenon, leadership must also be examined within the changing meanings of race and gender.

Future research must look more deeply at the potential benefits of diverse leadership. Commenting on the state of research in educational leadership, F. I. Ortiz (personal communication, 1993) notes that research to date has not specified why it is necessary for women and people of color to assume leadership positions in educational organizations; what women and people of color contribute to educational administration, schools, and society as leaders of educational institutions; and how women and people of color are to be integrated within the leadership ranks of the educational enterprise. Ortiz's point is well taken because, while it is clear that educational administration is stratified by race and gender, relatively little is known about the employment experiences of women and people of color within the dynamics of race and gender in schools. Additional information is needed about the socialization of women and people of color in the workplace. We also need to know more about the initiation process that women and minorities experience when they enter administrative positions.

The roles of minorities and women in our society are clearly changing, and those changes may be reflected in the career patterns and in the leadership and managerial styles and skills of educational leaders. A multicultural approach to research on educational leadership invites opportunities for researchers to use a multidisciplinary approach to examine the intersections of race and gender. Important insights can be gained from comparing and contrasting the experiences of women and people of color in educational leadership. A multicultural approach adds a new dimension to the study of leadership and provides a basis for developing more comprehensive and inclusive approaches for theory and practice.

While there continues to be a significant underrepresentation of women and people of color in educational leadership, firm explanations for the underrepresentation continue to elude us. In terms of advanced training, degrees held, number of years in the profession, and total numbers in the pool from which administrators are drawn, there is no justification for the small number of women and minority educational leaders. Research is needed to explicate the ways in which gender and race affect the recruitment, selection, and retention process for school administrators.

In conclusion, the study of women and people of color presents many challenges to researchers. It also holds out the promise that insights gained from such research will lead to more inclusive leadership that represents the diversity in our pluralistic society. As our knowledge about the experiences of women and minorities in educational leadership deepens, we may be better able to select, train, and nurture more effective leaders for schools in the 21st century.

REFERENCES

Adkinson, J. A. (1981). Women in school administration: A review of the research. *Review of Educational Research, 51,* 311–343.

American Association of School Administrators. (1960). *Profile of the school superintendent.* Washington, DC: Author.

American Association of School Administrators. (1985). *Women and minorities in school administration.* Arlington, VA: Author.

Ashmore, R. D., Del Boca, F. K., & Wohlers, A. J. (1986). Gender stereotypes. In R. D. Ashmore & F. K. Del Boca (Eds.), *The social psychology of female-male relations: A critical analysis of central concepts* (pp. 69–119). Orlando, FL: Academic Press.

Argyris, C., & Schön, D. A. (1974). *Theory in practice: Increasing professional effectiveness.* San Francisco: Jossey-Bass.

Astin, H. S. (1969). *The woman doctorate in America: Origins, career and family.* New York: Russell Sage Foundation.

Astin, H. S., & Leland, C. (1991). *Women of influence, women of vision.* San Francisco: Jossey-Bass.

Bales, R. F. (1950). A set of categories for the analysis of small group interaction. *American Sociological Review, 15,* 257–263.

Banks, C.A.M. (1991). *City school superintendents: Their career patterns, traits, and perceptions of leadership and managerial skill and style.* Unpublished doctoral dissertation, Seattle University.

Banks, C. M. (1988). *The Black school superintendent: A study in early childhood socialization and career development.* Unpublished doctoral dissertation, University of Pittsburgh.

Bass, B. M. (1981). *Stogdill's handbook of leadership.* New York: The Free Press.

Bayes, M., & Newton, P. M. (1978). Women in authority: Sociopsychological analysis. *Journal of Applied Behavioral Science, 14,* 7–20.

Beck, H. N. (1978). *Attitudes toward women held by California school district board members, superintendents, and personnel directors including a review of the historical, psychological, and sociological foundations.* Unpublished doctoral dissertation, University of the Pacific, Stockton, CA.

Bell, D. J. (1975). *Power, influence, and authority.* New York: Oxford University Press.

Bem, S. L., & Bem, D. J. (1975). *Training the woman to know her place: The social antecedents of women in the world of work.* (ERIC Document Reproduction Service No. ED 082 098)

Bernard, J. S. (1964). *Academic women.* University Park: Pennsylvania State University Press.

Biklen, S. K., & Brannigan, M. B. (Eds.). (1980). *Women and educational leadership.* Lexington, MA: D.C. Heath.

Blau, P. M. (1976). *Exchange and power in social life.* New York: Wiley.

Broverman, I. R., Broverman, D. M., Clarkson, F. E., Rosenkrantz, P. S., & Vogel, S. R. (1970). Sex-role stereotypes and clinical judgments of mental health professionals. *Journal of Consulting and Clinical Psychology, 34,* 1–7.

Broverman, I. R., Vogel, S. R., Broverman, D. H., Clarkson, F. E., & Rosenkrantz, P. S. (1972). Sex-role stereotypes: A current appraisal. *Journal of Social Issues, 28*(2), 59–78.

Brown, L. K., & Klein, K. H. (1982). Woman power in medical hierarchy. *Journal of American Medical Women's Association, 37,* 155–164.

Brown, S. M. (1979). Male versus female leaders: A comparison of empirical studies. *Sex Roles: A Journal of Research, 5*(5), 595–611.

Bulls, G. P. (1986). *Career development of the Black female superintendent.* Unpublished doctoral dissertation, University of Pennsylvania.

Burns, J. M. (1979). *Leadership.* New York: Harper & Row.

Butler, J. E., & Walter, J. C. (Eds.). (1991). *Transforming the curriculum: Ethnic studies and women's studies.* Albany: State University of New York Press.

Byrne, D. R., Hines, S. A., & McCleary, L. E. (1978). *The senior high school principalship.* Reston, VA: National Association of School Principals.

Chapman, J. B. (1975). Comparisons of male and female leadership style. *Academy of Management Journal, 18,* 645–650.

Clement, J. P. (1975). *Sex bias in school leadership*. Evanston, IL: Integrated Education Associates.

Clifford, G. J. (1982). Marry, stitch, die, or do worse: Educating women for work. In H. Kantor & D. B. Tyack (Eds.), *Work, youth, and schooling: Historical perspectives on vocationalism in American education* (pp. 223–268). Stanford, CA: Stanford University Press.

Collins, N. W. (1983). *Professional women and their mentors*. Englewood Cliffs, NJ: Prentice Hall.

Cunningham, L. L. (1990). Educational leadership and administration: Retrospective and prospective views. In L. L. Cunningham & B. Mitchell, *Educational leadership and changing contexts in families, communities, and schools* (pp. 1–18). Chicago: The National Society for the Study of Education.

Cunningham, L. L., & Nystrand, R. O. (1969). Toward greater relevance in preparation programs for urban school administrators. *Educational Administration Quarterly, 5*(1), 6–23.

Diaz, S. (1976). *The aspiration levels of women for administrative careers in education: Predictive factors and implications for effecting change*. American Educational Research Association, San Francisco. (ERIC Document Reproduction Service No. ED 119 376)

Doughty, R. (1980). The Black female administrator: Women in a double bind. In S. X. Biklen & M. B. Brannigan (Eds.), *Women and educational leadership* (pp. 165–174). Washington, DC: Lexington Books.

Douglas, L. D., & Simonson, S. V. (1982). *A comparison of life experiences and leader behaviors between male and female superintendents*. Unpublished doctoral dissertation, Seattle University.

DuBois, C., & Ruiz, V. L. (Eds.). (1990). *Unequal sisters: A multicultural reader in U.S. women's history*. New York: Routledge.

Dugger, K. (1991). Social location and gender-role attitudes: A comparison of Black and White women. In J. Lorber & S. A. Farrell (Eds.), *The social construction of gender* (pp. 38–59). Newbury Park, CA: Sage.

Eagly, A. L., Karau, S. J., & Johnson, B. T. (1992). Gender and leadership style among school principals: A meta-analysis. *Educational Administration Quarterly, 28,* 76–102.

Edson, S. K. (1987). Voices from the present: Tracking the female administrative aspirant. *Journal of Educational Equity and Leadership, 7,* 261–277.

Edson, S. K. (1988). *Pushing the limits: The female administrative aspirant*. Albany: State University of New York Press.

Epstein, C. F. (1970). *Woman's place: Options and limits in professional careers*. Berkeley: University of California Press.

Epstein, C. F. (1972). Positive effects of the multiple negative: Explaining the success of Black professional women. *American Journal of Sociology, 78,* 912–915.

Epstein, C. F. (1988). *Deceptive distinctions.* New Haven, CT: Yale University Press.

Epstein, C. F. (1991). Ways men and women lead. *Harvard Business Review, 69*(1), 150–153.

Evers, C. W., & Lokomski, G. (1991). *Knowing educational administration: Contemporary methodological controversies in educational administration research.* New York: Pergamon Press.

Feistritzer, C. E. (1990). *Profile of teachers in the U.S.: 1990.* Washington, DC: National Center for Education Information.

Fernberger, S. W. (1948). Persistence of stereotypes concerning sex differences. *Journal of Abnormal and Social Psychology, 43,* 97–101.

Fiedler, F. E. (1967). *A theory of leadership effectiveness.* New York: McGraw-Hill.

Fierman, J. (1990, December). Do women manage differently? *Fortune,* pp. 115–118.

Fleishman, E. A. (1953) The description of supervisory behavior. *Journal of Applied Psychology, 37,* 1–6.

Fleishman, E. A. (1957). A leader behavior description for industry. In R. M. Stogdill & A. E. Coons (Eds.), *Leader behavior: Its description and measurement* (pp. 89–120). Columbus: Bureau of Business Research, Ohio State University.

Forlines, A. H. (1984). *Superintendents' perceptions of public opinions toward women administrators and superintendents' opinions toward women administrators.* Unpublished doctoral dissertation, George Peabody College for Teachers, Vanderbilt University.

Franklin, J. H. (1993). *The color line: Legacy for the twenty-first century.* Columbia: University of Missouri Press.

Frasher, J. M., & Frasher, R. S. (1979). Educational administration: A feminine profession. *Educational Administration Quarterly, 2,* 1–13.

Freeman, J. (Ed.). (1984). *Women: A feminist perspective* (3rd ed.). Palo Alto, CA: Mayfield.

French, J.R.P., Jr., & Raven, B. (1960). The bases of social power. In D. Catwright & A. Zander (Eds.), *Group dynamics: Research and theory* (pp. 607–623). New York: Harper & Row.

Friedan, B. (1963). *The feminine mystique.* New York: Dell.

Gaertner, K. N. (1980). The structure of organizational careers. *Sociology of Education, 53,* 7–20.

Goode, W. J. (1960). A theory of role strain. *American Sociological Review, 25,* 483–495.

Goslin, D. A. (Ed.). (1969). *Handbook of socialization theory and research.* Chicago: Rand McNally.

Gross, E., & Etzioni, A. (1985). *Organizations in society.* Englewood Cliffs, NJ: Prentice-Hall.

Gross, N., Mason, W. S., & McEachern, A. W. (1958). *Explorations in role analysis: Studies of the school superintendency role.* New York: Wiley.

Gross, N., & Trask, A. E. (1976). *The sex factor and the management of schools.* New York: Wiley.

Hagen, R., & Kahn, A. (1975). Discrimination against competent women. *Journal of Applied Social Psychology, 41,* 362–376.

Halpin, A. W., & Winer, B. J. (1957). A factorial study of the leader behavior descriptions. In R. M. Stogdill & A. E. Coons (Ed.), *Leader behavior: Its description and measurement* (pp. 190–235). Columbus: Bureau of Business Research, Ohio State University.

Harragon, B. L. (1977). *Games mother never taught you: Corporate gamesmanship for women.* New York: Warner Books.

Helgesen, S. (1990). *The female advantage: Women's ways of leadership.* Garden City, NY: Doubleday.

Hemphill, J. K., & Coons, A. E. (1957). Development of the leader behavior description questionnaire. In R. M. Stogdill & A. E. Coons (Eds.), *Leader behavior: Its description and measurement* (pp. 147–163). Columbus: Bureau of Business Research, Ohio State University.

Hersey, P. (1984). *The situational leader.* New York: Warner Books.

Holden, R. L. (1977). *The Chicago schools: A social and political history.* Beverly Hills, CA: Sage.

Hollander, E. P., & Yoder, J. (1978). *Some issues in comparing women and men as leaders.* (ERIC Document Reproduction Service No. ED 185 883)

Holter, H. (1970). *Sex roles and social structure.* Oslo, Norway: Universitetsforlaget.

hooks, b. (1990). *Yearning: Race, gender, and cultural politics.* Boston: South End Press.

Horner, M. (1987). Toward understanding of achievement-related conflicts in women. In M. R. Walsh (Ed.), *The psychology of women* (pp. 169–184). New Haven, CT: Yale University Press.

House, R. J., & Baetz, M. L. (1979). Leadership: Some empirical generalizations and new research directions. In B. M. Staw (Ed.), *Research in organizational behavior* (Vol. 1). Greenwich, CT: JAI.

Huber, J. (1973). *Changing women in a changing society.* Chicago: University of Chicago Press.

Immegart, G. L. (1988). Leadership and leader behavior. In N. J. Boyan (Ed.), *Handbook of research on educational administration* (pp. 259–278). New York: Longman.

Jago, A. G. (1982). Leadership: Perspectives in theory and research. *Management Science, 28*(3), 315–336.

Janda, K. F. (1960). Towards the explication of the concept of leadership in terms of the concept of power. *Human Relations, 13,* 345–363.

Johnston, G. S., Yeakey, C. C., & Holden, R. L. (1979). An analysis of the external variables affecting the role of the Black school superintendent. *Educational Research Quarterly, 4,* 13–24.

Johnston, G. S., Yeakey, C. C., & Moore, S. E. (1980). Analysis of the employment of women in professional administrative positions in public education. *Planning and Changing, 11,* 115–132.

Jones, E. H. (1983). *Black school administrators: A review of their early history, trends, problems in recruitment.* Arlington, VA: American Association of School Administrators.

Jones, E. H., & Montenegro, X. P. (1982). *Recent trends in the representation of women and minorities in school administration and problems in documentation.* Arlington, VA: American Association of School Administrators.

Jones, E. H., & Montenegro, X. P. (1990). *Women and minorities in school administration.* (ERIC Document Reproduction Service No. ED 273 017)

Josefowitz, N. (1980, September/October). Management men and women: Closed vs. open doors. *Harvard Business Review, 58,* 56–62.

Kanter, R. M. (1977). *Men and women of the corporation.* New York: Basic Books.

Keim, A. S. (1978). *Women and the superintendency: A comparison of male and female career paths and expectations.* Unpublished doctoral dissertation, Lehigh University, Bethlehem, PA.

Komarovsky, M. (1973). Cultural contradictions and sex role: The masculine case. In J. Huber (Ed.), *Chicana women in a chicana society* (pp. 111–112). Chicago: University of Chicago Press.

Korah, S. (1990). Multiculturalism and the woman of colour: Can we bridge the gap between rhetoric and reality? *Tiger Lily: Journal by Women of Colour, 6,* 5–20.

Lesser, P. (1978). *The participation of women in public school administration.* (ERIC Document Reproduction Service No. ED 151 958)

Loden, M. (1985). *Feminine leadership or how to succeed in business without being one of the boys.* New York: Times Books.

Loewenstine, H. V., Ponticos, G. D., & Pauldi, M. A. (1982). Sex differences in graffiti as a communication style. *Journal of Social Psychology, 117,* 307–328.

Lomotey, K. (1989). *African-American principals: School leadership and success*. New York: Greenwood.

Lovelady-Dawson, F. (1980, December). Women and minorities in the principalship: Career opportunities and problems. *NASSP Bulletin, 64,* 18–28.

Mack, M. H. (1981). *A study of attitude toward women as school administrators*. Unpublished doctoral dissertation, Auburn University, AL.

Marshall, C. (1984). The crisis in excellence and equity. *Educational Horizons, 63,* 24–30.

McCamey, D. S. (1976). *The status of Black and White women in central administrative positions in Michigan public schools*. Unpublished doctoral dissertation, University of Michigan, Ann Arbor.

McCarthy, C., & Crichlow, W. (Eds.). (1993). *Race identity and representation in education*. New York: Routledge.

McCarthy, M., & Zent, A. (1981). School administrators: 1980 profile. *Planning and Changing, 12*(3), 144–161.

McGregor, D. (1960). *The human side of enterprise*. New York: McGraw-Hill.

McIntosh, P. (1988). *White privilege and male privilege: A personal account of coming to see correspondence through work in women's studies*. Wellesley, MA: Wellesley College Center for Research on Women.

Merton, R. K. (1957). *Social theory and social structure*. New York: Macmillan.

Millett, K. (1980). *Sexual politics*. New York: Ballantine. (Originally published 1969)

Millham, J., & Smith, L. (1981). Sex role differentiation among Black and White Americans: A comparative study. *Journal of Black Psychology, 7,* 77–99.

Mills, J. (1984). Self-imposed behaviors of females and males in photographs. *Sex Roles, 10*(7/8), 633–637.

Misserian, A. K. (1982). *The corporate connection: Why executive women need mentors to reach the top*. Englewood Cliffs, NJ: Prentice Hall.

Monteiro, T. (1977). Ethnicity and the perceptions of principals. *Integrated Education, 15*(3), 15–16.

Moody, C. D. (1971). *Black superintendents in public school districts: Trends and conditions*. Unpublished doctoral dissertation, Northwestern University, Evanston, IL.

Morsink, H. M. (1970). Leadership behavior of men and women principals. *NASSP Bulletin, 54*(347), 80–87.

Munson, C. E. (1979, March). Evaluation of male and female supervisors. *Social Work, 24,* 104–110.

Nasstrom, R. R., & Butler, W. E. (1975). The professionalism of women teachers. *Kappa Delta Pi Record, 12*(1), 6–8.

National Center for Educational Statistics. (1991). *The condition of education 1991: Vol. 2. Postsecondary Education.* Washington, DC: U.S. Department of Education.

Neely, M. A., & Wilson, A. E. (1978). *A program to overcome sex bias in women's qualifications for vocational administration posts.* (ERIC Document Reproduction Service No. ED 166 391)

Nichols, N. A. (1993). Whatever happened to Rosie the riveter? *Harvard Business Review, 71*(4), 54–62.

O'Leary, V. E. (1974). Some attitudinal barriers to occupational aspirations in women. *Psychological Bulletin, 81,* 809–826.

Ortiz, F. I. (1982). *Career patterns in education: Men, women and minorities in public school administration.* New York: Praeger.

Ortiz, F. I., & Covel, J. (1978). Women in school administration: A case analysis. *Urban Education, 13,* 213–236.

Ortiz, F. I., & Marshall, C. (1988). Women in educational administration. In N. J. Boyan (Ed.), *Handbook of research on educational administration* (pp. 123–141). New York: Longman.

Paddock, S. C. (1981). Male and female career paths in school administration. In P. A. Schmuck, W. W. Charters, Jr., & R. O. Carlson (Eds.), *Educational policy and management: Sex differentials* (pp. 35–52). New York: Academic Press.

Parsons, T. (1951). *The social system.* New York: The Free Press.

Pavan, B. N. (1982). *Certified but not hired: Women administrators in Pennsylvania.* (ERIC Document Reproduction Service No. ED 263 689)

Pavan, B. N. (1987). Mentoring certified aspiring and incumbent female and male public school administrators. *Journal of Educational Equity and Leadership, 7*(4), 318–331.

Pelz, D. C. (1952). Influence: A key to effective leadership in the first-line supervisor. *Personnel, 29,* 209–217.

Perkins, L. M. (1989). The history of Blacks in teaching: Growth and decline within the profession. In D. Warren (Ed.), *American teachers: Histories of a profession at work* (pp. 344–369). New York: Macmillan.

Peshkin, A. (1978). *Growing up American.* Chicago: University of Chicago Press.

Peterson, P. (1985). *The politics of school reform 1870–1940.* Chicago: University of Chicago Press.

Petty, M. M., & Miles, R. H. (1976). Leader sex-role stereotyping in a female-dominated work culture. *Personnel Psychology, 29,* 393–404.

Phillips, D. L., & Voorhees, S. V. (1986). *Attitudes toward female school administrators in the state of Washington.* Unpublished doctoral dissertation, Seattle University.

Pinar, W. F. (1993). Notes on understanding curriculum as a racial text. In C. McCarthy & W. Crichlow (Eds.), *Race identity and representation in education* (pp. 60–70). New York: Routledge.

Pitner, N. J. (1981). *Notes on the differences in behavior of women superintendents in suburban districts.* Paper presented at the annual meeting of the American Educational Research Association, Los Angeles.

Popenoe, D. (1971). *Sociology.* New York: Meredith Corporation.

Pratt, J.M.M. (1980). *A case study analysis of male-female leadership emergence in small groups.* Unpublished doctoral dissertation, University of Minnesota, Minneapolis.

Revere, A.L.B. (1985). *A description of the Black female superintendent.* Unpublished doctoral dissertation, Miami University.

Richardson, J.A.M. (1979). *Women superintendents of public schools in the United States: Factors contributing to obtaining the position.* Unpublished doctoral dissertation, Drake University, Des Moines, IA.

Rosen, B., & Jerdee, T. H. (1974a). Influence of sex role stereotypes on personnel decisions. *Journal of Applied Psychology, 59, 9–14.*

Rosen, B., & Jerdee, T. H. (1974b). Effects of applicant's sex and difficulty of job evaluations of candidates for managerial positions. *Journal of Applied Psychology, 59, 511–512.*

Rosen, B., & Jerdee, T. H. (1974c). Sex stereotyping in the executive suite. *Harvard Business Review, 52, 45–58.*

Rosen, B., & Jerdee, T. H. (1975). Effects of employee's sex and threatening versus pleading appeals on managerial evaluations of grievances. *Journal of Applied Psychology, 60(4), 442–445.*

Rosener, J. B. (1990). Ways women lead. *Harvard Business Review, 68(6),* 119–125.

Rossi, A. S. (1970). Sex equality: The beginning of ideology. In M. L. Thompson (Ed.), *Voices of the new feminism* (pp. 113–147). New York: McGraw-Hill.

Rost, J. C. (1991). *Leadership for the twenty-first century.* Westport, CT: Praeger.

Ruble, T. L. (1983). Sex stereotypes: Issues and change in the 1970s. *Sex Roles, 9,* 397–402.

Saks, J. B. (1992, December). Education vital signs. *The American School Board Journal,* pp. 32–45.

Schmuck, P. A. (1980). Changing women's representation in school management: A systems perspective. In S. K. Biklen & M. B. Brannigan (Eds.), *Women and educational leadership* (pp. 242–263). Lexington, MA: D. C. Heath.

Schmuck, P. A., Charters, W. W., Jr., & Carlson, R. O. (Eds.). (1981). *Educational policy and management: Sex differentials.* New York: Academic Press.

Schuster, D. J. (1987). *Male and female superintendents compared nationally: Career implications for women in educational administration.* Unpublished doctoral dissertation, Teachers College, Columbia University, New York.

Scott, H. J. (1980). *The Black school superintendent: Messiah or scapegoat?* Washington, DC: Howard University Press.

Scott, H. J. (1983). Views of Black school superintendents on school desegregation. *Journal of Negro Education, 52*(4), 378–382.

Shakeshaft, C. S. (1979). Dissertation research on women in educational administration: A synthesis of findings and paradigm for future research. (Doctoral dissertation, Texas A&M University, 1979). *Dissertation Abstracts International, 40,* 6455a.

Shakeshaft, C. S. (1985). Strategies for overcoming the barriers to women in educational administration. In S. Klein (Ed.), *Handbook for achieving sex equity through education* (pp. 124–144). Baltimore, MD: The Johns Hopkins University Press.

Shakeshaft, C. S. (1987). *Women in educational administration.* Newbury Park, CA: Sage.

Sizemore, B. A. (1986). The limits of the Black superintendency: A review of the literature. *Journal of Educational Equity and Leadership, 6*(3), 180–208.

Sleeter, C. E. (1993). How White teachers construct race. In C. McCarthy & W. Crichlow (Eds.), *Race identity and representation in education* (pp. 157–171). New York: Routledge.

Snyder, T. D. (1989). *Digest of educational statistics.* Washington, DC: National Center for Educational Statistics, Government Printing Office.

Spencer, G. (1986). *Projections of the Hispanic population: 1983–2080* (Current Population Reports, Series P-25, No. 995). Washington, DC: U.S. Bureau of the Census.

Stevens, K. M. (1988). *Profiles of Washington state women school superintendents.* Unpublished doctoral dissertation, Seattle University.

Stogdill, R. H. (1963). *Manual for the leader behavior description questionnaire —Form XII.* Columbus, OH: Bureau of Business Research, Ohio State University.

Stogdill, R. H. (1974). *Handbook of leadership: A survey of theory and research.* New York: The Free Press.

Taylor, S. S. (1971). *The attitudes of superintendents and board of education members in Connecticut toward the employment and effectiveness of women as public school administrators.* Unpublished doctoral dissertation, University of Connecticut, Storrs.

Toren, N. (1973). The bus driver: A study in role analysis. *Human Relations,* 26(1), 101–112.

U.S. Bureau of the Census. (1992). *Statistical abstract of the United States* (112th ed.). Washington, DC: Government Printing Office.

Valverde, L. A. (1974). *Succession socialization: Its influence on school administrative candidates and its implications to the exclusion of minorities from administration.* Austin, TX: University of Texas at Austin. (ERIC Document Reproduction Service No. 093 052)

Valverde, L. A. (1980). *Promotion socialization: The informal process in large urban school districts and its adverse effects on non-Whites and women.* Paper presented at the meeting of the American Education Research Association, Boston, MA.

Villani, D. (1983). *Mentoring and sponsoring as ways for women to overcome internal barriers to heightened career aspiration and achievement.* Unpublished doctoral dissertation, Northeastern University, Boston.

Vroom, V. H. (1976). Leadership. In M. Dunnette (Ed.), *Handbook of industrial and organizational psychology* (pp. 1527–1552). Chicago: Rand McNally.

Vroom, V. H., & Yetton, E. W. (1973). *Leadership and decision making.* Pittsburgh: University of Pittsburgh Press.

Weber, M. (1968). Economy and society: An outline of interpretive sociology. In G. Roth & C. Wittich (Eds.), *Wirtschaft und Gesellschaft* (E. Fischoff, Trans., pp. 28–72). New York: Bedminster Press.

West, C. (1993). *Race matters.* Boston: Beacon Press.

White, J. (1967). Women in the law. *Michigan Law Review, 65,* 1051.

White, L. T. (1950). *Educating our daughters.* New York: Harper.

Williams, J. E. (1982). An overview of findings from adult sex stereotype studies in 25 countries. In R. Rath, H. S. Asthana, D. Sinha, & J. B. Sinha (Eds.), *Diversity and unity in crosscultural psychology* (pp. 250–260). Lisse, Netherlands: Swets and Zeitlinger.

Woo, L. C. (1985). Women administrators: Profiles of success. *Phi Delta Kappan, 64*(4), 285–288.

Yukl, G. A. (1981). *Leadership in organizations* (3rd ed.). Englewood Cliffs, NJ: Prentice Hall.

17

GENDER AND SUPERVISION

Charol Shakeshaft
Irene Nowell
Andy Perry

COMMUNICATION BETWEEN women and men has long been the basis of both humor and folklore in the human drama of life. From the cry of "What do women want?" to the characterization of men as unable to express emotions, men and women have been stereotyped as people who talk and act differently.

Because these stereotypes have most often been hurtful to women, especially in the workplace, many of us who have struggled to help women achieve equity have resisted the notion of differences between males and females. Nevertheless, in a society that does not treat females and males the same, the impact of gender on behavior is worthy of study.

Based on our experiences as administrators as well as our collective and individual research, we believe that gender affects both supervisory style and outcome. In this article, we examine some of the ways in which gender may influence the supervisory act.

Sex and Gender

Sex is a biological description, one that divides most of humankind into two types of people—females and males. We say most, since even a variable such as sex, which seems to be easily distinguished, has some ambiguity depending upon the evidence used to determine who is male and who is female (Shakeshaft, 1989).

Gender is a cultural term (Shakeshaft, 1989). It describes the characteristics we ascribe to people because of their sex—the ways we believe they behave or the characteristics we believe they possess, based on our cultural expectations of what is male and what is female.

As far as we can determine from our work and the work of others, one's biological identification as male or female has little to do with how people behave and the work they do in schools. However, one's gender identification has a tremendous influence on behavior, perceptions, and effectiveness (Shakeshaft, 1989). In other words, being born female or male does not in itself affect how we will act as workers; however, the way we are *treated* from birth onward, *because* we are either female or male, does help to determine how we both see and navigate the world.

Although the supervision area abounds with theories and scripts, little has been written on the impact of gender on successful supervision. This issue seems particularly salient given the sex structuring of schools, which results in an organization in which males most often supervise females. It takes on added importance if we examine the stereotypic expectations of behavior and status and imagine what implications they might have when the norm is reversed and a female supervises a male.

Communication and Feedback Patterns

Gender and gender expectations may partially determine how supervisors interact with those they supervise. For instance, research suggests that the sex of participants affects what is communicated and how it is communicated (Borisoff & Merrill, 1985). The same words spoken by a male supervisor have different meanings to male and female teachers. Conversely, an interaction between a female principal and a male teacher is not the same as an exchange between a female principal and a female teacher.

Men and women communicate differently and they listen for different information (Borisoff & Merrill, 1985). In a supervisory conference in which a principal is discussing an instructional issue with the teacher, the woman participant may be listening for the feeling and the man for the facts. Given what we know of the values that males and females carry into their jobs in schools, the woman may be focused upon an instructional issue or a matter concerning the child, while the man may choose to discuss an administrative problem.

Further, research supports the notion that there may be discomfort in communicating with a member of the other sex. Male teachers tend to exhibit more hostility in dealing with female administrators than do female teachers, and women administrators have to work harder to get male teachers to "hear" them (Shakeshaft, 1987).

Perceptions of competence may also influence supervisory styles and effectiveness. Women are initially evaluated less favorably than equally competent men (Shakeshaft, 1987). These perceptions may unknowingly affect supervisory interactions, both when the woman is being supervised and when she is the supervisor.

Nowhere does the impact of gender on supervision become more evident than in the area of feedback. Men receive both more and more types than do women. Women are more likely to get nonevaluative feedback, or neutral responses. Men receive more positive and more negative responses (Shakeshaft, 1987).

A 1987 study found that male administrators are less likely to give direct feedback to females than to males (Shakeshaft, 1987). For instance, when a male subordinate makes a mistake or does not live up to the expectations of his boss, his supervisor tends to level with him, "telling it like it is." When a female errs, she often is not even informed. Instead, the mistake is corrected by others without her knowledge. The results of this behavior are two-fold. For the male, learning takes place instantly. He gets criticism and the chance to change his behavior. He learns to deal with negative opinions of his work and has the option to improve.

Females often do not hear anything negative, being given neutral or slightly positive cues, even if their performance is less than ideal. This results in a woman's misconception of her abilities or, at least, the level of her performance. If she is not given direct criticism, she has neither the opportunity to improve nor the opportunity to reassess her abilities.

These differential feedback patterns are not unique to the adult work setting. The work of Sadker and Sadker (1986) describes similar patterns throughout K–12 schooling, where boys receive more feedback and a wider range of feedback than girls. These early differences not only help us understand why we behave as we do when we become adult workers, they also help us understand women's reactions to criticism in the rare instances when they get it first-hand. (Women get criticism; the issue is whether or not they get to hear it.)

In interviews with women administrators (Shakeshaft, 1987), the women were found to take criticism hard. They tended to think it was an assessment of their very essence. The first time they received criticism or the first time they failed, the women administrators interpreted it as a sign that they were inferior and that they never should have tried to become an administrator in the first place. This is not surprising for two reasons.

First, females are less valued than males in this society. Consequently, from birth onward through school and into adult life, women receive subtle and not so subtle messages about their worth. These messages are one of the reasons that women have been found to have lower self-esteem than men (Andrews, 1984). Secondly, if, as girls, females received little direct criticism, they had few opportunities to learn not to take critical comments personally.

When male superintendents and principals were asked why they did not confront women with their misgivings and dissatisfactions, one of the major reasons given was the fear of women's tears (Shakeshaft, 1987). Most of the men were uncomfortable with the prospect of tears. When questioned about what they expected from men to whom they gave negative feedback, most anticipated anger. While none of the administrators in this study liked confronting anyone with negative feedback, the prospect of an angry response was easier for them to face than the prospect of tears. Male superintendents and principals said they did not like to deal with angry subordinates, but that they had the skills to do so. They reported being much less comfortable with crying, and, because of this discomfort, most failed to give women important corrective feedback that would have allowed the women to improve their performance as educators.

This information led to an examination of who cries and how often (Shakeshaft, 1989). The results suggested that there is not a great deal of crying in public schools, and that, although women cry in front of supervisors slightly more than men, the difference in frequency is very small. However, women are reported to cry equally often in front of females and males, while males cry only in front of women. Thus, the study suggested that it is the fear of tears—rather than overwhelming evidence of actual crying—that paralyzes male administrators. Also, since both men and women cry, it is not solely a "female" problem. Finally, although crying is not solely a female problem, and although nobody cries very much, the fear of tears (or the gender expectation about what women do) keeps women from getting honest feedback about their performance and impairs the supervisory effectiveness of male administrators.

Thus, gender perceptions are influencing behavior and interfering with effectiveness. The issues are difficult for both men and women. Women must be aware of the feedback loop and try to determine if they are getting helpful evaluative information. Men, on the other hand, often perceive themselves in a "no-win" position. If a man treats a woman as he does a man, he may be accused of being harsh or unfair. If he does not treat a woman as he does a man, he may be accused of not giving her helpful or corrective feedback. We need to examine our expectations about male and female behavior and confront the issue so that both men and women are as effective as they can be in a supervisory relationship.

Influence of Sexuality on Working Relationships

Another factor that may inhibit or interfere with the supervisory act is heterosexuality and our unspoken beliefs about men and women working together. In a study of the hiring practices of male superintendents (Shakeshaft, 1989), they were asked if they would hire a traditionally attractive female. The term "traditionally attractive" was used so that the superintendents could make their own decisions not only about what was attractive, but also about what was attractive within the acceptable range of school administrators. Almost all of the superintendents in the study said they would hire an attractive woman. When asked for what job, almost all suggested an elementary principalship.

In a follow-up question as to whether they would hire this imaginary woman as an assistant superintendent, in a role that worked very closely with the superintendent, very few of the superintendents said they would. The issue for these superintendents was the combination of the intensity of the working relationship and the attractiveness of the woman. Most of them said they felt uncomfortable in a close working relationship with an attractive woman.

One reason given for this lack of comfort was the superintendents' concern that school board members would see something unseemly in the relationship and that this perception would threaten their effectiveness with their boards. Another reason given by the superintendents was their worry that it would cause marital friction, and few wanted "trouble on the homefront" added to their already stressful lives. A third reason, and one that may hurt women the most, was an uncertainty on the part of most of the male superintendents about what their own feelings would be toward an attractive female subordinate. If they were sexually attracted to her, it seemed like a no-win situation. If she did not return the feelings, the superintendent ran the risk of being charged with sexual harassment. If the feelings were mutual, the superintendent's first two fears (school board disapproval and marital friction) might become reality. Thus, most of the superintendents concluded that it was not worth the risks to hire an attractive woman (and for many that translated into woman) into a position with which the superintendent worked closely.

Because of the lack of comfort men in school administration have with issues of sexuality, women have been advised to dress and act in ways that suppress or hide their own sexuality. Women's dress for success formulas are more like dress for asexuality than for any criteria associated with success. Men, on the other hand, are advised to wear "power suits," attire that has high sexual appeal among women (Shakeshaft, 1989).

From the woman's perspective, the issue of sexuality is also a problem. Women administrators are often cautious and suspicious of attention from male superordinates, since they are unclear about the underlying message. Whether or not there is a spoken or unspoken sexual message, women process the possibility and think about their responses and actions in light of that possibility (Shakeshaft, 1987).

In addition to the possible negative effects for women of sexual attraction, some positive ones are also possible. Being noticed initially because one is attractive might open professional doors. Just how much attractiveness helps or hurts women in school administration has not been comprehensively explored; however, sexuality issues may be evident in some supervisory interactions and roles. Therefore, women's notions about what is expected of them may get in the way of how they supervise as well as how they respond to supervision.

The discomfort and lack of knowledge in this area is not surprising. The United States is a country not altogether comfortable with sexuality. Sex integration rarely occurs in U.S. school systems. Starting in about the second grade, boys and girls move apart and segregate themselves along sex lines (Best, 1983). Little is done to change this pattern of segregation by sex, and observations of classrooms and playgrounds find ample evidence of boys competing against girls in spelling bees and athletics (Sadker & Sadker, 1986).

When males and females mix again during late adolescence, it is for sexual or romantic reasons. Men and women have little training or practice in working together as people, except as representatives of different sexes. It is not surprising, then, that sexuality (and particularly heterosexuality) gets in the way of easy working relationships between women and men.

This issue of sexuality comes to our attention because it helps to explain some of the reasons why men are reluctant to hire women into jobs that require working together closely. However, further exploration of sexuality highlights the importance of the cultural meanings we give to people because of their sex and the implications these meanings have for administrative behavior. We need to understand how the issue of sexuality overlays the behavior of men and women in organizations and explore how it both helps and hurts the players involved.

Gender Differences in Expectations

Another example of gender differences and the possible effects on supervision is found in a study by Garfinkel (1988). He attempted to determine whether men and women superintendents conceptualize their administrative teams differently and whether these superintendents and their team members value different traits. Garfinkel found that both men and women value competence and trust, but they give each a different priority. For women superintendents, competence is the first thing they look for in a team member; trust is lower on the list. Men superintendents, on the other hand, identify trust as their number one criterion for team membership and view competence as less important.

To complicate matters, especially for team members, men and women define trust differently. According to Garfinkel (1988), men, both superintendents and team members, were more likely to describe trust as the "ability and comfort to say what they wished to say, confident that the persons they were sharing their thoughts or opinions with would not ridicule or repeat these thoughts elsewhere" (p. 311). Women superintendents defined trust as "an expectancy, held by an individual, that the word, promise or written statement of another individual or group can be relied on" (p. 311).

These differing conceptions of trust call for different indicators of proof. For men to see a person as trustworthy, that person must not divulge information or discuss actions or conversations with others. Women did not interpret those actions as untrustworthy. They expected people to discuss conversations, actions, and feelings with others. What women saw as untrustworthy was someone failing to do what they said they would do, when they said they would do it. Men did not identify a person as untrustworthy if he or she did not deliver on time. Rather, men saw that as an issue of time management or competency.

Garfinkel's study indicates that differences do exist in how people evaluate the job performance of those with whom they work and how that evaluation may be related to gender. The results of this study as well as literature that describes women administrators as differing from men led to an investigation by the three of us of differences in the written evaluations of teachers by male and female principals. The work of Shakeshaft (1987) provided a guide for exploring this issue. This earlier research indicated the following:

1. Relationships with others are more central to all actions for female administrators than they are for male administrators;

2. Teaching and learning is more often the major focus for female administrators than for male administrators;

3. Building community is more often an essential part of the woman administrator's style than it is for the man.

In this study, we did a content analysis of the written evaluations of 108 female teachers by 8 principals (5 males and 3 females) to determine whether male and female principals highlighted different things. All of the principals worked in the same school district and had received the same amount of training in the Hunter (1984) technique. The evaluations were coded without knowledge of the sex of the principal; inter-rater reliability was 77 percent.

We did find some differences in the things that women and men focused on. Women were more likely than men to encourage the empowerment of their teachers, establish instructional priorities, attend to the social and emotional development of the students, focus on student relationships, attend to the feelings of teachers, include more "facts" in the evaluation, look for the teachers' effects on the lives of children, emphasize the technical skills of teaching, comment on the content and quality of the educational program, provide information gathered from other sources, involve the teacher in decision making, issue directives for improvement, provide immediate feedback on performance, and emphasize curricular programs. Men, on the other hand, were more likely than women to emphasize organizational structure and to avoid conflict (Shakeshaft, Nowell, & Perry, 1991). Thus, we found that the evaluations of teachers written by female principals focused on more items, and particularly more items concerned with teaching and learning.

These findings support the literature that women may approach the supervisory process by valuing different characteristics and, thus, may concentrate on a different set of criteria than do men. This study suggests that, even when trained in a similar approach to supervisory interaction, males and females may still bring with them expectations and behaviors based upon gender. While this study is in no way definitive, it does provide some additional support for the need to more fully understand gender in all aspects of school administration, especially supervision.

Summary

In our view, gender does make a difference in how administrators behave. Sometimes these behaviors are just different and interesting. At other times, they may signal treatment that is not only different but more favorable to one sex than to another. When the latter is the case, we need to reexamine practice.

To do this, we might first examine ourselves. Having been raised in a sexist society, it is not surprising that we have ideas about what women and men can do and be, how males and females act, and how to treat men and women. We need to acknowledge our backgrounds and training, understanding that we had no control over what we were taught by society, school, and family. We do, however, have control over our actions today.

One way to gauge whether we are applying different expectations and standards to a situation is to imagine a member of the other sex in that situation. For instance, if a woman is working with a man and wonders if she has lowered her expectations, she might pretend he is a woman and consider how that woman would be treated. Another way to gain insight is to transfer knowledge about racism to male-female situations. When characterizing a woman in a particular way, one might consider whether the same characterization would be acceptable when referring to a minority person. Although racism is still strong, Americans have become more cautious about expressing it publicly, and educators have become more able to identify it. The models learned in one area can help us in another.

Addressing these issues with school administrators is crucial if we are to effect change. Research demonstrates that inservice education on these issues has gone a long way toward changing behavior (Grayson, 1988). For a small investment in time and money, districts can reduce the negative effects of gender issues and enhance the positive ones. The result is an environment more supportive of teaching and learning.

REFERENCES

Andrews, P. H. (1984). Performance—self-esteem and perceptions of leadership emergence: A comparative study of men and women. *Western Journal of Speech Communications, 48*(1), 1–13.

Best, R. (1983). *We've all got scars*. Bloomington: Indiana University Press.

Borisoff, D., & Merrill, L. (1985). *The power to communicate: Gender differences as barriers*. Prospect Heights, IL: Waveland Press.

Garfinkel, E. (1988). *Ways men and women in school administration conceptualize the administrative team*. Unpublished doctoral dissertation, Hofstra University, Hempstead, NY.

Grayson, D. (1988). *The equity principal*. Earlham, IA: Graymill.

Hunter, M. (1984). Knowing, teaching, and supervising. In P. L. Hosford (Ed.), *Using what we know about teaching* (pp. 169–192). Alexandria, VA: Association for Supervision and Curriculum Development.

Sadker, M., & Sadker, D. (1986). Sexism in the classroom: From grade school to graduate school. *Phi Delta Kappan, 67,* 512–515.

Shakeshaft, C. (1987). *Women in educational administration.* Newbury Park, CA: Sage.

Shakeshaft, C. (1989). The gender gap in research in educational administration. *Educational Administration Quarterly, 25,* 324–337.

Shakeshaft, C., Nowell, I., & Perry, A. (1991). [Written evaluations of teachers by male and female principals]. Unpublished raw data.

PART FOUR

MORAL LEADERSHIP

BOOKS ON MORAL LEADERSHIP have sold very well in recent years, acknowledging what many see as a crisis of violence and cruelty in the schools. These authors discuss the need for learning more than just facts and figures in the classroom; moral leadership helps set standards of conduct and care that members of school communities abide by to function. Part Four gives some practical advice on how to make a strong and virtuous school in the chapter by Kevin Ryan and Karen E. Bohlin; transformational insight into moral leadership, stewardship, followership, and leading by example is discussed in chapters by Thomas J. Sergiovanni and by Robert Evans.

18

LEADERSHIP AS STEWARDSHIP

"WHO'S SERVING WHO?"

Thomas J. Sergiovanni

MANY SCHOOL ADMINISTRATORS are practicing a form of leadership that is based on moral authority, but often this practice is not acknowledged as leadership. The reason for this problem is that moral authority is underplayed and that the management values undergirding this authority are largely unofficial. When I asked Larry Norwood, principal of Capital High School, Olympia, Washington, to participate in one of my studies on leadership, he responded, "I have wrestled with this—and finally decided to pass. First, because I am so late in responding and, second, I can think of nothing of literary significance that I have achieved (in the way of leadership) in the past twenty-two years. My style is to delegate and empower, and my successes have been through other people. If I have a strength it is as a facilitator—that doesn't make good copy. Sorry." Larry Norwood is a successful school administrator. Although he does not think of himself as a leader, he is one.

I suspect that one of the reasons for Norwood's success may be that he implicitly rejects leadership, as we now understand it. The official values of management lead us to believe that leaders are characters who single-handedly pull and push organizational members forward by the force of personality, bureaucratic clout, and political know-how. Leaders must be decisive. Leaders must be forceful. Leaders must have vision. Leaders must successfully manipulate events and people, so that vision becomes reality. Leaders, in other words, must *lead*.

From time to time, there may be a place for this kind of direct leadership. But it is only part of the story. The leadership that counts, in the end, is the kind that touches people differently. It taps their emotions, appeals to their values, and responds to their connections with other people. It is a morally based leadership—a form of stewardship. Greenfield (1991) found this to be the case in his study of an urban elementary school. The moral orientation of its teachers was central in fixing their relationship with the principal and with each other. Greenfield comments, "Their persistence in searching out strategies to increase their colleagues' or their personal effectiveness in serving the needs of the school's children was motivated not by bureaucratic mandate or directives from superiors, but by moral commitment to children, rooted in their awareness of the needs of these children and their beliefs about the significance of their roles, as teachers, in these children's lives. Much of the principal's efforts to foster leadership among the teachers . . . was directed to further developing and sustaining this moral orientation among teachers" (p. 3). To those teachers, shared ideals and beliefs became duties to which they willingly responded. These findings parallel those of Johnson (1990). Morally based leadership is important in its own right, but it is also important because it taps what is important to people and what motivates them.

Stewardship in Practice

Implicit in traditional conceptions of leadership is the idea that schools cannot be improved from within: school communities have neither the wit nor the will to lead themselves; instead, principals and teachers are considered pawns, awaiting the play of a master or the game plan of an expert to provide solutions for school problems. In his chronicle of Madeline Cartwright, principal of Blaine School, Philadelphia, Richard Louv (1990) points out that too many teachers and administrators doubt the power of determination and the ability of schools themselves to make a difference. "It just won't work," they maintain, or "The central office won't let us," or "We can't do that because. . . ." Madeline Cartwright is one principal who thinks differently. For her, being a school administrator is a form of stewardship, and the responsibilities of stewardship simply require that obligations and commitments be met, regardless of obstacles. "I tell my staff don't tell me what I can and can't do. I can do something if I want to. It can happen. It's like people say to me, 'You cannot wash this child's clothes, put 'em in the washing machine and give him some clean clothes to put on.' I can do that" (p. 75). And that she does.

Shortly after becoming principal at Blaine, Cartwright organized a raffle to buy a washer and dryer for the school. They are used every morning, to launder the clothes of many of the children. Cartwright often does the washing personally, believing that this is the only way many of the children know what it is like to have clean clothes. In her words, "This is one of the things you can do to bring about a change. My kids look good" (p. 63). When Cartwright arrived at Blaine, she found a school that was "black as soot." She told the parents, "This place is dirty! How can your kids go to school in a place like this? We're going to clean this building this summer. Raise your hands if I can depend on you. Keep your hands up! Somebody get their names!" Eighteen parents showed up and began the work. "We cleaned it, and cleaned it good. I made these parents know that you don't accept anything less than that which is right because you live in North Philadelphia!" (p. 66).

Parental involvement at Blaine is high. Parents help supervise the yard in the morning and the hallway during the day. They work in classrooms, help prepare food, and decorate the school. "Everybody is involved in the washing" (p. 67).

What kind of leader is Madeline Cartwright? She is one who will do whatever it takes to make Blaine work and work well: "If a child isn't coming to school, I'll go into a home and bring kids out" (p. 74). On one such venture, Cartwright and a friend walked into an apartment she describes as follows: "This place was cruddy. I mean, beyond anything I could ever imagine for little children to live in. The kitchen was a hotplate sitting on a drainboard. I saw no refrigerator. There was no running water and no electricity. There were dirty dishes, food caked in piles. The bathroom had a bedspread wrapped around the bottom of the toilet and the toilet was full to the brim with human waste. To the *brim*. And the little girl had one foot on one side of the toilet, and one foot on the other and she squatted over this toilet while she used it, and it was seeping over the sides." She sent one of the persons in the apartment off to get a snake. Then, using a plastic container and buckets from the school, "we dug this mess out. . . . While we were in the apartment, we scrubbed the floors, took all the dirty clothes out, all the sheets off the beds, brought them back to the school, washed them up. And we left food for dinner from our school lunch. The mother came home to a clean house and clean children. This lady had gotten so far behind the eight ball she didn't even know where to go to get out" (p. 74).

Some experts on the principalship might comment, "All well and good, but what about Cartwright's being an instructional leader? What about her paying attention to teaching and learning, to charting, facilitating, and monitoring the school's educational program?" Cartwright does that, all right, and with a flair. As Louv points out, Cartwright maintains that there are two types of principals, "office principals" and "classroom principals," and she is clearly the latter. She is in and out of classrooms regularly, often taking over the teaching of classes. She not only communicates high expectations but also demands performance from her staff. She is a no-nonsense disciplinarian, as well as a devoted and loving one. But all this "instructional leadership" just is not enough to make this school work. What makes Blaine work is that Cartwright practices leadership by washing clothes, scrubbing the building, and, yes, cleaning toilets (one of the chores that Mahatma Gandhi cheerfully claimed for himself as part of his leadership in the Indian independence movement). Both Cartwright and Gandhi were practicing something called *servant leadership*. In the end, it is servant leadership, based on a deep commitment to values and emerging from a groundswell of moral authority, that makes the critical difference in the lives of Blaine's students and their families. As Louv explains (p. 74), "Maybe Madeline Cartwright's dreams are naïve, maybe not. But they do make a kind of mathematical sense: one safe and clean school, one set of clean clothes, one clean toilet, one safe house—and then another safe school . . . and another . . . and another. 'I'm tellin' you, there's things you can do!'"

The Many Forms of Leadership

The practices of Madeline Cartwright and Larry Norwood demonstrate one of the themes of this book: leadership takes many forms. Further, as has been argued, today's crisis in leadership stems in part from the view that some of these forms are legitimate and others are not. For example, a vast literature expounds the importance of practicing command leadership and instructional leadership. Both kinds provide images of direct leadership, with the principal clearly in control—setting goals, organizing the work, outlining performance standards, assigning people to work, directing and monitoring the work, and evaluating. This kind of direct leadership is typically accompanied by a human relations style designed to motivate and keep morale up.

Command and instructional leadership have their place. Heavy doses of both may be necessary in schools where teachers are incompetent, indifferent, or just disabled by the circumstances they face. But if command and instructional leadership are practiced as dominant strategies, rather than supporting ones, they can breed dependency in teachers and cast them in roles as subordinates. Subordinates do what they are supposed to, but little else. They rely on others to manage them, rather than acting as self-managers. This is hardly a recipe for building good schools.

Command leaders and instructional leaders alike are being challenged by the view that school administrators should strive to become leaders of leaders. As leaders of leaders, they work hard to build up the capacities of teachers and others, so that direct leadership will no longer be needed. This is achieved through team building, leadership development, shared decision making, and striving to establish the value of collegiality. The leader of leaders represents a powerful conception of leadership, one that deserves more emphasis than it now receives in the literature on school administration, and more attention from policymakers who seek to reform schools. Successful leaders of leaders combine the most progressive elements of psychological authority with aspects of professional and moral authority.

Servant Leadership

Virtually missing from the mainstream conversation on leadership is the concept of servant leadership—the leadership so nobly practiced by Madeline Cartwright, Larry Norwood, and many other principals. Greenleaf (1977) believes that "a new moral principle is emerging which holds that the only authority deserving one's allegiance is that which is freely and knowingly granted by the led to the leader in response to, and in proportion to, the clearly evident servant stature of the leader" (p. 10). He developed the concept of servant leadership after reading Herman Hesse's *Journey to the East*. As Greenleaf explains (p. 7),

> In this story we see a band of men on a mythical journey. . . . The central figure of the story is Leo, who accompanies the party as the servant who does their menial chores, but who also sustains them with his spirit and his song. He is a person of extraordinary presence. All goes well until Leo disappears. Then the group falls into disarray and the journey is abandoned. They cannot make it without the servant Leo. The narrator, one of the party, after some years of wandering, finds Leo and is taken into the Order that had sponsored the journey. There he discovers that Leo, whom he had known first as servant, was in fact the titular head of the Order, its guiding spirit, a great and noble *leader* [p. 7].

For Greenleaf, the great leader is a servant first.

Servant leadership is the means by which leaders can get the necessary legitimacy to lead. Servant leadership provides legitimacy partly because one of the responsibilities of leadership is to give a sense of direction, to establish an overarching purpose. Doing so, Greenleaf explains, "gives certainty and purpose to others who may have difficulty in achieving it for themselves. But being successful in providing purpose requires the trust of others" (p. 15). For trust to be forthcoming, the led must have confidence in the leader's competence and values. Further, people's confidence is strengthened by their belief that the leader makes judgments on the basis of competence and values, rather than self-interest.

When practicing servant leadership, the leader is often tempted by personal enthusiasm and commitment to define the needs of those to be served. There is, of course, a place for this approach in schools; sometimes students, parents, and teachers are not ready or able to define their own needs. But, over the long haul, as Greenleaf maintains, it is best to let those who will be served define their own needs in their own way. Servant leadership is more easily provided if the leader understands that serving others is important but that the most important thing is to serve the values and ideas that help shape the school as a covenantal community. In this sense, all the members of a community share the burden of servant leadership.

Schools should not be viewed as ordinary communities but as communities of learners. Barth (1990) points out that, within such communities, it is assumed that schools have the capacity to improve themselves; that, under the right conditions, adults and students alike learn, and learning by one contributes to the learning of others; that a key leverage point in creating a learning community is improving the school's culture; and that school-improvement efforts that count, whether originating in the school or outside, seek to determine and provide the conditions that enable students and adults to promote and sustain learning for themselves. "Taking these assumptions seriously," Barth argues (pp. 45–46), "leads to fresh thinking about the culture of schools and about what people do in them. For instance, the principal need no longer be the 'headmaster' or 'instructional leader,' pretending to know all, one who consumes lists from above and transmits them to those below. The more crucial role of the principal is as head learner, engaging in the most important enterprise of the schoolhouse—experiencing, displaying, modeling, and celebrating what it is hoped and expected that teachers and pupils will do." The school as learning community provides an ideal setting for joining the practice of the "leader of leaders" to servant leadership.

Command and instructional leadership, "leader of leaders" leadership, and servant leadership can be viewed developmentally, as if each were built on the others. As the emphasis shifts from one level to the next, leadership increasingly becomes a form of virtue, and each of the preceding levels becomes less important to the operation of a successful school. For example, teachers become less dependent on administrators, are better able to manage themselves, and share the burdens of leadership more fully.

The developmental view is useful conceptually, but it may be too idealistic to account for what happens in practice. A more realistic perspective is to view the expressions of leadership as being practiced together. Initially (and because of the circumstances faced) the command and instructional features of the leadership pattern may be more prominent. In time, however (and with deliberate effort), they yield more and more to the "leader of leaders" style and to servant leadership, with the results just described.

The idea of servant leadership may seem weak. After all, since childhood, we have been conditioned to view leadership in a much tougher, more direct light. The media portray leaders as strong, mysterious, aloof, wise, and all-powerful. Lawrence Miller (1984) explains:

> Problems were always solved the same way. The Lone Ranger and his faithful Indian companion (read servant of a somewhat darker complexion and lesser intelligence) come riding into town. The Lone Ranger, with his mask and mysterious identity, background, and lifestyle, never becomes intimate with those whom he will help. His power is partly in his mystique. Within ten minutes the Lone Ranger has understood the problem, identified who the bad guys are, and has set out to catch them. He quickly outwits the bad guys, draws his gun, and has them behind bars. And then there was always that wonderful scene at the end. The helpless victims are standing in front of their ranch or in the town square marveling at how wonderful it is now that they have been saved, you hear hoofbeats, then the *William Tell Overture,* and one person turns to another and asks, "But who was that masked man?" And the other replies, "Why, that was the Lone Ranger!" We see Silver rear up and with a hearty "Hi-yo Silver," the Lone Ranger and his companion ride away.
>
> It was wonderful. Truth, justice, and the American Way protected once again.
>
> What did we learn from this cultural hero? Among the lessons that are now acted out daily by managers are the following:
>
> • There is always a problem down on the ranch [the school] and someone is responsible.

- Those who got themselves into the difficulty are incapable of getting themselves out of it. "I'll have to go down or send someone down to fix it."

- In order to have the mystical powers needed to solve problems, you must stay behind the mask. Don't let the ordinary folks get too close to you or your powers may be lost.

- Problems get solved within discrete periodic time units and we have every right to expect them to be solved decisively.

These myths are no laughing matter. Anyone who has lived within or close to our corporations [or schools] knows that these myths are powerful forces in daily life. Unfortunately, none of them bears much resemblance to the real world [pp. 54–55].

One way in which the servant leader serves others is by becoming an advocate on their behalf. Mary Helen Rodriguez, principal of San Antonio's De Zavala School, provides an example:

A teacher came to Mrs. Rodriguez to discuss problems she had been having in arranging a field trip for her grade level. The teacher, in reality, had begun planning too late to get the bus and sack lunch requests conveniently through the district bureaucracy for the planned day of the trip. Mrs. Rodriguez first asked the teacher how important the field trip was for the students. After a bit of discussion, Mrs. Rodriguez and the teacher decided that a trip to the zoo was indeed important, given what students were studying in class at the time. Mrs. Rodriguez then immediately set about making the necessary preparations. Although it took a bit of cajoling over the telephone, sack lunches and busses were secured, and the teacher was most appreciative.

The remarkable thing about this episode is the extra effort Mrs. Rodriguez put in, even though it would have been perfectly reasonable to say, "No, I'm sorry. It's just too late." In a situation where another principal might have saved her powder and not fought the system, Mrs. Rodriguez proved to be a successful advocate for the teacher and her students [Albritton, 1991, p. 8].

Such ideas as servant leadership bring with them a different kind of strength—one based on moral authority. When one places one's leadership practice in service to ideas, and to others who also seek to serve these ideas, issues of leadership role and of leadership style become far less important. It matters less who is providing the leadership, and it matters even less whether the style of leadership is directive or not, involves others or not, and so on. These are issues of process; what matter are issues of substance. What are we about? Why? Are students being served? Is the school as learning community being served? What are our obligations to this community? With these questions in mind, how can we best get the job done?

Practicing Servant Leadership

Summarized in the following sections are practices that, taken together, show how servant leadership works and how the burden of leadership can be shared with other members of the school community.

Purposing

Vaill (1984) defines *purposing* as "that continuous stream of actions by an organization's formal leadership which has the effect of inducing clarity, consensus and commitment regarding the organization's basic purposes" (p. 91). The purpose of purposing is to build within the school a center of shared values that transforms it from a mere organization into a covenantal community.

Empowerment

Empowerment derives its full strength from being linked to purposing: everyone is free to do what makes sense, as long as people's decisions embody the values shared by the school community. When empowerment is understood in this light, the emphasis shifts away from discretion needed to function and toward one's responsibility to the community. Empowerment cannot be practiced successfully apart from enablement (efforts by the school to provide support and remove obstacles).

Leadership by Outrage

It is the leader's responsibility to be outraged when empowerment is abused and when purposes are ignored. Moreover, all members of the school community are obliged to show outrage when the standard falls.

Leadership by outrage, and the practice of kindling outrage in others, challenge the conventional wisdom that leaders should be poker-faced, play their cards close to the chest, avoid emotion, and otherwise hide what they believe and feel. When the source of leadership authority is moral, and when covenants of shared values become the driving force for the school's norm system, it seems natural to react with outrage to short-comings in what we do and impediments to what we want to do.

Madeline Cartwright regularly practiced leadership by outrage. In one instance, she was having trouble with teachers' attendance. She learned of another principal who solved this problem by answering the phone per-sonally, and she decided to follow suit: "I started answering the phone. I say, 'Good morning, this is the Blaine School, this is Madeline Cart-wright.' They hang right up. Two, three minutes later, phone rings again. 'Good morning, this is Blaine School and still Madeline Cartwright.' Hang right up. Next time the phone rang I said: 'Good morning, this is Mrs. Cartwright. If you're going to take off today, you have to talk to me. You either talk to me or you come to school, simple as that'" (Louv, 1990, p. 64). The school is the only thing that the kids can depend on, Cart-wright maintains, and for this reason it is important to make sure that the teachers will show up. She tells the teachers, "As old as I am, you haven't had any disease I haven't had, so you come to school, no matter what."

Some administrators who practice the art of leadership by outrage do it by fighting off bureaucratic interference. Paperwork is often the villain. Other administrators capitulate and spend much of their time and effort handling this paperwork. As a result, little is left for dealing with other, more important matters. Jules Linden, a junior high school principal in New York City, and Linda Martinez, principal of San Juan Day School, San Juan Pueblo, New Mexico, belong in the first group.

In Linden's words, "The only thing the bureaucracy hasn't tried to solve by memo is cancer. . . . My rule of thumb is, when people can't see me because of the paperwork demands, I dump [the paperwork]—and most of it is not missed" (Mustain, 1990, p. 14). Martinez has devised a unique filing system to handle the onslaught of memos, rules, directives, and the like, which she receives from above: "I decided to 'bag it.' Every Friday I would clear my desk. Everything would be tossed in a garbage bag, dated and labeled weekly." Should Martinez be contacted about something filed (and that is not often the case), the proper bag is opened and dumped on the floor, and the item is retrieved for further considera-tion. Linda Martinez remarks, "I had never really considered my 'filing system' of garbage bags to be associated with leadership. I've been told it borders on lunacy." In a redefined leadership, what first appears to be lu-nacy may not be, and vice versa.

Not all schools share the dire conditions of Blaine School, and not all are deluged with a mountain of paperwork. But every school stands for something, and this something can be the basis of practicing leadership by outrage. Many administrators and teachers believe that students do not have the right to fail—that, for example, it should not be up to students to decide whether to do assigned work. Unless this belief rests on the practice of leadership by outrage, however, it is likely to be an academic abstraction rather than a heartfelt value, a slogan rather than a solution.

How is failure to complete assigned work handled in most schools? Typically, by giving zeros—often cheerfully, and without emotion. It is almost as if we are saying to students, "Look, here is the deadline. This is what you have to do. If you don't meet the deadline, these are the consequences. It's up to you. You decide whether you want to do the assignments and pass, or not do the assignments and fail." Adopting a "no zero" policy and enforcing it to the limit is one expression of leadership by outrage. It can transform the belief that children have no right to fail from an abstraction to an operational value. When work is not done by Friday, for example, no zeros are recorded. Instead, the student is phoned Friday night, and perhaps the principal or the teacher visits the student at home after brunch on Sunday to collect the work or press the new Monday deadline. If the student complains that she or he does not have a place to do homework, homework centers are established in the school, in the neighborhood, and so on.

Just remember Madeline Cartwright, and follow her lead. Granted, not all students will respond, but I believe that most will, and those who finally do wind up with zeros will get them with teachers' reluctance. Even if the school does not "win them all," it demonstrates that it stands for something. The stakes are elevated when the problem is transformed from something technical to something moral.

As important as leadership by outrage is, its intent is to kindle outrage in others. When it is successful, every member of the school community is encouraged to display outrage whenever the standard falls. An empowered school community, bonded together by shared commitments and values, is a prerequisite for kindling outrage in others.

Power *Over* and Power *To*

It is true that many teachers and parents do not always respond to opportunities to be involved, to be self-managed, to accept responsibility, and to practice leadership by outrage. In most cases, however, this lack of interest is not inherent but learned. Many teachers, for example, have become jaded as a result of bad experiences with involvement. Louise E. Coleman, principal of Taft Elementary School, Joliet, Illinois, believes that trust and integrity have to be reestablished after such bad experiences. When she arrived at Taft as a new principal, the school was required to submit to the central office a three-year school-improvement plan, designed to increase student achievement:

> Teachers were disgruntled at first. They were not really interested in developing a school-improvement plan. They had been through similar exercises in shared decision making before, and that's exactly what they were—*exercises*. Taft had had three principals in three years. The staff assumed that I would go as others had in the past. After writing a three-year plan based on the staff's perceptions, influencing teachers by involving them in decision making, helping them to take ownership in school improvement, [we have] made some progress. Trust and integrity have been established. Most of the staff now has confidence in me. We have implemented new programs based on students' needs. The staff now volunteers to meet, to share ideas. Minority students are now considered students. Communication is ongoing. Minority parents are more involved. Positive rewards are given for student recognition. The overall school climate has changed to reflect a positive impact on learning.

Coleman was able to build trust and integrity by gently but firmly allowing others to assume leadership roles. She did not feel too threatened to relinquish some of her power and authority. Power can be understood in two ways—as power *over,* and as power *to.* Coleman knows the difference. Power *over* emphasizes controlling what people do, when they do it, and how they do it. Power *to* views power as a source of energy for achieving shared goals and purposes. Indeed, when empowerment is successfully practiced, administrators exchange power *over* for power *to.* Power *over* is rule-bound, but power *to* is goal-bound. Only those with hierarchically authorized authority can practice power *over;* anyone who is committed to shared goals and purposes can practice power *to.*

The empowerment rule (that everyone is free to do whatever makes sense, as long as decisions embody shared values), and an understanding of power as the power *to,* are liberating to administrators as well as teachers. Principals, too, are free to lead, without worrying about being viewed as autocratic. Further, principals can worry less about whether they are using the right style and less about other process-based concerns; their leadership rests on the substance of their ideas and values. Contrary to the laws of human relations, which remind us always to involve people and say that it is autocratic for designated leaders to propose ideas for implementation, we have here a game that resembles football: everyone gets a chance to be quarterback and is free to call the play; if it is a good call, then the team runs with it.

Wayne K. Myers, a principal in Madison, Georgia, welcomes teachers to the role of quarterback, but he is not afraid to call some plays himself. In the spring of 1989, he declared one week in August as International Week, having organized the major activities on his own. He contacted parents for volunteers, asked foreign students from the University of Georgia to come to the campus and make presentations, arranged an exhibit from UNICEF, and even asked the lunchroom to serve meals from the cuisines of different countries:

> In describing this week, I keep [saying] "I" because the major activities were completed by me, but the real success of the week came from the teachers. It was based on a general understanding I had gained from working with these teachers: that they felt the true spirit of schooling had been lost, and that we were committed to recovering it. I shared my idea with them only one month before the start-up date. But, within that month, each grade organized a fantastic array of activities for students. The media specialist located all the materials she had on foreign countries. The hallways were full of displays of items, made by the students, that represented other countries. Since each homeroom would have a visitor with information about another country, each teacher centered activities on that country. The real significance was that the general theme of the week may not have been [the teachers'] idea, but the response was unbelievable. They were, of course, free to take the idea and run with it. It became a learning experience for everyone—administrators, teachers, students, and the community. All were involved, and all enjoyed themselves. . . . I am not sure what type of leadership this is. All I know is that the results have been very positive. I do not believe in telling people what to do or how to do it, but I do believe that sometimes we all have ideas that need to be proposed, sometimes unilaterally.

Myers does not have to worry about leadership—that is, about who does what, or whether he is being too pushy or if he is passing the ball off to teachers. But he would have to worry if trust, integrity, and shared values were not already established in the school. Moreover, Myers understands the difference between charting a direction and giving people maps, between providing a theme and giving teachers a script. Finally, although human relations remain important, Myers is confident that if he acts from the standpoint of what is right and good for the school, human relationships will have a way of taking care of themselves.

The Female Style

It is difficult to talk about power *to* and servant leadership without also addressing the issue of gender. Power *to,* for example, is an idea close to the feminist tradition, as are such ideas as servant leadership and community. By contrast, the more traditional conceptions of leadership seem decidedly more male-oriented. Modern management, for example, is a male creation that replaced emphasis on family and community with emphasis on individual ambition and other personal considerations. As Debra R. Kaufman and Barbara L. Richardson (1982) explain, "Most contemporary social science models [of which modern school management is one]—the set of concepts that help social scientists select problems, organize information, and pursue inquiries—are based on the lives men lead." They go on to say, "In general, social science models of human behavior have focused on rather narrow and male-specific criteria regarding the relationships of ability, ambition, personality, achievement, and worldly success" (p. xiii).

Joyce Hampel (1988) argues that the concept of servant leadership is not likely to be valued in male-dominated institutions or professions. Relying on the research of Carol Gilligan (1982), Joyce Miller (1986), and Charol Shakeshaft (1987), as well as on her own experiences in schools, Hampel points out that men and women generally have different goals when it comes to psychological fulfillment. Men tend to emphasize individual relationships, individual achievement, power as a source for controlling events and people, independence, authority, and set procedures. Women, by contrast, tend to emphasize successful relationships, affiliation, power as the means to achieve shared goals, connectedness, authenticity, and personal creativity. For most men, achievement has to do with the accomplishment of goals; for most women, achievement has to do with the building of connections between and among people. Hampel quotes Miller as follows: "In our culture 'serving others' is for losers, it is low-level stuff. Yet serving others is a basic principle around which women's lives are organized; it is far from such for men" (p. 18).

Shakeshaft (1987), in her groundbreaking research on the topic, characterizes the female world of schooling as follows:

(1) *Relationships with Others Are Central to All Actions of Women Administrators.* Women spend more time with people, communicate

more, care more about individual differences, are concerned more with teachers and marginal students, and motivate more. Not surprisingly, staffs of women administrators rate women higher, are more productive, and have higher morale. Students in schools with women principals also have higher morale and are more involved with student affairs. Further, parents are more favorable toward schools and districts run by women and thus are more involved in school life. This focus on relationships and connections echoes Gilligan's (1982) ethic of care.

(2) *Teaching and Learning Are the Major Foci of Women Administrators.* Women administrators are more instrumental in instructional learning than men and they exhibit greater knowledge of teaching methods and techniques. Women administrators not only emphasize achievement, they coordinate instructional programs and evaluate student progress. In these schools and districts, women administrators know their teachers and they know the academic progress of their students. Women are more likely to help new teachers and to supervise all teachers directly. Women also create a school climate more conducive to learning, one that is more orderly, safer, and quieter. Not surprisingly, academic achievement is higher in schools and districts in which women are administrators.

(3) *Building Community Is an Essential Part of a Woman Administrator's Style.* From speech patterns to decision-making styles, women exhibit a more democratic, participatory style that encourages inclusiveness rather than exclusiveness in schools. Women involve themselves more with staff and students, ask for and get higher participation, and maintain more closely knit organizations. Staffs of women principals have higher job satisfaction and are more engaged in their work than those of male administrators. These staffs are also more aware of and committed to the goals of learning, and the members of the staffs have more shared professional goals. These are schools and districts in which teachers receive a great deal of support from their female administrators. They are also districts and schools where achievement is emphasized. Selma Greenberg (1985, p. 4) describes this female school world: "Whatever its failures, it is more cooperative than competitive, it is more experiential than abstract, it takes a broad view of the curriculum and has always addressed 'the whole child.'"

The female perspective on school leadership is important, for a number of reasons. The teaching force is predominantly female, and this raises moral questions about giving full legitimacy to management conceptions and leadership practice that take women's lived experience into account. Female principals need to feel free to be themselves, rather than have to follow the principles and practices of traditional management theory. The record of success for female principals is impressive. Women are under-represented in the principalship but overrepresented among principals of successful schools. Giving legitimacy to the female perspective would also give license to men who are inclined toward similar practice. The good news is that such ideas as value-based leadership, building covenantal communities, practicing empowerment and collegiality, adopting the stance of servant leaders, and practicing leadership by outrage are gaining in acceptance among male and female administrators alike.

Servant Leadership and Moral Authority

The link between servant leadership and moral authority is a tight one. Moral authority relies heavily on persuasion. At the root of persuasion are ideas, values, substance, and content, which together define group purposes and core values. Servant leadership is practiced by serving others, but its ultimate purpose is to place oneself, and others for whom one has responsibility, in the service of ideals.

Serving others and serving ideals is not an either-or proposition. Chula Boyle, assistant principal of Lee High School, San Antonio, Texas, for example, can often be seen walking the halls of the school with a young child in arm or tow. Student mothers at Lee depend on extended family to care for their children while they are in school. When care arrangements run into problems that might otherwise bar student mothers from attending class, Boyle urges them to bring the children to school. By babysitting, Boyle is serving students but, more important, she reflects an emerging set of ideals at Lee. Lee wants to be a community, and this transformation requires that a new ethic of caring take hold. Lee High School Principal Bill Fish believes that this type of caring is reciprocal. The more the school cares about students, the more students care about matters of schooling. When asked about the practice of babysitting at Lee, he modestly responds, "From time to time kids get in a bind. We are not officially doing it [babysitting] but unofficially we do what we can." His vision is to establish a day-care center in the school for children of students and teachers.

Administrators ought not to choose among psychological, bureaucratic, and moral authority; instead, the approach should be additive. To be additive, however, moral authority must be viewed as legitimate. Further, with servant leadership as the model, moral authority should become the cornerstone of one's overall leadership practice.

Stewardship

The "leader of leaders" and servant leadership styles bring stewardship responsibilities to the heart of the administrator's role. When this happens, the rights and prerogatives inherent in the administrator's position move to the periphery, and attention is focused on duties and responsibilities—to others as persons and, more important, to the school itself.

Stewardship represents primarily an act of trust, whereby people and institutions entrust a leader with certain obligations and duties to fulfill and perform on their behalf. For example, the public entrusts the schools to the school board. The school board entrusts each school to its principal. Parents entrust their children to teachers. Stewardship also involves the leader's personal responsibility to manage her or his life and affairs with proper regard for the rights of other people and for the common welfare. Finally, stewardship involves placing oneself in service to ideas and ideals and to others who are committed to their fulfillment.

The concept of stewardship furnishes an attractive image of leadership, for it embraces all the members of the school as community and all those who are served by the community. Parents, teachers, and administrators share stewardship responsibility for students. Students join the others in stewardship responsibility for the school as learning community. Mary Giella, assistant superintendent for instruction in the Pasco County (Florida) Schools, captures the spirit of stewardship as follows: "My role is one of facilitator. I listened to those who taught the children and those who were school leaders. I helped plan what they saw was a need. I coordinated the plan until those participating could independently conduct their own plans."

The organizational theorist Louis Pondy (1978, p. 94) has noted that leadership is invariably defined as behavioral: "The 'good' leader is one who can get his subordinates to *do* something. What happens if we force ourselves away from this marriage to behavioral concepts? What kind of insights can we get if we say that the effectiveness of a leader lies in his ability to make activity meaningful for those in his role set—not to change behavior but to give others a sense of understanding what they are doing, and especially to articulate it so that they can communicate about the meaning of their behavior?

Shifting emphasis from behavior to meaning can help us recapture leadership as a powerful force for school improvement. Giving legitimacy to the moral dimension of leadership, and understanding leadership as the acceptance and embodiment of one's stewardship responsibilities, are important steps in this direction.

REFERENCES

Albritton, M. *De Zavala Elementary School: A Committed Community.* Case study, Department of Education, Trinity University, 1991.

Barth, R. *Improving Schools from Within.* San Francisco: Jossey-Bass, 1990.

Gilligan, C. *In a Different Voice.* Cambridge, Mass.: Harvard University Press, 1982.

Greenberg, S. "So You Want to Talk Theory?" Paper presented at the annual meeting of the American Educational Research Association, Boston, 1985.

Greenfield, W. "The Micropolitics of Leadership in an Urban Elementary School." Paper presented at the annual meeting of the American Educational Research Association, Chicago, 1991.

Greenleaf, R. K. *Servant Leadership.* New York: Paulist Press, 1977.

Hampel, J. "The Administrator as Servant: A Model for Leadership Development." Unpublished manuscript, Department of Education, San Diego State University, 1988.

Johnson, S. M. *Teachers at Work: Achieving Success in Our Schools.* New York: Basic Books, 1990.

Kaufman, D. R., and Richardson, B. L. *Achievement and Women: Challenging the Assumptions.* New York: Free Press, 1982.

Louv, R. "Hope in Hell's Classroom." *New York Times Magazine,* Nov. 25, 1990, pp. 30–33, 63–67, and 74–75.

Miller, J. B. *Toward a New Psychology of Women.* Boston: Beacon Press, 1986.

Miller, L. M. *American Spirit: Visions of a New Corporate Culture.* New York: Morrow, 1984.

Mustain, G. "Bottom-Drawer Bureau." *Washington Monthly,* Sept. 1990, p. 14.

Pondy, L. R. "Leadership Is a Language Game." In M. W. McCall, Jr., and M. M. Lombardo (eds.), *Leadership: Where Else Can We Go?* Durham, N.C.: Duke University Press, 1978.

Shakeshaft, C. *Women in Educational Administration.* Newbury Park, Calif.: Sage, 1987.

Vaill, P. "The Purposing of High-Performance Systems." In T. J. Sergiovanni and J. E. Corbally (eds.), *Leadership and Organizational Culture.* Urbana: University of Illinois Press, 1984.

19

THE AUTHENTIC LEADER

Robert Evans

The true force that attracts others is the force of the heart.
—James Kouzes and Barry Posner (1987, p. 125)

TRANSFORMATION BEGINS with trust. Trust is the essential link between leader and led, vital to people's job satisfaction and loyalty, vital to followership. It is doubly important when organizations are seeking rapid improvement, which requires exceptional effort and competence, and doubly again to organizations like schools that offer few extrinsic motivators (money, status, power). And it is as fragile as it is precious; once damaged, it is nearly impossible to repair. When we have come to distrust people, either because they have lied to us or deceived us or let us down too often, we tend to stay suspicious of them, resisting their influence and discounting efforts they may make to reform themselves. In work groups, the more people doubt one another, the more they "ignore, disguise, and distort facts, ideas, conclusions, and feelings that [might] increase their vulnerability to others" (Kouzes and Posner, p. 147), increasing the likelihood of misunderstanding. Imagine two schools that are virtual clones, identical in faculty, administration, student body, community, budget, and physical plant, identical even in their problems and in the improvements they are undertaking. Now introduce a single difference: the principal in the first school is distrusted by the faculty. An abyss opens. Despite their resemblance, they are disparate institutions, different in climate, morale, energy level, and responsiveness to innovation. The contrast in the scope and complexity of the tasks confronting their two principals is vast.

Clearly, then, school leaders seeking change need to begin by thinking of what will inspire trust among their constituents. The answer is direct: we admire leaders who are honest, fair, competent, and forward-looking. Although these qualities seem so obvious that they are easy to gloss over, they are the basis of trust (Kouzes and Posner, pp. 16, 21). (Imagine how our national cynicism about politics would change if we found our elected officials to be honest, fair, and competent, not to mention forward-looking.) For "honest" we may read "consistent." Consistency is the lifeblood of trust. People who do what they say they will do—meet their commitments, keep their promises—are trustworthy; those who don't, aren't. Most of us prefer to be led by someone we can count on, even when we disagree with him, than someone we agree with but who frequently shifts his position (Bennis, 1985, p. 21).

Innovation can't live without trust, but it needs more than trust—it needs confidence. We cannot have confidence in those we distrust, but we do not necessarily have confidence in all those we trust. Some people whose sincerity and honesty are beyond reproach lack the capacity to translate their goals into reality. They may have lofty ideals, and even fulfill them in their personal lives, but be unable to communicate clearly to others or be inept at handling daily events. Their heart, as we say, is in the right place, but they lack something that makes us follow them. To transform schools, principals and superintendents must inspire such confidence along with trust.

The key to both is authenticity. Leaders who are followed are authentic; that is, they are distinguished not by their techniques or styles but by their integrity and their savvy. Integrity is a fundamental consistency between personal beliefs, organizational aims, and working behavior. It is increasingly clear that leadership rests on values, that commitment among constituents can only be mobilized by leaders who themselves have strong commitments, who preach what they believe and practice what they preach.[1] But they must also know what they're doing. Savvy is practical competence, a hard-to-quantify cluster of qualities that includes craft knowledge, life experience, native intelligence, common sense, intuition, courage, and the capacity to "handle things." Most of us seek in a leader this combination of genuineness and effectiveness. It makes him authentic, a credible resource who inspires trust and confidence, someone worth following into the uncertainties of change.

This chapter explores the concept of authentic leadership, its roots and its implications for practice. It sketches authenticity's essentials—integrity and savvy—and describes a process for discovering one's own authentic core, a process that highlights the personal, idiosyncratic nature of leadership. From this flow three consequences: that there are many ways to excel as a leader; that we must recast our notions of vision and strategy; and, most important of all, that effective leadership rests on a set of strategic biases that simplify leadership and make transformation possible.

Integrity: Character in Action

Integrity is a fundamental consistency between one's values, goals, and actions. At the simplest level it means standing for something, having a significant commitment and exemplifying this commitment in your behavior. Leaders who have no strong values and no aspirations for their school may provide a dull consistency, but this is not something we would confuse with integrity. Even if they manage daily details adequately, they inspire no special motivation or attachment that enhances performance or makes being part of the school valuable. They are, at best, maintaining, not leading. Followership is not just impossible under their administration, it is irrelevant.

In a different way, leaders who do claim to stand for something but whose goals and actions are not aligned with their stated values also lack integrity. Those who profess aspirations that do not truly matter to them are easily seen through. When a principal dutifully introduces a district priority that she herself does not share, the discrepancy between her announced aims and her underlying beliefs will be apparent to all who know her well, even if she tries to muster up sincerity. Her falseness will ultimately be as evident as if she were adopting a style that is not her own. Similarly, when leaders do not model the values they assert or the goals they proclaim—when a superintendent announces "respect for others" as a district goal but treats staff disrespectfully—they breed cynicism and resistance. The problem of inconsistency is so widespread that it needs little elaboration, except to note that it can occur unconsciously. A leader may be sincere about his goal and unaware that his behavior is contradictory. In such cases, the leader may seem "out of it" and incompetent more than cynical or manipulative, but he will still invite disrespect and resistance instead of followership.

Integrity can take many forms. Let us begin with two examples:

> Jane Carroll, principal of Worthington High School, is a strong believer in "challenge." A triathlon competitor and ardent chess player, she values self-discipline and perseverance. She is overt about rewarding

students and faculty who demonstrate these qualities: "Effort matters far more than talent—for teachers as well as students. Success comes from striving. As Aristotle said, 'Excellence is not an act, but a habit.'" Jane leads the school with a firm hand and engages herself in aspects of curriculum, assessment, and staff development that in many schools have more teacher involvement and control. Some faculty find her "cold," others "elitist and controlling," but she enjoys wide support, even among most of these critics, because her commitments are so clear, because she holds herself to them as firmly as she holds others to them, and because they have come to embody the school's pursuit of excellence. "She drives everyone hard," says a teacher, "but she sets the example, and we all feel the end result is an exceptional school."

Tom Russell, the principal of Jackson Elementary School, believes in individual development. He reveres Thoreau and sees school as a place where everyone, child and adult, should grow at their own pace through rich opportunities and the freedom to explore, not through pressure to produce. Jackson has comparatively few rules and requirements. Tom rarely issues an order, he tolerates others disagreeing with him, and he gives the faculty wide latitude to decide policy, even if this involves heated arguments. He is unhurried in his style but unwavering in his focus. Each year he meets with each student and each staff member (including custodians and secretaries) to talk about their growth, interests, and ideas for the school. Some teachers have found Jackson too "chaotic" and left; some who have remained find Tom too "unstructured." But most agree with the teacher who says, "This guy lives what he believes: growth, support, respect. Because of him, Jackson really nurtures people."

Few of the principals I know would want to be Jane or Tom. They might endorse qualities of each but would find both at least a bit extreme. I cite Jane and Tom here as exemplars not of the perfect principal but of integrity. For both of them, values, goals, and actions are congruent.

(Before going further, an important note: it is impossible to address the ethical dimensions of leadership that are a primary focus of this chapter without using terms that have been poisoned by politics. In the 1990s in America, *values* and *basic values* are among a constellation of terms that have been appropriated by various political groups and reduced to code words for particular viewpoints. But all of us see certain values—fairness, for example—as "basic," even if we define these values differently. There is no other way to describe them. I use all such phrases and all such words as *moral* in this primary, generic way, not to refer to a particular political or religious agenda.)

Values and personal integrity come first. At the deepest level, the values of authentic leaders are characterized by three things: personal ethics, vision, and belief in others (Badaracco and Ellsworth, p. 100). A firm set of personal ethical standards is a hallmark of most successful leaders. Over and over in the research literature, portraits of exceptional leaders describe people with unusually high standards, commitments they keep with a self-discipline that can seem excessive, even fanatical: "Outstanding leaders have sources of inner direction." They may not be terribly religious, but their beliefs give them a sturdy guide for their long-range planning and their routine problem solving (p. 100). Whatever the specific content of their views, honesty and fairness tend to be among their chief tenets. It is not that authentic leaders necessarily preach honesty and fairness as specific virtues, but they demonstrate them through the sincerity of their commitments. This is the basis of trust and loyalty in any group.

Leaders with strong values translate these into organizational vision. Like Jane and Tom, they typically hold the same standards for their school as for themselves. "Challenge and Excellence" might well serve as the motto both for Jane and for Worthington, "Freedom to grow" for Tom and Jackson. Such commitments are important; they are crucial to followership because they provide the larger purpose that gives work direction and meaning. Leaders like Jane and Tom are able to communicate very clearly a definite notion of their school and its potential.

Leaders with values and vision tend to believe that other people have the potential to be motivated by the same commitments, not just by narrow self-interest (financial gain, personal power). Though their beliefs are different, neither Jane nor Tom base their leadership on maneuvering or manipulating people through special incentives, political trade-offs, and the like. They have faith that everyone can respond, can benefit from the opportunity the school provides, can fulfill the vision in their own personal ways. This faith may take many forms—Tom offers a chance to blossom, Jane a challenge to excel—but in one way or another it conveys a confidence in the potential of people.

These same three qualities—ethics, vision, belief in others—that are central in the personal beliefs of authentic leaders are reflected in their organizational goals. By "goals" I mean both the kind of institution the leader seeks to build and the improvements he seeks to implement. Leaders with strong personal ethics who exemplify honesty and fairness generally reflect these in a meritocratic approach to management; they want competence to be rewarded. They expect high ethical standards to prevail throughout and believe that when in doubt about a decision or a problem, everyone should behave in accordance with the school's fundamental values. They acknowledge those who observe and fulfill these values, basing recognition on "what you do, not on who you are or who you know," as Jane says. At the same time, they expect members of the organization to come to share the same basic values and goals, and they are usually unambiguous and unembarrassed about this. Authentic school leaders do not necessarily champion a "my way or the highway" philosophy, but they are unwilling to sacrifice their priorities and goals, and when necessary they will challenge those who can't or won't come along. This can sometimes seem harsh and unfeeling, but for many leaders with integrity this approach is simply axiomatic: "buying in" is ultimately a basic condition of organizational membership. A case in point is this high school principal:

> Last year we pushed our restructuring up a big notch: we converted to a block schedule, four 90-minute periods per day, so we could really start implementing an integrated curriculum and in-depth teaching. We'd spent a full year debating it and most people were on board, but six were still strongly opposed. They were angry and terrified at having to face kids for that long and at having to change the curriculum they'd taught for twenty years and start collaborating with other teachers. I met with each. I made it clear that we needed absolutely everyone to be truly committed, that we had finally reached the rock and the hard place; it was "in or out." They were going to be miserable if they stayed. Thanks to a special agreement with the union, we had the option of transferring people. I offered to find each their first choice of another high school in the city if they wished. No hard feelings, no shame, no blame. Four chose to leave. I worked like a maniac, and I got all of them the schools they wanted. It wasn't all happy, but they are happier, and we've made much more progress.

In a similar way, authentic leaders embrace programs or projects that reflect their values and institutional goals. They concentrate on what matters to them, again without embarrassment. They have definite notions of what is important, and they pay attention to these targets. The principal above is committed to the essential schools philosophy, which to him means "real depth learning," and the conviction that "nothing is more important than making our classrooms places where kids and teachers deeply explore challenging, important ideas. Everything else is subordinate to that."

As this principal's example indicates, integrity requires action, behavior that embodies values. Indeed, it is chiefly through consistent beliefs and goals expressed in consistent actions that we perceive a leader's integrity. The importance of setting the example, of leaders' modeling what they value, is one of the most frequently repeated themes in leadership writing. Authentic leaders translate their beliefs and values into concrete actions at a fundamental level:

> Anthony Cortez became a superintendent reluctantly. After years as a teacher and then principal at Clayville Middle School, he filled in as acting superintendent and was offered the permanent position because he was so universally admired. His hesitation was simple: "I like kids. I like being around them. Everything a school does depends on community, which means that kids know they are known: they're missed when they're absent, they're appreciated for their uniqueness, they're helped when they need it, and they're held accountable to do their part. That can't happen unless the adults like the kids and are with the kids." He delegates large amounts of his "paper and policy work" and usually averages at least three school visits—"a real visit, not a sail-through"—per week (he sometimes reads to children in the elementary schools). When he urges Clayville teachers to "reach out to kids, invest in them, know them," his credibility is absolute; his actions have always spoken for him.

When the late Henry Scattergood retired as headmaster at the Germantown Friends School in Philadelphia, a colleague wrote, "His virtues are as simple and uncomplicated as they are rare. They originate in the quality of creating in others a loyalty and affection, and even sometimes a goodness, by being himself, a man of perfect honesty, integrity, and goodness. He does not merely advise virtue, he creates it in others by offering its example and practice. . . . It is the simple yet exceptional use of character in action" (Nicholson, 1995, citing Sharpless). Whether it is challenging thoroughly resistant staff or staying close to students or spending large amounts of time on the job—or exemplifying virtue—authentic leaders embody character in action: they don't just say, they do.

Savvy

In discussing integrity, I have already been referring to "authentic leaders"; but although integrity is the chief defining characteristic of authenticity, it is not the only one. Authenticity also demands savvy, a practical, problem-solving wisdom that enables leaders to make things happen. Savvy subsumes an array of qualities, ranging from knowledge of one's field to having a good "nose" for institutional problems.[2] It includes intangibles like knowing what constitutes a good solution to a dilemma, knowing "what to do and when to do it" (Sergiovanni, 1992, p. 15). These and related qualities are sometimes called "craft knowledge" and are in good part a product of professional experience, learned skills that come with years of practice. But to me, savvy also includes native strengths, basic aspects of temperament, personality, and intelligence that are reflected in qualities like common sense and empathic sensitivity (being able to "read" people), courage and assertiveness, and resilience. These, coupled with craft knowledge, establish a leader's bona fides. In my experience, educators will rarely follow leaders unless they seem to "know their stuff"—not the tricks of leadership but the realities of school life.

Educators want leaders who know education, who are current and well versed without falling victim to fads, but they especially want leaders who are "one of us," who can still see education from a teacher's point of view and are attuned to the real world of classrooms, students, and parents. And they also want leaders who offer proof or promise of being able to "make things happen," whether this means fixing problems, finding resources, or handling people. These traits build a basic platform without which a leader lacks presence and clout and is not taken seriously:

> Jim Colby became a superintendent after a brief stint as a math teacher and then many years as a district business manager (he was never a principal). A devout convert to Total Quality Management, he failed to make it work in two different districts. In both, principals and teachers felt that his goals were formulaic and empty and his expectations unrealistic, that he didn't really understand teaching itself or the running of a school, and that he couldn't manage people. Principals especially felt that he never grasped the daily dilemmas of school life, the intricacies and politics of translating ideas into action. In the words of one, "Jim was a hard worker, but basically out of it. He just didn't have it, and he just didn't get it. You couldn't respect him."

If Jim had been charismatic, one of his districts might have made a temporary exception for him. There are gifted visionaries who can truly inspire others by the power of their ideas, the force of their eloquence, and the depth of their conviction, even though they have little practical aptitude and little grasp of the nitty-gritty. People will sometimes exempt such a leader from the "savvy requirement" (especially if there is a good second-in-command who handles the details), but they will not do so indefinitely and especially not as innovation proceeds from early optimism to actual implementation, with its inevitable obstacles.

Becoming Authentic

Let us say, then, that authenticity is ideal. How does one achieve it? The question is paradoxical. Just as genuineness can't be artificially manufactured—it simply *is*—neither can authenticity: it can't be generated; it can only be discovered. (A person cannot *act* authentic.) Still, one may fairly ask, "How do I get there?" The answer leads us again, as did our discussion of charisma in the preceding chapter, to the personal nature and roots of leadership.

It also leads first to a blunt truth: not everyone can. Despite the popularity of technical notions of leadership, most of us believe that good leaders must have the "right stuff," the right personal qualities to lead, and that these, like savvy or charisma, are to some extent innate: you either have what it takes or you don't. Most of us react to leaders in this way in our daily experience. But this view is not just folk wisdom—experience and research confirm that leadership requires a definite aptitude (Drucker, 1986, p. 159). For example, a study of identical twins who were raised apart concluded that leadership is a trait "strongly determined by heredity" (Goleman, 1986, pp. C1–C2). A study of leaders who achieved significant change in their organizations highlighted the importance of temperament and predisposition and suggested that the impulse and capacity to lead stem largely from innate talents and early childhood experience (Gibbons, 1986). Other research emphasizes that successful leaders tend to be psychologically hardy (Evans, 1996, ch. 7). They are resourceful and resilient. Compared to less successful peers in equally stressful jobs, they are more resistant to illness and experience both a greater sense of control over events and of positive challenge in their work (Maddi and Kobasa, 1984, p. 31). Unmistakably, they have what it takes.

The right stuff, like charisma, is a concept that might seem to suggest that there is little point in trying to teach leadership (a notion widely deplored by those who see leadership as a matter of technique and therefore teachable). But it leads to three less extreme and very practical implications. The first is that *some* central aspects of leadership are innate and unteachable and that not everyone has all the necessary potential, which means that some people will always lead better than others and that some are simply ill-suited for the task. As ordinary as this seems, it is routinely ignored in discussions of preparing school administrators to lead change. To expect that every leader can become authentic or transformational is foolish. The second is to underscore the importance of hardiness: to be effective, leaders must demonstrate and foster it. We don't follow the timid, the indecisive, and those who avoid problems, and we rarely stay committed to causes that distress us (Kouzes and Posner, p. 68).

The third and most important implication is that leadership begins at one's center: *authentic leaders build their practice outward from their core commitments rather than inward from a management text.* In addition to their craft knowledge, all administrators have basic philosophies of leading, of school functioning, and of human nature, philosophies that are deeply rooted in their personal history and professional experience. These philosophies guide their behavior, but they usually remain tacit. They are the true source of their integrity. They include basic assumptions about human nature, group behavior, and the roots of excellence. "Like a geological deposit," they accumulate during years of experience in life and work. Although few leaders pause to spell out their philosophies explicitly, "these deep assumptions influence almost everything they do" (Badaracco and Ellsworth, p. 7). Sergiovanni echoes this view when he speaks of an administrator's "known and unknown theories of practice . . . bundles of beliefs and assumptions about how schools and school systems work, authority, leadership, the purposes of schooling, the role of competition, the nature of human nature, and other issues and concerns." These constitute what he calls "mindscapes," frames of reference that, though rarely thought about, are powerful forces that drive one's practice (1991, pp. 10–12).

A leader's philosophy remains tacit in part because none of us can be fully in touch with the entire range of our knowledge, perception, feeling, and skill. At any given moment, our reservoir of expertise is larger than we can encompass, our wellspring of inspiration deeper than we can fully tap. But it also stays hidden—even unconscious—because it is buried and discouraged by formal leadership theory taught in graduate administration courses and disseminated in leadership books. The received wisdom in the field, which emphasizes techniques and styles, encourages school leaders to overlook their personal philosophies and the "hard-earned insights" of their craft knowledge, with the result that they end up drawing upon a tiny portion of their potential (Bolman and Deal, p. 37).[3] Uncovering this wisdom is the key to becoming authentic.

The Testimonial: What Do You Stand For?

There may be many routes to accomplishing that uncovering of wisdom. I prefer to begin this way: Imagine that your colleagues and friends have decided to honor you at a testimonial dinner, simply because they respect and love you so much. The meal is over, you have already been "roasted" and toasted, and speakers have lavishly praised your skills. Now, your closest colleague, who knows you best, is to offer the final tribute. This person will move the focus away from your competence to your commitment, summarizing what you stand for: the essential principle or core value, the fundamental belief deep inside you that drives your work as an educator and a leader. What will he or she say? (Note: it cannot be something like "He likes people" or "She has always stood for change," unless just liking people or change for its own sake is truly your highest value, the thing you care about most—in which case it would not have earned you a testimonial! The goal is to find out what lies below these kinds of characteristics.)

The task is simple but not necessarily easy. It usually involves talking about values that are at once ordinary and complex, plain and profound. In taking several thousand educators through this exercise, I have found that many tend to begin at a relatively superficial level, describing skills, attributes, or very general beliefs. But when they are encouraged to persevere and to talk to each other in greater depth, their answers gravitate toward values that are much deeper and often disarmingly simple, what one principal called "apple pie and motherhood" values. "I feel corny and sentimental saying this stuff," he said, "but it's all true."

The kinds of "stuff" superintendents and principals and teachers say can lead in many directions. (At one seminar, a principal whose core belief was "everything you do in life should be fun" was seated next to a colleague whose deepest commitment was to "live in the light of Christ.") But frequently the answers cluster around two broad headings, which I summarize as "equity" and "excellence." Most educators share a heartfelt commitment to students and to the development of their full potential, but they differ in their emphasis. Some, like Tom Russell, stress the importance of opportunity, fairness, diversity, and community. They are likely to believe that "all children can learn," which often means to them a commitment to special outreach and compensatory opportunities for children who are disadvantaged. Others, like Jane Carroll, emphasize goals, challenge, responsibility, and striving. They are more likely to speak of "excellence" and "standards," of bringing out the best in children by measuring them against high benchmarks. Most educators share both values to some degree, although differences of emphasis can lead to significant differences in the kinds of schools they develop.

"What do you stand for?" is an excellent point of departure for exploring one's own philosophy of schooling and school leadership, but there are three other questions that I have also found to be useful:

1. *How do I define my role as a leader?* Am I at heart a mover, some-one who redesigns and reshapes, who tolerates—even enjoys—the fric-tion that change can cause? Or am I a maintainer, someone who prefers to keep things running smoothly, who may occasionally modify or en-hance things but who is by nature more inclined to accept things as they are? One's preference will of course be affected by the specific situation—a new principal at a school will see his task differently if he finds its programs and teachers weak than if he finds them strong—but by phi-losophy and temperament every administrator is more drawn in one di-rection than the other. As they reflect on their conception of their role, some see themselves as active promoters of change, others don't (Fullan, 1991, p. 167). It is important to be clear about this.

2. *What inspires the best in staff?* Is performance enhanced when a leader actively shapes the work of staff members, or is it best when they are given wide latitude? Should they be free to work as individual arti-sans, or should they be linked in close collaborative groups? There is a fa-mous distinction in human resource theory between three views of human motivation and performance. Theory X holds that people are basically lazy and unambitious, that they need and want to be led; managers must direct and control their work (as with Taylorism and the "expect and in-spect" model of management). Theory Y holds that people can be relied upon to show motivation, self-control, and self-direction, provided that essential human needs for safety, independence, and status are met by the workplace (McGregor, 1960, pp. 35–36). Theory Z places maximum emphasis on human potential, calling for higher levels of trust and for egalitarian work relationships and participatory decision making involv-ing stakeholders at all levels (Ouchi, 1981, p. 110). Here again, though local conditions will influence one's preference, each individual school leader will have a primary predisposition.

3. *What are my strengths?* An excellent way to clarify one's basic phi-losophy is to identify one's particular skills and abilities and the parts of one's role that are most rewarding. A tremendous amount of leadership training and school improvement work concentrates on correcting de-fects. Indeed, ruminating about problems and trying to overcome them consumes vast quantities of educators' time and energy. But a person try-ing to discover her core beliefs and values does far better to start with her strengths, the parts of herself that she feels best about in the exercise of her profession. It is there that the essence of what matters to her is to be found. Trying to articulate this essence is not only informative, it can be hugely satisfying. I love to see superintendents and principals as they de-

scribe where in their work they feel most competent and alive; their faces light up, their enthusiasm is infectious. "When I think about what I love about my work and what I do best, it's helping kids learn important lessons about life," said one principal. "And I realize that this is actually a commitment: nurturing them into healthy growth. I feel it's sacred, and it's also something I really know I can do."

There are a range of related inquiries that can help a leader flesh out the details of his personal leadership landscape. Among them are, How well do I understand the school and its community? How solid is my relationship with my constituents? Where do I think the school ought to be headed? How should the school be governed? How prepared am I to handle the school's problems? How can I improve my ability to advance the school? If he dares, he can even ask himself, Am I the right one to be leading right now?[4]

Where Does It Come From?

The corollary to these "What do you stand for?" questions is, "Where does it come from?" Whatever the answer to the first question, whether it points to equity or excellence or some other set of beliefs, its origin is almost always personal—deeply personal, both in how strongly it is believed and in how old it is. At heart people's philosophies tend to be "dogmatic," in the original sense of the term, notes Nisbet: "The springs of human action, will, and ambition lie for the most part in beliefs about universe, world, society, and man which defy rational calculations and differ greatly from . . . instincts. These springs lie in what we call dogmas. That word comes from Greek roots with the literal meaning of 'seems-good.'" As Cardinal Newman said, "Men will die for a dogma who will not even stir for a conclusion" (1980, pp. 8–9). I don't ask educators whether they will die for what they stand for, but there is little doubt of the depth of their conviction when they speak of the "seems-goods" that matter most to them.

When I ask about the origins of their philosophy, people invariably point to their experience—their experience as an adult, as an educator, and as a student, and primarily to their early experience growing up. Few think of their courses in graduate school. In fact, the actual behavior of administrators has relatively little to do with their formal training. "They [bring] *themselves* with them to graduate school . . . and they [take] themselves back to their schools . . . knowing some new things, perhaps, but still basically themselves (Blumberg, 1989, pp. 19–20, emphasis in original). The study of management contributes to what they know (and to their espoused values) but has a modest impact on how they act. Administration, after all, mostly involves not the application of theory and data but the "idiosyncratic use of the self in interactive work situations" (p. 183), and people start learning about using themselves in such situations early on in life. Basic ways of thinking, feeling, and behaving that shape one's approach to problems and one's perspective on the world begin early in childhood in the framework of the family, and they are firmly established long before one becomes an administrator (pp. 191–192). "The philosophy which is so important in each of us," as William James said, "is not a technical matter."

I am used to hearing teachers, principals, and superintendents confirm the nontechnical nature of their philosophy. Their stories are often quite wonderful, providing fascinating glimpses into the personal roots of leadership. One such account was offered by Lawrence Briggs, a high school principal, who explained his philosophy this way:

> I can tell you why equity is so important to me. Up through fourth grade our schools were segregated. In fifth grade we all got to go to what had been the white school. On the first day the teacher asked who wanted to perform for the class on the flutaphone. All the white children raised their hands—they had all had flutaphone lessons and music classes; we hadn't had either. I made up my mind I was going to learn to play. I found a woman to teach me and was $17 in debt to her before my parents even knew I was taking lessons. After Christmas, when the teacher asked again, I raised my hand and kept it up until she finally called on me. I stood up and played my song. Nobody is going to tell me that a kid in my school can't do something.

Lawrence is a man of imposing personal presence: big, outgoing, articulate, witty, confident. He would not, I think, claim to be the least directive, most participatory of leaders. But he enjoyed strong support among his faculty, students, and parents—in good part, I believe, because of his authenticity. Lawrence's unmistakable commitment to students—his belief in their potential and in the importance of giving them the opportunity to succeed—makes what we might call "graduate school sense": it is intellectually sound; it would readily find professional, theoretical, and research support. But its roots are far deeper, far more personal; his commitment is in his bones, and it reaches people at a level that is both immediate and fundamental.

Many Ways to Excel

Lawrence Briggs's example, and those of Jane Carroll and Tom Russell, all illustrate that authentic leadership is highly personal and therefore can take many forms, depending upon the specific commitments of particular school leaders. "Personal" here does not mean arbitrary or whimsical but individual. All leaders whose practice is rooted in deep values and strong beliefs will resemble each other in some important ways, no matter how different their philosophies. But they will also differ according to the content of their beliefs and their preferred ways of operating. Authenticity helps to reveal a wonderful, liberating fact of leadership life: there are many ways to excel.

Most leadership research has been conducted in "low-performing systems"—organizations in trouble. It generally attributes their problems in motivation, morale, communication, trust, and performance to the way a leader is working and assumes that a change in approach or style will correct things (Vaill, 1984, p. 102). But when we look at high-performing systems—successful organizations—we find that leadership style is rarely a determining factor in their performance; in fact, we find a wide range of styles among their leaders: "There are tyrants whose almost maniacal commitment to achieving the system's purposes makes one think that they'd be locked up. . . . There are warm, laid-back parent figures who hardly seem to be doing anything at all, until one looks a little more closely. There are technocrats . . . and dreamers. . . . Some are rah-rah optimists and others are dour critics who express their love for the system by enumerating its imperfections" (p. 102).

I know thriving, vital, high-achieving schools that are led by easygoing, democratic authority delegators and by demanding, strict perfectionists; by creative, roll-with-the-punches improvisers and by obsessive, keep-me-posted worriers; by eloquent, expansive preachers and by quiet, modest doers. Research has shown that principals who were successful change agents all fulfilled four key roles (resource provider, instructional resource, communicator, visible presence) but did so in very different ways. Some were "strong, aggressive, fearless," others "quiet, nurturing, supportive" (Fullan, 1991, p. 158). In stark contrast to situational leaders and practitioners of styles, the most successful leaders "are not human chameleons, but . . . people of distinctive personalities who behave consistently in accordance with that personality" (Badaracco and Ellsworth, p. 208). Their greatest assets are "their own passions for the organization and its mission and their own common sense when it comes to getting the most out of the people they have. Their unwillingness to turn themselves inside out to conform to some behavioral scientist's theory is remarkable" (Vaill, 1989, p. 19).

The corollary of "many ways to excel" is "every way has its weakness." Authentic leaders have shortcomings; they are usually aware of them, but they tend to emphasize their strengths and to find sufficient nourishment in their sense of themselves. One of the greatest flaws in style-based leadership theories is the assumption that one might somehow acquire and apply only the strengths of each particular style, that one might become a composite of stylistic virtues. In fact, every way of leading, like every way of being, has deficits as well as advantages, and these are inextricably linked. Principals with a genuine commitment to a participatory process can show remarkable patience and sensitivity but be poor at asserting themselves, at setting limits on those who abuse the process, and at taking firm action in a crisis. Superintendents with a take-charge capacity and an ability to tolerate conflict can demonstrate impressive courage and perseverance but ride roughshod over people, make enemies where they don't need to, and be ineffective at compromising when it is necessary. As I have already suggested, authentic leaders tend to be unapologetic about the inevitable downsides of being true to themselves. A superintendent I have known for years sometimes says, with both pride and resignation, "Like Popeye in the old cartoons, 'I am what I am.' I know what I want and what I'm good at. I also know what I'm not so good at, and I try to stick with my strengths." The authentic leader who is aware of her basic inclinations, including her limitations, is already better equipped to compensate for the latter but is unlikely to dwell on them.

Philosophy, Vision, and Strategy: What Do I Want?

To see authenticity as profoundly personal is to recast many of the premises that have come to be taken for granted about leadership and organizations, chief among them vision and strategy. In scarcely more than a decade these concepts have become ubiquitous in leadership theory, practice, and parlance. Like mission, culture, and change, they have become buzzwords. They are widely and correctly trumpeted as vital to leading innovation and are almost as widely misunderstood. Vision is seen as a product of rational planning, as deriving from a careful appraisal of the external environment (a company does a market survey, a school does a needs assessment). In fact, successful change agents rarely operate in this way. Largely overlooked in all the enthusiasm for vision is that it typically derives from "a personal and imaginative creativity that [transcends] analysis" (Badaracco and Ellsworth, p. 101). In charting an organizational course, successful leaders rely on processes that are more intuitive and holistic than ordered and intellectual, more qualitative than quantitative (Mintzberg, p. 52). Though they are typically adept at gauging needs and identifying markets, the way they meet needs and approach markets is their own: they construct their vision out of their own philosophy and commitment, their own experience and judgment, their own interests and strengths. In education, such leaders have a mental model of what they want for their school, and they trust their own assessment of the school against that model.

To misunderstand this personal source of vision is to misunderstand the origins of strategy. When, as it all too often does, strategic planning begins by identifying external goals and then moves on to analyzing internal strengths, it puts the cart before the horse. To capture its core mission—how it will relate to its environment—a group must first understand its own strengths (Schein, 1985, p. 55). Over my years of consulting in schools I have been repeatedly struck by how often successful new programs grow out of the conviction or interest of an individual principal or a small group of leaders rather than out of a formal planned change process.

The highly personal nature of vision is central to its success. The value of a vision is not just to clarify goals and plot a strategy but to inspire followers. To change, people must be "moved." This requires not just an idea but an advocate. Change begins not just with a goal but with a leader who communicates it, enlisting the organization's members in the pursuit of a compelling agenda. The leader's own commitment to the agenda is crucial to its adoption by followers:

> The greatest inhibitor to enlisting others in a common vision is lack of personal conviction. There is absolutely no way that you can, over the long term, convince others to share a dream if you are not convinced of it yourself. . . . The most inspirational moments are marked by genuineness. Somehow we all are able to spot a lack of sincerity in others. We detect it in their voices, we observe it in their eyes, we notice it in their posture. We each have a sixth sense for deceit. . . . So there is a very fundamental question that a leader must ask before attempting to enlist others: "What do I want?" [Kouzes and Posner, pp. 124–125].

A fundamental question, indeed. Character in action is always vital to leadership, but it is especially vital when innovation is under way: the leader must change first—or at least very early. The leader, that is, must not just advocate but exemplify the change before asking staff to do so.

Why should anyone take an initiative seriously if the leader doesn't? Yet it is astonishing how often innovation is imposed on schools without administrators' support and how rarely administrators are accorded—or take—the time and freedom to think through what they want, to identify their own commitment or at least develop a commitment in response to an external priority forced upon them.

This lapse could not be more counterproductive, because although the need for leaders to commit themselves to change applies universally, it is critical in schools, where veteran teachers have seen many highly touted reforms fizzle and have watched many administrators depart before their priorities reached fruition. These teachers are naturally suspicious, sensitive to signs of hypocrisy, and inclined to hold back, waiting for proof that for once the administration means what it says and will really persevere. This proof is most crucially needed from the principal.

Principals are widely seen as indispensable to innovation. No reform effort, however worthy, survives a principal's indifference or opposition. He is the leader closest to the action, the operational chief of the unit that must accomplish the change. His involvement legitimates the effort, giving it an official imprimatur that carries symbolic weight and confirms that staff should take it seriously. And he is often best suited to secure the whole array of supports, from the material to the spiritual, that implementation demands. Research on the principal's role generally finds that schools where innovation succeeds are led by principals who are true Renaissance people: they do everything well. They demonstrate strong knowledge of and commitment to the innovation, but they approach faculty in a collaborative spirit, fostering open communication. They demand high standards, but they offer high levels of emotional support. They hold staff accountable, but they provide strong assistance. They run good meetings, but they reduce the burden of administrative details. The only problem is that there are apparently so few of them.

This should come as no surprise. Most principals are untrained for leading change. They have been socialized to be maintainers, not encouraged to be what I call authentic. Risk taking, despite the theoretical vogue it enjoys among academics who write about school reform, has always been—and remains—rare in schools. Almost everything one learns as a principal reinforces the old congressional saw: to get along, go along. After all, principals face the classic double dilemma of middle managers everywhere: they are given more responsibility than authority (even without reform initiatives, they are assigned more than they can accomplish), and their success requires maintaining positive connections not just with their superiors but also with their staff (they have little to gain from challenging people too sharply). And when they are asked to lead projects they did not choose or develop and may not fully grasp or endorse, they are likely to be ambivalent, especially when these projects require them to change their own roles and become active in areas, such as pedagogy, where previous improvement schemes have met with little success (Fullan, p. 152).

All of which underscores the necessity for principals to be able to work through their concerns and doubts, to make change meaningful to themselves, to clarify their own commitments. This means that those above principals—superintendents, school boards, state officials—must remember the importance of allowing time for a district's whole administrative team, especially its principals, to thrash out questions of values and goals as these relate to specific programmatic changes. (It also means that teachers who press for reform on their own must realize the importance of bringing the principal along early and, if this fails, the unlikelihood of achieving schoolwide success.) And what is true for principals is true for other key leaders. All those who have responsibility for an innovation need a chance to get on board before it is adopted, to ask themselves "what do I (or we) want," and then to stay on board, to revisit their answers periodically during its implementation. These steps take time, to be sure, but to skip them is a false economy that reduces "vision" and "strategy" to empty shells and leaders to deceivers of their constituents.

Authenticity in Action: Strategic Biases for Change

Thus far I have concentrated on leadership's overarching concerns and underlying beliefs. But making change in a school is not just a matter of the high and the deep. What about the daily dilemmas of transition, the issues small and large where policy turns into action and change must actually be accomplished? Authenticity would be little more than a nice ideal if it offered no help with these. Clarifying one's philosophy does not automatically make one savvy any more than it makes one charismatic; it does not create the wisdom that comes from experience, say, or provide the gift of empathic sensitivity. But it does wonderfully enrich one's ability to make decisions and solve problems: it makes one, in the best sense of the word, biased.

Spelling out their basic assumptions and discovering their authentic core helps leaders develop strategic biases for action to guide their work and shape the implementation of change. This notion of bias I take from Badaracco and Ellsworth, who suggest that leaders are far more likely to excel if they approach problems with certain prejudices, that is, "with preconceived biases toward handling them in certain ways" (pp. 3–4).[5] As used here, *bias* refers to a general way of thinking and acting, a predisposition that guides decision making and problem solving. It is the natural outgrowth of authenticity: a reliance on biases represents not bigotry or small-mindedness but "a quest for integrity, an effort that is at once moral, philosophical, and practical," one that seeks "coherence among a [leader's] daily actions, personal values, and [organizational] aims" (pp. 3–4). Its advantage is that it simplifies leadership, accents its essentials. Instead of long lists of "cookie-cutter approaches devised to fit all situations," which overlook the complexity and disorder of real life (p. 8), the concept of bias leads to a small set of guiding principles that help a school leader direct change according to the larger purposes that motivate his work (and do so in a way that maximizes followership by modeling consistency).

Which guiding principles? Having a philosophy does not by itself guarantee effectiveness. Not all biases are equally apt. We need to know which action orientations on the part of a leader foster change. From the organizational research literature and from my own work with schools that are implementing significant reform, four stand out as essential: clarity and focus, participation without paralysis, recognition, and confrontation. None of them is novel, and none is an arcane orientation accessible only to the gifted. They represent a new look at old truths, a reemphasizing of basics about human nature and school life that we have always known but have too often strayed from. But, as the following chapters will show, when viewed through the lens of authenticity, each of these biases acquires a new and practical emphasis.

NOTES

1. The centrality of integrity to leadership has been explored by a number of writers, notably Kouzes and Posner and, with exceptional clarity, Badaracco and Ellsworth. This chapter and several that follow draw on both, but especially Badaracco and Ellsworth's excellent book *Leadership and the Quest for Integrity* (1989).

2. Arthur Blumberg (1989, pp. 55–69) offers a good summary of what it means for a school leader to have a good "nose" for the job.

3. For example, many leadership trainers have adopted Argyris's well-known distinction (1976) between "espoused theories," the premises leaders profess to hold and to use as guides for their practice, and "theories-in-use,"

the real beliefs and assumptions they actually rely on. It is common for the two to be quite discrepant but for people to be unaware of this discrepancy. Argyris proposed that leaders should be taught to modify their theories-in-use to make them more congruent with their espoused values, a proposal widely accepted in leadership training programs. Recently, strategic theorists, led prominently by Vaill, have begun challenging this view. Vaill argues that there are "many subtle modes and mixes of competency" in leaders' actual practice and that their private, personal theories contain much more wisdom than academics realize (1989, p. 35).

4. These questions are adapted from Kouzes and Posner, pp. 298–299.

5. Badaracco and Ellsworth use *prejudice* instead of *bias*. Several of the biases I advocate (notably "confrontation") correspond closely to theirs and owe a debt to them, but they also draw upon different sources (including, among others, Bolman and Deal) and focus on schools and innovation, not, as Badaracco and Ellsworth's do, on corporations and general leadership.

REFERENCES

Badaracco, J. L., and Ellsworth, R. *Leadership and the Quest for Integrity.* Boston: Harvard Business School Press, 1989.

Bennis, W., and Nanus, B. *Leaders: The Strategies for Taking Charge.* New York: Harper & Row, 1985.

Blumberg, A. *School Administration as a Craft.* Boston: Allyn & Bacon, 1989.

Bolman, L. G., and Deal, T. E. *Reframing Organizations.* San Francisco: Jossey-Bass, 1991.

Drucker, P. F. *The Practice of Management.* New York: Harper & Row, 1986.

Evans, R. *The Human Side of School Change.* San Francisco: Jossey-Bass, 1996.

Fullan, M., with Stiegelbauer, S. *The New Meaning of Educational Change.* New York: Teachers College Press, 1991.

Gibbons, T. "Revisiting the Question of Born vs. Made: Toward a Theory of Development of Transformational Leaders." Unpublished doctoral dissertation, The Fielding Institute, 1986.

Goleman, D. "Major Personality Study Finds That Traits Are Mostly Inherited." *New York Times,* Dec. 2, 1986, pp. C1–C2.

Kouzes, J. M., and Posner, B. Z. *The Leadership Challenge: How to Keep Getting Extraordinary Things Done in Organizations.* San Francisco: Jossey-Bass, 1987.

Maddi, S. R., and Kobasa, S. *The Hardy Executive.* Chicago: Dow Jones-Irwin, 1984.

McGregor, D. *The Human Side of Enterprise.* New York: McGraw-Hill, 1960.

Mintzberg, H. "Planning on the Left Side, Managing on the Right." In
H. Mintzberg, *Mintzberg on Management.* New York: Free Press, 1989.

Nicholson, C. "Henry Scattergood." *Germantown Friends School Alumni Bulletin,* 1995, 36(2), 13.

Nisbet, R. *The History of the Idea of Progress.* New York: Basic Books, 1980.

Ouchi, W. Z. *Theory Z.* Reading, Mass.: Addison-Wesley, 1981.

Schein, E. *Organizational Culture and Leadership.* (1st ed.) San Francisco:
Jossey-Bass, 1985.

Sergiovanni, T. J. *The Principalship: A Reflective Practice Perspective.* Boston:
Allyn & Bacon, 1991.

Sergiovanni, T. J. *Moral Leadership: Getting to the Heart of School Reform.*
San Francisco: Jossey-Bass, 1992.

Vaill, P. B. "The Purposing of High-performing Systems." In T. J. Sergiovanni
and J. E. Cobally (eds.), *Leadership and Organizational Culture.* Urbana:
University of Illinois Press, 1984.

Vaill, P. B. *Managing as a Performing Art: New Ideas for a World of Chaotic
Change.* San Francisco: Jossey-Bass, 1989.

20

BUILDING A
COMMUNITY OF VIRTUE

Kevin Ryan
Karen E. Bohlin

NEW YORK CITY, home of Carnegie Hall, Times Square, the Brooklyn Bridge, the Statue of Liberty, the Yankees, and the Mets, is celebrating its one hundredth anniversary with an outpouring of civic pride. And New Yorkers have reason to celebrate. Although it is certainly not without its flaws, the Big Apple is the "comeback kid" of American cities. Within ten years, New York City has gone from the murder capital of the nation and a town with a well-earned reputation for filth and inefficiency to an again-thriving tourist and economic Mecca. And behind the glitter and the crowing of the city's politicians are some solid changes, particularly a dramatic decline in violent crime and the rebirth of the city's neighborhoods.

What accounts for this surge in the moral life of the city? In his discussion of "defining deviance down," Daniel Patrick Moynihan, the senior senator from New York and an urban sociologist by training, points out that cracking down on the little things effects positive change in the moral life of a city. Getting the prostitutes and hustlers off the streets was the first step. Next went the intimidating beggars and squeegee men. Then it was loitering and drinking on street corners and stoops that was targeted. When the New York Police Department started taking graffiti, vandalism, and shoplifting more seriously, drug dealing in the streets plummeted. Mayor Giuliani remains committed to the "little things approach" and has recently asked for increased vigilance against jaywalkers to enhance safety in the streets. The police chief has written about making public places "learning environments."

Behind all these improvements is a citizenry that decided to change, to take its city back. Big Apple residents are rejuvenated and have invested themselves in restoring a stronger spirit of community. A case in point is the Bronx's Crotona neighborhood, which was devastated by tenement fires in the 1970s but has recently been brought back to life by its inhabitants. The *New York Times*[1] reports that it is thanks to scrappy community advocates like Mr. Astin Jacobo (a community overseer who grew up in Crotona), church groups, and organized tenant associations and housing programs that new construction has come to the neighborhood. The resulting new homes and modest gardens are the surest signs that after years of abandonment, this neighborhood is poised to rejoin a city that, in the latter part of the 1990s, is enjoying the bounty of more jobs, less crime, and growing optimism.

What are some other sure signs of a flourishing city or community? Clean parks and sidewalks, provisions for the homeless and vulnerable, a high percentage of registered voters, thriving church communities, and energized civic associations are among the key indicators. These indicators suggest that both a community's citizens and its public servants have a stake in and benefit from the city they inhabit. Good cities emphasize their citizens' responsibilities and protect their rights, enabling them to flourish both individually and collectively. Peace, prosperity, and freedom may be blessings, but they are also hard-earned achievements. That all this is a matter of degree is clear from the recent *celebration* that Brooklyn had gone a full week without a murder.

The early Greeks laid the foundation for our understanding of what a city is. The Greek city, or *polis,* consciously cultivated particular habits or virtues among its citizens, habits that the Greeks had learned were necessary for life in the city, or "civilized life." A city was more than a shared physical space. It was a group of people—citizens—who shared a vision of what constituted a good life. It was a safe place, particularly compared with the spaces outside the city walls, where people were vulnerable and had to stand alone against barbarism. And the Greeks were quite conscious that a just city did not come to be by chance. Then as now, good cities required a solid political and moral architecture. The *polis* was not merely a haven from barbarism and vulnerability but also a center of civic life and learning. To flourish, a society must rest upon a covenant of shared principles between citizens who are ready to fulfill their civic obligations. Personal and social responsibility, combined with allegiance to shared ideals, are integral to the moral fiber of the body politic. Therefore an education in one's culture and civic duties is essential.

History has shown us that societies, from classical Athens and Rome to twentieth-century Berlin and Sarajevo, fall when their moral framework crumbles. When a people or government fails to attend to what holds their city together, when citizens have little regard for the common good, when political leaders betray or distort the moral ideals and principles for which they supposedly stand, then as Yeats prophetically pointed out, "Things fall apart; the centre cannot hold / The best lack all conviction, while the worst / Are full of passionate intensity." History is full of examples of the dire consequences of that intensity, from the burning of Atlanta to the bombing of Baghdad.

Like a city, a school is "a thing made." It is a social construction, and as such, it can rise or fall. School communities are themselves microcosms of the city they inhabit. They, too, must be communities of virtue, built on a solid frame. This frame, similar to a city's moral and political architecture, arises from a school's set of core beliefs and principles (who its people are) and its driving purpose or mission (what they stand for). These principles are either upheld, in the same way that a city upholds its laws, ensuring order, safety, and equal opportunity for its citizens, or they are lost and thwarted in the face of competing priorities. When the members of a school community have ownership in core beliefs and principles and are committed to them—like the citizens of Crotona in the Bronx—there is a rebirth of learning and pride in the school. In contrast, when students, teachers, and parents are cut off from what goes on in their school or are not invested in it, the moral life of the school begins to fall apart.

Communities of virtue are both made and sustained by the moral ethos of the school, by its distinctive climate or atmosphere. The word *ethos* is borrowed directly from the Greek and means "character, a person's nature or dispositions." And the ethos of a school is a profound character educator. Building a strong moral ethos in classrooms and throughout an entire school community is what this chapter is all about. For as our colleague Charles Glenn puts it, "Only a school of character can aspire to foster character in its pupils."

The Teaching Power of a School's Ethos

As Gerald Grant put it in *The World We Created at Hamilton High*, "Much of what we have become as a nation is shaped in the schoolyard and the classroom." [2] Since environment has a profound impact on children's development, we need to pay strict attention to our schools' environments. School absorbs an enormous chunk of our children's lives. Beginning when they have barely moved from the Big Wheel to the tricycle and continuing on through their adolescence, children spend the majority of their waking hours in the environment of a school. Like the citizens of the Greek *polis,* members of a school community incur specific obligations that shape the way they habitually behave.

We are social beings and forge our lives in a social context. Classroom and school environments give rise to a variety of social relationships: among students, teammates, and cast and choir members; among teachers, administrators, and staff; between students and teachers; between students and bus drivers, cafeteria staff, and custodians. The connective tissue that sustains these relationships—whether it is trust, encouragement, mutual respect, cooperation, collaboration, and selflessness, or mistrust, fear, power, manipulation, competition, and antagonism—has a powerful character-shaping influence. In sum, the ethos of a school has both an inevitable and a potentially permanent educational power.

Unfortunately, sometimes the principles that govern a school's ethos do not draw out the best in its students. Sometimes, indeed, they provoke the worst. Students quickly pick up on the tacit values at work in their school community and build their patterns of behavior around them. For example, survival skills are cultivated in environments where older children bully younger children. Manipulation and cheating are heightened in schools where rank in class and academic achievement are prized above all else. There is no such thing as an ethos-less school. Within a given school community students will either learn to develop and thrive as persons of strong moral character or to slide by, manipulate the system, cave in under pressure, and compromise their family, their faith, or themselves.

With over 850 students in pre-K through second grade, Easterling Primary School, in Marion, South Carolina, serves a large population of youngsters. But that is the least of the school's challenges. Six housing projects feed into Easterling. Says Principal Zandra Cook, "Our children associate with people every day who do not live by the codes we live by here in the Easterling Primary School. The greatest challenge we face is to ensure that our children learn to transfer those skills and habits of character into environments that don't support them." Building students' confidence in their ability to make a difference is at the heart of Easterling's mission. "We tell our children," Cook continues, "when you know what's right, do what's right, and you can be a leader." All reports suggest that this message is getting through to Easterling students.

Actions That Support a Community of Virtue

How can schools support a community of virtue among their students? The following paragraphs provide a few suggestions.

There are a number of initiatives we can take to build a community of virtue. When these actions are intentional, we help to raise everyone's awareness about what matters most in our school community. A community of virtue is supported by a developed sense of the common good and a commitment to advancing it. The common good is those social practices that affirm our common humanity and provide for the betterment not only of individuals but also of all people. Advancing the common good is a basic project in a democratic society. And it is also the "unfinished" project that young people need to be invited to take up.

Aiming Higher

Without goals, we flounder. Without demanding goals, we settle for mediocrity. Schools must hold high expectations, both for academic performance and for character, and work consistently to help students live up to them. In Phoenix, Arizona, for example, the Mountain Pointe High School motto, "Purpose, Pride, and Performance" resonates throughout the school, bolstering everything from students' academic goals to their class discussions, soccer practices, and championship pep rallies. One student summed up her experience at Mountain Pointe this way:

> There are three things I live by. These three things have only been there for a few years, but I hear and see them every day: "Purpose, Pride, and Performance." *Purpose*—the word that reminds me of why I am here and what I have to accomplish. *Pride*—what makes me stand tall each time I hear my name. *Performance*—the actions I take to move forward in my life. I have had four years at Mountain Pointe High School to live by these vows, and they have definitely made me a better person. I may not be a "perfect" role model, but I feel I have accomplished more at this school than I have anywhere else.

Creating Resonance

A friend of ours returned from a piano lesson the other day and exclaimed proudly, "I'm working on 'digging in.'" "What do you mean?" we asked, puzzled. "My piano instructor said that anyone can make pretty sounds by gliding along the surface of the keyboard," our friend explained. "But to make beautiful music, you have to dig deep into the notes. . . . Then the sound resonates." Building a community of virtue is not simply about aiming high or having lofty goals; it is about "digging in." There is an intense concern to see that in all aspects of school life—from the cafeteria to the playground, from the classroom to the faculty lounge—virtue is modeled, taught, expected, and honored. In a school with a strong moral ethos, virtue and the opportunity to practice it resonates throughout the community.

Instituting Meaningful Service

"Community service," "service learning," "mandatory service hours," and the like are high on the agenda of educational reform. In today's highly politicized atmosphere, we caution schools not to approach service superficially. We do not want our students simply fulfilling a requirement or beefing up their resume. Service can become an empty ritual, or worse. And although it can be a powerful learning event for students, service is not simply about engaging our students in productive work. We need to help them reflect on why it is important to take responsibility for the school community and to take care of those who are less fortunate than they are. The school community is an ideal place to invite students to give more of themselves. There are numerous opportunities to work as a class: removing graffiti, planting a garden, managing the school recycling program. Giving older students an opportunity to read to or tutor younger students not only helps them acquire the habit of service but also builds friendships between grades. Further, it gives the younger students a close look at older, service-rendering role models.

Mound Fort Middle School, in Ogden, Utah, has transformed its ethos completely by linking its efforts to improve literacy with a service program. Six years ago the faculty agreed they needed to focus aggressively on reading, because most of their students were illiterate. In addition to bringing in reading specialists to train the teachers, students were trained to read aloud. Now students practice and share their skills each week by reading stories to the elderly in a local nursing home and to children in the neighboring elementary school. Not only have scores skyrocketed, says Principal Tim Smith, but also violence in the school has plummeted. Perhaps one of the most telling results of this schoolwide effort comes from a parent who was astounded to discover her previously television addicted, thirteen-year-old son reading to his little sister instead of watching his favorite shows.

Encouraging Student Ownership

To build a community of virtue, students must have a stake in its construction. They must "buy in" rather than be forced in. They need to understand and embrace the principles behind their school's moral code.

Regardless of how a school community chooses to label its code, it should be grounded in principles everyone understands and embraces. When students have ownership of their code, anyone in the school community can ask them with confidence, "This is our school, so how can we solve this problem together?" "What might you do differently next time?" "What do you think is the best thing to do?" Moral maturity and freedom require more than mere adherence to the law; they require an understanding of the why and wherefore of its rules and regulations—the principles that make it worthy of their allegiance.

Bailey Gatzert Elementary School, in Seattle, Washington, serves a diverse student population. Five years ago, says one veteran teacher, "the playground was like a battlefield." There has since been a radical improvement in student behavior and academic performance, due largely to the school's Four Promises program. Everyone in the school community promises to act in a safe and healthy way, to respect the rights and needs of others, to treat all property with respect, and to take responsibility for their learning. It was not the four promises alone that effected change. The administration, teachers, and playground staff were also committed to teaching children how to play fairly. Additionally, the in-school counseling and family support workers join the staff in constantly referring to these four promises. By invoking the notions of honor and commitment, however, the school has tapped a deeper motivation than compliance with rules and regulations. When students feel ownership of their school's ethos, teachers are not the ones who say, "We don't do that here!" Students will become invested in a world they help create.

Remembering the Little Things

The moral life of a community is made up of many little things, and a community of virtue attends to those little things. On the academic front, everything from helping students see the importance of finishing their work neatly, completely, and on time to teachers' keeping their word about quiz dates, deadlines, and grading criteria falls under the umbrella of "the little things." Emphasizing the school's appearance is another constant invitation to grow in virtue. Hanging student work attractively, putting tables and chairs back where they belong, leaving the blackboard clean, and returning books to the library are among the long list of daily responsibilities that should be shared by everyone in the school community. Just as paying attention to the little things helped change the moral life of New York City, it will also improve the moral ethos of a school community and foster pride in its members.

Building Close Relationships

Warm friendships and close relationships are part of the connective tissue that sustains a community of virtue. In recent decades, schools have attempted to break down the walls between people through sensitivity training in an array of areas, from ethnic, religious, and cultural diversity to sexual orientation and gender identity. This was and continues to be done to promote tolerance and healthy relationships. But, quite frankly, we have found just the opposite to be the end result of these efforts. Programs that point up our differences rather than celebrate what we have in common can, in fact, be a hollow experience, ignored by teachers and mocked by students. As one student put it, "after we went to our diversity seminars, everyone split for lunch and sat at tables with students from their own ethnic groups."

We agree that tolerance of civil dissent is critical to public discourse in a democracy. Tolerance is not a virtue in and of itself, however. Children as well as adults seek not to be tolerated but to be trusted and respected, to be understood and befriended. Tolerance demands very little of us. We may tolerate—put up with—a man sitting next to us on a train who is speaking very loudly, but that doesn't mean we respect him. Furthermore, if we teach our children to tolerate all differences, they may never learn that some things in life—such as genocide, character assassination, or torture, for example—are simply intolerable. With overzealous efforts to sensitize them to differences, we may end up desensitizing them to important moral distinctions. As Ogden Nash aptly put it in "Yes and No" (in the 1936 collection *I'm a Stranger Here Myself*):

> Sometimes with secret pride I sigh
> to think how tolerant am I;
> Then wonder which is really mine:
> Tolerance or a rubber spine.

Lynn Lisy-Macan, principal of the Brookside Elementary School in Binghamton, New York, built her school's character education effort on the cohesiveness resulting from closer bonds among the people in her building. "I saw a real need to work on relationships with each other—teachers with teachers and teachers with students," she explained. Their focus has proved fruitful. "There's a certain feeling here at Brookside. Kids hold doors for adults. They speak to adults, and they are respectful. . . . There is a strong sense of community in the way children interact. As a staff we're making strides, but as adults it's hard to change. . . . We still fight, but I believe our foundation is stronger. Students and teachers feel closer. There is a strengthened connectedness. . . . We used to call character education a program. Now it's part of our culture."

Caring Enough to Correct Others

In an address to his students at the opening of the fall term, F. Washington Jarvis, our headmaster friend, explained to an auditorium filled with junior and senior high school students, "People who take the time to criticize you are often, in my experience, the ones who love you the most."[3] It is also an era that underestimates the resilience and realism of youth. To build a community of virtue, we certainly need to take the time and the interest in our students (and colleagues) to offer a word of encouragement and sincere praise when it is warranted. But we also need to be ready to correct them—and be skilled at doing so—and offer advice that will help them grow in virtue. Helping a student get an objective picture of the consequences of his rude behavior is not easy. Trying to do it entirely through positive comments is impossible.

Conditions That Create a Negative Ethos

Movies, newspapers, and the nightly television news have given many of us a negative stereotype of our urban schools. Images immediately come to our minds of children trying to learn in hostile environments, of danger lurking outside the schoolhouse door (and inside it, too), of disruptive boys and girls, indifferent teachers, and ineffective administrators. The attention given on TV to burly police officers, metal detectors, and surveillance cameras wrongly suggests that our urban schools are nothing less than junior state penitentiaries. This is not only a hackneyed image but a gross and destructive one as well. In fact, many urban public schools have a wonderful and constructive ethos. Suburban and private schools, meanwhile, tend to benefit from the opposite stereotype. Yet more than a few of these schools are afflicted with serious moral problems. Ethos varies enormously from school to school. What follows is an anecdote that illustrates how easily we can be deceived about the ethos of a school.

We heard an account some time ago from a high school teacher who had been tenured for many years in a quite comfortable suburban school district. Her high school was famous as a "lighthouse school" because of its reputation for excellence and its students' high academic, artistic, and athletic achievement. She told of an encounter with a senior, a boy she had taught when he was a freshman and at the time of this incident was teaching in a senior English elective. It was late in the school year, and concerned because he was becoming more and more withdrawn, she asked him to see her during a free period in her room. She was aware, too, that although he was one of the school's most outstanding students, he had recently lost a competition for the school's top college scholarship. The teacher acknowledged that although he had been one of her students for over a year and a half, she really didn't know him that well. She knew that he was very disciplined, as he had to balance a job at a 7-11 with his commitments to the debate squad and the wrestling team, which he captained. The teacher had heard, too, that the reason he worked was because there was no father at home and he needed to help out. Apparently, he had started a lawn maintenance business when he was in the eighth grade and now was able to make real money during the summer months. She related that she just wanted to give him a "little pep talk to get him out of his funk."

Their talk started slowly, with her asking a number of probing questions. After several monosyllabic answers and long pauses, he stared at her and said sardonically, "I mean no disrespect, but you don't get it, do you? You think you know what is going on in this school, but you're like the rest. You don't have a clue." Offended and somewhat defensive, she challenged him to back up his charge. And he did. He was clearly outraged by the unprincipled behavior of the majority of his classmates and some of the school's teachers. When she pushed him for specifics, he first got red in the face and then related chapter and verse about the prevalence of cheating and plagiarism among his classmates. The young woman who had been awarded the scholarship was apparently a notorious cheater. So were several others among the school's academic cream. He also insisted that although most of the teachers let it happen because they were too lazy to seriously monitor exams or adequately correct written work, he knew of three teachers that students claimed had caught them cheating but just wouldn't go to the trouble of making them pay the consequences.

He claimed that the vice-president of the student council had told him late one night when they were away at a debate tournament that since the ninth grade a handful of their classmates who had over and over been elected to prestigious positions in student government and various clubs had cynically set out to garner those positions. And they had been astonishingly successful. A debate team mate said that one of the school's history teachers had acted as an informal political advisor to these kids and seemed to get a big kick out of their political intrigues and machinations. He spoke of how teachers and administrators backed down whenever one of the well-connected kids got in trouble and pointed out how ironic it was that they always had to "make an example" of other kids. He talked about how much effort went into educating the talented kids while the rest just got scraps of attention from teachers—"unless, of course, they're important to the team." It came pouring out for a half hour. Finally, he said, "Lookit. I've got to get to work. But come on. Face it. The kids all know it. This place is a moral garbage can." The teacher could say nothing to the boy. She was stunned and paralyzed and as embarrassed as she had ever been.

What, then, contributes to a school with no soul, a school in danger of becoming a "moral garbage can"? The following are a few of the warning signs.

No Shared Vision or Ideals

When a shared vision or set of ideals is not embedded in a school community, then "Who cares?" and "Why bother?" become the silent mantra of many students. When disrespect ("dissing" peers and adults) is common, when "please," "thank you," "excuse me," and holding doors are all just remnants of a stuffy propriety that's gone out of style, when cheating and "getting by" are the norm, we can say with sad confidence that the school ethos does not foster respect, thoughtfulness, and diligence. We suggest posting the school's vision and mission statement prominently and referring to it frequently in both class meetings and faculty meetings.

Competition Run Amok

Cutthroat competition—on the sports field, in spelling bees, or in the AP calculus classroom—undermines community. Coaches who habitually fight with referees or storm off the court, swearing, after a loss send a clear signal to students: winning is what counts the most. Students who are both pushed to "look out for number one" and systematically rewarded for doing so are trained to be selfish and arrogant rather than cooperative and understanding. Character-building schools recognize students for their improvement, commitment, and sportsmanship, not simply for their successes and wins.

Little Opportunity to Serve

When students are not expected to remove the toilet paper from the trees in front of the school after a big victory or to monitor a class of younger students at recess, when teachers accept homework hastily done with a sigh ("at least she turned it in"), then a subtle message is reinforced: school is your right, not your responsibility. If students are not given an opportunity to "adopt a grandparent" at a nearby nursing home or to tutor a younger student, then they miss a chance to develop responsibility, generosity, and compassion. In a community of virtue, service is simply a way of life, not an occasion for bells and whistles. Meaningful service has its own intrinsic rewards.

No Traditions

Traditions are the backbone of school spirit, and school spirit is essential to loving the good. Schools without traditions are communities without heart, without a spirit of family, without a respect for history in the making, without a desire for memory making. A school community that does not take advantage of opportunities to celebrate and honor virtue, achievement, and service cannot provide a true framework for building character. Schools of character institute memorable traditions, annual events involving family and school community members, that potentially mark young people for life.

No Student Voice

Schools that do not welcome students' dialogue, inquiries, and recommendations deprive young people of the opportunity to develop self-knowledge, integrity, good judgment, and the ability to deliberate soundly. It's a mistake to tell students that their school or classroom is a democracy—it cannot and never will be. But children need to learn how to participate in a community and to prepare themselves for democratic citizenship. When schools make mere compliance with rules (rather than students' moral maturity) a priority, they sow the seeds of passivity rather than virtue. On the other hand, students become committed to an ethical community through such activities as drawing up classroom constitutions or refining school policies on open lunch.

Neglect of School Grounds and Property

A school's appearance is not everything, but it does make a strong statement to students, teachers, families, and visitors. If the front steps of the school are littered with candy wrappers and cigarette butts, if the school foyer features last year's student work, if scraps of paper and plastic cups litter the hallways, and if it is generally expected that "somebody else" will pick it all up, then students and teachers alike become indifferent to their school community. In character-building schools, students take pride in their classrooms and school grounds. They participate in lunchroom cleanup and the upkeep of the playing fields, and so on.

Ineffective Character Educators, or "Miss-the-Mark" Schools

Society's deepening worry about our children in recent decades has inspired some educational efforts notable for their good intentions, their ability to capture headlines, and their complete inability to create schools of character. Without thoughtful consideration of what character education means, schools may occasionally play pretty music, but their haphazard efforts never truly resonate in the lives of their students. Following are three approaches that run such a risk.

The Social Services Mall

Particularly in large middle and high schools, the school community can be conceived of as a social services agency rather than an educational institution. Increasingly, teachers of all disciplines and grade levels spend long hours (and their school's limited financial resources) attending professional training programs on drug and alcohol abuse, pregnancy prevention, and AIDS awareness. Additionally, students spend class time on small-group and private sessions in which they receive "peer support" and psychological counseling. The fires of social problems rage fast and furious, and these schools strive to keep up with all the technical and curricular support available that promises to put out the blaze. These deeply moral issues are often presented and dealt with in a value-free manner ("Here are the facts, now you make up your own mind"), hindering any real moral or intellectual growth.

The Substitute Nanny School

A second popular model that holds firm in a number of our elementary schools is that of the school as child care provider. Given the depressing trends in youth crime and the declining moral influence and very existence of the nuclear family, many public schools have done their best to offer a safe haven for children for six to nine hours a day. Providing early morning and afternoon child care as well as government-subsidized meals, the school community's function becomes one of keeping kids off the streets and out of trouble rather than educating them. Although it is a worthy goal to provide material needs for children whose parents cannot do so, it is not the schools' essential mission. This approach can lead to students' sensing that they are simply being parked in school for the day. In such schools, the goals of character development and academic growth are frequently given little attention.

The Achievement-at-All-Costs School

Some schools take an extremely laissez-faire approach to community building. Ignoring the need to build character and schoolwide esprit de corps, they believe their sole purpose is to drill students in academics. Such schools can become nothing more than hard-driving information dispensers. Often they take the stance that parents, religious groups, and youth organizations have sole responsibility for children's moral development. They are much more concerned with the "three Rs" and technology training than with character education. Their fundamental belief is that if the schools provide the academic knowledge and skills training people need to succeed in the workplace, then they are doing fine by their students.

None of these approaches, either alone or in combination, provides a positive character-forming influence. But there is an alternative model— the school as a community of virtue—in which academics and character are developed hand in hand. Fusing these two goals creates a synergy in which each objective advances the other. Thus we believe that a community of virtue provides a much richer context for students' intellectual and moral growth than do any of these other approaches.

"Lesser Places" Where Character Education Takes Place

In addition to the obvious place—in the classroom—character education of some sort or another can occur in a number of other, unexpected places in the school. Just as attention to the "little things" contributes to the moral life of the community, so does attention to its "lesser places." What follows are discussions of potentially miseducative environments in and around the school, each accompanied by a set of questions that invite the reader to transform these lesser places into corners of character building.

The School Bus

Many students are bused to and from school every day, and here they learn yet another moral code. Some schools have assertively addressed "bus issues" with their students. But more often than not, taunting, ridiculing, yelling obscenities, and just plain harassing other students are characteristic pastimes on the ride to and from school. Some parents complain; some bus drivers initiate a zero-tolerance policy concerning swearing and horsing around. On many buses, however, the intervention occurs long after the emotional (and sometimes physical) damage has already been done. Here again, children learn to either fight back or retreat from trouble. Others steel themselves and step onto the bus with fear in their guts. Threatened by their assailants not to tell their parents or teachers what has happened or they'll get it worse next time, children who are picked on on the bus have yet another reason to dislike school. The code of the school bus is survival of the psychologically fittest, or as one student told us, "It's put down or be put down."

To turn a bad bus climate around, consider these questions:

1. Are the bus drivers treated as important members of the school community? For example, are they recognized at annual assemblies or thanked by parents, students, and school staff?

2. Does the school respond immediately to a problem on a bus by calling a meeting with the students involved and their parents?

3. Are the bus drivers supported and recognized by the school as character educators? Are they encouraged to uphold the school's code of expectations and virtues on the bus?

4. Do parents back the school and the bus driver when they are asked to speak with their child about misbehavior on the bus?

5. Do older students look out for new and younger students who are riding the bus for the first time? What can be done to foster this kind of Big Sister, Big Brother tradition on the bus?

6. Do students feel safe on the bus? If not, why? Are these issues being addressed proactively?

The Hallways

In one urban school we've visited, students walk silently through the hallways, in single file, accompanied by stern-faced teachers armed with walkie-talkies. The teachers look more like prison guards escorting inmates through a penitentiary than teachers leading sixth graders from class to class. A college senior recounted for us her experience in a private high school that prided itself on its students' intellectual achievements and its impressive list of Ivy League acceptances. All the students knew that there was one hallway you shouldn't walk down alone because a particular group of boys liked to play "gang rape" in a closet down that way: "They didn't actually rape anyone. But they liked to bang on the walls and make a lot of noise, sometimes pulling a girl in to get a few good screams going as well. . . . I couldn't figure out why they got such a kick out of it. That is just one example among many of the sick things kids did and got away with. None of the teachers knew; or if they did, they didn't do anything about it."

Here are a few things to ask yourself about your school's hallways:

1. Do teachers and administrators make eye contact with students and greet them in the hallways?

2. Are the hallways clean and safe?

3. Do the adults in the school make an effort to keep student work posted neatly?

4. Is there zero tolerance for vulgar language and gestures? Are public displays of affection tolerated? Are these issues discussed among the faculty and staff so as to promote a coherent character-building effort, or simply as disciplinary problems?

5. Are the hallways clear during class time? Could adults circulate the hallways more frequently—not necessarily as police agents but as reminders to students that the adults in the building care about where they are and how they are spending their time?

Study Halls

Monitoring study halls is among the least desirable jobs teachers have to assume, especially in schools where students have two or more study halls a day. In some schools, students perceive quiet study halls as either a cruel punishment or an exciting challenge to see what they can get away with. Everything goes, from roaming the halls under the pretense of going to the lavatory to flipping through *Seventeen* magazine, *TV Guide,* or, yes, even *Hustler.* The lessons here are many: "You don't have to take the study hall monitor seriously, because she's not your teacher." "You can do whatever you want." "Study hall is a free zone."

Ask yourself these questions to help turn your school's study halls around:

1. Are students being assigned adequate (and engaging) homework, so that they have something to do when they arrive in study hall? Are students taught that using study halls well is an effective way to learn to manage their time and improve their study habits?

2. Are students required to arrive in study hall with books, pens, papers, and necessary supplies? Is there a reasonable way for students who want to work on a group project to do so without distracting the rest of the class?

3. Are the study hall monitors alert to what students are doing in class? Do they permit note writing or inappropriate magazines?

4. Have the teachers met to discuss the issues and challenges of leading a quiet study hall? Have they worked out a policy and set of expectations in keeping with the school's core virtues?

The Lavatories

Another frequent "free zone" is the lavatory. "Everybody knows that smoking ain't allowed in school"—except in the bathrooms. Starting as early as the fifth grade, students learn many creative ways to smoke in school. A popular one is to climb up onto the toilet, light up, and blow the smoke into the vents. If an adult happens to enter, a quick drop and flush eliminates the evidence immediately. What else goes on in this free zone? For younger students, the boys' and girls' rooms offer students their first encounter with four-letter words and dirty drawings. Students are maligned by a few words etched on stall doors—"For a good time call . . ." Fights start, gossip soars. Not too long ago, it was reported that some sixth-grade boys had taken obscene Polaroids of willing sixth-grade girls and then sold the kiddie porn to other boys in their school.

Here are a few points to consider to help turn your school's lavatories around:

1. Are the bathrooms in the school safe, clean, and in working condition? That is, are the doors on their hinges, do the lights and faucets work, and do the windows open?

2. Are there adequate supplies of soap, paper towels, and toilet paper?

3. If the walls are covered with graffiti, can each class participate in a "bathroom beautification" project, scrubbing or repainting the walls? Activities like this can conclude with a picnic, pizza lunch, or sundae party sponsored by the PTO.

4. Are the bathrooms properly monitored by adults or responsible students to ensure that smoking, gossip, vandalism, and other inappropriate activities are nipped in the bud?

The Playground

The playground is a powerful place in elementary school. Here the rules of the student community are forged. Students pick their best friends to be on their kickball team. Some students are always picked last or left free to drift to the sidelines as loners. A stray student punches another child and leaves him bruised and crying. When the bell rings, all scramble to line up and file back inside to their classroom. At least two students have taken a moral lesson away from the playground: "Might makes right" and "No one cares about me, so I've got to look out for number one."

If this sounds like your school's playground, ask yourself these questions to help turn it around:

1. Is the playground an inviting and clean area in which students can play safely?
2. Can a few games or sports be organized and overseen by older students or playground monitors to minimize exclusion and maximize student involvement?
3. Do teachers and monitors take time out to discuss positive and negative playground incidents (with individual students or the whole group, depending on the situation)?
4. Do monitors and older students stop fights, foul language, and littering immediately?
5. Can different grade levels be assigned to clean up and spruce up an area of the playground as a class project?

The Cafeteria

In the 1970s cult film *Animal House,* John Belushi popularized "food fights" in schools across the country. Projectile food remains high on the list of fears harbored by teachers on lunch duty. In many elementary, middle, and high schools, lunchtime is for the most part sheer bedlam. Cafeteria employees brace themselves before the crowds descend on them. Fifth graders jostle younger students to get ahead of them in line. Shouting is the accepted mode of discourse. Territorial about their tables, children rush to save seats for their best friends. Although it's understandable that children need to release pent-up energy at lunch, the pushing, shoving, name-calling, and generally raucous behavior seen in a great number of cafeterias fosters an élan of aggression rather than self-control and courtesy. Lunchtime becomes more an effort to fend for oneself than to celebrate time together as a community.

Here are some questions to help you tame a rowdy cafeteria:

1. Are the school's core virtues and code of expectations posted in the cafeteria?

2. Do teachers and other adults in the school speak with students and visit tables for friendly conversation during lunchtime?

3. Are students assigned jobs in the cafeteria on a rotating basis? For example, different students could be responsible for reminding classmates to throw their trash away when they're finished eating, distributing drinks or lunches, sweeping the floor, wiping down tables, or pushing chairs back under the tables when lunchtime is over.

4. Do the cafeteria monitors remind students to speak and act with courtesy and to wait their turn in line?

5. Are there logical consequences for serious misbehavior in the cafeteria?

The Faculty Room

The teachers' room is perceived by some younger students as a mysterious adult hideaway or a hallowed ground upon which they dare not tread. Although the office space and facilities for teachers vary widely from school to school, it is clear that the faculty lounge can have a pervasive culture of its own. We are concerned here with the teachers' room that looks more like a swill pit than a place of work. When the faculty room becomes the seat of gossip and complaints about students and parents and administrators and fellow teachers, when dirty jokes are more common than collegial exchanges about lesson plans and units, then the health of the school community is being infected from within.

If this sounds like your faculty lounge, ask yourself these questions:

1. What steps can be taken to make the faculty room a more inviting place to work?

2. Can teachers and staff use more professional discretion and care when discussing issues related to students and their parents? Would a faculty honor code or pledge facilitate such a commitment?

3. What initiatives can be taken to promote collegiality and awareness of other teachers' work and talents? Are there planned social events for the teachers and staff?

Examples of Schools of Character

Not all schools of character look the same. What follows are two pictures of very different schools that have taken *who they are* and *what they stand for* seriously and built a community of virtue that expresses their distinctive character.

The Hyde School

In 1966 Joseph W. Gauld, concerned that America's schools were failing to inspire excellence in students, founded the Hyde School—a private boarding high school that is perhaps best known for its success in working with "troubled" youth. Today the Hyde School has two campuses—one in Bath and the other in Woodstock, Connecticut—and a national reputation. Five other schools have adopted some elements of the Hyde "character first" curriculum.

The Hyde School is based on the principle that we each have dignity and a "unique potential that defines a destiny." Helping students achieve this potential means putting "character first." All students are expected to develop these traits:

- The *courage* to accept challenges
- The *integrity* to be truly themselves
- *Concern* for others
- The *curiosity* to explore life and learning
- *Leadership* in making the school and community work

At Hyde, character development is fundamentally a family affair. "We do not take kids unless parents make a commitment to go through our character development program," says Gauld. Parents gather monthly for parent meetings, retreats, and family weekends. Hyde asks parents to look within themselves, find their strengths and weaknesses, and strive to better themselves, for their own sake as well as for their child's. "You have to start with the principle that parents are the primary teachers and home is the primary classroom. . . . If you get to the parents, you get to the kids," says Gauld.

The Hyde faculty know—and students quickly learn—that achieving excellence is not easy. A sign hanging in the school simply reads, "The truth will set you free, but first it will make you miserable." Says Gauld, "I learn the most about myself by facing challenges." Students are not the only ones held to the school's high standards of truth and responsibility; teachers and staff are as well. Students are expected to accept challenges—including mandatory participation in athletics and performing arts. The "building blocks" of excellence in a Hyde education are as follows:

1. *Motions.* The individual is expected to follow the motions of responsible behavior.
2. *Effort.* The individual begins to take pride in meeting his or her given challenges.
3. *Excellence.* The individual begins to pursue his or her best. One discovers and acts on a unique potential.

How does the Motions-Effort-Excellence model look in practice? Malcolm Gauld—the founder's son and the current headmaster—describes taking over the Hyde women's soccer program in the mid–1980s: "The program was in shambles. The girls not only did not want to play soccer but held great disdain for Hyde's mandatory sports policy." At the first practice, he called the girls together and said:

> Okay, I know that many of you would prefer not to be out here. I'm not going to waste my time explaining why this will be good for you or why I think you could begin to develop a love for soccer or athletics. For the next two months, we are simply going to do the things that soccer players do. What do soccer players do? They show up on time. They bring their cleats and leave their purses at home. All of you will be expected to wear special Hyde Soccer T-shirts, which I will order. In short, I expect you to behave like soccer players and keep your attention on task while you're out here on the field.

Although initially he met with great resistance, the coach held them accountable for the motions of responsibility he had outlined. After several weeks, a group of girls made the step from the Motions to the Effort phase, displaying a positive attitude and a greater work ethic at practices. At the end of the season, three girls asked to join a local winter league—they wanted to move up to the Excellence stage. The following season, the three players at the Excellence level served as exemplars for the rest of the team, and a group of Effort-level girls wanted to compete for starting positions. Soon, 90 percent of the players displayed a norm of consistent effort and hard work. This was the beginning of a tradition of championship soccer teams.

When you walk through the halls of Hyde, you may see a student scrubbing the floor or cleaning a bathroom. "All students have jobs here," says Gauld. Students are expected to take responsibility at every level—including taking responsibility for other students. The concept is called "brother's keeper." One student described it this way: "If I respect this person and I love this person, then I want them to go after their best. If it's someone who's going out and drinking, they're not going after their best. I'm going to hold them to that. You view it more as 'How can I help this person?' than 'How can I snitch on this person?'" Says Gauld, "America is a freedom-of-choice society; [Hyde] is a 'choosing-well' environment." At Hyde, students, faculty, and parents believe that "we're trying to make the best choices possible, and it's my responsibility to let you know when you are not making good choices."

The "Hyde Solution" goes beyond rhetoric: it embodies a fundamental commitment to individual character development. At Hyde, the purpose of academics is to allow students to develop their unique potential—to help them answer the questions, "Who am I? Where am I going? How am I going to get there?"

Easterling Primary

During an in-class discussion about honesty, a second-grader at Easterling, visibly upset, explained to her teacher, "Mommy made me wear these shoes out of the store. I told her it wasn't honest. But she told me to shut up and do as I'm told." As noted earlier in the chapter, Easterling Primary School may serve little people, but its challenges are big. The school song—"Where Little People Do Big Things"—truly captures the spirit of this Title 1 school in rural Marion, South Carolina.

The whole school environment reflects Easterling's belief that "children are our highest priority." Easterling is, as Principal Zandra Cook and others report, "one big family." In each classroom, children cooperatively design job charts and assign responsibilities. The classrooms are warm and inviting. Everywhere you turn, it is evident that people care. "Even the janitors see children as primary" Cook explains. Furthermore, she adds proudly, "Easterling is a beautiful school." The children's work is displayed on banners in the hallways at all times. A garden designed by an environmental architect in honor of an assistant who died adorns the front of the library. A magic carpet and fairy tale scenes decorate the library walls. Painted by a volunteer outside the community, "Wee Fox Cafe" (the Easterling mascot is the Wee Fox) is emblazoned across the large awning that serves as the entrance to the cafeteria, and each of the dining room walls brightly features one of the four seasons.

What is the key to their character education effort? "Everything meshes," Cook answers decisively. "We try to integrate everything, to make sure that it's consistent. The children have to understand. This is what makes us strong." Easterling has been diligent in their effort to make things "mesh." The first meshing point is the staff's involvement. Easterling has a faculty character education team, and "they take their job very seriously." The whole school began strategic planning for character education three years ago, and they continue to assess and refine their efforts. Since it opened, Easterling has been surveying parents on their needs and values. As a result, the school's motto, rules, and "common core of human values" represent shared priorities:

WEE FOX MOTTO
I will treat others the way I want them to treat me.

WEE FOX RULES
1. I am honest
2. I cooperate
3. I show respect
4. I am responsible

COMMON CORE OF HUMAN VALUES
respect
responsibility
justice
kindness
honesty
loyalty

In addition, these values are made a vital part of daily life at Easterling. Teachers weave this core into all their curricular activities. Manners and social skills are taught through the Spanish and drama classes, where students role-play how to "voice an opinion in a kind way or to listen attentively." Schoolwide assemblies and multicultural luncheons provide an occasion for students to appreciate one another's differences. It's not just about costumes and food, however; it's about exploring the history and culture of diverse ethnic groups in an engaging way.

Parent outreach is a third significant feature of Easterling's character education effort. Easterling provides a variety of workshops for parents, on topics ranging from discipline to the content and methodology of its Heartwood Values–based literature program and its Second Step curricula, which teach children to problem-solve and empathize. Consequently, Cook reports, "Our parents know very well how to delve into characterization while reading a story to their children. They know to ask their children, 'How did so and so solve this problem?' or 'What traits did this character possess?'" A parent resource center with books and tapes on child development is open to all families. In keeping with the school's emphasis on early learning, prevention, and parental support, a parent-community group disseminates approximately thirty hospital packets a month to parents of newborns. Easterling's home-school liaison even makes house calls in the school's van, which was purchased with money awarded through the Target 2000 initiative. "We work very hard with our parents," Cook explains. Easterling Primary believes that "the family is the primary influence in society."

Next to parent education, perhaps the most powerful way the school promotes parents as character educators is through its morning television program. Each Friday, fathers visit the school to read stories on the air. "The children love it," Cook says enthusiastically. In fact, the school's daily television program is an effective tool for showcasing models of good character in the school. Each week, for example, a second grader is selected by his or her peers as "Citizen of the Week" and appointed to co-anchor the program for those five days.

The school has also effectively meshed the business community into their coordinated effort. "We have someone from a business visit each day," Cook explains. Visiting business leaders remind children that "working together, caring for what you do, attendance, consideration for others, and working hard" are essential to being a good employee.

What are the results? Total disciplinary actions are down significantly from last year. But more important, Cook says, "We see a difference in the children's understanding of what character is. They don't know manners, how to express their feelings appropriately, before they come here. No one talks to them much. What we see now is their ability to handle things, to work cooperatively without arguing. We see growth. . . . Especially in children with emotional and behavioral problems, I have seen remarkable changes."

The first of the core beliefs articulated by Easterling Primary reads, "We have an obligation to make a positive difference in the lives of others." Clearly, Easterling Primary is making that difference.

The Framework for a Community of Virtue

What does it take to change the ethos of a school and develop it into a community of virtue? What follows are what we believe to be the key elements and factors that need to be in place:

A Relevant Mission Statement

Revisit your mission and vision statements. Do they articulate shared principles and ideals, such as *who we are* and *what we stand for?* Revise them to reflect the centrality of character in academic and personal development.

Core Values

Identify the core virtues that are consistent with your identity and purpose as a school community, specifying those habits that you would like to see practiced among all the members of the school. Most school communities choose to engage in a democratic process of discussing and selecting these core character traits. These virtues (such as respect, perseverance, loyalty, self-discipline, and kindness) will become your starting point in shaping a strong moral ethos.

Partnerships with the Home

Invite parents to collaborate with teachers in a joint effort to help students acquire virtue and develop integrity. Schools need both the commitment and the trust of parents to help children become morally responsible. Parents and teachers must work together to help students understand what it means to take pride in their work and to be personally accountable for what they choose to do or not to do. They can also jointly assist students in their development of intellectual virtues and skills, such as diligence, concentration, listening, planning, and organizing.

Teamwork

Divide teachers and administrators into either grade-level or subject-area teams. Have these teams brainstorm possible ways to create a stronger moral ethos in the classroom. Together they should carefully go over the school's curriculum, assessing its moral richness (or poverty). Then they should work together to develop and exchange lesson plans that tap the moral dimensions of a particular story, event, experiment, or topic. Science teachers need to ask themselves, for example, how conducting a science lab can become a character-building experience for students. Teamwork with one's lab partner, responsibility and care for the instruments and materials used in the experiment, diligence in striving to get the best possible results are among the many lessons that can be included in a science lab.

A Formal Launch

Introduce your character education initiative at a formal assembly for the entire school community. Parents, as well as school, political, and religious leaders, should be invited to celebrate this new effort. This is not intended to serve as a pep rally but rather as a forum to acquaint the community with the school's mission statement, core virtues, policy revisions, and plans for implementing character education schoolwide.

Regular Meetings and Assessment

Make character education a priority item in regular faculty meetings. Discuss and assess the school's moral ethos as well as students' internalization of its core virtues. Individual teachers and staff members should regularly reflect on the following questions:

- Do I strive to integrate the core virtues into my teaching and professional development?
- Do my professional and social relationships with colleagues, students, and parents reflect the principles of character and integrity we hope to instill in our students?
- Do I consistently demand academic and personal excellence from my students?
- Do I foster opportunities for moral reflection during formal and informal classroom activities?

Involved Staff

Involve your library, custodial, administrative, and cafeteria staff, as well as volunteers and bus drivers, to achieve greater resonance. Their work, example, and daily involvement with students should embrace character education. Bus drivers should insist on courteous behavior. Cafeteria workers should expect students to clean up after themselves. Librarians can work with teachers to feature books of characters that inspire students.

Involved Students

Give students a stake in the school's character education initiative. Engage students in creating classroom constitutions and defining behavior expectations. Make sure they know that the school counts on their insights, feedback example, and leadership in sustaining a community of virtue. Invite students to fill out surveys each year with candid comments on the school's climate, academic classes, and extracurricular activities. Invite them as well to describe how they use their time and their level of engagement in school life. Students need to see that the quality of friendships and relationships in the school is key to the quality of life at the school. Therefore, the school's mission and core virtues should be regularly and carefully reviewed with them.

Integrated Extracurricular Activities

Athletics, performing arts, and clubs all provide opportunities for students to practice the school's core virtues. Students need to see that there is a larger purpose than fun and games behind these activities—to help them develop good habits and good character. The language of virtue and high expectations should be maintained in all of the school's sponsored activities, events, and field trips.

Relevant Evaluation

Some people like to begin with the hard-and-fast data: academic achievement scores, attendance records, number of disciplinary actions, student surveys. We suggest that it is more important to return to your mission statement and core virtues, to reflect on where your school is and where it is heading as a community. What can be done, for example, to promote greater collegiality and support among all the adults in the school? Take a look at absenteeism in your school (among both students and teachers), the condition of the school grounds, the tenor of schoolwide events, the atmosphere in the cafeteria, the language and social interactions in the hallways, the state of the lavatories—to what extent do these corners of your school's life represent who you are and what you stand for?

At this point we would like to risk introducing yet another metaphor, one that may help you to answer this question. In the last decade, American corporations have transformed themselves and become the envy of the world. They have done it in large part by transforming their ethos. In the corporate world, a strong ethos is what distinguishes a mediocre business from an outstanding one. A company's ethos is inspired by its core values and purpose. The extent to which these are embedded in the staff's thinking has a great impact on their job satisfaction and productivity. Three best-selling business books, Collins and Porras's *Built to Last,* Tom Chappel's *Soul of a Business,* and Stephen Covey's *Principle-Based Management,* speak precisely to this point. The first identifies the habits of visionary companies. The second emphasizes the importance of involving all stakeholders in the process of building the corporate culture. What matters most in a successful corporation is not its competitive edge but the community and commitment it creates. Evaluation, then, is not only about assessing results; more importantly, it is about how the company is doing in relation to its identity and purpose. The problem with mediocre corporations is not the lack of a mission but a mission that is not shared deeply. And this, Covey argues, is "the seedbed of most other problems."

Like outstanding corporations, the schools of character we have found are able to state with confidence *who they are* and *what they stand for.* It is these shared ideals and principles that govern these schools' lives and serve as their social glue. Building a community of virtue requires a commitment to these shared ideals, ongoing reflection, understanding, and assessment. A community of virtue is sustained and communicated through relationships of trust and respect—the connective tissue that binds together students, teachers, administrators, staff, and, by extension, parents and community members.

NOTES

1. Gonzalez, D. "New Life, Far from the Bright Lights." *New York Times,* Jan. 25, 1998, Sect. 15, p. 28.

2. Grant, G. *The World We Created at Hamilton High.* Cambridge, Mass.: Harvard University Press, 1988, p. 195.

3. Jarvis, F. W., from his headmaster's address to the student body at the opening of fall term, 1996.

PART FIVE

SHARED LEADERSHIP

MANY SCHOOLS ARE experimenting with more democratic means of leadership, including allowing teachers, students, and the community to have more of a say in school governance. This section focuses mainly on sharing leadership with teachers, a topic examined in the piece by Ann Lieberman, Ellen R. Saxl, and Matthew B. Miles and in the piece by Judith Warren Little. Carol H. Weiss and Joseph Cambone study six principals who have adopted Shared Decision Making (SDM) in their schools. This part also looks at shared management or shared (or team) governance in the Margaret Wheatley selection.

21

GOOD-BYE, COMMAND AND CONTROL

Margaret Wheatley

OLD WAYS DIE HARD. Amid all the evidence that our world is radically changing, we cling to what has worked in the past. We still think of organizations in mechanistic terms, as collections of replaceable parts capable of being reengineered. We act as if even people were machines, redesigning their jobs as we would prepare an engineering diagram, expecting them to perform to specifications with machinelike obedience. Over the years, our ideas of leadership have supported this metaphoric myth. We have sought prediction and control, and have also charged leaders with providing everything that was absent from the machine: vision, inspiration, intelligence, and courage. They alone had to provide the energy and direction to move their rusting vehicles of organization into the future.

But in the late 1990s, we are surrounded by too many organizational failures to stay with this thinking. We know, for example, that in many recent surveys senior leaders report that more than two-thirds of their organizational change efforts fail. They and their employees report deep cynicism at the endless programs and fads; nearly everyone suffers from increased stress from the organizational lives we have created together. Survey after survey registers our loss of hope and increased uncertainty for every major institutional form in our society. Do we know how to organize anything anymore so that people want to engage in productive and contributing work?

But there is good news as well. We have known for nearly half a century that self-managed teams are far more productive than any other form of organizing. There is a clear correlation between participation and productivity; in fact, productivity gains in truly self-managed work environments are at minimum 35 percent higher than in traditionally managed organizations. And in all forms of institutions, Americans are asking for more local autonomy, insisting that they, at their own level, can do it better than the huge structures of organizations now in place. There is both a desire to participate more and strong evidence that such participation leads to the effectiveness and productivity we crave.

With so much evidence supporting participation, why isn't everyone working in a self-managed environment right now? This is a very bothersome question because it points to the fact that over the years leaders have consistently chosen control rather than productivity. Rather than rethinking our fundamental assumptions about organizational effectiveness, we have stayed preoccupied with charts and plans and designs. We have hoped they would yield the results we needed—but when they have failed consistently, we still haven't stopped to question whether such charts and plans are the real route to productive work. We just continue to adjust and tweak the various control measures, still hoping to find the one plan or design that will give us what we need.

Organizations of all kinds are cluttered with control mechanisms that paralyze employees and leaders alike. Where have all these policies, procedures, protocols, laws, and regulations come from? And why is it so difficult to avoid creating more, even as we suffer from the terrible confines of overcontrol? These mechanisms seem to derive from our fear—our fear of one another, of a harsh competitive world, and of the natural processes of growth and change that confront us daily. Years of such fear have resulted in these byzantine systems. We never effectively control people with these systems, but we certainly stop a lot of good work from getting done.

In the midst of so much fear it's important to remember something we all know: people organize together to accomplish more, not less. Behind every organizing impulse is a realization that by joining with others we can accomplish something important that we could not accomplish alone. And this impulse to organize so as to accomplish more is not only true of humans but is also found in all living systems. Every living thing seeks to create a world in which it can thrive. It does this by creating systems of relationships where all members of the system benefit from their connections. This movement toward organization, called self-organization in the sciences, is everywhere, from microbes to galaxies. Patterns of relationships form into effective systems of organization. Organization is a naturally occurring phenomenon. The world seeks organization, seeks its own effectiveness. And so do the people in our organizations.

As a living system self-organizes, it develops a shared understanding of what's important, what's acceptable behavior, what actions are required, and how these actions will get done. It develops channels of communication, networks of workers, and complex physical structures. And as the system develops, new capacities emerge from living and working together. Looking at this list of what a self-organizing system creates leads to the realization that the system can do for itself most of what leaders have felt was necessary to do to the systems they control.

Whenever we look at organizations as machines and deny the great self-organizing capacity in our midst, we as leaders attempt to change these systems from the outside in. We hope to change our organization by tinkering with the incentives, reshuffling the pieces, replacing a part, or retraining a colleague or group. But these efforts are doomed to fail, and nothing will make them work. What is required is a shift in how we think about organizing. Where does organization come from? Organization occurs from the inside out, as people see what needs to happen, apply their experience and perceptions to the issue, find those who can help them, and use their own creativity to invent solutions. This process is going on right now, all over our organizations, in spite of our efforts at control. People are exercising initiative from a deeper desire to contribute, displaying the creativity that is common to all living things. Can we recognize the self-organizing behaviors of those in our organizations? Can we learn to support them and forgo our fear-based approaches to leadership!

Belief in the System

To lead in a self-organizing system, we have to ask ourselves, How much trust do I really have in the people who work here? Have they demonstrated any of these self-organizing behaviors already? The question of trust leads to a moment of deep reflection for any leader. Those leaders who have embraced a more participative, self-organizing approach tell of their astonishment. They are overwhelmed by the capacity, energy, creativity, commitment, and even love that they receive from the people in their organization. In the past they had simply assumed that most people were there for the money, that they didn't care about the welfare of the whole enterprise, that they were self-serving and narrowly focused. No leader would voice these assumptions, but most leader behaviors reveal these beliefs. Does the leader believe that his or her vision is required to energize the whole company? Does the leadership team keep searching for new incentives to motivate employees as if they have no intrinsic motivation? Does the organization keep imposing new designs and plans on people and avoid real participation like the plague?

Every so often we open ourselves to a moment of truth and realize the conflict between our behaviors and our deeper knowledge. As one manager of a Fortune 100 company said to me: "I know in my heart that when people are driving in to work they're not thinking, How can I mess things up today? How can I give my boss a hard time? No one is driving here with that intent, but we then act as if we believed that. We're afraid to give them any slack."

Most of us know that as people drive to work they're wondering how they can get something done for the organization despite the organization—despite the political craziness, the bureaucratic nightmares, the mindless procedures piled up in their way. Those leaders who have opened to participation and self-organization have witnessed the inherent desire that most people have to contribute to their organizations. The commitment and energy resident in their organizations takes leaders by surprise. But in honoring and trusting the people who work with them, they have unleashed startlingly high levels of productivity and creativity.

Strategies for Change

If we think of organizations as living systems capable of self-organizing, then how do we think about change in these systems? The strategy for change becomes simpler and more localized. We need to encourage the creativity that lives throughout the organization, but keep local solutions localized. Most change efforts fail when leaders take an innovation that has worked well in one area of the organization and attempt to roll it out to the entire organization. This desire to replicate success actually destroys local initiative. It denies the creativity of everyone except a small group. All living systems change all the time, in new and surprising ways, discovering greater effectiveness, better solutions. They are not acting from some master plan. They are tinkering in their local environments, based on their intimate experience with conditions there—and their tinkering shows up as effective innovation. But only for them. Information about what has worked elsewhere can be very helpful. However, these solutions cannot be imposed; they have to remain local.

This highly localized change activity does not mean that the organization spins off wildly in all directions. If people are clear about the purpose and true values of their organization—if they understand what their organization stands for and who it shows itself to be through its actions—

their individual tinkering will result in systemwide coherence. In organizations that know who they are and mean what they announce, people are free to create and contribute. A plurality of effective solutions emerges, each expressing a deeper coherence, an understanding of what this organization is trying to become.

Mort Meyerson, chairman of Perot Systems, said that the primary task of being a leader is to make sure that the organization knows itself. That is, we must realize that our task is to call people together often, so that everyone gains clarity about who we are, who we've just become, who we still want to be. This includes the interpretations available from our customers, our markets, our history, our mistakes. If the organization can stay in a continuous conversation about who it is and who it is becoming, then leaders don't have to undertake the impossible task of trying to hold it all together. Organizations that are clear at their core hold themselves together because of their deep congruence. People are then free to explore new avenues of activity, new ventures and customers, in ways that make sense for the organization. It is a strange and promising paradox of living systems: clarity about who we are as a group creates freedom for individual contributions. People exercise that freedom in the service of the organization, and their capacity to respond and change becomes a capability of the whole organization.

If we as leaders can ensure that our organization knows itself, that it's clear at its core, we must also tolerate unprecedented levels of "messiness" at the edges. This constant tinkering, this localized hunt for solutions does not look neat. There is no conformity possible unless we want to kill local initiative. Freedom and creativity create diverse responses. We have to be prepared to support such diversity, to welcome the surprises people will invent, and to stop wasting time trying to impose solutions developed elsewhere.

People always want to talk about what they do, what they see, how they can improve things, what they know about their customers. Supporting these conversations is an essential task of leaders. It's not about you, "the leader," developing the mission statement or employing experts to do a detailed analysis of your market strategy. These exercises, because they exclude more people than they include, never work as planned. Only when everyone in our organization understands who we are, and has contributed to this deep understanding, do we gain the levels of commitment and capacity we so desperately need. As a leader supports the processes that help the organization know itself, the organization flourishes.

It's also notable that when we engage in meaningful conversations as an organization, and when we engage our customers, suppliers, community, and regulators in these conversations, everything changes. People develop new levels of trust for one another that show up as more cooperation and more forgiveness. People stop being so arbitrarily demanding when they are part of the process, when they no longer are looking in from the outside trying to get someone's attention.

Moving to Action

Leaders put a premium on action. Organizations that have learned how to think together and that know themselves are filled with action. People are constantly taking initiative and making changes, often without asking or telling. Their individual freedom and creativity become critical resources to the organization. Their local responsiveness translates into a much faster and more adaptable organization overall.

But leaders need to know how to support these self-organizing responses. People do not need the intricate directions, time lines, plans, and organization charts that we thought we had to give them. These are not how people accomplish good work; they are what impede contributions. But people do need a lot from their leaders. They need information, access, resources, trust, and follow-through. Leaders are necessary to foster experimentation, to help create connections across the organization, to feed the system with rich information from multiple sources—all while helping everyone stay clear on what we agreed we wanted to accomplish and who we wanted to be.

Most of us were raised in a culture that told us that the way to manage for excellence was to tell people exactly what they had to do and then make sure they did it. We learned to play master designer, assuming we could engineer people into perfect performance. But you can't direct people into perfection; you can only engage them enough so that they want to do perfect work. For example, a few chemical plants that operate with near-perfect safety records for years at a time achieve these results because their workers are committed to safety. It becomes a personal mission. The regulations, the EPA, and OSHA are all necessary parts of their system, but they can never spell out the route to perfect safety. That comes from hundreds and thousands of workers who understand their role in safety, who understand the whys of safety, who understand that it's up to them.

For all the unscripted events—an irate customer, a leak, a winter storm —we depend on individual initiative. Ultimately we have to rely not on the procedure manuals but on people's brains and their commitment to doing the right thing. If they are acting by rote or regimen, they actually have lost the capacity for excellence. Imposed control breeds passivity. But people do have to know what right means. They have to know what safety really means. If they know what's right, then we have engaged their intelligence and heart on behalf of the organization.

No More Quick Fixes

Self-organization is a long-term exploration requiring enormous self-awareness and support. This is true partially because it represents such a fundamentally different way of thinking about organization and partially because all changes in organization take much longer than we want to acknowledge. If we've learned anything in the past twenty years it's that there are no quick fixes. For most organizations, meaningful change is at least a three-to-five-year process—although this seems impossibly long for many managers. Yet multiyear strategic change efforts are the hard reality we must face. These things take time. How long, for instance, has your organization been struggling with total quality? At Motorola, it's been more than a decade. How many years have you been working with the concept of teams? (Jack Welch, for one, understood that it would take at least ten years to develop the capacities of GE's people. In the crazed world of the late 1980s, that was a radical insight and a shocking commitment.)

Most CEOs aren't trying simply to squeeze their organizations for short-term profitability or shortsighted outcomes that don't endure. Most leaders would never say, "I just want this organization to perform well for a few quarters." More and more, leaders talk about their legacy. They talk about a deep desire for their work to have meant something. This has been a difficult time in which to be a leader. Leaders are not immune to the terrible destruction we've visited on many organizations. A senior executive of a major industrial firm, speaking for many, said in a meeting: "I've just destroyed what I spent twenty years creating." Who among us wants to end a career with that realization?

But if we are to develop organizations of greater and enduring capacity, we have to turn to the people of our organization. We have to learn how to encourage the creativity and commitment that they wanted to express when they first joined the organization. We have to learn how to get past the distress and cynicism that's been created in the past several years and use our best talents to figure out how to reengage people in the important work of organizing.

The Leader's Journey

Whenever we're trying to change a deeply structured belief system, everything in life is called into question—our relationships with loved ones, children, and colleagues; our relationships with authority and major institutions. One group of senior leaders, reflecting on the changes they've gone through, commented that the higher you are in the organization, the more change is required of you personally. Those who have led their organizations into new ways of organizing often say that the most important change was what occurred in themselves. Nothing would have changed in their organizations if they hadn't changed.

All this seems true to me, but I think the story is more complex. Leaders managing difficult personal transitions are usually simultaneously opening new avenues for people in the organization. They are moving toward true team structures, opening to more and more participative processes, introducing new ways of thinking. They are setting a great many things in motion inside the organization. These ripple through the system; some work, some don't, but the climate for experimentation is evident. A change here elicits a response there, which calls for a new idea, which elicits yet another response. It's an intricate exchange and coevolution, and it's nearly impossible to look back and name any one change as the cause of all the others. Organizational change is a dance, not a forced march.

Leaders experience their own personal change most intensely, so I think they report on this as the key process. But what I observe is far more complex. In the end, you can't define a list of activities that were responsible for the organization shifting, and you certainly can't replicate anyone else's exact process for success. But you can encourage the experimentation and tinkering, the constant feedback and learning, and the wonderful sense of camaraderie that emerges as everyone gets engaged in making the organization work better than ever before, even in the most difficult of circumstances.

Sustainability, Not Employability

I believe there is one principle that should be embraced by all organizations as they move into the future, and that is sustainability. How can we endure over time? What about us is worth sustaining long term? This focus flies in the face of current fashion. Our infatuation with fleeting "virtual" organizations misses an important truth: we cannot create an organization that means something to its people if that organization has no life beyond the next project or contract. We cannot promise people, for instance, only three years of employment—with vague assurances of their future employability—and expect the kind of energy and commitment that I've described.

Employability in lieu of mutual commitment is a copout. We seem to focus on it as a response to the grave uncertainty we feel about the future.

Because we can't predict markets, products, customers, governments, or anything, we decide not to promise anything to anyone. Too many leaders are saying, in effect, "We don't know what the future will be or how to manage this uncertainty, so let's think of our employees as negotiable commodities." What they've really said is, "Let's buy flexibility by giving up loyalty."

Commitment and loyalty are essential in human relationships. So how can we pretend we don't need them at work? The real issue is that we don't know yet how to engage people's loyalty while maintaining the flexibility we require. But leaders should be searching for creative answers to this dilemma, not ignoring it by settling on the nonsolution of so-called employability. Employability is a far more destructive practice than we have imagined. The organizations that people love to be in are ones that have a sense of history and identity and purpose. These are things that people want to work for. The belief that a company has stood for something in the past is a reason to want to move it into the future.

The Real Criteria for Measuring Change

You know when you walk in the door of an organization whether people want to be there or not. The sense of belonging (or not) is palpable. Yet few change efforts take that into account—and far too many end up killing the organization's capacity for more change. To measure whether a change effort has been successful, we need to ask, Are people in the organization more committed to being here now than they were at the beginning of this effort? In terms of sustainability, we need to ask if, at the end of this change effort, people feel more prepared for the next wave of change. Did we develop capacity or just stage an event? Do people feel that their creativity and expertise contributed to the changes?

If we're focused on these questions as indicators, we can create organizations that know how to respond continuously to shifts in markets and environments, organizations that have learned how to access the intelligence that lives everywhere in the system. We will have supported people's innate capacity to deal with changing conditions because we will have learned how to engage people. We will have honored their innate capacity for self-organization. And they will respond with the initiative and creativity that is found only in life, never in machines.

22

TEACHER LEADERSHIP:
IDEOLOGY AND PRACTICE

Ann Lieberman
Ellen R. Saxl
Matthew B. Miles

THE "SECOND WAVE" of school reform has been characterized by much talk of restructuring schools and professionalizing teaching. Commission reports from business, education, and statewide policy groups are calling for major changes in the ways schools go about their work and the ways teachers are involved in their decision-making structure (Darling-Hammond, 1987). There is clearly an attempt to change the organizational culture of schools from one that fosters privatism and adversarial relationships between and among teachers and principals to one that encourages collegiality and commitment (Lieberman & Miller, 1984; Little, 1986; Lortie, 1975; Rosenholtz, in press). On the political level, some states and school districts are creating new roles and new structures in an attempt to change the social relations of the people who do the work at the school level. The leap from report to reality, however, is a difficult one, for there are few precedents, few models, and no guidelines. We are literally learning by doing. What is needed, then, is a beginning description of this work and some understanding of the people involved—what they know and do, what the dynamics of their interactions look like—as these new forms come into being. What are these new structures? What can we learn about the meaning of these new roles for teachers? What is teacher leadership? What actually happens when teacher-leaders help other teachers? Our purpose here is to understand some of these new roles and begin to answer some of the questions now being raised as we look at a particular group of successful teacher-leaders in a major metropolitan area. We consciously use the term *teacher-leaders* to suggest that there is not only a set of skills that are teacherlike, but a way of thinking and acting that is sensitive to teachers, to teaching, and to the school culture.

The Skills of Teacher-Leaders

From 1983 to 1985 we had a unique opportunity to study 17 former teachers who played leadership roles in a variety of schools in a large eastern city (see Miles, Saxl, & Lieberman, in press). (We have continued to work with some of them for an additional two years.) Within that time, we were able to collect a great deal of information about who these people were, what they had learned in their new roles, what they did in the context of their school, and even, in their own words, their view of being teacher-leaders. The 17 teacher-leaders worked in three different programs, and all were considered successful in the work they did within their schools. The criteria for success varied, depending on the context, all the way from creating a healthy climate, to making organizational change, to raising achievement scores.

The programs represented three different approaches to working with school people. The first was based on the "effective schools research," the second had as its major strategy the formation of a large school site committee with a broad constituent group, and the third utilized an organic approach to working with teachers on a one-to-one as well as a group basis—providing support and expanded leadership roles for teachers. Despite the differences in strategy, we looked to see if there was a core of skills that was common to these people in their roles as teacher-leaders. (Skills to us meant knowing how to do something rather than knowing that something was appropriate to do. Our focus was on the *capabilities* of these people to activate strategies for change.) We reasoned that, as leaders, these people had to have or develop both process and content skills and that they had to be able to adapt to different contexts and different situations. It is important to note that although these people were very experienced, they learned from both their new role and the context of their particular program.

First, it was necessary to separate out what these teacher-leaders knew when they came to the job from what they had learned while on the job. This gave us not only a sense of the possible criteria that were used in choosing these leaders, but what their new learnings had been as they worked to create these new roles and structures. Ultimately, we were looking for what skills would be teachable to new teacher-leaders in the future.

We found that these leaders had a broad range of skills, abilities, and experience, which included teaching children at several grade levels as well as adults. They were truly "master teachers." In addition, many had been involved in *curriculum development* in the past, as well as having held positions that enabled them to teach new curriculum to others. Their enthusiasm for learning was made manifest by an impressive array of *academic pursuits* and accomplishments. They held many academic degrees, as well as having attended a broad spectrum of courses, conferences, and workshops on topics as diverse as conflict resolution, teacher effectiveness, and adult development. They came to their work knowledgeable about schools, the change process, and how to work with adults. Most had held positions in which they had gained experience in *administrative and organizational skills* and had learned something about the complexity of school cultures. They were knowledgeable about community concerns as well as schools, some having served as school board members, community organizers, and in a variety of support positions in schools.

These leaders were risktakers, willing to promote new ideas that might seem difficult or threatening to their colleagues. Their *interpersonal skills*—they knew how to be strong, yet caring and compassionate—helped them legitimate their positions in their schools amidst often hostile and resistant staffs.

On-the-Job Learning

In spite of this impressive array of skills and abilities, it was significant that these leaders had so much to learn to cope with their new positions. Where before, working in a variety of roles, they had been sensitive to individual personalities and perspectives, now they had to be aware of the interests of teachers, principals, and the community as a whole. These new conditions made it necessary for them to seek new ways of working, which, in turn, led them to find new sets of learnings. They found that what had worked in more narrowly defined positions would not work in the pursuit of a larger, common vision.

LEARNING ABOUT THE SCHOOL CULTURE. Without exception, these leaders learned about the school culture as if it were a new experience for them. They saw how isolated teachers were in their classrooms and what this isolation did to them. They realized how hard it would be to create a structure to involve them, to build trust within the staff, and to cut through the dailiness of their work lives. They were confronted with the egalitarian ethic held by most teachers—the belief that teachers are all alike, differing only in length of service, age, grade level, or subject matter, rather than function, skill, advanced knowledge, role, or responsibility (Lortie, 1975). They saw that, while some principals understood the need for teacher involvement in their own growth and for allocating time during the school day for reflection and adult interaction, other principals pressed for "outcomes"—with or without a structure or process for teachers to learn being in place. In some schools, they saw literally no one supporting anyone. It came as no surprise then that some of these leaders said that the school climate and the administrator's style were the two most critical components of the school culture.

NEW SKILLS AND ABILITIES. All of these leaders learned a variety of techniques for gaining acceptance by teachers and principals. They learned to break into the everyday activities and provide hands-on experiences to get teachers interested. They provided new environments and activities in which people could communicate with one another and learned how to facilitate both group and individual learning and involvement. They learned to be part of the system, but not get co-opted by it—a difficult but essential ability. They struggled with the collegial/expert dichotomy, one that clearly contradicts the egalitarian ethic that was being disrupted. In working with adults, they tried hard to listen more and suggest less and to resist jumping in with too many solutions. In spite of a high self-regard, several reported that they had not realized how much they did not know (Goodwin & Lieberman, 1986).

These new leadership roles tend to expose the powerful infantalizing effects on teachers of the existing structure of most schools. It is not that no one is in charge, or that people are inherently distrustful, but that the structure itself makes it difficult for adults to behave as adults. Rather than work collectively on their problems, everyone must struggle alone. This ubiquitous isolation dramatizes what "restructuring schools" means. New organizational forms enabling people to work together are certainly necessary, but in order for them to be established, the teachers must be organized, mobilized, led, and nurtured, with the principal's support, participation, and concern and the support and concern of all who share in the life of the school.

SELF-LEARNING. In addition to the techniques, skills, abilities, and new understandings that these leaders learned in their schools, they strongly expressed the feeling that they had learned a great deal about themselves as well. Many spoke of a new confidence that they felt in their own abilities. Some thought that they had acquired a more complex view of how to work with people. One said, "I can't believe I have learned to motivate, to lead, to inspire, to encourage, to support, and yes, even to manipulate." Assuming leadership in schools, then, may provide the means for greatly expanding one's own repertoire. Providing and facilitating for other people in the school offers opportunities for learning how to work with others, how to channel one's time, how to develop one's own abilities—to stretch both intellectually and personally.

It is paradoxical that, although teachers spend most of their time facilitating for student learning, they themselves have few people facilitating for them and understanding their needs to be recognized, encouraged, helped, supported, and engaged in professional learning. Perhaps this is what we mean by "professionalizing" teaching and "restructuring the work environment" of teachers. Maybe the opportunities for participating in the leadership of schools, and the structures created as a result, are the means to break the isolation of teachers and engage them in collective efforts to deal with what surely are large and complex problems.

Building Colleagueship—A Complicated Process

Researchers have found the building of collegiality to be essential to the creation of a more professional culture in schools (Little, 1986; Rosenholtz, in press). They have also documented that norms of collaboration are built through the interactions created by the principal's facilitation of collegial work. In Little's now-classic study, she describes how these norms were built as daily routines of isolation were replaced by talking, critiquing, and working together. In Rosenholtz's study, schools were differentiated as being of two kinds—"collaborative" or "isolated." In "collaborative settings" teachers perceived the principal to be supportive, concerned with treating any problems as collective schoolwide opportunities for learning; in "isolated settings" teachers and principals were alienated, with teachers feeling that any requests they made threatened the principal's feelings of self-esteem.

Since our study focused on the introduction of a new role that expanded the structure of leadership in a school, we were looking for the kinds of skills, abilities, and approaches that these leaders utilized in building collegiality in schools. In our search to understand how these teacher-leaders worked, we created sets of clusters, each cluster representing different skills, abilities, and approaches to building collegiality among the faculty. Although their contexts and styles were different, the similarity of the ways these leaders worked has added to our understanding of the complexities involved in changing a school culture when the leadership team is expanded beyond the principal.

The clusters were drawn from 18 different skills that were manifested by these leaders (Saxl, Miles, & Lieberman, in press). They include:

Building trust and rapport

Organizational diagnosis

Dealing with the process

Using resources

Managing the work

Building skill and confidence in others

Building Trust and Rapport

A very important cluster, this set of skills appears early in the development of the work of all teacher-leaders. We found that these leaders did a variety of things to gain the trust of the people in their buildings and that, even when the person was previously known to all the teachers, the same kind of work was still necessary. Because these leaders, in every case, did not have a teaching load, they were immediately suspect: "How come this person doesn't have a class load like me? What are they supposed to be doing anyhow?" Thus the first problem to be faced was how to clarify the expectations of their role for the teachers in the school.

To begin with, the leaders had to figure out for themselves what they could realistically do in the school. Then, they tried to explain to the teachers what they were going to do, describing in a broad way why they were there and what might be the effects of their work. In some ways, perhaps, it is like the beginning of school, where the students want to know what kind of teacher this is, what will be expected of them, and what will go on in the classroom. The relationship here is similar, in that these expectations are negotiated over time, but different, in that the adult culture in schools is not kind to newcomers, especially those of their own rank. The image and the reality of a new role (a teacher without a class) is not the norm, and it is often easier to use a new person as the source of one's frustrations rather than to accept her or him as a helper, go-between, or leader of a different kind.

Just as in the teacher/class relationship, the leader must come to be seen by the teachers as legitimate and credible. They try to accomplish this by finding various ways to demonstrate their expertise and value to the teachers. For some, it is giving a make-or-break workshop—one that they know will either give them immediate credibility if it is successful or set them back for months if it fails. For others, it means becoming a "gofer" and providing resources: going to the library, bringing new materials, keeping the coffee pot going and the cookie jar filled. Somehow they have to do enough to show the staff that they are "good"—experts and helpers, important enough to belong in "their" school. It is at this point that these leaders must learn to deal with *addressing resistance,* for they are coming into a social system with well-developed formal and informal ties. Sometimes this resistance is based on old disappointments and unfulfilled promises from past years. Other times a newcomer takes the brunt of all kinds of existing tensions in a school, caused by everything from lack of adequate communication to complaints about space, resources, time, and so forth.

Engaging in open supportive communication is part of building trust. These leaders found ways of working with teachers and proving to them that they were capable of being open without betraying trust—that they were there for the staff in a helping nonevaluative way. As they worked with the teachers, they began to *build a support group,* people who came to see that they could work together, struggle collectively, and feel comfortable working as a group rather than alone. For many leaders this meant finding teachers who could be experts in their own right, teachers who could teach other teachers things that they had learned. In the process of facilitating for others, the leaders began to *develop shared influence* and shared leadership. The idea that there are problems common to teachers and problems in a school that can be addressed collectively began to take hold, and teacher-leaders began to build a set of *productive working relationships.*

The abilities mentioned above appear to be necessary to the building of trust and rapport, which are the foundation for building collegiality in school. Regardless of the size or complexity of the school, the age or experience of the staff, or the differences in the programmatic thrust, the same kinds of skills were used to legitimate the leadership role.

Organizational Diagnosis

This set of skills—an understanding of the school culture and the ability to diagnose it—is crucial if a leader is to have the basis for knowing how and where to intervene to mobilize people to take action and begin to work together. Leaders did this in very different ways. Some people had an intuitive awareness of the formal and informal relationships in a school, while others consciously worked out strategies to help them collect data to help them better understand the school social system.

Depending on the specifics of the program, the methods of collection ranged from a formal needs assessment that asked teachers what they would find useful, to an informal collection of information about the principal, curriculum, resources, and so on. However it was accomplished, some initial *data collection* gave teacher-leaders a beginning awareness of the school environment. All were involved in picking up cues from staff, bulletin boards, teachers rooms, principals, parents—anyone who could provide information.

> In the beginning . . . I had to overcome my own personality—the tendency to move too quickly and speak out.

> When you are a teacher, you only know your classroom problems. Now I look at the whole system. . . . When I was in the classroom, I controlled it; the higher you go, the less control you have.

As we can see, collecting information while being conscious of one's self within the larger system was a strategic part of the teacher-leaders' way of working. Either as an insider or as one who came to a school with a leadership role, these people came to form some kind of a *conceptual scheme* in their minds—a map of what the school looked like, who one might work with, where the trouble spots were, who was open to thinking about working on schoolwide problems. As they collected information about the school by being there, hanging around, talking to people, and so on, they began to get enough information to *make a diagnosis*.

If action and change were what their diagnosis called for, these leaders had to find ways to engage key school people with their observations, to *share the diagnosis* with them to see if it was theirs as well. This series of steps, not always consciously thought out, formed the basis for action plans for the school. We begin to see a process: understanding the school, collecting information about the people and how they work, constructing a valid picture of the organization, sharing the picture with others and planning a strategy for action.

Dealing with the Process

Critical to the work of teacher-leaders were their understanding of and skill in managing the change process. Since this meant, among other things, promoting *collaborative relationships* in schools where people had little experience in working together, it involved the use of *conflict mediation* and *confrontation skills*. They soon learned from the realities of their work that, when one tries to get people to work together where they have previously worked alone, conflicts arise, and that their job was to find the means to deal with them. As they worked in their schools, building and modeling collaborative work, they were called upon to weave their way through the strands of the school culture. This involved many types of interactions with teachers, staff members, and administrators.

The relations with the principal varied according to the style of the principal and the structures for collaboration that were being created. When the structure called for working as a team and the principal had been used to working alone, the teacher-leader had to show the principal the benefits to the school of shared decision making. Where a teacher center had been created, the principal had to learn to give support for teachers to work independently without feeling that the existence of this room threatened her or his perceived role as "instructional leader." The tact, skill, and understanding of the teacher-leader was crucial to the involvement of the principal in supporting these new modes of collaboration.

Sometimes the school was in conflict from the start: "The first mission was to bring teachers together to talk to each other. There was a general distrust of the administration by the teachers." Sometimes the job entailed helping the faculty work through conflicts. "At committee meetings, many conflicts come up. He helps us talk them out. . . . We ventilate and direct our energy in a specific way."

Collaboration does not come as a natural consequence of working in a school. It must be taught, learned, nurtured, and supported until it replaces working privately. There were times when these teacher-leaders were the ones who had to confront negative information and give feedback where it was appropriate. Where conflicts appeared as a result of personal incompatibilities or differing interests, their job was not merely to smooth them over, as had often been the case in the past, but to find areas of agreement based on a larger view of the school and its problems.

They worked hard to *solve these problems* by making decisions collaboratively. This was a key skill: Who will do what, how will we do it, when will we make it happen, and how will we come to agree? They found that it took more than a vote to build consensus. It was always necessary to be alert to discontent and to practice and work on being open, communicating together, and finding ways to bring people, as individuals, to think of themselves as part of the group with group concerns.

Using Resources

The fourth cluster of skills involved the use of resources. This refers to people, ideas, materials, and equipment—all part of the school, but often not utilized in the pursuit of collective goals. The teacher-leaders found themselves engaged in providing material things for teachers that helped to link them to the outside world.

> I'm a reader. I need follow-up materials from the literature to find out about good ideas.
>
> They needed a lot of resources.
>
> I would attend conventions, day and weekend seminars and collect handouts.
>
> I keep on top of things. What texts are good?

They did workshops for teachers, demonstrated techniques, and provided follow-up. They also looked inside the school to plug people in to what was already there and, where appropriate, to link people together.

In the process of finding resources and using existing staff to help, these teacher-leaders also began to build a *resource network,* which included developing active linkages between teachers and other members of the school community. It was not just knowing where or who to go to for help, but choosing the right person or right thing at the right time. Matching local needs and capabilities became the key skill.

Finally, it was necessary to help people make good use of the resources. Just getting the "stuff" there was not enough. The leaders had to perform a brokerage function and then follow-up to see that the resources were being used. As we observed, this cluster of skills is part of a complicated process: from finding people and materials, both inside and outside the school, to building networks with these resources, to seeing that whoever, whatever, and wherever they were, they were available and utilized.

Managing the Work

The teacher-leaders worked hard to maintain a balance between the process of getting people to work on collective problems and providing the content or substance around which they worked. Managing this work required a subtle blend of skills, including managing time, setting priorities for work, delegating tasks and authority, taking initiative, monitoring progress, and coordinating the many strands of work taking place in their schools. (It should be noted that these leaders differed in the amount of time they spent in a school. Some spent four days a week in one school, while others spent one day a week in four schools.)

Administrative/organizational skills, although part of their qualifications, were far more complex in these roles than the teacher-leaders had faced before. Time was a persistent problem. How much time does one spend with people having difficulties, or getting resources, or making arrangements for workshops, or demonstrating, or troubleshooting? This proved to be a formidable task, with the successful teacher-leaders we studied gaining great skill in allocating their time as they became experienced in their role.

Managing and controlling skills were needed to organize and manage the work. The teacher-leaders had to learn to move from thought to action. Some used charts to keep track of their activities; some did not. But all of them had to learn how to mobilize the staff and coordinate the many activities, while walking the fine line between exerting influence and "overmanaging" the process of change.

Although contexts differed, these leaders shared the skill of being proactive, that is, having a bias for action. This included modeling specific new techniques as well as promoting a general vision of more productive ways of working. Maintaining momentum in their work, without usurping the authority or the prerogatives of other leadership in the school, required them to take initiative while negotiating their way through the delicate yet tough relationships between and among teachers and principal.

Building Skill and Confidence in Others

The last cluster of skills involved the continuous monitoring and *individual diagnosis* of teachers' communication needs and concerns, while attending to the general organizational health of the school. Working for several years in the same schools, these leaders tried to make normative the notions that it was both legitimate to have technical assistance and necessary to have in place some structure for problem solving. They were attempting to socialize a whole staff to have individual teachers look at themselves critically and take action on their own behalf, while continuing to build supportive structures to better carry out the work as a whole.

They tried to involve as many people as possible in leadership roles by institutionalizing a process or mechanism for dealing with improvement goals, at the same time trying to make sure that constructive changes occurred that would be visible to the whole school. They were concerned with building a support network for the school community, based on commitment and involvement, that was sensitive to individual teachers and other members of the community and, at the same time, promoted organizational change. This required constant vigilance: building networks for support, continuously recognizing and rewarding positive individual efforts that improved the school, helping to create short-term goals, and always working to institutionalize individual and collective efforts at improvement so that they would become "built into the walls."

Teacher-Leaders in the Context of Their Schools

The skill clusters we have been describing are based on interview and observational data from the 17 teacher-leaders we studied from 1983 to 1985. We can get another view, perhaps more integrated and dynamic, by being there, by seeing these people in their own contexts. We did several case studies of these teacher-leaders in 1985 and 1986. The following summary of two of them will help round out the picture we have drawn thus far (Miles, Saxl, James, & Lieberman, 1986).

Urban High School

Urban High is a large comprehensive high school that also serves as the special education center for the entire area. It is in a blighted area in a large urban city. There are 3,500 students in the school, 62 percent Hispanic and 30 percent black. Achievement is low overall. The majority of the students (2,000) are enrolled in general education. Reading, math, and writing scores are low. The principal is young, energetic, and extremely receptive to innovative ideas and any means to improve the school. He is very concerned with raising the level of instruction and increasing the professionalism of teachers through staff development and increased teacher control of the curriculum.

In March 1985, a teacher center opened in the school. Brenda C., a former English teacher at Urban, became the teacher-specialist—a full-time teacher-leader hired to run the teacher center and work with the staff. Because the school was in the process of reorganizing from departments to clusters, experienced teachers were becoming the coordinators or heads of special projects, causing them to leave teaching and move to these new positions. (Given the harsh conditions of the school context—crime, purse snatchings, noise, pitted chalkboards, lack of necessary supplies, prisonlike rooms, and other difficult teaching conditions—it is not hard to see why teachers would want these positions.) When they left new teachers replaced them.

Brenda wanted to do three things during her first year: improve morale, facilitate communication between the various groups in the school, and encourage the staff to utilize the center for professional growth. Subtle resistance plagued her efforts in the beginning. There was the natural resistance to being "improved," as well as the notion that being a high school teacher—a subject-matter specialist—somehow made one already expert.

She began, during her first month, by just offering free coffee and refreshments to the teachers. (The principal had supplied a large room and the coffee.) She spent a great deal of time and money (her own) buying materials that would be of interest to the teachers. She tried hard to get materials that would engender self-help as much as possible, attempting to be sensitive to the sensibilities of her peers. She spoke at department meetings to advertise the availability of these materials to the teachers.

Little by little the teachers began to come to the center. At first they came only for coffee. Brenda wrote personal notes to people to encourage them to come back and to participate in other activities. To enhance communication, she formed a site committee made up of representatives from the various cluster groups. (Finding a common meeting time for everyone was impossible, so staggered meetings went on during the day.)

With encouragement from the director of the teacher center consortium, Brenda helped create a workshop, given after school was over in June, to teach teachers about the latest research on classroom management, mastery learning, and learning styles. The workshop was planned in such a way that the teachers had an obligation to attempt one or more of the ideas in their classrooms in the fall. In this way, Brenda hoped to begin to build a core group of teachers, encourage professional development in the center, and work on greater communication among the teachers.

The impact of these efforts, and others, has been to draw more and more teachers to the center. They read the bulletin boards, look at materials, use the machines, plan lessons, talk together, and work with Brenda. Informally, teachers come for afterschool courses from other schools, which indicates that the center is reaching out to a larger network in the district.

Teachers from the site committee have been instrumental in disseminating information about the center to other teachers. New teachers have talked about being offered nonjudgmental assistance by Brenda in the center. Experienced teachers have spoken about the amenities that make their life easier: a quiet place to work, rexograph machines, and new materials and supplies. All of this has greatly increased the morale of the staff. (An indication of the center's growing popularity was the success of a party for the staff that was given at the end of June. Almost all the teachers came—a highly unusual occurrence.)

Brenda, who has been a teacher at Urban High for 23 years and knows the social system of her school as an insider, has been using this knowledge to create an "oasis in the desert." We see the special role that a teacher in a leadership position can play—encouraged and supported by a sensitive principal—as she gently and cautiously plans for and takes on the function of building morale and professionalism among the staff. She helps alleviate the tensions of a large, experienced staff trying to deal with the tremendous problems that exist in a school in a depressed community. She builds trust among the faculty, recognizing not only the classical resistance to new ideas, but also the special nature of high school teachers (subject-matter specialists with advanced degrees who have their own special reasons to resist being "improved"). Although just a beginning, Brenda's leadership has begun to fill in the tremendous gap between a professional environment and the bare level of subsistence in a complex, difficult high school.

Parkridge Elementary School

At Parkridge Elementary School, Andrea G., a teacher-leader who came from another part of the city, also runs a teacher center. She has been at her school for four years. Her school has always been known as the showcase school of the district. It is a school with 1,500 children. The ethnic mix of the neighborhood has changed over time from Jewish and Italian to Hispanic and black, with a small percentage of Caucasian children.

The school has many fine teachers, many of whom have been there since the 1960s, when additional resources were given to particular schools, including this one, to help with their special problems. These teachers were attracted to the school because of the supply of specialists and the support they would be given. They came because they felt it would be a good place to teach. To this day, the school is still quite special for the area, but it is manifesting problems that are eroding the quality of the program. (Because of the positive reputation of the school, many parents want to send their children there; as a result, the school is suffering from serious overcrowding.) The principal is known to be a real "professional." He is very hard working and the school is remarkably stable. The principal has been there for fifteen years, which is almost unheard of in this area.

Andrea, unlike Brenda, came from the outside to work at Parkview, but, like Brenda, she, too, had the problem of legitimating her presence to the teaching staff. Because the staff was large, and because many had been there for a long time, there were numerous cliques among the teachers. There was also a group of eight new teachers who had taken over classrooms with little preparation for the job. (There was a massive teacher shortage in this city at the time.) An all-day kindergarten program had just been implemented, and the district had called for the school to involve the parents in working with their children at home.

In looking over this situation and figuring out her goals for the year, Andrea decided that the new teachers would be a focus for her work. She also decided to take on the responsibility for working with the parents of the kindergarten children to facilitate better understanding of what the school was doing and what the parents could do to reinforce student learning. In addition, she continued to maintain the teacher center—although it was a small, crowded room, teachers would know that at least there was a place to come where they could give and get help, put their feet up, and share some hot soup from the corner deli.

Everyone speaks of Andrea as the "glue" of the school: "She has made the school a family. Everyone feels a sense of gratitude and loyalty to her." Because she is a very giving person, her mere presence and her way of working fill a great void in this large, three-story building. Her first words are always, "How can I help you?" An hour and a half with her illustrates the point.

> On this day Andrea arrives at the center at 8:15 A.M. She is immediately involved in a "major" problem. One of the teachers, who has a refrigerator in his room, is complaining that because people leave food in it his room smells, thus disturbing him and the students. Andrea gets into the conversation to try to sort out who is responsible for cleaning the refrigerator and what needs to be done to get it cleaned. (This may seem like an insignificant problem, but no problem is insignificant. The message to the teachers is that all problems can be worked on in the center.)
>
> Andrea goes downstairs to the auditorium. She is due to hold a meeting there to teach parents how to provide for reading-readiness activities for their children. When she gets there she finds someone else is rehearsing a play.
>
> Instead of complaining that the auditorium was reserved for her, she quickly negotiates with the teacher to use his room and runs to the front door to alert the parent sitting there to tell the parents what

room to go to. Stopping off at the photocopy room to see that the materials are being run off for the parents, she finds a paraprofessional having trouble with the photocopy machine and also with someone in the office. Andrea helps her fix the machine and then intervenes to ease the problem with the staff person. She then makes her way to the new room, where several parents are waiting, and quickly makes arrangements for one of the parents to translate for one who does not understand English.

In this one-hour period, Andrea has already made four interventions that do not go unnoticed. She has helped a teacher (with the smelly refrigerator), changed her room (by negotiating with the teacher in the auditorium), helped the paraprofessional with the photocopy machine (and a small problem with an office person), and provided for a translator (so that her work with the parents could go on in two languages). Such sensitivity does not go unnoticed, even in a faculty of this size. As a matter of fact, it turns out to be a mode of leadership that is felt by everyone. The principal is extremely respectful of Andrea's good work with the faculty. The supervisors find her presence welcome, since she helps them with their work without overstepping her authority. The specialists know that Andrea and the teacher center can support their work and also help them deliver services. And the new teachers come to the center because they know they can get help and support from both Andrea and other teachers who serve as a support group for them.

The Teacher-Leader as Learner

From this initial look at teacher-leaders, we see that they are not only making learning possible for others but, in important ways, are learning a great deal themselves. Stepping out of the confines of the classroom forces these teacher-leaders to forge a new identity in the school, think differently about their colleagues, change their style of work in a school, and find new ways to organize staff participation. As we have documented, it is an extremely complicated process, one that is intellectually challenging and exciting as well as stressful and problematic. Changing the nature of an occupation turns out to have the possibilities for both "high gain and high strain" (Little, 1988). The gain is mostly in the personal and professional learnings of the leaders themselves: the technical learnings about teachers, instruction, and curriculum; the social learnings about schools as social systems, including how to build collegiality and manipulate the system to help teachers do a better job; the personal learnings about their own professional competence as they learn new skills and abilities and find new approaches to being a leader among their peers; and even, in some cases, the satisfaction of learning how to create structures that alter the culture of the school.

But the strain is there, too. Building trust among teachers, who have long felt that they have little or no voice in choosing what is best for their students or themselves, is not easy. Initial hostility and resistance is always there, and it is hard not to take some of it personally. (What works with students does not necessarily work with adults.) Dilemmas of being a colleague and also being an "expert" are not easily negotiated. Being nonjudgmental and helping are often in conflict with making value judgments that affect the priorities for one's work. Listening to teachers— rather than giving advice—and working with them *on their terms* is sometimes in conflict with personal style. Learning to negotiate from a position of leadership—in a school where there is little precedent for teacher leadership—without threatening those in existing administrative positions takes skill, courage, and nerve. Teacher-leaders have to learn that these tensions and dilemmas are an inevitable part of the drive to professionalize schools and of the change process itself.

The Teacher-Leader as Professional Model

Part of the ideology developed in these new roles is the belief that there are different ways to structure schools and different means to work with teachers and other members of the school community. This involves such characteristic themes as:

Placing a nonjudgmental value on providing assistance

Modeling collegiality as a mode of work

Enhancing teachers' self-esteem

Using different approaches to assistance

Building networks of human and material resources for the school community

Creating support groups for school members

Making provisions for continuous learning and support for teachers at the school site

Encouraging others to take leadership with their peers

We are only beginning to understand the nature and impact of these new roles in schools and the subtleties of fashioning new ways of working with the school community. From studying these teacher-leaders, we see that some sort of team, teacher center, or site committee—a structural change—appears necessary to the creation of collegial norms in a school. More cooperative work, increased interaction across department lines, and support groups for new teachers require new modes of collaboration to replace the existing isolated conditions prevailing in most schools.

What we have, then, is a new leadership role that can help in the creation of new collaborative structures. It appears that a combination of these new roles and structures is necessary to professionalize the school culture and to bring a measure of recognition and respect to teachers— who may be, in the final analysis, the best teachers of teachers as well as children.

REFERENCES

Darling-Hammond, L. (1987). Schools for tomorrow's teachers. *Teachers College Record, 88*(3), 354–358.

Goodwin, A., & Lieberman, A. (1986, April). Effective assistance personal behavior: What they brought and what they learned. Paper presented at the annual meeting of the American Educational Research Association, San Francisco.

Lieberman, A., & Miller, L. (1984). *Teachers: Their world and their work.* Alexandria, VA: Association for Supervision and Curriculum Development.

Little, J. W. (1986). Seductive images and organizational realities in professional development. In A. Lieberman (Ed.), *Rethinking school improvement: Research, craft, and concept* (pp. 26–44). New York: Teachers College Press.

Little, J. W. (1988). Chapter 5 in A. Lieberman (Ed.), *Building a Professional Culture in Schools.* New York: Teachers College Press.

Lortie, D. (1975). *School teacher.* Chicago: University of Chicago Press.

Miles, M., Saxl, E., James, J., & Lieberman, A. (1986). *New York City Teacher Center Consortium evaluation report.* Unpublished technical report.

Miles, M., Saxl, E., & Lieberman, A. (in press). What skills do educational "change agents" need? An empirical view. *Curriculum Inquiry.*

Rosenholtz, S. J. (in press). *Teacher's workplace: A social-organizational analysis.* New York: Longman.

Saxl, E. R., Miles, M. B., & Lieberman, A. (in press). *ACE—Assisting change in education.* Alexandria, VA: Association for Supervision and Curriculum Development.

23

PRINCIPALS, SHARED DECISION MAKING, AND SCHOOL REFORM

Carol H. Weiss
Joseph Cambone

When schools adopt shared decision making (SDM), principals' authority is limited. Nevertheless, all six principals in the SDM high schools we studied supported SDM, at least in part because they had chosen to serve in an SDM school. The three principals who were most supportive of SDM also had ambitious visions of instructional reform. After 1.5 to 2 years, the high schools in which these principals served experienced a heightened level of conflict among the faculty. In large part, the conflict was due to these principals' efforts to use SDM as a vehicle to foster large changes. Teachers resisted major change, and principals became impatient with the participatory process and tried to promote their own versions of reform. Only a modest degree of reform was achieved, but it was more than was achieved by SDM principals without a reform agenda. Reformist principals in non-SDM high schools implemented modest reforms as well, although at the expense of suspicion and antagonism after changes were introduced. We explore the dilemmas that reformist principals face and suggest policy implications.

○

SHARED DECISION MAKING (SDM) is a reform of significant proportions, altering as it does the balance of power in schools. When schools shift to a system of SDM, some of the principal's authority is transferred to the teacher-administrator decision-making group. Johnson (1990, p. 143) writes: "As teachers' formal powers are augmented and administrators' authority is abridged, the role of the principal will be redefined." The redefinition inevitably reduces the domains in which the principal holds unilateral sway (Cohen, 1987; Levine & Eubanks, 1992; Levine & Lezotte, 1990).

In the study to be reported here, the principals of six SDM high schools, despite abridgement of their usual authority, supported the SDM process and cooperated with teachers in the new arrangements. One reason, clearly, was that their position as principal of an SDM school was voluntary. Either they had participated in the creation of SDM or were early implementers of it or they came to a school at which SDM was already in operation with a good notion of what they were getting into. SDM was not imposed on them. Therefore, although there was some variation in commitment to the process, the principals generally were willing participants.

The big difference among the six principals was the degree to which they embraced SDM as a vehicle for improving teaching and learning in the school. Half championed SDM for this reason, expecting that teachers' participation in school decisions would lead to changes that encouraged good teaching for all students. The other three principals supported SDM largely for its own sake, that is, to democratize schools and share power with teachers.

The reformist principals' emphasis on instructional and curricular improvement seems like a worthy stance. As Shanker (1994) recently wrote:

> Is student learning better in schools where there are democratic school councils or in schools where the principal runs the show? . . . The whole point of school reform is to have students learn more. If this doesn't happen, the experiment is a failure, no matter how happy the children, the parents and teachers and the reformers are. (p. E7)

However, our study demonstrates the great difficulties high school staff experience as they labor toward democratic decision making. Is that complicated work confounded when principals simultaneously advocate fundamental changes in teachers' practices? In fact, when SDM principals become strong advocates for change in teacher practice, do they risk undermining the consensual nature of SDM? Do they end up being perceived by teachers as wielding the same authority they previously had but disguising it with procedures of participatory decision making?

In this article, we analyze six high schools with SDM and the roles that principals played in decision-making processes. We compare developments in the three high schools whose principals sought to use SDM as a pathway to instructional and curricular reform and the three high schools whose principals viewed SDM as a democratizing measure without links to a reformist agenda. By the end of the study, the three principals who were highly committed to SDM and had an explicit reform agenda engendered high conflict among participants. Only modest changes were achieved in curriculum and instructional practice. The three schools whose principals supported SDM but had no explicit reform agenda did not experience the same level of conflict, nor did they make much change in practice. In all six schools, SDM was continuing as a mode of school governance, but not one of the schools was making significant progress toward major reform in curriculum or teaching.

By way of comparison, we report briefly on the six other high schools in our study, which had no SDM structures. In three of these high schools, principals attempted instructional reform through traditional means of governance. These principals also generated conflict within the school, and they managed modest change in instructional practice as well.

Our analysis suggests that principals and policymakers must understand the magnitude of the change that SDM involves for high school teachers and recognize that establishing democratic processes in schools is a significant reform in itself. The analysis also suggests that principals—and advocates of reform—might consider uncoupling issues of governance and of classroom curriculum and instruction. Contrary to Wohlstetter and Odden's (1992) recommendation that school-based management be joined with curriculum and instructional reform "as part of a coordinated effort to improve school productivity" (p. 541), our suggestion is to recognize the time that schools need to learn their way into SDM. Even though we are committed to improvement in student learning as the long-term goal of any school innovation, we nevertheless suggest that it is important to recognize teachers' concerns and doubts about SDM and the effort it takes for them to become comfortable and competent with it. Drawing on several published analyses of SDM as well as our own, we explore policy implications. Also, we discuss possible strategies for establishing effective participatory processes and for reform of curriculum and instruction.

The Empirical Study

The data for this study were derived from a longitudinal investigation of 12 public high schools in the United States, half of which have instituted a system of SDM and half of which are operating under traditional leadership. A main intent was to find out how and what kinds of decisions were made, on what topics, and with what consequences. The study ran for 5 years, from 1988 to 1993.

We chose six high schools in different parts of the country that had adopted SDM at least 2 years earlier. These schools were in Miami, Denver, Seattle, a Boston suburb, Salt Lake City, and rural Maine. At the time of our first visit, one school had been operating with SDM for 2.5 years, two schools for 3 years, one for 4 years, one for 5 years, and one (Merit High School[1]) for 13 years. For comparison, we selected six schools that were operating under traditional patterns of leadership and that approximated the demographic features of the SDM schools. They were located in San Antonio; Chicago[2]; Monroe, Louisiana; Boston; an Oklahoma City suburb; and rural Virginia. The socioeconomic status of students' families, as reported by school staff, was low to working class or low to middle class in nine schools, mainly middle class (although with sizable low- or working-class enrollments) in two schools, and middle to upper-middle class (again with notable working-class enrollment) in one school. Three schools served populations composed almost exclusively of students of color. Seven others had substantial minority populations (up to 81 percent), and two were predominantly White.

At each school, we conducted individual interviews with teachers, principals and assistant principals, and other staff members such as guidance counselors and librarians. We asked each person to talk about a schoolwide decision in which she or he had been involved (or, in default of involvement, knew a good deal about). The decision did not need to have been resolved. We asked them to identify, wherever possible, a decision concerned with curriculum or program, but only 35 percent did so. Interviews were structured, following a predetermined sequence, from the origin of the issue through the stages of its discussion and (when appropriate) its resolution and consequences. Questions called for open-ended responses, and probes pursued the details of each particular narrative. Auxiliary questions were asked about leadership in the school. Interviews ran from 35 minutes to 2 hours, averaging 45–50 minutes. The last set of interviews was conducted an average of 17 months after the initial interview. In these 12 schools, we completed 193 interviews. All were taped, transcribed, coded, and entered into a computer program for analysis. Analysis proceeded from the individual school, to the two sets of schools (SDM and non-SDM), to a cross-set comparison, to the total sample.

One of the goals of the study was to investigate claims that inclusion of teachers in school decision making would move schools toward reform of curriculum and instruction. Those results have been reported elsewhere (Cambone, Weiss, & Wyeth, 1992; Weiss, 1993a, 1993b; Weiss,

Cambone, & Wyeth, 1992; Wyeth, 1992). Briefly, we found that SDM enhances teachers' opportunities to influence decisions in the school but that a relatively small number of teachers become active in the process. SDM takes a great deal of their time and energy and, to some degree, diverts their attention from the classroom. The types of decisions reported in schools with and without SDM were only modestly different. SDM schools discussed somewhat more innovative decisions, but the new ideas were more likely to have come from principals than from teachers. Teachers tended to be reluctant to accept innovations and acted as a brake on reform. A main consequence of participatory decision making was to slow down changes that school administrators sought to introduce (Weiss, 1993a).

Note: The schools had different labels for their SDM bodies. For simplicity, we call the decision-making bodies on which teachers and administrators served "the team."

Principals' Attitudes Toward SDM

Although one possibility for principals confronted with diminution of their authority would be to oppose the change, no principal in our study did so. Nor did teachers in any of the schools claim that their principal was antagonistic. The principal at Merit High School was initially the least supportive. He was philosophically and psychologically uncomfortable with SDM. He had been a principal in a traditional school and was accustomed to exercising authority unchecked. He came into a school that had been operating under SDM for 13 years, and he found it onerous to have to take all matters to the team. On many matters, he was out of sympathy with other team members, and, in his first year at the school, votes of 5–1 against him were common. He angered other members of the team by violating the norm of expressing consensus in public; he told the rest of the school when he had opposed a decision and been overridden. Respondents reported that meetings of the team during his first year were characterized by "a lot of shouting."

By a year and a half later, much had changed. The principal had come to appreciate the strength of the system, although he still chafed a bit at restrictions on his authority. He said,

> I think I'm more effective now. . . . I know how to play the game. And
> I am also not stupid enough to think that this isn't a good system. And
> I will play the game and make it as good a system as I know how.

He had also managed to recruit two like-minded teachers to the six-person team so that he was not outvoted as often or as easily as he had been before. He was functioning in the collective decision-making structure with relatively good grace and more appreciation of its value.

The five other principals were initially more cooperative. They all indicated that they supported the SDM apparatus. The extent of their cooperation varied, with the principals at Marble, Copper, and Waters High Schools strongly supportive and the other two more passively acquiescent. The three strong supporters were generally viewed as the guiding force behind the SDM process. The Waters High School principal had been the initiator of the SDM idea for the school; the principal at Copper had taken the lead early; and the Marble principal had been appointed to the principalship at least in part because of her commitment to SDM in order to implement the plan.

The other two principals were going along. The Flanders High School principal was seen as fully supportive at the time of our first visit to the school, but his ardor diminished over the period of our study. During the same period, support from the district office and teachers' union, the original proponents of SDM, also flagged. As support for SDM declined, team meetings increasingly turned from issues of restructuring and instructional change to routine matters such as parking and test schedules. Before the end of our fieldwork, the principal left the school.

At Utley High School the principal supported SDM, but teachers believed that his support, although real, was superficial. His school was not allowed much autonomy by the district, and he seemed to be as concerned about the superintendent's approval as he was with teachers' wishes.

In every school, some disgruntled respondents believed that the principal was manipulating the system or evading it. And not without some reason. Even the most supportive principals acknowledged that there were some things they had to do on their own. A crisis called for an immediate decision, matters came up over the summer, or only they had the requisite knowledge. They granted that they sometimes had to delay or table a team decision because it would run afoul of state or district regulations or the union contract or would involve legal liability. One principal said, "Somebody always has to be the leader, has to take the role and be responsible for what's going on. It's how you do that. And sometimes it's done by manipulation." The principals were responsible for the school and accountable to the superintendent, and, in certain cases, they believed that their judgment had to prevail.

Thus, the six principals all indicated a willingness to work with the SDM machinery. Three pressed hard to get the system working; they prodded teachers into participating and encouraged them to continue when progress seemed slow. The other three saw advantages in having teachers involved in decisions, and they were content to cooperate so long as things did not get out of hand.

All of the principals voiced support for SDM at least part of the time and usually worked to sustain the process and move it along. This is not to gainsay that, from time to time, they worked around it. As one person said of the principal at Marble High:

> [She] is not above making a top-down decision. . . . When she gets frustrated with the process, and it's not working, finally she'll say, "OK, we'll do it this way." . . . But she has a high tolerance level. . . . She very rarely will push those panic buttons.

The principal at Waters summed up the positive, if occasionally ambivalent, feelings that the principals generally displayed:

> I think that this school will make a transition into, you know, that cooperative participatory mode without any problem at all. . . . We've come a long way. And I've come a long way. Because it was—it's very threatening when it—not threatening so much as it is, you know, stuff's going on out there. You're not really sure what it all is. And some of it can be pretty hairy. And some of it's really neat. And it's exciting.

In fact, these principals apparently have a greater commitment to the representation of teachers in decision making than do most of the teachers themselves. Teachers' allegiance to SDM seemed to cool over time. While many of them were positive about SDM when we first interviewed them, as time went by more and more of them articulated a sense that the principal should make decisions. They wanted to be consulted and wanted their voice to be heard and acknowledged, but many wanted the principal to decide "and let's get on with it." Over and over, teachers said that administrators know how to make decisions, they have the big picture, they are paid to make decisions, and they have the time to make decisions. They also said that principals are legally responsible for the school, so let them do their jobs. According to one department head:

> If you haven't got a captain to steer the boat, the boat is going to go on the rocks. . . . Somebody has got to make the decision, whether it is right or wrong for the building. . . . It is the principal . . . the principal has got to give direction and has to make the final decision on everything.

Especially as the time demands of SDM piled up on teachers and diverted them from their responsibilities in the classroom, teachers became exhausted by—and resentful of—the added burdens of participation. Furthermore, the fruits of their participation were not very visible. Many of them did not feel as though they had been very influential or effective. They believed that an elephantine amount of talk sometimes brought forth a small "mouse" of results. Sometimes they suspected that they were being manipulated by administrators. At one point or another, large numbers of teachers yearned for the days when a responsive principal listened to their ideas and then made the decisions him- or herself.

A Sidebar on Gender

The principals who were most supportive of SDM were the three women principals. Of course, the sample is much too small to support generalizations, but these data support other studies on women in school administration (Bossert, Dwyer, Rowan, & Lee, 1982; Fauth, 1984; Gilbertson, 1981; Gross & Trask, 1976; Lee, Smith, & Cioci, 1993; Marshall & Mitchell, 1989; Shakeshaft, 1989; M. S. Smith & Andrews, 1989). Earlier studies have shown that women principals generally adopt a more participatory style of leadership, and they have been found to spend more time with teachers and visiting classrooms than do male principals (Fauth, 1984; Pitner, 1981; Shakeshaft, 1987).

The three women principals in our study worked hard to stimulate participation, to encourage new ideas, and to make clear to teachers that any disagreement with administrators was fine and would not be met with retribution. They put up with delays; they tried hard to find resources to free participants for team activities; and they sought funding to implement the team's decisions. While two of the men also made cooperative moves, the impulse for sustaining SDM came more from teachers than from them. The women were seen by their staffs as most committed to SDM processes.

All three of the women were the initial implementers of SDM in the school. Only one of the men was the first to put SDM into effect; the other two men came in after the system was well established. Thus, in large part the women's enthusiasm for SDM reflects a process of selection. Those who liked the idea of working cooperatively with teachers either helped to develop SDM or chose to apply for the principal's job in the early stages of restructuring. They selected themselves into a system with which they were in sympathy, and district officials chose *them* in part because they had sympathy for the new plan.

Moreover, early involvement was a two-way process. The very fact of being involved early seems to engage principals' interest and allegiance. Early on, when plans are fluid and the structure inchoate, principals and teachers work out understandings and mutual accommodations that appear to lead to heightened principal support. In two schools, SDM came to be seen as the "principal's baby," and her reputation and respect were tied up with making the system work.

The women principals did not talk about SDM in terms of personal relationships or connections with others. Rather, they talked about SDM in abstract and intellectual terms. Their discussions were sprinkled with phrases about "democracy," "teacher professionalism," and "appropriate governance." When teachers talked admiringly about them, as many did, they referred to their managerial skills, their leadership qualities, and their vision of education.

Although there was little talk about feminine caring and connectedness, SDM has characteristics that are linked to what many see as women's ways of thinking, knowing, and doing. When the women principals spoke forcefully of their advocacy of SDM, and when their actions supported their words on many harried occasions, they were evidencing commitment to a system of nonhierarchical relationships. SDM tends to level the playing field between administrators and teachers and to allow each person to contribute. The substratum of SDM is permeated with notions of equality of participation. Its ideal image is of a group of people coming together in mutual respect to reach consensus on what is best for students.

In order to make SDM work to bring about reform, principals must forge bonds with fellow members of the team. They have to bolster the position of those who are already on their side and listen carefully to opponents, not to refute them but to incorporate their objections and ideas into a revised proposal that has a better chance of success. Much of this kind of small-group, relationship-oriented, politically sensitive work is congruent with the "feminine" side of management. Our data, although based on a very small sample, reinforce other studies that show that women administrators are committed to—and adept at—this kind of leadership.

Relationship Between Support for SDM and Support for School Reform

SDM is a reform that is often embraced not so much for its own sake (i.e. to give teachers more power) as to bring about improved teaching and learning in the school. The expectation of its advocates is that teachers' participation in school decisions will focus attention on instruction and curriculum and thus lead to important changes in the classroom (Barth, 1990; Darling-Hammond, 1987; Futrell, 1988; Liontos, 1993; Little, 1988; Rallis & Highsmith, 1987). Our study suggests that efforts to link SDM to curricular and instructional reform may overburden SDM, at least in its early stages.

We recognize that this suggestion differs from the recommendations of other scholars who want to see school-based management and SDM linked to student performance and who urge that schools be held accountable for making plans and meeting goals (Hill & Bonan, 1991; Wohlstetter & Odden, 1992). Nevertheless, on the basis of our data, we are impressed with the slowness of the process by which teachers come to trust the authenticity of power sharing through SDM and gain confidence in their own ability to provide direction and implement plans.

The principals of Marble, Copper, and Waters High Schools, who were the most committed to SDM, were also the principals who had serious agendas for school reform. Their schools had experienced and capable staffs who cared about kids, and, while the schools were all in urban settings and had sizable minority populations, not one of them were dogged with the sense of hopelessness that afflicts some large-city schools. They all recruited hard-working teachers to serve on the team without additional compensation, and they all collaborated with the team to try to bring about changes in curriculum, schedule, and organization of the school day. Interdisciplinary teaching was one change they all wanted to introduce, and one or another of them was interested in developing schools-within-the-school, block scheduling, cooperative learning, special programs for at-risk students, and similar items on the current reform agenda. Their primary aim was to make the school more responsive to the needs of students.

The other three principals did not have an explicit agenda of their own. Two of them also served in big-city schools with sizable minority enrollments, and one was employed in a rural school. These principals were apparently content with incremental changes, whether initiated by other administrators and teachers or by themselves.

The three principals with reform agendas looked upon SDM as a way station to reformation of the school. They wanted teacher participation in order to engage teachers in a major overhaul of traditional forms of instruction. They believed that only if teachers have a voice in restructuring the school will they "buy in" and implement the radical ideas being promoted by the principals. SDM was part of the package of reform that they were fostering.

So far, this seems like a hopeful picture, much in line with the prescriptions of academic writers and commissions. But the consequences of support for SDM and support for serious reform were not uniformly happy. One of the effects was a heightened degree of conflict in the school.

Visible Tensions

SDM schools in which principals were pushing for serious reform experienced the most conflict of any schools in the study (Weiss et al., 1992; see also Peterson & Warren, 1994). In schools in which principals were not strong proponents of SDM, no strong agenda for reform was on the table. Principals and teachers involved in governance were content to deal with incremental changes on relatively modest matters. Although there were differences of opinion, relative calm reigned on the team and in the · school.[3]

Copper High School, an SDM school, went through spasms of resentment and uproar. The principal was intent on supporting innovative programs to meet the needs of students who were not prospering in the regular program. In one of her first moves, she empowered a few young, untenured teachers to develop a special program for at-risk youth; she also secured an outside grant to pay for the program, allowed a relaxation in school rules for participating students, and reduced teaching schedules for the teachers. These and similar acts alienated members of the informal "power structure" of the school—department heads, union representatives, and others—who objected to what they saw as favoritism to a select few (Weiss, 1993b). After a major blowup, she agreed to a reconfiguration of the team, with greater representation of department heads. Then, when the new body started on a course for which she had little sympathy, people alleged that she let the team lapse. After a time, another new team was formed. This body, supported by many of the teachers and informal leaders in the school, delayed many of the reforms she was trying to introduce. At one point, she became so frustrated that, in violation of her own principles of shared governance, she unilaterally decided to institute block scheduling. She gave the team the opportunity to choose which kind of block schedule should be adopted. They studied alternative schedules and winnowed alternatives down to three. The entire teaching staff voted on which of the three to introduce. A big change was made, but at the expense of considerable divisiveness. Other changes she strove to implement (e.g., schools-within-the-school) were either not implemented or were confined to one or two classrooms, and she left the school for another position.

In Marble and Waters High Schools, which also had crusading principals, conflict was not so pronounced. Nevertheless, the principals' proposals to change teachers' accustomed ways of work generated opposition among significant portions of the faculty. Each of these schools went through episodes of serious friction. In defense of SDM, the Marble High principal said that SDM merely brought into the open conflict that had been latent:

> I believe that there's always dissension out there. It's underneath and people just keep it quiet or complain about it in the faculty meetings. You can't do anything about it until you know what it is, so we should provide some possibility that dissension can be resolved. Sometimes that's very hard.

Thus, the paradox is that schools in which the principals were most committed to SDM were also the schools with the most conflict. The reason is that these principals envisioned SDM as one part of a larger reform package. They believed not only that SDM was good and right in itself but that it was a useful strategy for reforming other aspects of the school. When their other proposals for reform came on line, the implications for disturbing teachers' usual working arrangements became apparent. Many teachers responded with antagonism.[4]

On the other hand, it is possible that these principals' zeal for substantive reform was necessary for sustaining their commitment to SDM during its many squalls. Without expectations for improving teaching and learning, they might not have been willing to devote so much energy to nurturing the SDM process.

The Consequences of SDM for Reform

Of course, conflict need not be all bad. Despite most teachers' preference for serene civility with their colleagues, the eruption of dispute can be a sign that people are confronting serious issues and beginning to "unfreeze" obsolete ways of work. As scholars of organizations have noted, organizations can probably not undertake important change without a heightened level of conflict (e.g., Pfeffer, 1981; Pfeffer & Salancik, 1983). If conflict leads to real improvements in the school, it serves a useful function.

In schools in which principals gave full support to SDM and had their own vision of reform, some change did occur, although not as much as the principals had hoped or planned to achieve. The opposition of many teachers on the team and elsewhere in the school delayed some of the changes, modified others, and prevented still more from coming into effect. Nevertheless, more change occurred than under less supportive principals. After 3 or 4 years, the SDM schools were at somewhat different places than they previously had been. A few interdisciplinary courses were being offered or planned at all three of the schools. A new program went into effect in one school, block scheduling arrived in another, and a special 2-week all-school curriculum was mounted in a third.

Schools in which the principal's relationship with the team was less cooperative also underwent changes, but the changes tended to be more tangential. One of these schools started with an initial spurt of activity, developing a system for peer evaluation of teachers and a collective process of budgeting in the first 2 years. Participants had high expectations for continuing the progress. However, over the next 2 years, the bloom faded. The extraordinary time demands not only of SDM but of some of the changes they had introduced became overwhelming. Furthermore, not all of the changes worked out as well as expected, and some of the early confidence drained away. As the district and the teachers' union lost interest in SDM, the principal's support wavered, and the team reduced its aspirations to second- and third-order matters.

Reform Without SDM

Schools with committed principals managed to implement somewhat more changes and more innovative changes in curriculum and schedule than schools with more status quo principals. What about reformist principals in schools without SDM? Did they have more or less success than the reformers in SDM schools?

Of the six traditional high schools we studied, two had principals intent on major changes, and a third principal undertook one significant change (viz., ending "basic" courses for low-achieving students). These three principals pushed their reforms through. Without the need to win support from teacher representatives on a team, they moved ahead unilaterally. The last category of schools—traditional schools whose principals did not seek change—stayed much as they were.

In a few cases, traditional schools made more extensive changes than did SDM schools. The principal of one traditional school, Vanguard High, wanted to introduce an interdisciplinary curriculum. She had the superintendent's backing, and she found four teachers who were willing to begin interdisciplinary teaching. She decreed the new curriculum, starting with ninth grade and adding another grade each year. While the SDM schools were still arguing and debating over the same kind of reform, the changed curriculum went into effect. In another non-SDM school, the principal mandated portfolio assessment throughout the school; the change was made, accompanied by agonized complaints from teachers. A third school, at the administrators' initiative, gradually eliminated its basic courses for "slow learners," even though many teachers chafed at accommodating these students in heterogeneous classrooms.

In all of these cases, many of the teachers, probably a majority, were opposed to the change. Rumors flew around the school about what was happening, and many teachers were suspicious and anxious about what the change would mean for them. When the changes became more visible (e.g., ninth-grade interdisciplinary courses), some teachers voiced strong discontent. In one school, teachers filed grievances with the union about the requirement for portfolios. Morale deteriorated. Whereas the SDM schools experienced conflict during the course of discussion, teachers in the non-SDM schools were hit with a change first and became angry or bitter afterward. The comments of teachers in the non-SDM schools suggest that the changes will be hard to sustain. Many teachers continue to oppose them.

SDM, on the other hand, although often slowing down change, had the advantage of defusing opposition. By the time the change was implemented, even though it might have been modified and watered down, teachers in SDM schools tended to accept it. They had made it their own. While this is not the stuff of fanfares and fireworks, it is not an inconsequential achievement. As Elmore and McLaughlin (1988, p. 44) have written: "Experience has shown that unless teachers are committed to a reform effort, desultory compliance or complete disregard is the likely result." Teacher acceptance is a big step forward.

Reformist Principals' Dilemmas

When principals wanted to sustain both SDM and a program of school reform, they often became frustrated. The energy they put into encouraging teacher participation and engaging teachers in decisions on serious issues too often resulted in glacial movement—or no movement at all—on school reform.

Several of the principals worked hard at making SDM work. They tried to be facilitators. They encouraged people to participate and gave them real decision-making power. They continually reached out to people and engaged them in activities and then turned over the reins once the process had a life of its own. They provided the vehicles for SDM to work (in the words of one person, "providing days away, providing lunches, providing resources, consultants when needed"). Still, often nothing much happened.

Many teachers refrained from participating, others sat passively through meetings, and few volunteered to serve on action subcommittees. When they did speak out, it was often to oppose change. The tendency of the team was to listen to objections to proposals, propose further study, and delay action. Our respondents said that teachers were "conservative" and that the climate was one of "inertia."

It is easy but probably wrong to blame the teachers for their opposition to reform efforts. Their position can be viewed as holding their ground against the untested ideas of academic reformers as transmitted through the principal. Experience with the school reforms of the last 40 years suggests that caution may well be in order. Teachers have seen too many fads come and go to be willing to embrace the latest nostrums with enthusiasm. As they told us, principals stay in schools for a relatively short time; teachers have to stay around and pick up the pieces.

The Flanders principal unobtrusively reclaimed some of the authority that had been delegated to the team. Without any single episode or turning point, it became obvious over the months that team meetings dealt with more and more routine matters. Other SDM principals handed down occasional decisions by fiat. They were unhappy with their retreat from democratic procedures but unable to tolerate interminable delay. Principals felt driven to show *something* for all the effort that they and participating teachers were expending on the process. They had to prove to themselves as well as to others that SDM was worth the candle. When their patience was exhausted, they made unilateral decisions in order to get things moving.

The tension between principals' belief in SDM and the occasional decision to override it left some of them acutely uncomfortable. Yet they could see no way out of the impasse. They were aware of the cynicism of many of the teachers and felt smothered by spoken and unspoken complaints (e.g., "See, all this time and effort is going into SDM, and nothing ever comes out of it"). They felt forced to counter this endemic perception by demonstrating real change. If the team was not going to move, they would have to do it on their own.

Trice and Beyer (1991) wrote about the difference between innovation leaders and maintenance leaders. Innovation leaders sell others on their ideas. Maintenance leaders are more apt to sit back and facilitate the plans of others. Innovation leadership "usually arises in situations of perceived crisis while maintenance leadership tends to occur when people see no crisis or a manageable one" (p. 165). These principals wanted to be innovation leaders, but SDM required that they be facilitators of a participatory process. The combination was frustrating. When teachers would not be "facilitated" into change, they faced the necessity of giving up one value or the other.

The three activist principals wanted democracy, but they also wanted the school to better meet the needs of students. Often the need for change seemed more compelling. SDM was not an end in itself but a means to achieve longed-for improvements in teaching and learning. One gets the suspicion, although none of the principals articulated it, that over time there was a tug of war between support for SDM and support for change in curriculum and instruction. To a degree, the two "reforms" were vying for primacy. Given the always-limited time and energy of school people, both administrators and teachers, it began to seem as though a zero-sum game was in progress; time and energy spent on making SDM work were taken away from instructional reform. In our schools, we saw a number of principals who expended much of their political capital in pushing through and maintaining SDM. They had to prod and push to get teachers to participate, to get committees to take responsibility for action, and to keep moving the team along to resolution of issues. In a sense, they "used up" their credits on trying to make SDM work when their real goals were bringing about changes in teaching and learning. Yet, interestingly, none of them expressed a wish to abandon SDM or redirect it strictly toward curriculum development.

Summary

The three principals who were most committed to SDM all saw SDM as one part of a larger package of reform. They intended to use SDM to help them institute major changes in the curriculum and structure of the school. Because of their commitment to many of the items on the current reform agenda, these principals ran into a good deal of flak from teachers. Considerable conflict plagued their attempts to change courses, programs, and the organization of the school day. While an active group of teachers supported their plans and, in some cases, actually provided the ideas and the initial push, most teachers tended to be conservative, wanting to maintain things much as they had been, with minor changes to take care of problems (Cambone et al., 1992; Weiss et al., 1992). A line of cleavage running through all of the schools was the division between those people who thought the school was fine as it was and those who saw problems that required basic change. Among teachers and administrators who thought the school was doing well, SDM was an opportunity to remedy annoyances and distractions and smooth daily operations, not rock the boat. Relatively few teachers saw a need for basic change, and the ambitious plans of the three campaigning principals were blunted by the pervasive complacency.

But when the crusading principals persevered, and when they had the support of a coterie of committed and hardworking teachers, they sometimes managed to wring change out of the system. It was a slow process fraught with uncertainties, and many plans went down the tubes of the SDM machinery. Still, these schools accomplished somewhat more change than schools whose principals were content to go along with the minor modifications that they and teachers were likely to initiate. The relatively greater movement in schools whose principals were committed to SDM was due less to SDM, or their support for it, than to their unremitting efforts to establish a vision for the school and to stimulate teacher innovation in line with that vision. They were only occasionally successful, but even the occasional successes distinguished them from other schools.

Reformist principals in schools without SDM were able to implement changes more rapidly because they did not need to negotiate with teachers. Reforms did not go through the heated debates that attended efforts at reform in SDM schools, nor were they diluted or slowed down to meet teacher objections. However, their long-term staying power is questionable. Principal-mandated reforms evoked suspicion and unease in the early stages, as teachers heard rumors about what was going on, and often led to grumbling and bitterness during implementation. In the case of sizable principal-ordered changes, such as the introduction of portfolios or change in the number of periods in the school day, teacher resentment was serious enough to suggest that changes would not survive long.

Policy Implications

SDM is frequently looked upon as a vehicle for change. In all of the SDM high schools included in this study, the idea of change and improvement was an explicit rationale for the system. These six schools demonstrate that SDM does not lead to change by itself. It can become merely a system for venting grievances, dealing with minor annoyances, or even transferring to the team unpleasant responsibilities that administrators are reluctant to shoulder alone, such as deciding where the budget should be cut. Bringing about change, particularly on central issues of instruction, curriculum, and school organization, requires effective change-oriented leadership. Those schools that had principals with strong commitment both to SDM and to school reform managed to institute some changes.

The rhetoric of SDM suggests that teachers should take leadership; however, in almost all of the schools studied here, principals were the leaders of reform. In only one school was leadership exercised by teachers through the team. This was Merit High School, with its long history of teacher participation. There teacher leadership was being contested by a new principal who believed that the principal should have major authority. Over the course of 2 years, he came a considerable way toward acceptance of SDM and the authority of the team, at the same time that he was reshaping the team to be a closer reflection of his own preferences.

In all of the other schools, principals were the leaders of schoolwide change. They had the resources to make plans and gain attention for them that teachers lacked: time, contacts within and outside the school, a podium from which to speak, easy access to information, and the historical tradition that assigned authority to their office. Even when a few committed teachers had important ideas and worked hard to implement them, they made headway only to the extent that the principal adopted their ideas and gave them momentum.[5]

SDM provides advantages as well as headaches for a reform-minded principal. First, it gives the staff a chance to shape the proposed innovation to fit the practices and culture of the school. Little as the principal may appreciate what seems like a "watering down" of the innovation, it does improve the match between the innovation and the school environment in which it is to be implemented. Second, it gives teachers a sense of ownership of the innovation. After they have argued, amended, and adopted the plan, they tend to "buy in" to it. It has become their own. Third, with the sense of ownership comes a greater commitment to implementation. Teachers are more likely to carry out the innovation with resolve.

A main implication for future action concerns the mix of SDM and school reform. Problems arose when the two were conflated. SDM had been introduced under the banner of instructional improvement, and the lack of instructional improvement disappointed not only the reformist principals but their staff supporters in the school. Even in the three SDM schools whose principals were not promoting a particular reform agenda, a number of the teachers most active in SDM were discouraged that their efforts were not giving rise to important instructional changes.

SDM produces benefits that have little or nothing to do with instructional reform. As one principal told us, it is just plain right. It is a form of democracy, and it allows people who will be affected by decisions the opportunity to participate in making those decisions. As one principal said, "I think that until all schools take a tack toward participation and democracy, and until that's done, American education is going to stay in the paralyzed place that it is."

Perhaps SDM and school reform need not be explicitly linked, at least in early years. In the high schools we studied, emphasis on first changing the structure may have diverted principals' and teachers' attention from instruction and sapped their energies. Maintaining the machinery of SDM became so demanding in some cases that, like Charlie Chaplain in *Modern Times,* they had to race around feeding this machinery rather than devoting attention to instruction. And SDM made demands on teachers that were outside their usual sphere of competence. Teachers are rarely strong on matters of structure, administrative issues, rules and regulations, or even group process. They went into teaching because of an interest in youngsters and their own subject. Most do not feel capable of or choose to focus their efforts on making decisions on schoolwide issues. The curriculum-oriented SDM processes that Hannaway (1993) studied are more congenial to most teachers and more likely to be rewarding to them than are what they view as administration-oriented decision making.

The resistance of teachers to SDM may also reflect doubt about its reality. SDM promises that power will be shared among faculty and administrators. Teachers were inevitably skeptical about the promise. After many years of working in hierarchically organized schools in which the principal was the "boss" (and most teachers had been around for more than 15 years), they needed considerable convincing to believe that their word in fact carried weight. Principals committed to SDM tried to build their trust. They encouraged creative ideas from teachers and allowed teachers many opportunities to take charge. But when ideas were in short supply or provoked controversy or when teachers were chary of straying far from conventional patterns of schooling, the reform-minded principals became impatient. They came to see teachers as laggards and turned to their own blueprints about what school reform should look like. They believed that they needed to give the school some direction for change; they needed to show movement from the expenditure of time and effort in SDM.

Their impatience, understandable as it was, and their fallback on their own vision of school reform tended to disrupt the slow cumulation of teachers' trust in SDM. Teachers began to think: Whose change is it that we are talking about here? Is it our change or their change? Whatever the new lingo and the schedule of committees and meetings, is this the same old story, where we are expected to ratify what the principal wants to do?

Even the best-intentioned principals seemed ready to abandon SDM principles occasionally, at least for a time, when the system did not lead to what they saw as progress. Unwittingly, they thus undermined the long, slow, uncertain process of teacher reflection that might have led, painstakingly and perhaps painfully, to plans that fitted *teachers'* diagnoses of needed change.

Principals' time horizons were short. It takes time for teachers to develop trust in a new mode of decision making and to see school change as attractive and possible. Teachers, with their focus on the classroom, can in time begin to formulate ideas about how to improve classroom teaching and learning and figure out what kinds of support and organizational change are needed to sustain such change. But first they have to believe that their ideas are really valued and that the suggestions they make will be implemented. This may take a long period of patient nurturance without expectations for schoolwide instructional reform.

Just as time horizons were short, expectations for change were large. Furthermore, change was expected at the level of the school—something large and visible—rather than at the classroom level. Many teachers felt inadequate to share in schoolwide decisions because they believed the principal had "the big picture." What may be needed is not so much the big picture as a whole school-full of "little pictures" grounded in classrooms. These "little pictures" can form the basis of teacher plans and activities that benefit each teacher and student.

As Pauly (1991) has written, education takes place only in classrooms, and what happens among teachers and students in the classroom determines whether policies succeed, fail, or are totally refashioned. Pauly makes a strong case against across-the-board prescriptions and for policies that support the particular needs of particular classrooms. If teachers analyze their daily concerns and figure out what they need in order to improve teaching and learning, they can collectively build individualized plans and a supportive organizational structure that sustains learning in each classroom. Over time their small improvements can be expanded to encompass a larger vision of school reform.

Those are our hopes, but we realize that they may sound quixotic in today's urban high schools with their climate of skepticism and inertia. In only a few scattered high schools do we hear of teacher communities that assume this kind of leadership. Sustained teacher planning and decision making over long periods of time in ordinary schools everywhere will require a system of supports well beyond any available in the schools we studied. It will require that teachers be paid for the time they devote to the effort, which is rarely the case now. It will require that they be able to plan their ongoing staff development so as to link it directly to the issues with which they are coping, something that is not done in these schools at all. It will require assurance that principals, district officials, and superintendents will continue to support SDM over the long haul, even when budget pressures are severe. Teachers in these schools currently see repeated indications that support for SDM is fragile and, in some cases, fading.

Murnane (1993) reviewed Honda's successful experience with worker decision making at its U.S. automobile plant and derived just these kinds of lessons for American education. Honda of America pays workers for daily meetings to discuss and solve problems and provides resources to follow through on solutions. It invests in practical training to facilitate workers' changes in the way work is done. And management commits itself to long-term support of worker initiatives. Murnane views these policies as directly relevant to U.S. education.

Honda of America believes that improvement in quality will come not from grand changes but from continuous implementation of a great many ideas from workers. If schools adopted Honda's policies of paid time for decision making, resources for implementation, focus on the content of the job, self-directed training, and long-term administrative support, teachers might be able to build up from changes in the classroom to broader visions of school reform.

Still, a brake on the potential of SDM in these schools is the age of the teaching force. Many teachers were more interested in planning for retirement than in planning for educational improvement. It may take an influx of new and enthusiastic teachers to reinvigorate some of these schools. When schools have a renewed sense of excitement and potential, resources available to pay for time and installation of changes, training connected to decisional tasks, and sustained administrative support, teachers could yet lead the way to significant educational reform. Then the task for principals will be to stimulate teachers to develop their own classrooms and then build the supports—financial, structural, informational, and developmental—that allow those visions to take shape.

NOTES

This article is a revision of a paper presented at the annual meeting of the American Educational Research Association, Atlanta, Georgia, April 1993. The research was supported by the U.S. Office of Educational Research and Improvement through a grant to the National Center for Educational Leadership at Harvard University. The article was revised while the senior author was a fellow at the Center for Advanced Study in the Behavioral Sciences, and she thanks the center and the Spencer Foundation for their support. We thank Alexander Wyeth for research assistance.

1. All names of high schools are pseudonyms.

2. The Chicago school was chosen because, on the basis of reports on Chicago school reform, it was expected to be an SDM school. However, after we completed the first round of interviewing, we realized that, in operation, it did not fit the category, and we classified it as a non-SDM school. It remained a principal-run school throughout the fieldwork.

3. Certain conflicts erupted in two schools during our study that were due to district actions. We have excluded these events from our analysis.

4. A subsidiary explanation for the association of SDM with conflict is that many teachers were unprepared to cope well with the demands of participation. Long habituated to hierarchy and deference to superiors, they had neither the incentive nor the skills to participate appropriately in decision making (Cambone, Weiss, & Wyeth, 1992). As they attempted to participate, they had to make preliminary psychological shifts to accommodate to new roles and behavior. Such intrapersonal discomfort may have helped engender interpersonal friction.

5. Discussion of teachers' reluctance to embrace change at the school level is not to suggest that they were similarly opposed to change in their classrooms. Our study focused on decisions that required schoolwide action rather than classroom innovation.

REFERENCES

Barth, R. (1990). *Improving schools from within.* San Francisco: Jossey-Bass.

Bossert, S. T., Dwyer, D. C., Rowan, B., & Lee, G. V. (1982). The instructional management role of the principal. *Educational Administration Quarterly, 18*(3), 34–64.

Cambone, J., Weiss, C. H., & Wyeth, A. (1992). *We're not programmed for this* (Occasional Paper 17). Cambridge, MA: National Center for Educational Leadership, Harvard Graduate School of Education.

Cohen, M. (1987). Improving school effectiveness: Lessons from research. In V. Richardson-Koehler (Ed.), *Educators handbook: A research perspective.* New York: Longman.

Darling-Hammond, L. (1987). Schools for tomorrow's teachers. *Teachers College Record, 88,* 354–358.

Elmore, R. F., & McLaughlin, M. W. (1988). *Steady work: Policy, practice, and the reform of American education.* Santa Monica, CA: RAND.

Fauth, G. C. (1984). Women in educational administration: A research profile. *Educational Forum, 49,* 65–79.

Futrell, M. H. (1988). Teachers in reform: The opportunity for schools. *Educational Administration Quarterly, 24*, 374–380.

Gilbertson, M. (1981). The influence of gender on the verbal interactions among principals and staff members: An exploratory study. In P. A. Schmuck, W. W. Charters, Jr., & R. O. Carlson (Eds.), *Educational policy and management: Sex differentials* (pp. 297–306). New York: Academic Press.

Gross, N., & Trask, A. (1976). *The sex factor and the management of schools.* New York: Wiley.

Hannaway, J. (1993). Decentralization in two school districts: Challenging the standard paradigm. In J. Hannaway & M. Carnoy (Eds.), *Decentralization and school improvement: Can we fulfill the promise?* (pp. 135–162). San Francisco: Jossey-Bass.

Hill, P. T., & Bonan, J. (1991). *Decentralization and accountability in public education.* Santa Monica, CA: RAND.

Johnson, S. M. (1990). Redesigning teachers' work. In R. E. Elmore & Associates (Eds.), *Restructuring schools: The next generation of educational reform* (pp. 125–151). San Francisco: Jossey-Bass.

Lee, V. E., Smith, J. B., & Cioci, M. (1993). Teachers and principals: Gender-related perceptions of leadership and power in secondary schools. *Educational Evaluation and Policy Analysis, 15*, 153–180.

Levine, D. U., & Eubanks, E. E. (1992). Site-based management: Engine for reform or pipedream? Problems, prospects, pitfalls, and prerequisites for success. In J. J. Lane & E. G. Epps (Eds.), *Restructuring the schools: Problems and prospects* (pp. 61–82). Berkeley, CA: McCutchan.

Levine, D. U., & Lezotte, L. W. (1990). *Unusually effective schools: A review and analysis of research and practice.* Madison, WI: National Center for Effective Schools Research and Practice.

Liontos, L. B. (1993). Shared decision-making. *OSSC Bulletin, 37*(2), 1–42.

Little, J. W. (1988). Assessing the prospects for teacher leadership. In A. Lieberman (Ed.), *Building a professional culture in schools.* New York: Teachers College Press.

Marshall, C., & Mitchell, B. (1989, April). *Women's careers as a critique of the administrative culture.* Paper presented at the annual meeting of the American Educational Research Association, San Francisco, CA.

Murnane, R. J. (1993, May). *Improving American education: Lessons from Honda of America.* Paper presented at Harvard University, Cambridge, MA.

Pauly, E. (1991). *The classroom crucible: What really works, what doesn't, and why.* New York: Basic Books.

Peterson, K. D., & Warren, V. W. (1994). Changes in school governance and principals' roles: Changing jurisdictions, new power dynamics, and conflict in restructured schools. In J. Murphy & K. S. Louis (Eds.), *Reshaping the principalship: Insights from transformational change efforts* (pp. 219–236). Newbury Park, CA: Sage.

Pfeffer, J. (1981). *Power in organizations.* Boston: Pitman.

Pfeffer, J., & Salancik, G. R. (1983). Organization design: The case for a coalitional model of organizations. In J. R. Hackman, E. E. Lawler, & L. W. Porter (Eds.), *Perspectives on behavior in organizations* (pp. 102–111). New York: McGraw-Hill.

Pitner, N. J. (1981). Hormones and harems: Are the activities of superintending different for a woman? In P. A. Schmuck, W. W. Charters, Jr., & R. O. Carlson (Eds.), *Educational policy and management: Sex differentials* (pp. 273–296). New York: Academic Press.

Rallis, S., & Highsmith, M. (1987). The myth of the "great principal," *American Educator, 11*(1), 18–22.

Shakeshaft, C. (1987). *Women in educational administration.* Newbury Park, CA: Sage.

Shanker, A. (1994, March 13). Where we stand: The Chicago reform. *New York Times,* p. E7.

Smith, W. F., & Andrews, R. L. (1989). *Instructional leadership: How principals make a difference.* Alexandria, VA: Association for Supervision and Curriculum Development.

Trice, H. M., & Beyer, J. M. (1991). Cultural leadership in organizations. *Organization Science, 2,* 149–169.

Weiss, C. H. (1993a). *Interests and ideologies in educational reform: Changing the venue of decision making in the high school* (Occasional Paper 19). Cambridge, MA: National Center for Educational Leadership, Harvard Graduate School of Education.

Weiss, C. H. (1993b). Shared decision making about what? A comparison of schools with and without teacher participation. *Teachers College Record, 95,* 69–92.

Weiss, C. H., Cambone, J., & Wyeth, A. (1992). Trouble in paradise: Teacher conflicts in shared decision making. *Educational Administration Quarterly, 28,* 350–367.

Wohlstetter, P., & Odden, A. (1992). Rethinking school-based management policy and research. *Educational Administration Quarterly, 28,* 529–549.

Wyeth, A. (1992). *The department head and high school leadership.* Unpublished doctoral dissertation, Harvard Graduate School of Education, Cambridge, MA.

24

ASSESSING THE PROSPECTS FOR TEACHER LEADERSHIP

Judith Warren Little

THIS CHAPTER BEGINS with a simple proposition: it is increasingly implausible that we could improve the performance of schools, attract and retain talented teachers, or make sensible demands upon administrators without promoting leadership in teaching by teachers.

Teacher Leadership and the Professionalization of Teaching

Debate over the prospects for teacher leadership threads its way through larger discussions of the professionalization of teaching (see, e.g., Soltis, 1987). Three sets of professionalization problems form the context for questions of teacher leadership (see Figure 24.1). They are:

Conditions of membership in the occupation

The structure of the teaching career

Conditions of productivity in schools

This chapter is based on research conducted at the Center for Action Research, Boulder, Colorado, under Contract NIE-G-82-0020, and at the Far West Laboratory for Educational Research and Development under Contract 400-83-003, both with the National Institute of Education, U.S. Department of Education. The views expressed herein are not necessarily the views of that agency.

Figure 24.1. Targets of Change in the Professionalization of Teaching Arenas for Teacher Leadership

Conditions of Membership in the Occupation

- Recruitment
- Preservice admission and exit standards
- Licensure/certification
- Testing and assessment tied to a knowledge base in teaching
- Teacher evaluation

Structure of the Teaching Career

- Structure of opportunity for advancement/promotion
- Structure of opportunity for expanded responsibility or job enlargement
- Access to meaningful (professional) reference groups in and out of school

Conditions of Productivity in Schools

- Structure of leadership and decision making that includes well-qualified teachers
- Administrators' roles in the support of teachers and teaching
- Collective responsibility for student achievement
- Reward structure that promotes teacher-to-teacher collaboration and accountability

Membership in the Occupation

Teachers have been invited—or pressed—to take a larger role in regulating membership in the teaching occupation. Teachers are increasingly involved in planning and conducting preservice teacher education. In some states, teachers now participate (or soon will) on assessment teams that make decisions governing teacher licensure. Teachers and administrators in some districts have reached agreements governing teachers' participation in teacher evaluation. All of these changes are in accord with the recent proposition that, "it is only by regulating [those who become] *teachers* that we will be able to deregulate *teaching*" (Darling-Hammond, 1987, 356; emphasis in original).[1]

Restructuring the Teaching Career

Efforts to diminish the "careerlessness" of teaching (Sykes, 1983) have spawned a wide array of career-ladder plans and special roles or assignments for experienced teachers. Such plans typically present options for teacher leadership as possible steps in an individual career. Over time, according to most plans, some teachers will advance to senior positions on the basis of their demonstrated knowledge, skill, energy, and commitment. Their new positions will be recognized by distinctive titles, access to discretionary resources, and expanded responsibility and authority. The number of such positions will be limited, and teachers will necessarily compete for them.

The development of career-ladder and other incentive plans has been prompted by fears that attractive (and accessible) career options will lure both prospective and practicing teachers away from teaching and by hopes that the promise of career advancement will slow the attrition.

Career ladders and other competition-based incentive systems for teachers were announced with considerable fanfare following the flurry of reform reports in 1983,[2] but they have subsequently drawn criticism. It is probably a myth, Susan Rosenholtz (1985b) argues, that "competition between teachers for career advancement and higher pay is a sound way to improve the quality of their teaching" (p. 351) or that "career ladders and incentive pay will attract more academically talented people into the teaching profession" (p. 353). Further, critics have questioned the incentive value of plans that provide attractive options for only a small proportion of the teaching force, and then often after long tenure in the classroom.

Certainly it is hard to detect a groundswell of support from teachers for most of the career-ladder proposals; policy makers, educational reformers, and researchers have been the most vocal advocates.

The element of competition contained in career-ladder plans may be only one of several reasons for their lukewarm reception from teachers. The "promotion and advancement" vision of career reflected in such plans does not necessarily match teachers' conceptions of career. Studies of art and science teachers in British secondary schools conclude that professional identity and career satisfaction derive in part from meaningful contact with professional reference groups outside the school, for example, working scientists or artists or university-based educators (Bennet, 1985). American teachers interviewed by Stanford researchers appear to be less interested in hierarchically arrayed positions than in a richer pool of professional opportunities for all classroom teachers (Yee, 1986).

Conditions of Productivity in Schools

A third set of problems (and recommendations) centers on the professional environment of the school, or workplace conditions. Among the recommendations are ones calling for richer teacher-student ratios and greater amounts of planning and preparation time; these are conditions that would permit teachers time for critical reflection and closer collaboration. Other recommendations call for differentiated staffing or for school-level "leader-teacher" roles. The idea behind such proposals is that promoting leadership by teachers in the context of the school will satisfy two needs: it will present attractive opportunities and rewards for teachers, and it will direct greater institutional attention to the quality of teaching.

Such recommendations treat leadership less as a matter of individual career trajectories than as a matter of rigorous professional relations among teachers. Teachers are expected to exert the kind of influence on one another that would enhance success and satisfaction with students. In that respect, workplace reform proposals challenge longstanding patterns of teacher isolation and individual autonomy. They fly in the face of most cultural, institutional, and occupational precedents (Feiman-Nemser & Floden, 1986).

Some recommendations, particularly those centered on differentiated staffing and the development of lead-teacher positions, have drawn the same criticisms as career ladder, and for some of the same reasons. On the whole, however, the workplace reform recommendations, like the career-ladder proposals, have been deemed by many states and localities to be important enough to deserve a serious trial (Darling-Hammond, 1987; Carnegie Forum, 1986).

Professionalizing Teaching by Professionalizing the Workplace

This chapter emphasizes the third of the three potential arenas for reform activity: conditions of productivity in schools. It is in this arena that the public interest in teacher leadership is most pressing. There are three main arguments underlying "school workplace" reforms.

First, experiments in teacher leadership will prove to be marginal and ephemeral if they are not demonstrably (and soon) linked to benefits close to the classroom. Teachers themselves test reform proposals by trying to anticipate the effect they might have in their own work. Other observers, including school board members and state legislators, will reasonably ask: What are the promised gains for students, their parents, and their communities when teachers assume greater leadership in the day-to-day life of schools?

Second, the work of schoolteaching is characteristically "professional" work; it is complex and subtle, requiring informed judgment by well-prepared practitioners in circumstances that are often ambiguous or difficult. Current arrangements often retard rather than advance teachers' professional capacities for sound judgment when they restrict opportunities for joint study and problem solving and when complex issues are tackled primarily through the exercise of bureaucratic rule making. The proposed alternative arrangements are held out with the promise that they will produce more successful solutions to problems of student learning and student socialization, at the same time that they build teachers' commitments to teaching.

Finally, we know something about the professionalization of organizations (Benveniste, 1987). These are reforms that are actionable. Despite some increase in real costs, they are reforms that will require clear vision, persistence, and good will far more than money.

In sum, the professionalization of the larger occupation rests in important ways on our ability to professionalize the organizations in which teachers work. Questions of theory, research, policy, and practice coincide in an examination of the prospects for professionalizing the daily work—and workplace—of teaching.

Even the most conservative of the workplace reform proposals requires that teachers, individually and collectively, act differently toward their work and one another. In some fashion or other, each proposal calls for teachers to take the lead in advancing the understanding and practice of teaching.

What are the prospects that such proposals, with their element of leadership by teachers, could be tested on a large enough scale in American schools to guide districts and states in their policy and program choices, or to guide professional associations in building their agendas?

The rest of this chapter assesses the prospects from one standpoint: the likelihood that teachers will accept one another's initiative on matters of curriculum and instruction and do so in ways that demonstrably affect their own classroom choices.

I have relied primarily on teachers' own perceptions of and participation in school leadership, collected as part of four separate studies.[3] The major source is a two-year study of instructional leadership in eight secondary schools. The study included leadership attitudes and practices by both administrators and teachers. The second is a study of "teacher advisors" who were charged with promoting and assisting teacher development in nineteen school districts. The third study examined the introduction of school-level instructional leadership teams in a single district. And the last is a two-year study of the California Mentor Teacher Program.

This collection of studies, and others' work on related topics, reveal some of the conditions required to promote and sustain rigorous professional relations among teachers that yield benefits for students.

Work Worth Leading: Targets of Teacher Leadership

Leadership is an empty term when there is nothing to lead, nowhere to go, and no one who follows. Do teachers have reason to lead the work of teaching, and thus have reason to lead one another? Advocates of teacher leadership, it appears, have largely underestimated the magnitude of the change their proposals represent.

Are Schools Organized to Influence Teaching?

When we promote leadership by *teachers,* we may assume that such an arrangement is an alternative to present conditions—that principals, for example, may have to relinquish some of their own influence as instructional leaders in order to make room for teachers. There is some doubt, however, whether teaching is now led at all, in any meaningful sense, in more than a few exceptional schools.

History would lead us to be skeptical about schools' influence on teaching (Cuban, 1985). This is not to say schools are not organized. Schools have been increasingly well organized for several purposes that are dear to the public interest. Most are organized to provide a humane, safe, orderly environment for students to learn. More and more schools are organized to teach basic academic and social skills. Finally, most schools are organized to maintain good relations with parents and the local public.

Schools are organized, then, for many important functions. Influencing teaching—the long-term directions as well as the daily classroom decisions that affect students—is not typically one of them (Bird & Little, 1986; Feiman-Nemser & Floden, 1986). Teachers are far less likely to defer to another teacher's view of curriculum or instruction than to rely upon habit and personal preference. There is rarely anything in the immediate professional environment that overcomes the effect of other influences on teachers' decisions. Such influences range from the teacher's own experience as a student (Lortie's "apprenticeship of observation"), to students' attempts to "bargain" the curriculum, to teachers' interpretations of parental interests, to personal predilections regarding curriculum content, instructional method, or the social organization of students for learning.

Schools that are organized to influence teaching are relatively rare. There are few precedents in the occupation or in the organization of schools that would encourage teachers to take initiative with regard to the classroom choices made by their colleagues. The arrangements that would underscore teachers' mutual interdependence, such as shared instructional assignments, are few. Traditional authority relations in schools and districts, as well as conventional teacher evaluation procedures, communicate a view of teaching as an individual enterprise. Finally, few of these rare institutions appear able to sustain their productive work norms and structures when the building principal or key teaching staff depart.

Teachers Who Lead

Recall that the task here is to consider how teacher leadership might be promoted in ways that improve productivity conditions in schools. The target of teacher leadership is the stuff of teaching and learning: teachers' choices about curriculum, instruction, how students are helped to learn, and how their progress is judged and rewarded.

Teachers who lead leave their mark on teaching. By their presence and their performance, they change how other teachers think about, plan for, and conduct their work with students.

Teachers invited to lead may well fail to do so. Examples abound. Leadership programs turn out to be mini grant competitions in which successful competitors pursue topics and problems of individual interest and "lead" the same way they teach: alone. Or a position described as "mentor," bearing all the powerful imagery and promise of that term, is steadily diminished in the eyes of teachers as its holder is seen to do little more than ordinary curriculum writing ("extra work for extra pay"). Or a teacher asked to assist first-year teachers worries so much about being "threatening" that he or she turns out to be useless instead.

Teachers placed in positions that bear the titles and resources of leadership display a caution toward their colleagues that is both poignant and eminently sensible. The relation with other teachers that is implied by terms like *mentor, advisor,* or *specialist* has little place in the ordinary workings of most schools. Even the simple etiquette of teacher leadership is unclear.

Teachers face a task of considerable magnitude in giving meaning to leadership within their own ranks. Imagine two teachers, one of whom has been accorded a title of "master teacher." Having seen each other teach rarely or not at all, the two teachers must worry about what they will discover about one another. The leader must worry about whether he or she has anything to offer that is not already fully at the command of the person presumably to be led. Having seldom or never talked about teaching in any depth, the two must now quickly learn to communicate in ways that match their complex and subtle sense of teaching; anything less will not satisfy them, because it will fail even to incorporate the accomplishments each has managed alone and because it will not take their work further than either one could carry it alone.

Teachers contemplating a rigorous mutual examination of their teaching may well have good reason to believe it will be difficult, even troublesome, and little reason to believe that the yield could be worth the trouble.

In a paper titled "The Lead Teacher: Ways to Begin," Kathleen Devaney (1987) describes six arenas in which teachers might reasonably demonstrate leadership at the school level. While some have more well-established precedents than others, each of the six has been described in prior studies of school organization. This is a plausible inventory of possibilities. It offers a balance between leadership that advances a school *program* by making it more suitable or rigorous, and leadership that moves *people* by strengthening their knowledge, skills, and commitment. In Devaney's view:

1. *Lead teachers continue to teach and to improve their own teaching.* They gain their legitimacy by remaining credibly in touch with life in the classroom. They work consistently to apply best practice, and they engage in planned experimentation, often as members or leaders of small groups of colleagues. The California Mentor Teacher Program requires that mentors continue to teach at least a 60 percent load. Programs that release teachers full time to work in a "mentoring" or "advising" capacity (see Kent, 1985) promote demonstration lessons and other classroom consultation as one means of establishing the mentor's legitimacy in the eyes of teachers.

2. *Lead teachers organize and lead well-informed peer reviews of school practice.* In practice, such activity has been most fruitful where it develops quickly from review to revision. In one school, teachers described two-year "innovation cycles." The cycle began when a group of five or six teachers decided that some aspect of student progress deserved their collective attention and set out to "get smarter" about the problem and the prospects for solving it. The cycle typically led to clearer formulation of the problem, potential avenues of improvement, skill training where appropriate, and selective classroom experimentation. Experiments that "worked" were marketed to others on the faculty. At the secondary level, we have observed reviews and improvement activities profitably organized by department as reviews of subject-area teaching. (For a discussion of the master teacher as curriculum leader, see Klein, 1985.)

3. *Lead teachers participate productively in school-level decision making.* They work with administrators and teachers to arrive at decisions

that are well targeted, well informed, and well accepted. Shared decision making has taken a range of forms, from formally organized and specially scheduled goal-setting sessions to a once-a-week staff meeting that engaged principal and grade-level team leaders in the routine decision making that kept an entire school roughly headed in the same direction.

4. *Lead teachers organize and lead inservice education* that is meaningfully related to the student population and the school program. A faculty effectively organized for its own learning, it appears, can make reasonable use of external staff development options that would otherwise have weak effect (e.g., the one-time workshop).

5. *Lead teachers advise and assist individual teachers* through methods that have come to be called mentoring, coaching, or consultation. The literature on coaching has been growing steadily following Joyce and Showers' (1981) review of staff development practices, culminating in their prediction that classroom impacts would remain small unless skill training were accompanied by the kind of classroom assistance and consultation that would enable teachers to establish the "fit" between new ideas and established habits (see also Showers, 1983; Goodwin & Lieberman, 1984). On the whole, the logic underlying mentoring or coaching has been readily accepted (especially when applied to support for beginning teachers), but teachers have remained ill prepared and ill supported to assume mentoring responsibilities (Bird & Little, 1986).

6. *Lead teachers participate in the performance evaluation of teachers* by providing appropriate appraisal and feedback. Peer evaluation is promoted as one hallmark of a professionalized occupation, in which standards of performance are monitored by the members of the profession in exchange for substantial guarantees of (collective) autonomy. Evaluation of teaching and teachers is the most problematic of the proposed domains for teacher leadership, though not unknown in our studies, in studies of effective teacher evaluation (Wise et al., 1984), or in current statewide reform initiatives (Connecticut State Department of Education, 1984).

Teachers' Acceptance and Support of Leadership by Colleagues

Much has been made of teachers' probable (and sometimes demonstrated) opposition to any large-scale change in the occupation or the organization of schools that would introduce status differences among teachers based on demonstrated knowledge and skill. And recently, administrators have made the news with their own opposition to leadership schemes that they believe will usurp site administrators' authority to conduct personnel and program evaluation.

In the past, studies of teacher leadership experiments at the school or district level have produced mixed results and limited practical guidance. One study of organized teacher teams in open-space schools documented teachers' ambivalence about team leaders assigned by building principals (Arikado, 1976), while other studies have attributed the vigor of a school program to the work of teacher-led teams in which the leaders were also designated by the principal (Lipsitz, 1983). There are more skeptics than enthusiasts represented in the literature, but it would be too strong an indictment to say it has been tried and did not work. There have been few serious trials.

This section examines the support for teacher leadership in the day-to-day social organization of schools. One can gauge the prospects for teacher leadership on a school-by-school basis in light of teachers' responses to two possibilities.

First, the prospects for leadership can be judged in part by whether teachers have developed, or are prepared to develop, a close working knowledge of one another's teaching, based on observation and in depth discussion. To assess the prospects for leadership in a school, then, one might ask: Is the very act of teaching public enough (or might it become so) to support vigorous leadership that affects classroom practices?

Classroom observation among teachers serves as a bellwether practice: of all the possible interactions among teachers, it is perhaps the clearest signal that the traditional norm of privacy may have been displaced. A school's culture is conducive to leadership by teachers when teachers are in one another's classrooms for purposes of seeing, learning from, commenting on, and planning for one another's work with students.

Second, the prospects for teacher leadership can be judged by teachers' acceptance of initiative by specially designated leaders in their midst. Here, we examine the possibility that teachers who are recognized as leaders by some special title ("master teachers," "mentors," "teacher advisors") would, by word and deed, attempt to influence improvements in curriculum and instruction and thus influence the day-to-day classroom work of other teachers. A school's culture is conducive to leadership by teachers when such initiative is acceptable. To assess the prospects for leadership in a school, then, one might ask: What latitude will teachers accord a colleague who is clearly recognized as a "master teacher"?

Teachers' attitudes toward classroom observation, and their attitudes toward leadership initiative by specially selected teacher leaders, are not the only grounds on which one might assess prospects for leadership, but they are crucial ones. Teachers' acceptance of and participation in regular classroom observation reveals their fundamental orientation toward teaching as a private or public activity. Teachers' acceptance of initiative regarding curriculum and instruction reveals their orientation to the very idea of leadership, that is to the rights and obligations that teachers inherit by virtue of membership in the profession.

Making Teaching Public

Teaching has long been described as a private activity, both in planning and execution. Veteran teachers report having worked 30 years with no other adult in the classroom except on incidental business. Yet schools that are discovered to be vital, adaptable institutions have been consistently found to support vigorous professional exchanges among teachers. Teachers in these schools talk in depth about teaching and about students' progress, plan for teaching together, observe one another's work in classrooms, and learn from one another. They eschew oversimplified war stories that defy analysis, concentrating instead on straightforward assessments that reveal the true complexities of a situation and yield new options (see Rosenholtz & Kyle, 1984).

While classroom observation is clearly not the only route to a more public, collective version of teaching, we anticipate that the rate and rigor with which teachers watch and discuss one another's classroom work with students are important indicators of teachers' acceptance of teacher leadership.

THE SIGNIFICANCE OF LEADERSHIP CLOSE TO THE CLASSROOM. We consider the classroom observation data to be significant in principle for three reasons. First, structured classroom observations have been promoted as one of the most prominent and potentially powerful vehicles for instructional leadership. Second, classroom observation directly and literally tackles the main consequences of the closed classroom door. The closed door isolates students and fragments their learning; the closed door offers teachers only a truncated, impoverished understanding of one another's abilities and activities. Third, teachers argue that leaders must demonstrate that they have something to offer that is worth following—and that the demonstration will not be persuasive unless it is credible in the classroom. Teachers who aspire to lead must be able to display their own mastery of classroom challenges. They must be able to grasp and describe other teachers' intentions and accomplishments. And they must be willing and able to recognize and act on opportunities to improve their own and others' work with students. In the end, teachers are unlikely to accept leadership at too great a distance from the classroom.

DO GOOD COLLEAGUES STOP AT THE CLASSROOM DOOR? An exploratory study of interactions among teachers tells of Jim and Bill, whose close personal and professional relationship almost dissolved after Jim's first foray into Bill's classroom (Zahorik, 1987, p. 391). The study concludes that collegiality may stop at the classroom door. Others, too, have observed that what passes for collegiality may not add up to much (Hargreaves, 1984; Little, 1987; Rosenholtz & Kyle, 1984) and that access to classrooms is problematic (Little, 1985).

Across the country, schools are experimenting with peer observation, peer coaching, and other programs designed to get teachers into one another's classrooms. For teachers in many schools, the idea of classroom visitation has strong appeal. For an even larger number, I suspect, the idea is met with skepticism, indifference, or outright opposition. One might ask what prior experience those teachers have encountered that would lead them to respond in any other way.

In eight secondary schools, we examined teachers' assessment of the observation practices they typically encountered in their schools, and we asked teachers to indicate their relative approval or disapproval of specific classroom observation practices by department heads and by peers. Nearly 500 teachers in eight middle and high schools recorded their preferences and their actual experiences with regard to nine aspects of observation, including frequency and duration, methods of observation, arrangements for feedback or consultation, the nature of follow-up, approaches to praise and criticism, and the qualifications of the observer.[4]

The picture that emerges from the findings belies the stereotype of the closed classroom door. The door opens, it appears, to colleagues and other observers who will neither waste the teacher's time nor insult the teacher's intelligence. The door remains open when full professional reciprocity is established—when observers work as hard to understand and describe classroom events as teachers are working to plan and conduct them.

THE PRECEDENT SET BY ADMINISTRATORS. When teachers consider observation by other teachers or by department heads, they look first to the precedent set by those who have observed them before. In most instances, the precedent has been set by administrators. For good or ill, the perspectives and practices of administrators carry substantial weight in teachers' estimates of the potential usefulness of observation by colleagues.

Among the eight schools in the instructional leadership study, the greatest support for observation of teachers by teachers came in two junior high schools in which administrators had worked hard to establish a record of thoughtful, thorough, well-informed classroom observation over a period of years. In contrast, teachers in the three urban high schools were generally unimpressed by any form of administrator observation they had had and were correspondingly unenthusiastic about observation by chairs or teachers.

Observers, whether administrators or teachers, have more latitude than they usually exploit. For almost every aspect of classroom observation, from how often it occurs to the nature of its link to formal evaluation, teachers approve a more rigorous scrutiny of classroom teaching than they typically encounter. In six of the eight schools surveyed, the greatest latitude is accorded to administrators; in two large suburban schools, department heads bear substantial responsibility for instructional leadership and supervision, and teachers reserved their highest expectations and most generous observation options for them. This pattern suggests that the greatest approval attaches to the role with formal and legitimate authority for observation; the preference for administrator over teacher as observer may well be an artifact of prevailing authority relations in schools, subject to systematic experimentation.

Does Classroom Observation Change Classroom Teaching?

Teachers find that spending productive time in others' classrooms is a labor-intensive business, one that is rarely accommodated well by the school's master schedule. Does spending time in others' classrooms yield enough benefits to compete well with other demands on teachers' time? How powerful is an observer's commentary as an influence on a teacher's planning and performance? Consider the following item as one measure of the relative salience of commentary on teaching: "In my school, teachers ignore feedback on their teaching."

In three urban high schools with no strong tradition of close involvement in classrooms (or, put another way, a longstanding tradition of independent/isolated work in classrooms), teachers and administrators are uncertain whether teachers take feedback seriously but are inclined to believe they do not. (In at least one of the urban high schools, administrators and department chairs are fairly certain that teachers *do* ignore feedback.) Observation is a ritual event, conducted only by administrators and associated almost exclusively with the triennial teacher evaluation.

Casual or infrequent classroom visitation, it appears, offers weak support for teacher leadership. (Indeed, there is some evidence that classroom observation of this sort may serve as a disincentive for teacher leadership, since it convinces teachers that they have little to gain from the occasions when teachers or administrators enter their classroom or presume to talk to them about their work with students.)

A strong contrast is provided by three small city schools, where secondary administrators (as part of an informal study group) have worked to make teaching "public" through frequent observation and discussion. Teachers in these schools firmly deny that teachers ignore feedback on teaching. The survey findings for these schools are consistent with case-study observation, and have led us to draw the following conclusion:

> In one of five [case-study] schools, classroom observation is so frequent, so intellectually lively and intense, so thoroughly integrated into the daily work, and so associated with accomplishments for all who participate, that it is difficult to see how the practices could fail to improve teaching. In still another school, the observation practices approach this standard. In three of the five schools, however, the observation of classroom life is so cursory, so infrequent, so shapeless and tentative that if it were found to affect instruction favorably we would be hard-pressed to construct a plausible explanation. (Little & Bird, 1986, p. 122)

Teachers who are newly selected in potential leadership roles—mentors, teacher advisors, resource teachers, and others—understand that the test of their worth will be in the classroom. But these emerging leadership roles have been ambiguous, particularly with regard to the expectations for entering other teachers' classrooms or becoming involved in any way with another teacher's work. (Mentors in California have been described as enacting a play for which there is no script.) Some districts have a long history of special-assignment positions that serve as an admirable precedent for the new generation of leadership roles. Some districts have developed the position of grade-level chair or department head as a good role model for successful leadership on curriculum, instruction, and classroom organization; more often, they do not. Individuals have been left to carve out identities and build support from teachers or administrators on a case-by-case basis.

In the absence of some commonly understood, affirmative ground for working with other teachers on matters affecting the classroom, most new leaders are hesitant to move toward another teacher's classroom unless invited, or to offer more than the most modest invitation to other teachers to observe them in their own classrooms. Teachers, meanwhile, refrain from making any request of the leader until they are certain of how it will be received and how it will be interpreted by others. In the absence of traditions for mutual work in classrooms, what transpires might be coined the "teachers' lounge waltz."

Teachers have more latitude than they have acted on to enter one another's classrooms. In any of the eight schools surveyed, teachers could enter one another's classrooms by satisfying stringent but quite practical conditions. These conditions establish professional reciprocity between observer and observed. For example, teachers who were observed wanted to be able to comment on the quality of the observation, in the same manner and spirit in which the observers would comment upon the teaching they witnessed.

Returning to the tale of "Jim" and "Bill" in Zahorik's recent study, I am led to underscore the importance of the ground rules and other preparations that make it acceptable to watch others at work. One might have concluded that collegiality need not have stopped at the classroom door, but that Jim and Bill's relationship—alleged to be a sturdy one—was barely sturdy enough to survive a clumsy first attempt at moving the action into the classroom.

In some schools, the entrance to the classroom is well trafficked. In one junior high school, for example, teachers reported that their high expectations for observation were in fact being met by colleagues who observe them. Teachers tended to observe one another in the course of work they were doing jointly to refine the curriculum—an endeavor that had already paid off handsomely in the form of increased test scores, improved daily classroom performance, and a virtual elimination of discipline problems. When participating in structured observations for one another (a kind of professional service), teachers took for granted that they would provide a written record of what transpired; they would take the time to engage in a properly thorough and deferential discussion afterward, concentrating on the response elicited from students. In order to see a set of related lessons unfold, they would devote at least 20 minutes to the observation and would try to observe for two or more days in a row. Further, teachers in this school have been known to observe and critique one another not only in classrooms, but also in conducting in-service workshops.

Teachers in all the surveyed schools shared high but reachable expectations when their colleagues observe. Teachers expect that:

- Observers will describe what they've seen and invite the teacher's commentary.

- Observers who find something to admire or praise will say so directly.

- Observers who have suggestions to make will help teachers to act on them by providing demonstrations or by joint planning.

- Teachers who observe will request feedback on their *observation* practices (reciprocity).

In follow-up videotape study of observation in action, we detected some of the moment-by-moment interactions among teachers that enabled leadership "close to the classroom" to emerge. This study of ten teacher advisors at work with teachers showed (1) how explicit ground rules built tolerance and trust and (2) how payoff escalated as teachers became "skillful pairs" with a common language and organized set of routines for describing, analyzing, and planning for teaching.

Taken alone, classroom observation (even at its most frequent and intense) is not an adequate avenue by which to expand a school's influence on teaching. Its most fruitful ground is the entire pattern of shared responsibility among teachers and the pattern of shared professional tasks, which give larger purpose to time spent in classrooms. Teachers' support for arrangements that bring them sensibly into contact with others, under conditions that they can reasonably accept, has been demonstrated in the data. Most responded that they "definitely would" agree to work with one or more colleagues under these conditions: "You and another member of your faculty have been asked to share your ideas and methods for teaching, to assemble the best methods that the two of you can come up with, and to use those methods and techniques well in your work. You will have some choice about the person with whom you are to work."

Acts of Leadership: Initiative by "Master Teachers"

A long-standing element of the culture of teaching is the maxim: "you don't interfere with another teacher's teaching." Teachers may offer their assistance to others under special circumstances and with special care. To a new teacher, it is widely acceptable to say, "Ask me if you need anything," but less so to say, "It's important to the school and to you that you get off to a good start here. I propose that we work together pretty closely for the first semester." In few schools would one teacher say to others, as a matter of course, "I've been studying some ways to help our kids with their writing, and I want to propose that we try some of them this year."

In fewer still, "I've noticed that you've really been struggling with that class. Let me help." In the culture that prevails, "don't interfere" and "ask if you need help" bound teachers' initiative toward one another. Teacher autonomy, in this view, is interpreted as freedom from scrutiny and the right of each individual teacher to make independent judgments about classroom practice.

Missing from this scenario is an affirmative construction of professional obligations that is other than intrusive ("interference") or loosely invitational ("ask if you want"). The prospects for school-based teacher leadership rest on displacing the privacy norm with another that might be expressed this way: "It's part of your job to ensure that all the teaching here is good teaching." Teacher autonomy, in this view, is interpreted as the right of the teaching *profession* to construct and uphold standards of good teaching (Sykes, 1983) and the obligation of individual teachers to examine closely their own and others' professional judgments. In schools, teachers would in fact expect to be their brothers' keepers.

To examine the possibilities for a norm favoring closer mutual examination of teaching by teachers, this chapter stresses the central problem of *initiative* by teachers on matters of curriculum and instruction. Initiative among teachers is construed here not as a problem of individuals' character, energy, and knowledge (though certainly they matter), but as an institutional problem of teachers' obligations, rights, opportunities, and rewards. Data from the two-year study of instructional leadership in secondary schools provide our first systematic test of teachers' acceptance of initiative by colleagues.

Teachers were confronted with the following statement, and then asked to judge a set of options for action: "In every school there are teachers who are known to be highly informed, creative, and skillful. These 'master teachers' routinely produce unusually good results. How should they and how do they interact with other teachers?"

Of the nine options that teachers were presented, the two most conservative options required almost no initiative on the part of the master teacher. They required at most that teachers recognize that some teachers in their midst might deserve the reputation of master teacher and that the master teacher "respond when asked by another teacher for suggestions, but otherwise not offer advice." Somewhat more initiative is envisioned by the options that place the master teacher at work with beginning teachers and then with experienced teachers, both at the behest of the principal. The most assertive options call for the master teacher to circulate materials, organize and lead inservices, and offer help independently to a teacher having difficulty.

Teachers in six schools (N = 282) recorded their relative approval or disapproval of each of the specific options and indicated the extent to which they encountered such behavior in their own school.[5]

A PATTERN OF HESITANT APPROVAL. Teachers in five of the six schools did not flinch from the prospect that masterful teaching would be publicly recognized or that an acknowledged master teacher would be assertive in dealings with others. All but one of the nine options generated mean ratings from the group at large that were well into the "approval" range (+1 to +3). Nonetheless, the findings are best summed up as a pattern of hesitant approval. Teachers did not vigorously or uniformly embrace any of the options (none of the overall means exceeds +2, and the range of individual responses is considerable).

Judging by the three schools that offer both case-study and survey data, teachers' responses to others' leadership may correspond closely to their day-by-day experience as colleagues. The most confident endorsements of teacher-to-teacher initiative came from teachers in a junior high school that boasted a seven-year history of vigorous collaborative work among teachers. Elsewhere in the survey findings, teachers in this school were distinguished with regard to other professional practices: more than teachers in other schools, teachers here reported (1) two teachers getting together for a few minutes each day to share teaching plans for the day, (2) teachers negotiating ground rules to guide their work together, (3) teachers commenting on each other's course materials and tests, (4) exchanges or advice among experienced teachers, and (5) teachers praising one another's work. The most skeptical response came from an urban high school in which a variety of work conditions induced more competition than cooperation and in which teachers were formally observed only every three years.

Overall, teachers more readily gave their approval to those options that acknowledged a master teacher's skills and talents but did not anticipate truly assertive behavior toward other teachers. Offering help when asked, therefore, received uniformly high teacher approvals, while offering help without being asked drew the same level of approval from teachers in only two of the six schools.

Support for beginning teachers is one arena in which teachers have found status differences based on knowledge and skill to be defensible and leadership roles therefore sensible; these data are consistent with other case-study findings that support mentoring relationships directed at induction-year assistance. Thus teachers at five of the six schools registered solid support for the master teacher who helps a new teacher get off to a good start, while only two schools granted that same level of support for work to improve the performance of an experienced teacher.

As predicted, the school with the greatest shared responsibility for the students, curriculum, and instruction (as determined by case-study findings) also showed the greatest involvement in leadership by teachers. In that school, teachers accept the principal's action in asking skilled teachers to present faculty inservice and said it happens often. Teachers give their approval to peers who circulate professional articles they have found useful. Teachers approve when some of their number are invited to provide inservice at other schools and believe that it happens reasonably often.

Yet even at this school, some doubt or hesitation remains about the possibility of the principal's asking a master teacher to meet regularly with an experienced colleague to help improve the other teacher's work; it almost never happens. The master teacher who offers help without being asked receives less approbation than the teacher who waits to be invited. And the master teacher who distributes copies of his or her own successful lesson plans may be looked at askance, although other professional materials a teacher has found useful or informative are welcomed.

BUILDING ON PRECEDENT: THE DEPARTMENT HEAD. When principals were recently encouraged to find ways of sharing their leadership with teachers (Acheson & Smith, 1986), one prominent suggestion was to capitalize on school-level positions that—at least in name, if not always in practice—already present opportunities for teacher leadership. Department heads, resource teachers, project directors, and grade-level chairs are among the examples of positions that may permit special recognition of talent and experience and that may have the requisite discretionary resources attached to them.

All six of the six secondary schools surveyed in the instructional leadership study gave some role to formal department heads, but only the two large suburban high schools emphasized the role of the department head as a leader in curriculum development and instructional supervision. In these two schools, department heads stood out as a distinctive reference group, more ready than teachers to approve of high initiative but still less cautious than the administrators. (In other schools, department heads' responses were virtually indistinguishable from those of other teachers.)

Asked about the possibility of giving assistance to an experienced teacher, department heads were more closely aligned with administrators than with teachers; judging by the responses, chairs were likely to overestimate the support they would receive from teachers for agreeing to work with a teacher in difficulty.

In questions targeted precisely to the department head's role, teachers were asked to review six options for behavior. Like the options regarding new leadership roles for classroom teachers, these reflect varying degrees of initiative. The most conservative (or lowest initiative) option called for the department head to act as a buffer, dealing with administration so that teachers can get on with teaching. Department heads were also depicted as encouraging participation in conferences or workshops, suggesting specific improvements to individual teachers, organizing teachers in small groups to study new options for teaching, arranging for a district supervisor to work with a department member, and using a department meeting to deliver a workshop.

The most aggressive profile of the department head came from one of the two suburban schools with a long history of using department heads to carry the weight of instructional leadership. Even in that school, however, support fell off when the chair was depicted as moving from one-on-one consultation to the leadership of the group as a whole. The lowest level of support for the department head came from the high school where that position rotates among teachers and is regarded as a "paper-work position."

When the options required group leadership (as in assembling a study group or conducting a workshop), schools with a strong recent history of teacher-to-teacher collaboration (but no particular emphasis on the department head position) stood out in their level of support; it appears that the collaborative history had established an environment in which the head's position could be invested with greater responsibility and latitude than it had enjoyed to date.

Assessing the Prospects for Teacher Leadership

Teacher leadership has become a hot topic. Grand schemes, with equally grand titles, promise a new enticement for talented teachers and a new resource for the improvement of schools. In writing this chapter, however, I have had in mind a less grand scheme. I paint a picture of ordinary life in schools. And in doing so, I am led to draw four conclusions about the prospects for teacher leadership.

"High Gain, High Strain"

The *gain* in teacher leadership derives from teachers' classroom orientation, from their wealth of practical knowledge, and from their sheer numbers. The *strain* in teacher leadership derives from the inherited traditions of an egalitarian profession, from the persistent belief that teaching is just a matter of style and from the pervasive privacy and isolation of teaching. To talk in terms of teacher leadership is to introduce status differences based on knowledge, skill, and initiative in a profession that has made no provision for them.

The sources of strain often outweigh the felt gains, leading newly designated leaders to downplay their special status and the expertise that it signals.

The strains are compounded when teacher-leaders are recruited straight out of the classroom and attempt to earn their title after the fact with little preparation and support.

The strains are compounded when the principal is cut out of the action. Principals are pressed to be instructional leaders—and now are asked to move over and make room for teachers. When teacher leadership reaches the bargaining table, negotiators often require that the organizational "territory" occupied by teacher-leaders look so different from that occupied by administrators as to make any sensible discussion (or cooperation) between the two suspect. The more useful perspective is the well-led school.

Finally, the strains are compounded when the pace of implementation is fast—a year or less where legislative money is at stake. To gain endorsements for a program, well-intended school professionals reach agreements that move a program forward but defeat the interests of schools and students. (One example is the provision for confidentiality regarding any dealings between a first-year teacher and his or her mentor.)

Through the Eyes of the Principal

When confronted directly about the prospects of expanded teacher leadership in their schools, what do administrators say?

Sweeping proposals for changes in teachers' titles, responsibilities, compensation, and relationships to principals have, predictably, generated worried speculation in administrators and school board members. Most commonly, administrators protest that a school's standing in its community will be jeopardized by the public impression that no one is properly "in charge" and that the best teachers are no longer available to teach children. Teachers' potential encroachments on traditional domains of principals' authority, especially teacher evaluation, have even led to legal opposition. Studies of larger leadership initiatives, such as the California Mentor Teacher Program, detect considerable ambiguity in the teachers' new role and uncertainty among teachers and principals about their proper relation to one another (Bird, 1985).

But sweeping proposals produce equally sweeping responses. Case-study observations and closely situated survey measures have permitted us to "get down to cases" with regard to administrators' support of or opposition to specific teacher leadership possibilities.

Principals in case-study schools conceived and implemented a range of faculty configurations that offered teachers both the reason and the opportunity (including time) to lead. The configurations were varied, including teacher-led interdisciplinary teams or subject-area study groups, schoolwide instructional support teams, and intensified use of department heads. Asked in interviews and through survey measures about specific practices by which teachers, or principals and teachers acting in concert, might take initiative to improve the quality of teaching, principals responded in distinctly favorable terms. These principals, like the principals of other team-based schools (Johnson, 1976), were inclined to say that their influence over classroom teaching had been enhanced, not diminished, by involving teachers in decision making on matters of curriculum and instruction.

Principals and assistant principals in six secondary schools were confronted with the same small set of "teacher-initiative" survey items that were presented to teachers in their school. The items explored faculty and administration approval for advice giving by recognized leaders and for assistance to both beginning and experienced teachers. They presented options that included leadership in curriculum and lesson development as well as formal inservice training.

In their responses to the selected teacher leadership options, administrators were more sanguine than teachers, displaying more support for teacher initiative than teachers themselves displayed and believing that such acts of potential leadership occurred with more regularity than teachers themselves reported.

It is probable that administrators' support for teacher initiative is overestimated by these findings. The consistently high approval rates among the administrators on survey measures (despite considerable variations in observed practice) suggest that we have not yet constructed a set of measures that will tap the threshold of administrator's tolerance for teacher initiative. There are no scenarios among these items, for example, that directly require administrators' support for peer evaluation by teachers. In addition, these measures capitalize on a long history of school-level autonomy that may be steadily eroded by initiatives that centralize curriculum policy, leaving neither principals nor teachers much of significance to lead.

The Public Interest in Teacher Leadership

Teacher leadership will be supported when teachers and school boards believe that it deserves local tax dollars: that public interest, professional interest, and personal interest all are served by singling out leaders from the ranks of teachers. The prospects for teacher leadership remain dim if no one can distinguish the gains made for students when teachers in large numbers devote their collective attention to curriculum and instruction. Each of the schools we have studied works with a staffing formula that makes the intelligent development of teacher leadership an exercise in creative organization (and occasionally creative insubordination). Underlying the staffing formula is a public conception (legitimized in board policy) of teachers and teaching that is satisfied almost exclusively by time spent in classrooms with children.

The most volatile issue in formal teacher leadership initiatives has been teacher selection. Witness the elaborate arrangements for the selection of mentor teachers in California and the careful provisions made for selection and promotion in the first stages of the Charlotte-Mecklenburg career-ladder plan. The selection of leaders has been cast both as a technical problem (what are the acceptable criteria for performance?) and as a political problem (who will teachers accept as leaders, if anyone?), and substantial space has been devoted to describing its solutions (Schlechty, 1984).

One might see the selection problem, however, as an artifact of isolated work in schools, a problem that only arises when teachers have no sensible grounds on which to grant or deny someone the right to lead them. Thus classroom teachers who are recruited or selected into positions with titles that signal leadership (mentor) display a wondrous ability to diminish their new status and to downplay the leadership opportunities and obligations that (inescapably) accompany the title (Bird, 1985). To the extent that the selection problem remains at the forefront of discussions of teacher leadership, and elaborate selection strategies remain the heart of implementation plans, we can expect that the prospect of teacher leadership will decline.

What will defeat teacher leadership? Past efforts have had a "checkered history" (Griffin, 1985, p. 2), and current initiatives proceed by fits and starts (Bird, 1985). School-level arrangements that have fostered leadership by teachers, with apparent benefit to students, have proved fragile and unstable (Little, 1987; Cohen, 1981). The professional teacher responsibilities and relationships anticipated by the Carnegie Forum and by many state initiatives (including California's Mentor Teacher Program) are a sufficient departure from current practice to produce a backlash (Bird, 1985).

Among the conditions that will advance or erode the prospects for teacher leadership, these five are prominent:

1. *The work that leaders do:* Prospects will be diminished by describing as "leadership" tasks that are trivial and inconsequential, that are only peripheral to the important problems and tasks that schools and districts face, or that do not match in their own complexity the intellectual and social demands of teaching and learning. Prospects will be advanced by work that is widely and properly held to be important and difficult.

2. *The symbolic role that leaders assume:* Prospects will be rapidly lessened if teacher leaders serve as "hit men," engaged in activities designated to fix, punish, or remove the incompetent or intransigent. Prospects will be strengthened by roles that invest leaders with dignity and by activities that show them to be exemplars of rigorous, rewarding professional relationships.

3. *Agreements for getting started:* Teacher leadership will be jeopardized by well-intended but restrictive agreements (compromises) concerned largely with protecting the separate interests of teachers and administrators. A more sturdy platform will be provided by public, and concrete, demonstrations of shared interests and by specific ground rules for doing business together in the leadership of schools. For example, the relationship among principals, first-year teachers, and mentors can be thwarted by blind adherence to a confidentiality rule, but made effective by a careful consideration of each person's obligations to both of the others.

4. *Incentives and rewards:* Prospects for teacher leadership must be judged in large part by the incentives for teachers to favor collaborative work over independent work and to lend their support to teachers who take the lead on some shared task or problem. There are substantial disincentives in the present organization of work in most schools. Among the most powerful examples is Cusick's (1983) description of the disincentives to cooperation created by the proliferation of electives in the high school curriculum. Faculties that are relatively cohesive or polarized over appropriate ends and means for student learning are likely to provide

quite different environments for teacher leadership, but those relationships have gone largely unexplored (see Metz, 1978).

5. *Local policy support:* Prospects for teacher leadership will be directly affected by district policies and practices, particularly those governing the principalship: the recruitment, selection, placement, and evaluation of building principals, and the provisions, if any, for transitions in leadership. In prior studies, effective but atypical faculty configurations have been quickly unraveled when the building principal departs (Cohen, 1981; Little, 1987) unless districts place special emphasis on preserving teacher leadership and evaluate principals accordingly (Little & Long, 1985).

Organized Preparation and Support

In effect, districts and schools face a two-part challenge. Policy and program support can be organized to meet both. One challenge is to introduce capable people to a new role. Leading a group, a school, or an occupation is not the same as teaching a class well. Training programs for new teacher leaders ensure that leaders have something to offer by helping them recognize, organize, and display their knowledge and skill to others (Bird & Little, 1985a). They ensure that new leaders work as successfully with colleagues as with students. And finally, they ensure that leaders have access to discretionary resources and are able to invent good strategies for using them.

A second challenge is to introduce a new role to an institution and an occupation. Leadership by teachers will require a more common pattern of teacher-to-teacher work in the daily operations of schools, as the basis on which teacher leadership comes to be found sensible and feasible. It will require shifts in authority relations in schools, in the bases for power and prestige. It will require changes in long-standing and firmly held conceptions of teaching, learning to teach, and teacher education.

NOTES

1. Descriptions of teachers' involvements in preservice teacher education can be found in Lanier, 1983, and in "Teacher Induction Programs and Research," the January–February 1986 issue of the *Journal of Teacher Education.* On teachers' involvement in teacher licensure, see Furtwengler, 1985, and the Connecticut State Department of Education, 1984. On teachers' involvement in teacher evaluation, see Wise et al., 1984.

2. The Office of Educational Research and Improvement (OERI) is preparing a summary of the experience of 55 "teacher incentive" planning grants, most of which were targeted to career ladders. The Career Ladder Clearinghouse of the Southern Regional Education Board has recently prepared an update on its earlier state-by-state review (Career Ladder Clearinghouse, 1986). Wagner (1985) provides an overview of the California Mentor Teacher Program. Other well-established programs have promoted special roles based on teachers' demonstrated knowledge and skill (see Kent, 1985). The most celebrated recent example of "career restructuring" is the "lead teacher" recommended by the Carnegie Forum in its report *A Nation Prepared* (1986). Following the Carnegie proposal, Devaney (1987) has prepared a discussion paper for use by local constituencies in deciding an approach to teacher leadership at the school and district level.

3. The following discussion is based on research conducted at the Center for Action Research, Inc., Boulder, Colorado, under Contract NIE-G-82-0020, and at the Far West Laboratory for Educational Research and Development, under Contract 400-83-003, both with the National Institute of Education, U.S. Department of Education. The views expressed herein are not necessarily the views of that agency.

   In the first year of the instructional leadership study (Bird & Little, 1985b), case studies were completed in five schools (two districts). In the second year, surveys were completed in the five case-study schools and in three additional schools (four districts). The districts included a small city district, two large suburban districts, and a large urban district. In other related studies, the Professional Development Studies Group investigated the California Mentor Teacher Program (Bird, 1985), a countywide teacher advisor project (Little, 1985; Kent, 1985), and school-level instructional support teams (Little & Long, 1985). The studies described were conducted in partnership with my colleague, Tom Bird. The arguments developed here reflect his thinking in ways I am no longer able to untangle after 14 years of collaboration.

4. The survey was completed by 476 teachers and 22 administrators in eight schools. Return rates varied from 50 percent to 100 percent. (Six of the eight schools had return rates of 77 percent or above; in three schools, all teachers completed the survey.)

5. The results that follow were obtained in a second survey in six schools. The survey was completed by 282 teachers and 14 administrators; return rates were above 70 percent in each of four schools, and 44 percent and 65 percent in the remaining two schools.

REFERENCES

Acheson, K. A., & Smith, S. C. (1986). *It is time for principals to share the responsibility for instructional leadership with others.* Eugene, OR: Oregon School Study Council, University of Oregon.

Arikado, M. S. (1976). Status congruence as it relates to team teacher satisfaction. *Journal of Educational Administration, 14*(1), 70–78.

Bennet, C. (1985). Paints, pots or promotion? Art teachers' attitudes toward their careers. In S. J. Ball & I. F. Goodson (Eds.), *Teachers' lives and careers* (pp. 120–137). London: Falmer Press.

Benveniste, G. (1987). *Professionalizing the organization.* San Francisco: Jossey-Bass.

Bird, T. (1985). *The mentor's dilemma.* San Francisco: Far West Laboratory for Educational Research and Development.

Bird, T., & Little, J. W. (1985a). *From teacher to leader: Training and support for instructional leadership by teachers.* San Francisco: Far West Laboratory for Educational Research and Development.

Bird, T., & Little, J. W. (1985b). *Instructional leadership in eight secondary schools.* Final report to the National Institute of Education, Contract NIE-G-82-0020, Boulder, CO: Center for Action Research.

Bird, T., & Little, J. W. (1986). How schools organize the teaching occupation. *Elementary School Journal, 86*(4), 493–511.

Career Ladder Clearinghouse. (1986). *1986—Incentive programs for teachers and administrators: How are they doing?* Atlanta: Southern Regional Education Board.

Carnegie Forum on Education and the Economy. (1986). *A nation prepared: Teachers for the twenty-first century.* New York: Author.

Cohen, E. (1981). Sociology looks at team teaching. *Research in Sociology of Education and Socialization, 2,* 163–193.

Connecticut State Department of Education. (1984). *The beginning year teacher support and assessment program.* Hartford, CT: Author.

Cuban, L. (1985). *How teachers taught.* New York: Longman.

Cusick, P. A. (1983). *The egalitarian ideal and the American high school: Studies of three schools.* New York: Longman.

Darling-Hammond, L. (1987). Schools for tomorrow's teachers. *Teachers College Record, 88*(3), 354–358.

Devaney, K. (1987). *The lead teacher: Ways to begin.* New York: Carnegie Forum on Education and the Economy.

Feiman-Nemser, S., & Floden, R. (1986). The cultures of teaching. In M. Wittrock (Ed.), *Handbook of research on teaching* (3rd ed.) (pp. 505–526). New York: Macmillan.

Furtwengler, C. (1985). Tennessee's career ladder plan: They said it couldn't be done. *Educational Leadership, 43*(3), 50–56.

Goodwin, L. A., & Lieberman, A. (1984, April). *Effective assister behavior: What they brought and what they learned.* Paper presented at the annual meeting of the American Educational Research Association, New Orleans.

Griffin, G. (1985). The school as a workplace and the master teacher concept. *Elementary School Journal, 86*(1), 1–16.

Hargreaves, A. (1984, October). Experience counts, theory doesn't: How teachers talk about their work. *Sociology of Education 1984, 57*, 244–254.

Johnson, R. (1976). *Teacher collaboration, principal influence, and decision-making in elementary schools* (Technical report No. 48). Stanford, CA: Stanford Center for Research and Development in Teaching, Stanford University.

Joyce, B., & Showers, B. (1981, April). *Teacher training research: Working hypotheses for program design and directions for future study.* A paper presented at the annual meeting of the American Educational Research Association, Los Angeles.

Kent, K. (1985). A successful program of teachers assisting teachers. *Educational Leadership, 43*(3), 30–33.

Klein, F. (1985). The master teacher as curriculum leader. *Elementary School Journal, 86*(1), 35–43.

Lanier, J. E. (1983). Tensions in teaching teachers the skills of pedagogy. In G. Griffin (Ed.), *Staff development: Eighty-second yearbook of the National Society for the Study of Education* (pp. 118–153). Chicago: University of Chicago Press.

Lipsitz, J. (1983). *Successful schools for young adolescents.* New Brunswick, NJ: Transaction Press.

Little, J. W. (1985). Teachers as teacher advisors: The delicacy of collegial leadership. *Educational Leadership, 43*(3), 34–36.

Little, J. W. (1987). Teachers as colleagues. In V. Koehler (Ed.), *Educator's handbook: A research perspective* (pp. 491–518). New York: Longman.

Little, J. W., & Bird, T. (1986). Instructional leadership "close to the classroom" in secondary schools. In W. Greenfield (Ed.), *Instructional leadership: Concepts, issues, and controversies* (pp. 118–138). Boston: Allyn and Bacon.

Little, J. W., & Long, C. (1985). *Cases in emerging leadership: The school level instructional support team.* San Francisco: Far West Laboratory for Educational Research and Development.

Metz, M. H. (1978). *Classrooms and corridors: The crisis of authority in desegregated secondary schools.* Berkeley: University of California Press.

Rosenholtz, S. (1985a). Effective schools: Interpreting the evidence. *American Journal of Education, 93,* 352–388.

Rosenholtz, S. (1985b). Political myths about education reform: Lessons from research on teaching. *Phi Delta Kappan, 66*(5), 349–355.

Rosenholtz, S. J., & Kyle, S. J. (1984). Teacher isolation: Barrier to professionalism. *American Educator, 8*(4), 10–15.

Schlechty, P. (1984, April). *A school district revises the functions and rewards of teaching.* Paper presented at the annual meeting of the American Educational Research Association, New Orleans.

Showers, B. (1983). *The transfer of training: The contributions of coaching.* Eugene, OR: Research and Development Center for Educational Policy and Management.

Soltis, J. (Ed.). (1987). *Reforming teacher education: The impact of the Holmes Group report.* New York: Teachers College Press.

Sykes, G. (1983). Public policy and the problem of teacher quality. In L. Shulman & G. Sykes (Eds.), *Handbook of teaching and policy* (pp. 98–125). New York: Longman.

Teacher induction programs and research. (1986). *Journal of Teacher Education, 37*(1), entire issue.

Wagner, L. (1985). Ambiguities and possibilities in California's Mentor Teacher Program. *Educational Leadership, 43*(3), 3–29.

Wise, A. E., Darling-Hammond, L., McLaughlin, M. W., & Bernstein, H. T. (1984). *Teacher evaluation: A study of effective practices* (R-3139-NIE). Santa Monica: The Rand Corporation.

Yee, S. M. (1986). *Teaching as a career: Promotion versus development.* Stanford, CA: Stanford University School of Education.

Zahorik, J. (1987). Teachers' collegial interaction: An exploratory study. *Elementary School Journal, 87*(4), 385–396.

Grateful acknowledgment is made for permission to reprint the following:

From *On Leadership* by John W. Gardner. Copyright © 1990 by John W. Gardner. Reprinted with the permission of The Free Press, a Division of Simon & Schuster, Inc. and with the permission of Sterling Lord Literistic, Inc.

From *The Fifth Discipline* by Peter M. Senge. Copyright © 1990 by Peter M. Senge. Used by permission of Doubleday, a division of Random House, Inc. and by permission of The Random House Archive & Library, a Division of the Random House Group Ltd.

From *Out of the Crisis* by W. Edwards Deming by permission of MIT and The W. Edwards Deming Institute. Published by MIT, Center for Advanced Educational Services, Cambridge, MA 02139. Copyright 1986 by The W. Edwards Deming Institute.

From *The Quality School* by William Glasser. Copyright © 1990 by William Glasser, Inc., Joseph Paul Glasser, Alice Joan Glasser, and Martin Howard Glasser. Reprinted by permission of HarperCollins Publishers, Inc.

"Leadership as an Organizational Quality" by Rodney T. Ogawa and Steven T. Bossert from *Educational Administration Quarterly,* vol. 31, no. 2 (May 1995), pp. 224–243. Copyright © 1995 by The University Council for Educational Administration. Reprinted by permission of Corwin Press.

"People and Organizations" from *Reframing Organizations* by Lee G. Bolman and Terrence E. Deal. Copyright © 1991 by Jossey-Bass Inc., Publishers. Used by permission of the publisher.

From *Leading to Change* by Susan Moore Johnson. Copyright © 1996 by Jossey-Bass Inc., Publishers. Used by permission of the publisher.

"Interstate School Leaders Licensure Consortium, Standards for School Leaders, Adopted by the Full Consortium, 11/2/96. Used by permission of the Interstate School Leaders Licensure Consortium.

"The Unheroic Side of Leadership," by Jerome T. Murphy from *Phi Delta Kapan,* May 1968, pp.654–659. Used by permission of the author.